The ESSENTIAL MARKETING AND ADVERTISING DICTIONARY

es-sen-tial ADJ. Of the utmost importance.

The ESSENTIAL MARKETING AND ADVERTISING DICTIONARY

es-sen-tial ADJ. Of the utmost importance.

Jerry M. Rosenberg

SPHINX® PUBLISHING
AN IMPRINT OF SOURCEBOOKS, INC.®
NAPERVILLE, ILLINOIS
www.SphinxLegal.com

Copyright © 2010 by Lisa Holton
Cover and internal design © 2010 by Sourcebooks, Inc.®

All rights reserved. No part of this book may be reproduced in any form or by any electronic or mechanical means including information storage and retrieval systems—except in the case of brief quotations embodied in critical articles or reviews—without permission in writing from its publisher, Sourcebooks, Inc.® All brand names and product names used in this book are trademarks, registered trademarks, or trade names of their respective holders. Sourcebooks and the colophon are registered trademarks of Sourcebooks, Inc.®

First Edition: 2010

Published by: **Sphinx® Publishing, An imprint of Sourcebooks, Inc.®**

Naperville Office
P.O. Box 4410
Naperville, Illinois 60567-4410
(630) 961-3900
Fax: (620) 961-2168
www.sourcebooks.com
www.SphinxLegal.com

This publication is designed to provide accurate and authoritative information in regard to the subject matter covered. It is sold with the understanding that the publisher is not engaged in rendering legal, accounting, or other professional service. If legal advice or other expert assistance is required, the services of a competent professional person should be sought.
From a Declaration of Principles Jointly Adopted by a Committee of the American Bar Association and a Committee of Publishers and Associations

This product is not a substitute for legal advice.
Disclaimer required by Texas statutes.

Library of Congress Cataloging-in-Publication Data

Rosenberg, Jerry Martin.
 The essential marketing and advertising dictionary / by Jerry M. Rosenberg. — 1st ed.
  p. cm.
 Rev. and updated ed. of: Dictionary of marketing and advertising. c1995.
 (pbk. : alk. paper) 1. Marketing—Dictionaries. 2. Advertising—Dictionaries. I. Rosenberg, Jerry Martin. Dictionary of marketing and advertising. II. Title. III. Title: Marketing and advertising dictionary.
 HF5415.R577 2008
 658.8003—dc22
                  2008040014

Printed and bound in the United States of America.
RRD 10 9 8 7 6 5 4 3 2

This volume is dedicated, with love, to Bess, my first grandchild

CONTENTS

Preface ix
Introduction xiii
Definitions 1
Abbreviations 745

PREFACE

The Essential Marketing and Advertising Dictionary

Creations of commerce over the past two hundred years, marketing and its companion activity advertising; are usually identified with the nations of the Western world. These fields have captured the imagination of promoters, who attempt to move manufactured goods and evolving services from beginning stages to consumer purchases. Whether it be free markets, managed trade, national control of exports and imports, or, for that matter, the concepts of social and not-for-profit agencies, marketing and advertising have profoundly influenced and altered the way our modern life evolves.

Directly or indirectly, people worldwide have been influenced by others who promote and develop tactics for implementing ideas, gathering and processing raw materials, producing and selling merchandise and services, and, ultimately, distributing these human achievements to distributors, wholesalers, conveyors of services. The marketing and advertising of goods and services have become central activities of modern-day commerce.

More recently, traditional approaches have been re-examined and often replaced with newer strategies, and, consequently, new terminology. Globally, the fields of international marketing and advertising have not only expanded, but have also created a new demand for a greater awareness of overseas forces and a jargon rarely used, nor previously required, by the domestic marketer or advertiser. This situation is changing quickly, however, as the marketing of items and services has become regionalized and has been affected by the completed Uruguay Round of the General Agreement of Tariffs and Trade, and its 1995 replacement, the World Trade Organization. The July 2008 collapse of the Doha Round will alter the advance of globalization and change the marketing of world products.

To prepare this volume, considerable assistance has come indirectly from authors of books, journal articles, and reference materials. They are too numerous to be named here. On a more personal level, I thank the various individuals whom I used as a sounding board to clarify my ideas and approach; they offered valuable suggestions and encouraged me to go on with this project. Erin R. Shanahan, Esq., Editorial Manager of Sphinx Publishing, was instrumental in the preparation of this volume, as was Elise Jajuga, my editor. A special thanks to publisher Dominique M. Raccah, who reached out and agreed to publish this work.

There is my precious wife Ellen of forty-eight years, who remains my inspiration, sharing my adventures and joys of life. Others in my family include my daughters Lauren and Liz, their husbands Bob and Jon, and my four grandchildren—Bess, Ella, Celia, and Rita. Only in their presence do I at times find myself lacking in the proper verbal expression of true love. Once again, I look forward to hearing from readers with suggestions, both for changes and for future entries.

Jerry M. Rosenberg, PhD
July 2008
New York, New York

INTRODUCTION

Essential Marketing and Advertising Dictionary

This work of approximately five thousand entries has been prepared with the hope that awareness of the accepted meaning of terms may enhance the sharing of information and ideas. Though it cannot eliminate the need for the user to determine how a specific writer or speaker is treating a word, such a dictionary shows what usages exist. It should assist in stabilizing terminology. Most important, it should aid people in saying and writing exactly what they intend with greater clarity.

A word can take on different meanings in different contexts. There may be as many meanings as there are areas of specialization. A goal of this dictionary is to be broad and to establish core definitions that represent the variety of individual meanings of each word, thus enhancing parsimony and clarity in the communications process.

Many terms are used in different ways. I have tried to unite them without giving one advantage or dominance over another. Whenever possible (without creating controversy), I have stated the connection among multiple usages.

Commonly used acronyms and abbreviations are included. Foreign words and phrases are given only if they have become an integral part of our English vocabulary.

This work reaches throughout the world, incorporating terms from both government and private-sector organizations, making this dictionary an all-inclusive lexicon of international marketing and advertising.

Among the areas receiving special attention beyond traditional domestic aspects of marketing and advertising are regional trade blocs, other global partners, and the World Trade Organization.

This is a defining work rather than a compilation of facts. The line is not easy to draw because in the final analysis, meanings are based on facts. Consequently, factual information is used where necessary to make a term more easily understood. All terms are presented in the language of those who use them. The level of complexity needed for a definition will vary with the user; one person's complexity is another's precise and parsimonious statement. Several meanings are sometimes given—relatively simple definitions for the layperson, and more developed and technical explanations for the specialist.

I have organized the dictionary to provide information easily and rapidly, while keeping in mind two categories of users: the experienced person who demands precise information about a particular word; and the newcomer, support member, teacher, or student who seeks a general explanation. I have, in most cases, supplied both general and specialized entries to make this work a useful reference.

DEFINITIONS

.15. N. A symbol for the fifteen-second radio or television commercial, as shown on the program script.

60. N. The designation for a sixty-second television or radio commercial, as shown on the broadcast script.

800-number (eight-hundred number). N. A toll-free telephone number created for a company who pays for this service, enabling a consumer to order goods and services.

AAA

AAA. ABBRV. American Academy of Advertising.

AAAA. ABBRV. American Association of Advertising Agencies.

AA rating. ABBRV. Average audience rating.

ABA. ABBRV. Area-by-area allocation.

abandoned call. N. See *no-op*.

abandonment stage. N. The final stage in a product"s life cycle, when the profit potential is such that management decides that the best course is to discontinue marketing it.

abandon rate. N. The percentage of telephone calls from an automatic dialing unit to prospective customers or by customers to a telemarketer that are not intercepted by a live operator prior to disconnection by the customer.

ABC. ABBRV. Audit Bureau of Circulations.

ABC inventory management. N. Dividing inventories at the time of purchase into categories, A, B, and C, based on relative high or low usage or high or low costs.

abeyance order. N. The request for commercial television time when that particular time slot is not available when the request is made.

above the line. N. (1) For firms, all incomes and expenses before taxes. (2) In advertising, the promotional expenses associated with advertising in one of the media.

above the market strategy. N. See *market-plus pricing*.

absence of demand. N. Within a market, the situation where a major segment of the market finds no possibilities of benefits from a product and is completely disinterested in the product. Synonymous with *no demand*.

absolute advantage. N. (1) An advantage of one nation or area over another in the costs of manufacturing an item in terms of used resources. See also *comparative advantage*. (2) The advantage enjoyed by a country because it can produce a product at a lower cost than can other countries.

absolute frequency. N. In marketing research, the number of data elements in a given subunit that has clear boundaries.

absolute product failure. N. The failure of an item to recover in the marketplace the investment made in its development, manufacture, and marketing.

absolute sale. N. An agreement between the buyer and seller where both concur that there should be no conditions or restrictions affecting the sales transactions. See also *approval sale*, *conditional sale*.

absorption costing. N. A type of product costing that assigns fixed manufacturing overhead to the units produced as a product cost. See also *product costing*.

abstract. N. An abridged summary of information omitting unessentials.

abuses. N. In the overseas marketing of products and services, unfair practices by one nation against another following the completion of a trade agreement. Examples are: (a) directly or indirectly imposing unfair purchase or selling prices or other unfair trading conditions; (b) limiting product, markets, or technical development to the prejudice of consumers; (c) applying dissimilar conditions to equivalent transactions with other trading parties, thereby placing them at a competitive disadvantage; and, (d) making the conclusion of contracts subject to acceptance by the other parties by supplementary obligations that, by their nature or according to commercial usage, have no connection with the subject of such contracts. Rectifying such abuses may require the assistance of an international trade court or commission.

accelerator principle. N. States that the final consumer demand affects several layers of organizational consumers. See also *marginal propensity to consume*.

acceptance. N. (1) The acknowledged receipt by a shipment's consignee resulting in the termination of the common carrier contract. (2) In marketing, a positive reception of a product, brand, or line of products by the public. (3) In marketing, an agreement to purchase goods at a stated price and under stated terms.

acceptance sampling. N. The usage of a given pattern of statistical sampling as part of the inspection procedure of a manufacturing organization that purports to set the acceptance or rejection of specific lots of materials or products. See also *decision rule*.

accessibility. N. One of the four characteristics of a market segment if it is to deserve specific marketing attention. Other features are measurability, substantiality, and uniqueness.

accessible site. N. Where a retail store can be readily reached by customers and employees. Distance is a factor, along with driving time and parking facilities.

accessorial service. N. A service rendered by a carrier in addition to a transportation service, such as assorting, packaging, precooling, heating, storage, or substitution of tonnage.

accessories. N. In retailing, items that coordinate with a basic article of clothing to make it more appealing, and therefore, more attractive. Includes items such as gloves, stockings, scarves, etc.

accessory equipment. N. Portable industrial capital goods used in the production process that require a moderate amount of consumer decision making, are less costly than installations, last a number of years, and do not become part of the final product or change form.

accidental exporting. N. In international marketing, an export business obtained through no effort of the exporter.

accommodation area. N. In retailing, the area devoted to providing additional services to customers, such as wrapping of packages, validating parking tickets, etc. Synonymous with *accommodation desk, service area*.

accommodation desk. N. See *accommodation area*.

accordion fold. N. A method for folding an advertising page so that the panels fold alternatively inward and outward. See also *accordion insert*.

accordion insert. N. An advertising circular, leaflet, or other advertising brochure folded in an accordion fold that will be bound into a periodical or for placement in an envelope as a piece in a direct mail campaign. See also *accordion fold*.

account. N. (1) A record of all the transactions, and the date of each, affecting a particular phase of a business, expressed in debits and credits, evaluated in money, and showing the current balance, if any. (2) In marketing, a customer of a supplier or vendor firm from which the consumer obtains specific materials or services. (3) In marketing, a customer with whom the marketer does business. (4) In advertising, the client of an advertising agency or an organization that places promotional material directly with the media. (5) In advertising, an advertiser. (6) See *client*.

account classification. N. The evaluation of retailers or other buyers according to existing and, in particular, potential business.

account conflict. N. Problems created when two directly competing items or services are handled by the same advertising agency. Agencies servicing competitive firms may be in conflict and often one of the accounts will be withdrawn by a manufacturer.

account executive. N. (1) In advertising, the member of an agency who supervises the planning and preparation of advertising for clients and is responsible for contacts between the agency and the advertiser. (2) In broadcasting, a broadcast-station time salesperson who is usually paid a commission on the funds spent by a sponsor for purchasing commercial time. (3) See *account representative*. ABBRV. *AE*.

account management policies. N. (1) In marketing, policies that specify whom sales people should contact, what kinds of selling and customer service activities should be engaged in, and how these activities should be carried out. (2) In advertising, policies used by an agency's account executive in dealing with clients.

account opener. N. A gift given by a bank or other financial institution to a potential depositor opening a new account or adding funds to an existing account. See also *direct premium*.

account planning. N. A means of evolving advertising where the agency research acts as a major part of the creative team; involves personal interviews with select members of the target market. The objective is to design advertising that parallels the concerns and desires of the consumer.

account representative. N. See *account executive*.

accounts payable. N. A current liability representing the amount owed by an individual or a business to a creditor for merchandise or services purchased on an open account or short-term credit.

accounts receivable N. (1) Money owed to a business enterprise for merchandise bought on open account. (2) In advertising, funds due to an agency on client billings.

account supervisor. N. An advertising agency executive responsible for the work of several account executives. Actively involved in client relationships, but not necessarily on a regular basis.

accuracy. N. A criterion used to judge whether a market research study is logical and presents correct information.

achieved penetration. N. A marketing measure of the ratio of existing users (or buyers) to current potential users (or buyers) of a product class.

ACI. ABBRV. Advertising Council, Inc.

ACK. ABBRV. Acknowledgment.

acknowledgment. N. (1) A statement that a proper document has been submitted. (2) A written confirmation from a manufacturer to a buyer dealing with the buyer's merchandise order; informs the buyer that the order was received and is being processed, or that any inquiries or complaints are being handled. ABBRV. *ACK*.

A.C. Nielsen Company. N. See *Nielsen*.

acquisition N. (1) The takeover of one company by another. (2) In sales, a means of expanding a firm's sales by securing other firms, product rights, or technological advances; a means of enhancing corporate growth other than via international expansion.

acquisition budget. N. Money set aside for advertising and promotion in the securing of potential customers.

acquisition cost. N. The cost to a company of securing business; primarily commissions to agents and agencies.

across-the-board. ADJ. A broadcast program aired every day of the week at the same time; often also applied to such broadcast activity five or more times per week. Since a program fills in a strip in a broadcast schedule, it is synonymous with *strip programming*. See also *media planning*.

action. N. (1) The last step in the communication process, entailing implementation of the communication. (2) In advertising, the resulting effort from an advertising agency. Its primary function is to lead to some altered form of behavior, usually to get consumers to purchase a product or service.

action device. N. Part of a marketing promotion to encourage reader involvement through the performance of an action, such as filling out a questionnaire. The concept suggests that greater involvement leads to a higher response from readers. Synonymous with *involvement device*. See also *scratch and sniff*.

action item list. N. An aid to implementing a market plan, consisting of three columns: (a) the task; (b) the name of the person responsible for completing the task; and, (c) the date by which the task is to be finished.

action plan. N. See *marketing plan*.

action program. N. Part of a marketing strategy; steps taken to achieve the plan's goals.

active. ADJ. A customer is considered active when he or she makes a purchase within a stated time period.

active buyers. N. In direct marketing, customers whose last purchase were made within the past twelve months. Synonymous with *active customers*, *actives*.

active customers. N. See *active buyers*, *actives*.

actives. N. See *active buyers, active customers.*

active search. N. Securing information by a prospect or customers in buying an item or service that lacks sufficient feedback to help in making a buy decision. At this point, the customer who is actively searching for information is highly sensitive to advertising and commercials.

active subscriber. N. A customer committed to receiving regular magazine, book, etc., delivery or services for a time period.

activities, interests, opinions. N. A discipline for understanding consumers' lifestyles and their ensuing purchasing behavior. Activities include occupation and hobbies, interests relate to community and family, and opinions deal with issues and politics. Advertisements are often directed to the activities, interests, and opinions characteristics of the target group. ABBRV. *AIO.*

activity quota. N. A measure of the salesperson's success in terms other than from sales and the monies generated. Includes letters and telephone calls to prospects, offering of demonstrations, visits to potential buyers, etc. See also *call report, sales quota.*

act of God. N. In contractual language, an irresistible superhuman cause, such as no reasonable human foresight, prudence, diligence, and care can anticipate or prevent.

actuals. N. Merchandise and other items available for immediate purchase and subsequent sale.

actual total loss. N. In marketing, a loss that occurs when an item is totally destroyed or destroyed sufficiently to become useless.

ad. ABBRV. Advertisement.

ad-a-card

ad-a-card. N. A trademark for printed tear-off coupons affixed to advertisements; traditionally placed in newspapers.

adaptation. N. A design that reflects the dominant feature of a style that inspired it but is not an exact copy.

adaptive-control model. N. A means for establishing an advertising budget to determine the sales impact of advertising costs. The budget remains flexible and is often reevaluated to permit for the changing marketing situation.

adaptive product. N. A variation of another offering of the same firm, designed to broaden the company's market share. See also *emulative product, multiple brand entries*.

adaptive selling. N. A need-satisfaction sales presentation involving adjusting the presentation to fit the selling situation.

added gravy. N. Resulting from added selling; sales resulting from items used to provide satisfaction from another item, such as linens for outfitting a queen-size mattress.

added selling. N. Hoping to sell more products or services to a customer who has just made a purchase. See also *added gravy*.

added-value tax. N. See *value-added tax*.

additional mark-on. N. An increase in the retail price of merchandise above the price placed on it when it was originally accepted for sale.

add-ons. N. In retailing, further purchases added to the account of a charge account customer before the previous balance in the account has been completely paid.

address coding method. N. A technique developed by direct marketers that contains the actual or potential beginning and ending house numbers, block groups, zip codes, and other codes for city delivery service streets.

addressing. N. One of the costs to be considered particularly in direct-mail advertising; the manual, mechanical, or automatic inscription of the name and address of the recipient on the face of an envelope or mailing piece.

adequate sampling. N. (1) When a test group is sufficiently large enough to reach precision, it reduces the element of chance as a variable affecting the obtained data. (2) In advertising, the test group of people to determine which audience adequately represents a market about to be tested.

adjacencies. N. Programs that precede or follow a specific broadcast time period.

adjustment. N. (1) A change in an account to correct an incorrect entry or for some other sound reason. (2) In marketing, the satisfying of a customer's claim that a shipment was not as ordered or that the price was improperly charged, by an agreeable financial settlement. (3) In sales, correcting mistakes involving the wrong recording of invoices or wrong dating of purchases bought on open account.

adjustment allowance. N. The appropriate compensation given to a customer to settle a claim or complaint.

admass. N. High-pressure advertising and promotion in the media to increase sales, with a damaging impact on the culture of the society.

administered channel system. N. A set of relationships in ordering, supply, and payment between the producer and channel intermediaries; purports to retain the autonomy of each channel member while at the same time allowing informal and lasting organization arrangements to upgrade efficiency and encourage loyalty.

administered price. N. The price established under situations of imbalance competition wherein one business has some degree of control. See also *price leadership*.

administered vertical marketing. N. A vertically aligned group of organizations, not necessarily vertically integrated, that performs as a unit to lower the costs inherent in merchandising a line or classification of goods.

adnorm. N. The percentage of readers of a specific publication who recall a particular advertisement found in the publication; represents a proportion of an accepted norm for advertisements of a similar nature.

adopter categories. N. Persons or firms that adopt an innovation are often classified into five groups according to the sequence of their adoption of it: (a) innovators (the first 2%–5%); (b) early adoptors (the next 10%–15%); (c) early majority (the next 35%); (d) late majority (the next 35%); and, laggards (the final 5%–10%). The numbers are percents of the total number of actual adopters, not of the total number of persons or firms in the marketplace. There is wide disagreement on the exact percentage in each category. See also *adoption of innovation*.

adoption of innovation. N. The process by which an innovation spreads throughout a population. It consists of adopter categories (innovators, early adopters, etc.) and a specific process of adoption by each adopter. See also *adopter categories*.

adoption process. N. The awareness that occurs when a person first becomes aware of an innovation until he or she is willing to accept it; usually in the instance of real things, purchasing them. See also *AIDCAS process, awareness, diffusion process, evaluation*.

adoption process segmentation variables. N. Consumer stages that are completed in the process of becoming a regular user of a product or service. The stages include awareness, interest, evaluation, trial, and adoption.

ad-slick. N. A camera-ready advertisement prepared for distribution to firms of an association for placing in the local print media. Ad-slicks often have a blank space where the advertiser inserts its address, telephone number, and other relevant but brief information. See also *dealer listing*.

ad valorem tariff. N. A tariff based on a percentage of the value of the goods imported.

advance bill. N. (1) In marketing, a bill of exchange drawn prior to the shipment of merchandise. (2) In sales, the invoice presented before the items or services itemized have been delivered or carried out. It is usually requested by purchasers for tax reasons.

advance canvass. N. In advertising, when retailers are contacted prior to the introduction of a new promotional campaign so as to create an emotional high for the forthcoming program, and, indeed, to capture support from the store.

advance dating. N. The added time allowed by a vendor to pay for goods, enabling the purchaser to receive a cash discount. Such extensions are usually arranged before the goods are shipped. Synonymous with *seasonal dating, season dating*.

advance freight. N. In international sales, freight paid for in advance. It permits the shipper to endorse the bill of lading with a freight release, and the importer to take immediate delivery.

advance order. N. The sales order placed sufficiently ahead of the requested date for delivery, thereby often entitling the buyer to a substantial discount.

advance premium. N. The premium offered to a potential customer by a home-service route firm in the hope that it will be earned by later purchases.

advance renewal. N. Resubscribing to a periodical, prior to the termination date.

advantage. N. In salesmanship, the way an item or service can assist in solving problems or fulfilling needs.

advertise. V. (1) To promote; to solicit, usually without payment, i.e., a radio announcer promoting the qualities of a wine he or she experienced in a restaurant. (2) In advertising, applying some form of message or communication to attract the attention of an individual or group to a product, service, concept, institution, etc., with the expectation of some form of behavior or action; usually to purchase the item or service, or to gain support for the concept or idea. See also *advertised*.

advertised. ADJ. The promotion of a product or service, without cost, such as hearing a radio announcer praise a bottle of wine that he experienced in a local restaurant. See also *advertise*, *advertisement*.

advertised brand. N. The promotion, usually by recommendation of a brand used by an individual.

advertised price. N. (1) In advertising, the cost to buyers for the item or service presented in a commercial or advertisement. (2) In broadcasting, the set price for the advertiser. A formula is often applied combining the time purchase (the volume), the cost to advertise the item or service, and the number of times the commercial is presented.

advertisement. N. A public announcement or sale offer in a public area or medium, expressed in print, by other visual means, or

advertising

orally. Major locations of advertisements are in newspapers, magazines, and journals, and on signs, billboards, radio, and television. Similar to but not synonymous with commercial. An advertisement is usually paid for. See also *advertise, advertised, commercial.* ABBRV. *ad.*

advertiser. N. Anyone who engaged to pay for advertising. See also *account, client.*

advertising. N. (1) A paid-for or nonpersonal presentation or promotion of goods, services, or ideas. It is usually paid for by an identifiable sponsor. Decisions evolve around what is to be said and where to place the advertising. See also *promotion, publicity.* (2) Often used to include messages promoting concepts and causes; containing three basic objectives: (a) to inform consumers about new items, product uses, available services, or other information of use to the consumer; (b) to persuade an audience to buy an item, change brand preferences, or perceive an item or service differently; and, (c) to remind consumers about the need for an item or service where it can be bought. See also *advocacy advertising, aisle advertising, bait advertising, bait and switch advertising, burst advertising, business-to-business advertising, classified advertising, commercial advertising, comparative advertising, comparison advertising, consumer advertising, coop advertising, cooperative advertising, corporate advertising, deceptive advertising, demonstration advertising, direct-action advertising, direct advertising, direct-response advertising, endorsement advertising, end-product advertising, ethical advertising, false advertising, financial advertising, generic advertising, impact advertising, indirect action advertising, indirect advertising, institutional advertising, keyed advertising, local advertising, mail-order advertising, manufacturer's cooperative advertising, merchandising the advertising, name advertising, national advertising, noncommercial advertising, outdoor advertising, patronage institutional advertising, perimeter advertising,* *personalized advertising, POP advertising, positioning advertising, postmark advertising, prestige advertising, primary advertising, primary demand advertising, product advertising, product reputation advertising, professional advertising, promotional advertising, public relations institutional advertising, public service advertising, reinforcement advertising, retail advertising, selective demand advertising, shortage advertising, spot advertising, subliminal advertising, subordinate product advertising, teaser advertising, tie-in advertising, tombstone advertising, trade advertising, trade paper advertising, transit advertising, transportation advertising, vertical advertising, vocational advertising, want advertising, word-of-mouth advertising, yellow page advertising.*

advertising agency. N. A specialized institution that aids businesses or organizations in all phases of promoting sales of a product or service. An agency usually receives a 15% commission on the total billing, and the client pays for direct costs on a cost-plus basis. There are full-service agencies providing a complete range of creative, production, research, planning, and buying functions; and limited-service agencies providing only one form of service. See also *fifteen and two, full-service agency, sales promotion agency.*

advertising agency recognition. N. A perception of an advertising agency, based on a medium; its purpose is to receive approval to receive commissions on advertisements placed with the medium by the agency. Factors include credit worthiness, professional qualifications, and clients ready to advertise employing that agency. See also *fifteen and two.*

advertising allowance. N. A discount in price or payment given to a store to help meet the expense of the store's advertising of a product. Such allowances are most often granted when new products are being introduced or when manufacturers are attempting to increase promotion of their products. See also *promotional allowance, cooperative advertising, trade promotion*.

advertising appeal. N. The central concept of an advertisement that communicates to the potential consumer what the advertised item or service provides and gives the reasons why it should be bought.

advertising appropriation. N. See *advertising budget*.

advertising art. N. The illustrative matter of a creative nature, such as drawings, photographs, layouts, decorative designs, hand-lettering, and retouching specifically prepared to use in advertising.

advertising budget. N. The amount of money an advertiser chooses to spend on advertising in a fixed time period, often one year. Synonymous with *advertising appropriation*.

advertising campaign. N. The planned use of varying media and advertising methods to solicit acceptance for an idea or item or to increase the sales of a product or service; running for months or as long as several years. Campaigns feature a variety of advertisements on the same theme and sales message. See also *campaign*.

Advertising Checking Bureau. N. A New York City–based organization that releases reports on print advertising, on the Internet, and yields tearsheets on advertising in newspapers throughout the United States.

advertising contract. N. (1) An agreement between the supplier of advertising space or time and the advertiser, providing details of content, cost, and placement of the advertisement. Both parties, once the contract is signed, are bound by these written terms. (2) An agreement between a supplier and retailer where the retailer agrees to advertise the merchandise over a fixed time period for a stated amount of money.

Advertising Council, Inc. N. Begun as the War Advertising Council in 1941, a not-for-profit organization of advertisers and agencies that designs and controls the distribution of public service advertising programs. ABBRV. *ACI.*

advertising credit. N. The mention of a store's name in the advertisement of a producer.

advertising effectiveness. N. A measure of the consumers' recall of advertising messages that they have been exposed to, along with the persuasiveness of the message; often determined at differing stages of the campaign. See also *advertising testing, concept testing.*

advertising exposure. N. The actual presentation of an advertisement to an audience. See also *advertising impact.*

Advertising Federation of America. N. A federation of member divisions representing different advertising agencies. ABBRV. *AFA.*

advertising goals. N. See *advertising objectives.*

advertising impact. N. One of three characteristics in determining advertising exposure and advertising response, the other being reach and frequency. Impact is qualitative and quite difficult to determine. It varies based on the receiver's perception and the sender's context of intent. See also *advertising exposure.*

advertising manager. N. The title given to the individual in the advertising firm with major responsibility for advertising. He or she works closely with the advertising agency and is responsible to the firm's director of marketing or a similarly titled person. Advertising managers usually report to the firm's marketing vice president.

advertising media. N. (1) Various publications, devices, and structures that carry messages to intended recipients (e.g., newspapers, television, billboards, etc). See also *media.* (2) The class of vehicle where the advertiser's message is carried to its audience. Advertising media are usually categorized into (a) print media; (b) broadcast media; and, (c) position media. Synonymous with *persuasion vehicles*.

advertising media costs. N. Expenditures involved with placing messages in media. They are related to the length or size of an advertisement, as well as the characteristics of the chosen media.

advertising medium. N. See *advertising media*.

advertising message. N. The creative aspect of an advertisement campaign. The purpose of the message is to discharge the advertising objectives of the product or service. The message purports to secure the consumer's attention and interest. See also *advertising target market*.

advertising models. N. Today, computerized systems assist in advertising decision making, from helping to determine budgets, to media scheduling, to expectations of sales and profits.

advertising network. N. The grouping of advertising agencies, noncompeting and independently owned, who share ideas and services in the interest of their clients, and save themselves considerable expense.

advertising novelty. N. See *advertising specialty*.

advertising objectives. N. Reasons behind an advertising campaign; usually to stimulate the consumer into purchasing a product or service. These objectives, once thrashed out, are ultimately translated into specific goals and product positioning.

advertising opportunity. N. Conditions suggesting that a product or service would benefit from advertising. They are: (a) favorable primary demand for the product or service category; (b) the product or service to be advertised can be significantly differentiated from its competitors; (c) the product or service has hidden qualities or benefits that can be portrayed effectively through advertising; and, (d) there are strong emotional buying motives for the product or service. See also *hyperreality*.

advertising platform. N. The main issues or selling aspects desired by an advertiser when preparing an advertising campaign.

advertising quadrangle. N. From the advertising theorists, where advertising is examined as containing four parts: the sender or advertiser, the message or advertisement, the receiver or prospect, and the medium. From the marketing theorists, the four parts are: the product, the prospect, the sponsor, and the channel of distribution. Synonymous with *quadrangle*.

advertising rates. N. Charges for advertising time, advertising space, or both. These rates, often subject to a surcharge when a preferred position is secured, are discounted when the advertiser makes volume purchases. These rates are basic costs for air time and space, and are traditionally negotiable between the medium and the advertiser.

advertising readership measurement service. N. A commercial service designed to measure the quantitative or qualitative readership of advertising appearing in any issues of a business publication for the purpose of providing advertisers, agencies, and publishers with some knowledge of the relative effectiveness of the advertising and of the publication in developing interest among readers.

advertising record sheet. N. A worksheet for monitoring either daily, weekly, monthly, or all three orders for merchandise received as a result of a particular advertisement.

advertising register. N. One of the directories of national advertisers or agencies published on a steady basis.

advertising research. N. See *advertising testing*.

Advertising Research Foundation. N. A not-for-profit membership organization, based in New York City; overseas media research and works toward "more profitable marketing through more effective research." ABBRV. *ARF*.

advertising reserve. N. Funds set aside by the advertiser to be used in an emergency or a special unexpected situation.

Advertising Review Board. N. Composed of advertisers, agencies, and media specialists, to which advertisements claimed to be misleading or untrue may be referred. With any legal authority, the board publicizes its decisions. ABBRV. *ARB*.

advertising space. N. The portion of the total page-space in print (newspaper, magazine, etc.) allocated to advertising rather than editorial or news matter.

advertising specialty. N. A low-cost item (e.g., a ballpoint pen) on which the seller's name, address, and telephone number are printed to promote awareness of the seller's name and location. Synonymous with *advertising novelty, specialties, specialty*.

advertising specialty distributor. N. See *specialty distributor*.

advertising stage. N. See *spiral stage*.

advertising substantiation. N. Documentation provided by advertisers to the Federal Trade Commission to support their advertising claims. This paperwork must show that this data is the basis for the creation of the advertisement.

advertising target market. N. The specific audience toward which an advertising message is aimed. See also *advertising message*.

advertising testing. N. A means of determining the effectiveness of individual advertisements or full campaigns. There is pretesting to determine the appropriateness and projected effectiveness before the placing of advertisements; there is posttesting to determine their impact following an appearance in the marketplace. See also *advertising effectiveness, eye camera*.

advertising theme. N. A major idea behind an advertising campaign as presented to its potential audience. It purports to prove the superiority of the value of the item, idea, or service being offered.

advertising time. N. The portion of the total broadcasting time given to advertising instead of programming.

advertising weight. N. The measure of the number of exposures planned or actually completed from an advertising promotional campaign.

advertorial. N. (1) A print article produced by the medium's advertising unit and financed by the firm's sponsors. The sponsoring organization pays to be quoted in the text, which appears as editorial material but is referred to as advertising. (2) An advertisement appearing in layout format to resemble news copy. Can be read at a news column and therefore is a deceptive practice. See also *advocacy advertising, reading notice*.

advice note. N. A supplier's listing of items that is sent to a customer prior to an invoice, either accompanying the merchandise or preceding it, identifying the nature and quantity of the goods but not giving prices.

advocacy advertising. N. Advertising whose goal is the support of a specific idea, philosophy, or course of action on the part of its audience. Intends to induce or discourage particular forms of activity with regard to controversial issues, e.g., a person purchases magazine advertising to attack the availability of handguns to teenagers without proper regulations. See also *advertorial*.

advocate channel. N. An individual communication channel composed of a firm's sales force contracting purchasers in the target market.

AE. ABBRV. See *account executive*.

AFA. ABBRV. See *Advertising Federation of America*.

affective component. N. The emotional feeling of favorableness or unfavorableness that results from a person's evaluation of an object.

affiant. N. One who swears to an affidavit.

affidavit. N. A written, notarized, dated, and sworn statement of the facts pertaining to a financial transaction or civil event. Such a statement must show the name and address of the affiant, must be signed by that person, and must bear the signature of the attesting official (e.g., a notary public).

affidavit of performance. N. A notarized statement in which an employee of a station or network swears that the advertiser's message or program was actually broadcast as ordered. The affidavit is sent to the advertiser or his or her agency along with the invoice of charges as proof of services rendered.

affiliate. N. (1) An organization whose management is connected by contract with that of another organization. (2) In international marketing, a unit, either partially or wholly owned by a multinational enterprise. It includes subsidiaries, branches, joint ventures, and any other legal form implying at least partial control over the entity. (3) In advertising, a broadcast station that belongs to or carries the programs of a national network. Affiliates can be independently owned or are a division of a network. Affiliates provide commercial time, and the networks then sell it to national advertisers. Networks desire affiliates to attract large advertisers by securing for themselves large viewing audiences in numerous markets.

affiliated wholesaler. N. (1) The wholesaler who acts as initiator of a voluntary chain. See also *voluntary chain*. (2) A wholesaler who has an association with other wholesalers utilizing a common trade name for merchandising purposes.

affinity. N. Marketing a strategy that allows a consumer to emphasize his or her identification with some organization; for example, when organizations issue credit cards with their names on them.

affirmative disclosure. N. A Federal Trade Commission procedure for regulating advertising. It stipulates that, should the information contained in an advertisement be considered inadequate or insufficient by the commission, it can demand that the firm identify limitations of its product or service within its subsequent advertising. This attempts to protect the consumer by providing data for judging both negative and positive attributes.

affirmative dumping decision. N. The decision that a nation has deliberately marketed products below their fair market value and is therefore subject to antidumping duty orders or other measures.

affixed merchandise. N. In advertising, items attached to a display in a fixed manner so that the display remains intact.

affordable method. N. A method of settling marketing budgets based on what a firm can afford to spend.

aforos. N. In overseas marketing, a customs value for computing ad valorem levies in some South American nations. The customs value is different from market value and is applied to designated classes of imports.

afternoon drive. N. In broadcasting, the time from 3:00 p.m. to 7:00 p.m. weekdays; a key prime time for radio. See also *day parts*.

agate line. N. In printed newspapers and periodicals, the standard unit of area used to determine the cost of advertising space.

age and life-cycle segmentation. N. A marketing strategy utilizing different marketing approaches for different age categories or different life-cycle segments within the population.

age cohort. N. A group of consumers of the same approximate age who have undergone similar experiences.

agency commission. N. (1) The fee that an advertising agency charges its clients for the work completed in choosing and supervising the production work carried out by another firm, such as a film recorder, printer, etc. (2) The compensation received by an advertising agency by the media for purchases of time or space completed for clients. This commission represents the basic financial structure of the advertising agency business. See also *commission, fee basis*.

agency group. N. See *agency network*.

agency network. N. Advertising agencies separately affiliate to serve as local offices in primary locales to provide appropriate services for other members of the same network.

agency of record. N. Where an advertiser secures the services of several advertising firms, one of them acts as primary coordinator for the entire program. The agency of record is chosen by the advertiser, who then prepares all media contracts and receives payment from the other agencies involved for the media placement of their advertising.

agency–produced program. N. In broadcasting, a program made by an advertising agency as contrasted with a program by an independent production firm, a local station, or a local network. The agency-produced program is usually bought as a complete package to the network or station, thus allowing the advertising agency to place its client's commercials in the commercial time slots.

agency recognition. N. Acceptance by or having met the highest standards for an advertising agency.

agency reinstate. N. See *agent's reinstatement*.

agent. N. (1) An individual authorized to act on behalf of another person, the principal. (2) In marketing, a middleman who does not take title to the goods he or she sells. (3) In wholesaling, a wholesaling intermediary that does not take title to merchandise ,but serves primarily to bring buyers and sellers together and facilitate exchanges.

Agent/Distributor Service. N. An export/marketing promotion service industry of the U.S. Department of Commerce's International Trade Administration; its goal is to locate foreign companies to serve as agents and distributors of American products.

agent's cancellation. N. The cancellation of an agent's order, either at the customer's request or at the agent's request when payment of a bill is not received. Cancellations are often applied against commissions paid. See also *agent's order, agent's reinstatement*.

agent's clearance. N. See *agent's order*.

agent's order. N. A single order, or orders, submitted by the subscription agency for fulfillment processing. Synonymous with *agent's clearance*. See also *agent's cancellation*.

agent's reinstate. N. See *agent's reinstatement*.

agent's reinstatement. N. A reordered periodical or magazine subscription that was canceled because the payment had been received too late to maintain the flow of subscription. See also *reinstatement*. Synonymous with *agency reinstate*.

agent's summary. N. A report presented with the agency's order that reviews subscription orders for quantity, price of sale, terms, and dollars received or billed.

aggregate demand. N. (1) The total spending within an economy. (2) The total of personal consumption expenditures, business investments, and government spending.

aggregate economics. N. See *macroeconomics*.

aggregate supply. N. The capacity of a country's total resources to produce real goods and services.

aggregation. N. A marketing method based on the concept that consumers in a particular market are alike. Mass advertising and mass product distribution often result from this assumption, especially when low price is considered the primary appeal leading to the greatest number of consumers.

aggressive philosophy. N. In consumer behavior, the concept where a firm attempts to increase market share by engaging in significant competition, utilizing all legal and ethical strategies available. See also *passive philosophy*.

agio. N. In overseas sales, the premium paid for the exchange of one nation's currency for that of another's.

agree and counterattack technique. N. See *yes, but technique*.

agreeing and neutralizing technique. N. See *yes, but technique*.

Agreement on Anti-Dumping Practices. N. Impacting on international marketing; a 1980 international agreement, following the Tokyo Round of General Agreement on Tariffs and Trade; established conditions under which anti-dumping duties can be legally imposed by a nation as its defense against what it claims are dumped imports.

Agreement on Customs Valuation. N. Impacting on international marketing; a 1980 international agreement, following the Tokyo Round of General Agreement on Tariffs and Trade; replaced numerous systems of customs valuation with transparent regulations to afford participating members a fair, neutral, and uniform process of valuing items for the purpose of levying customs duties. The agreement harmonized numerous goods.

AIDA process. N. Attention, interest, desire, and action process. In marketing, a concept of how prospects purchase, based on a series of mental activities. They are attention, or zeroing in on the salesperson and listening for the presentation; interest, or desiring further information; desire, or a need to secure the salesperson's offering; and, action, or placing the order. See also *AIDCAS process*.

AIDCAS process. N. Attention, interest, desire, action, conviction, and satisfaction process. The next step after the AIDA process to incorporate conviction, or the conclusion that the salesperson's offering offers benefits as good as or superior to those of any other offering that is available; and, satisfaction, or the pleasure from the purchase in the belief that the correct choice was made and the expected benefits were received. See also *AIDA process*.

aided recall. N. A method to survey the impression made by an advertisement or other media communication whereby an interviewer presents an advertisement or other aid to memory. See also *diary method, unaided recall, copy testing, recognition*.

AIO. ABBRV. Activities, interests, opinions.

air. N. In broadcasting, the time a program goes over the air waves.

air bubble packing. N. Packing materials made of plastic with air pockets for cushioning.

air check. N. A permanent record of a broadcast, program, or commercial to determine the quality of production and delivery time or date.

air date. N. The date when a broadcast program of a commercial is to be shown or heard.

airedale. N. *(slang)* A high-pressure salesperson who often dresses sharply, talks fast, and is aggressive in behavior. See also *bird dog*.

air waybill. N. Used in global sales; a transport document that covers both domestic and international flights transporting goods to a specified destination. This is a nonnegotiable instrument of air transport that serves as a receipt for the shipper, indicating that the carrier has accepted the goods listed and obligates itself to carry the consignment to the airport of destination according to specified conditions.

aisle advertising. N. In-store item display to attract attention and make the item accessible to purchasers; usually has the same copy and graphics used in other promotional efforts produced by the sponsoring product. See also *POP advertising*.

a la carte agency. N. An advertising agency that provides services in parts as needed on a negotiated basis. Synonymous with *modular service agency*.

alien company. N. When marketing overseas, the incorporated company that is formed and operated under the regulations of a foreign nation.

allied products. N. In retailing, items associated with one another in the same use category. See also *complementary products*.

allocate. V. To distribute, assign, or allot.

allocation. N. (1) Assigning one or more items of cost or revenue to one or more segments of an organization, according to benefits received, responsibilities, or other logical measure of use. (2) In broadcasting, the range of wavelengths assigned by the Federal Communications Commission to a broadcast system. (3) In merchandising, the lowering of price to a retailer by the manufacturer or wholesaler based upon some unique agreement. Traditionally it is used to compensate the retailer for expenses in marketing the item.

allocation rights. N. The authority given to managers in the area of purchasing to incorporate strategies.

allonge. N. A paper affixed to a bill on which further endorsements are written.

allotment. N. (1) The separation of anticipated revenue among specific classes of expenditure. (2) An assignment of pay for the benefit of dependents. (3) In outdoor advertising, the unit of sale composed of a showing in a given market. Often a poster or two based on the market size and its traffic flow.

allowable order cost. N. The amount spent on convincing a customer to purchase something, without diluting the desired profit margin.

allowance. N. (1) In merchandising, a deduction from the weight or value of merchandise; a reduction permitted if the carrier does not supply appropriate equipment and the shipper then produces the equipment for use. (2) In sales, any price reduction.

all-purpose revolving account. N. In retailing, the charge account for which the agreement with customers provides that no service charge will be imposed if the account is paid in full within a given time period following the presentation of a statement. Synonymous with *flexible charge account, retail installment credit account, revolving charge account.*

all-you-can-afford method. N. A technique for evolving a promotional budget where all nonpromotional marketing expenses are budgeted initially and the remaining funds are allocated to promotional activities.

Alpha test. N. The testing of a new product in-house, not with potential users (Beta test). The testing may be in a laboratory setting or (as in the case of glues or computers) in some part of the developing firm's regular operations.

alternate bundles run. N. In print media advertising, when two differing versions of the advertiser's message are printed in separate phases of a press run and then alternately commingled when bundled for circulation delivery; used to measure the effectiveness of one message over another message.

alternate sponsorship. N. Two sponsors sharing a program, usually each one taking a week. Permits exclusivity for the duration of the sponsorship.

alternate weeks. N. The advertiser's instructions to a broadcasting media to run a commercial for one week, then skip one week, and then run it again. After a three-week period, the advertiser pays for a two-week exposure.

alternative media. N. Advertising media that does not fall into clear categories, such as advertisement on shopping mall carts. Alternative media evolved in response to increasing competition by different manufacturers for purchases by consumers. See also *media, out-of-home media.*

alternative tariff. N. When marketing overseas, the tariff containing two or more rates from and to the same points, on the same goods, with authority to use the one that produces the lowest charge.

altruistic display. N. (1) A display for items of advertisers other than the ones who pay for the display. (2) A store-wide occurrence giving seasonal items including the advertiser's product without specifically naming it.

AMA. ABBRV. American Marketing Association.

ambiguous statement. N. An advertising method utilizing a statement that can be interpreted in differing ways to mean different things. This may be deliberate on the part of the advertiser, especially when the item or service has no clearly defined target market. Often consumers that are indifferent or do not possess a strong feeling toward a brand or particular service are attracted to ambiguous statements.

American Academy of Advertising. N. The professional organization of academics and practitioners in advertising concerned with advancing advertising education. ABBRV. *AAA*.

American Advertising Federation. N. An advertising association of fifty thousand members; promotes rights of advertisers; based in Washington, D.C.

American Association of Advertising Agencies. N. A trade association of leading advertising agencies in the United States; purports to improve standards of advertising by its members. ABBRV. *AAAA*.

American goods returned. N. A provision of the U.S. Tariff Schedules that allows the duty-free return of merchandise of American manufacture. The goods must not have been manipulated or advanced in value, except for the packaging of the item.

American Marketing Association. N. A national professional organization for persons engaged in the practice and teaching of marketing. It also publishes the *Journal of Marketing*, the *Journal of Marketing Research*, and a twice-monthly newsletter. ABBRV. *AMA*.

American Research Bureau. N. A television-rating service utilizing both the viewer diary method and an electronic recording and tabulating device, called Arbitron. See also *diary method*. ABBRV. *ARB*.

American selling price. N. In international sales, the price charged by U.S. producers for goods, used to determine the duty to be paid on a similar item brought into the United States, rather than determining the duty on the actual cost of the item to an importer. ABBRV. *ASP*.

American Telemarketing Association. N. An association of telephone marketing businesses and related firms; promotes the use of telephone sales and purports to upgrade the industry's public and private image. ABBRV. *ATA*.

amplification and details. N. The section of verbal copy of an advertisement that supplements and extends, usually in considerable length, the idea presented by the headline. Frequently follows the subheadline should one be used.

AMS. ABBRV. Analytical Marketing System.

ANA. ABBRV. Association of National Advertisers.

analogy advertising. N. The way of broadcasting a commercial utilizing an extraneous example of one item in a comparison to explain the advertised merchandise.

analysis of covariance. N. In marketing research, an extension of methods used in the analysis of variance to include two or more related variables. See also *analysis of variance*.

analysis of variance. N. In marketing research, a method for determining whether the differences found in a dependent variable, when it is exposed to the influence of one or more experimental variables, exceed what may be expected by chance. See also *analysis of covariance*.

Analytical Marketing System. N. One of four systems of a firm's marketing information system. It consists of a statistical bank and a model bank for analyzing marketing information and issues. Deals with new product sales forecasting, choosing a site, sales-call planning, media mix, and marketing mix budgeting. ABBRV. *AMS*.

analytical research. N. A form of marketing research that focuses on why consumers purchase the products they do.

anchor. N. As used by consumers to evaluate communications; often employed as a "rule of thumb" concept, such as "the higher the price for an item, the better its quality." An advertiser, aware of anchors used by the target markets, can increase positive reactions and avoid negative ones.

ancillary customer services. N. Optional services provided for customers to increase the noncompetition activities of the sellers; always of a nonessential variety. Some stores do and other, do not charge for such services.

ancillary services. N. See *ancillary customer services*.

Andy awards. N. Awards of the Advertising Club of New York for the best commercial on radio and television, and the best overall commercial from all entrants.

angled poster. N. A poster placed so that it is viewed by traffic moving in one direction only.

announcement. N. The second stage of the product launch cycle; used to introduce the product or service to the public.

announcer voice over. N. See *voice over*.

annual rebate. N. A discount of approximately 12%–13% granted by the major radio and television networks to sponsors who use network facilities for at least fifty-two consecutive weeks, and applied to the gross cost of time purchased by advertisers during the year.

anthropology. N. A branch of social sciences that examines the development of people and their customs. Used in marketing where data from this discipline is used to avoid mistakes in the use of symbols, cultural themes, and the encroachment into taboos.

anticipation of demand. N. Requires a firm to do consumer research on a regular basis in order to develop and introduce offerings desired by consumers.

anticonsumption. N. The actions taken by consumers that involve the deliberate defacement or mutilization of products.

Antimerger Act. N. A consumer protection amendment from 1950 to Section 7 of the Clayton Act that applied federal legislation barriers to corporate mergers that impaired or impeded market competition. Synonymous with *Celler-Kefauver Act*.

antitrust acts. N. Federal legislation that regulates trade in order to maintain competition and prevent monopolies. Advertising and promotional allowances are allowed as long as they offer prices for rendered services on an equal basis, and without prejudice, under such legislation. See also *consumer protection legislation*.

apathetic shoppers. N. One of four classifications of consumers; indicates those with little interest in making comparisons. The consumer here is happy to patronize the most convenient store. See also *economic shoppers, ethical shoppers, personalizing shoppers*.

appeal. N. (1) The motivation of a sales pitch with the expectation that the potential customers will become favorably disposed

applause mail

toward the product or service. (2) The advantage of purchasing a product or service as given in the sales message for that item or service.

applause mail. N. Letters of praise received by advertisers or broadcasters.

appraiser. N. One who determines the value of goods.

approach-approach conflict. N. Used in consumer behavior analysis, a situation in which a person is drawn toward two potentially satisfying goals that are at least partially incompatible, e.g., to buy or lease a car. See also *approach-avoidance conflict*, *avoidance-avoidance conflict*.

approach-avoidance conflict. N. Used in consumer behavior analysis, a situation in which a person delays making a decision. May require motivation to resolve this conflict, which involves a goal that can be secured only at a cost. See also *approach-approach conflict*, *avoidance-avoidance conflict*.

approach phase. N. The part of a sales presentation that includes the announcement and rapid sales work of the seller, the firm, and the product to gain customer interest.

approval sale. N. In retailing, the sale to a customer where the person has unlimited returns privileges. See also *absolute sale*.

apron. N. (1) An open area within the store where displays are set, either on free-standing units, or built entirely of items from the floor up. (2) In outdoor advertisements, the lattice or other decorative finish set below the bottom of the display area.

ARB. ABBRV. (1) Advertising Review Board. (2) American Research Bureau.

arbitrary allocation. N. See *arbitrary method*.

arbitrary method. N. A technique for allocating a company's promotional budget where the amount to be spent on promotion over a given time frame is the result of deriving an executive decision rather than from scientific analysis. Synonymous with *arbitrary allocation*.

arbitration. N. The process whereby parties to a conflict agree to present their dispute before, and have the matter adjudged by, an independent third party that is not a court of law.

arbitration clause. N. In international sales, the clause found within the sales contract between an exporter and an importer that specifies the method under which disputes relevant to the contract in question will be settled.

Arbitron. N. A technique for acquiring television program measurements immediately by means of an electronic apparatus placed in multiple homes and connected to a central measurement unit. See also *American Research Bureau*.

area-by-area allocation. N. A means for defining the advertising budget, where advertising dollars are assigned to be spent in markets in direct proportion to the advertiser's projected or current product or sales in those areas. Synonymous with *market-by-market allocation*. ABBRV. *ABA*.

area sample. N. (1) A probability sample in which respondents are chosen at random from a complete list of the population in a specific geographic area. (2) In marketing research, a random selection of a population in which the small geographical units chosen determine which subjects are included in the selection. See also *quota sampling, random sample*.

area sampling. N. See *area sample*.

area selection. N. See *area sample*.

area structure. N. The natural resource specialization based on the anticipated marketing returns on them, leading to a specific location for each institution in the agency structure.

arousal method. N. A technique of copy testing by which a galvanometer (a machine that purports to measure the changes in electrical resistance of the skin) records the reaction of a consumer subject to an advertisement or radio or television commercial; designed to determine the extent to which an advertising message will influence a consumer before the advertisement is run by recording the changes in sweating in the palms of the hands caused by emotion accompanying the reading or hearing of the message.

arrears. N. (1) Monies due but unpaid; a real or contingent obligation that remains unpaid at the date of maturity. (2) In advertising, complimentary issues of a magazine sent to consumers whose subscriptions have expired; permits publishers to meet their rate base, which guarantees the advertiser of the publication an agreed-upon circulation.

art director. N. The senior person working on the graphics side in the creative unit of an advertising agency; usually reports to the creative services vice president.

articles of mixed status. N. Items manufactured within a free trade zone of components of more than one status (the product of several factors). Upon withdrawal of the items fabricated within a zone, the finished item is assessed duties in accordance with the status of the merchandise from which it was composed.

artificial obsolescence. N. The decline in market acceptance of an item brought about because of change in the item or a new version of the item introduced to replace the old one on the belief that it is better to lose sales of a product to a new one of one's own firm than to that of a competitor. See also *planned obsolescence*.

art service. N. A firm specializing in the creation of advertising art for use by agencies and advertising departments. See also *advertising art*.

aseptic packaging. N. Germ-free packaging that allows products to be sealed in paper containers and stored for extended periods of time without refrigeration.

as is. N. Items that have no warranty and may be damaged or shopworn.

asked price. N. The price that is officially offered by a seller.

ASP. ABBRV. American selling price.

aspect ratio. N. The ratio between the width and height of a television or motion picture screen.

assembling. N. (1) Putting together different parts of an article or machine. (2) In marketing, the activities involved in gathering supplies or assortments of items or services to assist in sales or purchases.

assessment technique. N. A means of arriving at an advertising budget by adding a specific, arbitrary amount of money for each unit to be sold. Can be applied as well to the evolution of the budget for the total marketing mix.

ASSESSOR. N. A computer model for predicting the market share of a new packaged good brand using laboratory test market data.

asset turnover. N. The ratio of sales to total assets available.

assigned mailing date. N. In direct marketing, the date when a list user is to mail a specific purchased list, by virtue of a prior agreement between the list owner and the user. The user cannot mail

assimilation-contract concept. N. A theory where consumers reject an advertisement requiring an extreme attitude shift. Such a message is seen as more extreme than it actually is, further reinforcing the rejection process.

association advertising. N. A type of horizontal cooperative advertising, e.g., milk promoted by the U.S. Dairy Association, carried out by trade associations to promote a primary demand for a class of products or services.

association advertising format. N. A form of advertisement that conveys its message by setting a relationship between an event, an activity, or an image, and the product being promoted.

Association of National Advertisers. N. A national organization of advertisers, with most members being among the largest manufacturers. ABBRV. *ANA*.

assorting. N. Performed usually by wholesalers or retailers to supply an assortment of items, e.g., an automotive supply store carrying hundreds of related items for the car user. It purports to evolve a heterogeneous inventory of products for the convenience of customers. See also *sort*.

assortment. N. (1) Various forms of the same general type of item, such as the depth and width of the merchandise offering. Depth is about variety, an array of styles, colors, and prices; width is about different product categories such as towels, hats, or lotions to accompany the sale of bathing suits. (2) Relating to a specific consumer, the particular combination of items and services seen as needed to maintain or improve one's living standard, e.g., toothbrushes and hair spray.

assortment plan. N. Items of one type established to meet the requirements of customers by a determination of inventory levels. See also *assortment, basic stock, model stock*.

assumptive close. N. In sales, a close accomplished without a buyer's verbal agreement. This becomes presumed when the purchaser fails to protest the salesperson's beginning to prepare the order or to wrap the merchandise.

ATA. ABBRV. American Telemarketing Association.

at best. N. In global marketing, the instruction with a buying or selling order indicating that it should be carried out quickly at the best possible price. Synonymous with *at the market*.

atmosphere. N. The sum total of the physical characteristics of a retail store or group of stores that are used to develop an image and draw customers.

atmospherics. N. External factors from the environment that are designed to establish a specific mood or image or to stimulate sales. These factors include layout, architecture, colors, and other sensory inputs.

ATR. N. Awareness-trial-repeat.

attention. N. The reader-viewer's response to an advertisement.

attention, interest, desire, action. N. See *AIDA process*.

at the market. N. See *at best*.

at-the-market prices. N. In retailing, prices that are generally the same for all stores within a location. See also *market-minus prices, market-plus pricing*.

attitude. N. (1) Feelings that express whether a person likes or dislikes objects in his or her environment. (2) A lasting, learned

attitude study

predisposition to behaving in a consistent way toward a given class of objects or persons. This condition has a direct effect on feeling and action, and refers to an aspect of personality that may account for persistent and consistent behavior.

attitude study. N. See *attitude survey*.

attitude survey. N. A method for ascertaining consumer's perceptions of products and services, usually by use of questionnaires or interviews.

attribute analysis. N. A bundle of idea-generating techniques built on the concept that any product improvement is a change in the attributes of its predecessor. Dimensional analysis and the checklist are the most popular techniques.

attribute-based shopping products. N. Products for which consumers get information about and then evaluate features, warranties, performance, options, and other factors.

attribute mapping. N. In the planning of new products, a statistical means of analyzing a market in an effort to find openings for new items. Existing items are placed on a chart, and open spaces that indicate gaps point to where potential new products can be introduced. Synonymous with *market position analysis*.

attribution theory. N. The concept that consumer assumptions about a product are drawn from the customer's experience, personality, or attitudes.

auction. N. (1) A unique trading market in which there is one seller and many potential buyers. (2) In sales, a means of selling products to the highest bidder.

auction company. N. A wholesaling intermediary that sells merchandise on an agency basis by means of auctions.

audience. N. (1) The sum of people who are exposed to an advertising message delivered by a medium or combination of media. See also *reach*. (2) The target group at which a promotional message is aimed. Synonymous with *target audience*.

audience accumulation. N. The total net audience reached by an advertisement from all sources of the media. Should an advertising campaign for an item or service run for a six-week period and uses a combination of media, the audience accumulation is the total number of persons who were exposed to an advertisement or commercial at least one time.

audience composition. N. (1) In advertising, the mix of people, classified by age, sex, or other characteristics, who are reached by an advertising approach. See also *customer profile, mix*. (2) In broadcasting, the breakdown by program of the listening and viewing audience based on age and sex.

audience duplication. N. The number of the same listeners reached by two or more programs of the same sponsor; important in media planning. Audience duplication is desired when the advertiser wishes to reach a target audience over and over again.

audience flow. N. The gain or loss of a broadcast audience during a program or from one program to another. See also *hold-over audience, share of audience*.

audience fragmentation. N. Separating an audience into smaller groups because of the wide spectrum of media outlets. With more audiences becoming fragmented, broadcast networks are pushed to find new revenue sources.

audience holding index. N. A means for measuring how well a program keeps its audience interested; measured on a minute-by-minute or fifteen-minutes basis by the researcher. The index becomes critical in that many people start watching a program, but soon after its commencement may turn to another broadcast, thereby impacting the audience for the commercial or advertisement.

audience measurement. N. Determining audience numbers exposed to advertising in a particular medium. See also *rating*.

audience-participation program. N. A type of radio or television show, the form and entertainment value of which are based upon the cooperation of the studio audience.

audience profile. N. See *audience composition*.

audience rating. N. The percent of listeners in the market that a specific radio station gets at a certain time period. See also *audience share*.

audience share. N. The number of listeners of a particular radio station at a given time compared to the station's potential audience. Usually audience share is electronically measured by a device attached to a radio or television, by telephone interviews, or direct mail studies. See also *audience rating, share, total audience*.

audience study. N. A form of analysis to determine the characteristics and attitudes of listeners, viewers, or readers of advertising media. See also *Arbitron, Hooperating, Nielsen rating, Trendex, Videodex, media analysis*.

audience turnover. N. The ratio between the cumulative and average audiences for a specific broadcast.

audimeter. N. An electromechanical unit used by A.C. Nielsen Company to record station turning of radio and television receivers by tapping a sample of home users. A.C. Nielsen radio listening efforts were discontinued in 1964, while they were first used for television audience estimates in 1950. See also *Nielsen rating, share of audience, coincidental telephone method.*

Audit Bureau of Circulations. N. An independent nonprofit auditing organization established in 1914 to audit and validate circulation figures for the benefit of its members. ABBRV. *ABC.*

audited net sales. N. The total amount of sales for a specified period, computed after returns and allowances have been deducted. These totals are circulated by the auditing department of a store and credited to the book inventory of each department.

audition. N. In advertising, a means by which the advertiser determines the feasibility of sponsoring a specific radio or television program by listening to a trial performance of the program and then deciding if the program meets his or her goals of the item or service.

augmented product. N. (1) The core product together with its attendant benefits and services. See also *core product.* (2) An expected product that has been enhanced by a set of benefits that consumers do not expect or that exceed their expectations.

authorized dealer. N. A middleperson who has received a franchise to represent or sell a manufacturer's products.

autocratic decisions. N. Those purchase decisions that are made almost exclusively by one or the other spouse.

automatic group. N. In marketing research, a reference unit where the person belongs because of sex, education, race, etc. See also *negative group.*

automatic markdown. N. The lowering of price taken by a retailer according to a predetermined time schedule.

automatic merchandising. N. See *automatic selling.*

automatic renewal. N. A means of renewing subscriptions to magazines and periodicals without asking the subscriber's authorization after the initial order. Subscribers are charged for each renewal by credit card number. Publishers using automatic renewal methods are required to keep proof of prior subscriber authorization at the time purchasers first ordered the reading material. See also *automatic reorder*.

automatic reorder. N. An order for staple goods issued on the basis for reaching an established minimum inventory quantity. The reorder quantity is predetermined. See also *automatic renewal*.

automatic selling. N. The retail sale of items or services through machines operated by the consumer utilizing credit cards, funds, or any other authorized method.

automatic vending. N. A type of nonstore, nonpersonal retailing of goods and services using coin-operated, self-service equipment. Examples of merchandise are cigarettes, candy, condoms, and sodas.

Automobile Information Disclosure Act of 1958. N. U.S. legislation that prohibited car dealers from inflating the factory prices on new automobiles.

autonomous consumption. N. Consumption that is independent of income; the part of total consumption that is unrelated to income.

auxiliary dimensions of a product. N. Those features of a product, other than the item itself, that add to the product's attractiveness and utility to the consumer.

availability. N. (1) In outdoor advertising, units such as showings or bulletins that a plant operator has open for contract. (2) The broadcast time offered to an advertiser for sponsorship. Ratings and prices are based on the most recent ratings of the shows, as given by rating services.

available market. N. People who can afford the item or service, who have ready access to it, and who have shown an interest in using or owning it.

avails. N. The proceeds from a discounted note. ABBRV. In advertising, short for *availabilities*.

average. N. In market research, the measure of central tendency, showing the middle value around which numbers are grouped. See also *mean, median, mode*.

average audience rating. N. One of several kinds of A.C. Nielsen Company ratings indicating the average size of the audience on a minute-by-minute basis. Provides a splendid measure of the size of an audience for a specific advertisement or commercial. ABBRV. *AA rating*.

average cost. N. The sum of all output costs divided by the quantity of production.

average fixed costs. N. Production costs that do not depend on the amount produced divided by the quantity produced. Average fixed costs decline as production grows.

average frequency. N. The average number of times a consumer or prospect has been shown a commercial in any medium that is part of an advertising campaign.

average gross sales. N. The dollar amount of gross sales divided by the number of sales transactions that created the gross sales.

average mark-on. N. The mark-on obtained when the costs and retail prices of several purchases are combined.

average net paid circulation. N. A measurement of the average number of copies of a magazine, periodical, or newspaper sold per issue; determined by dividing the total number of subscription and newsstand-sold copies for all issues of the period by the total number of issues.

average paid circulation. N. See *average net paid circulation*.

average profit margin. N. Used to assess the value of a campaign or advertisement. A means of determining the profit margin per item bought by applying an equal proportion of the total expenses of the seller against each item that has been sold.

average quarter hour persons. N. The number of people estimated to listen at home or away to a radio or television station for a minimum of five minutes within a given fifteen minutes.

average revenue. N. The sum of revenues divided by the quantity sold; often presented as an average revenue curve, with quantity plotted on the horizontal axis and average revenue on the vertical.

average stock. N. The quantity representing the midpoint between the highest and lowest inventory levels for a stated time period. Average stock is calculated by adding each month's opening stock figure plus the closing stock figure for the last month. The total is divided by the number of months being considered.

average variable cost. N. The cost per unit of production of inputs such as labor, materials, and utilities, which are used in increasing amounts as production increases.

avoidance. N. Used to explain consumer preferences, the administration of a reinforcement that prevents the occurrence of an undesirable behavior.

avoidance-avoidance conflict. N. Used in consumer behavior analysis, a situation in which a person, in moving away from one's undesirable path, must move toward another undesirable path. See also *approach-approach conflict*.

awareness. N. In the marketing cycle, the recognition by a consumer that he or she has a need or problem and wishes to have it satisfied. Awareness is the first stage in the adoption process. See also *adoption process*.

awareness-trial-repeat. N. An explanation for the behaviors of a consumer in adopting a service or item. The individual goes from being uninformed of the product or service to becoming a regular user after learning of the item or service's assets and availability (awareness), trying the item or service (trial), assuming the trial usage is beneficial, and purchasing the item or service again (repeat). ABBRV. *ATR*.

B

baby boomers. N. In advertising, people who were born in the years immediately after 1945, at the end of the second World War; in the 1980s and 1990s, a major target audience for advertisers.

baby boomlet. N. The generation of children born in 1977 and later.

back card. N. The advertising message found on a card fixed to the back of a merchandiser, projecting above the merchandiser to show the communication at eye level.

back cover. N. The outside back of a periodical or magazine that is frequently read and consequently often sold at a premium. Advertisers prefer this placement and, whether or not color is used, pay for this expensive back cover. Synonymous with *fourth cover*.

back dating. N. (1) Placing on a statement a date prior to the date on which it was drawn up. (2) In sales, commencing a subscription to a magazine or other periodical with an issue prior to the current issue; helps lower back inventory. Synonymous with *back start*.

back-door selling. N. When the salesperson deliberately avoids the purchasing department and places a call to people in the department that he or she assumes can use the item.

back end. N. (1) Following a customer's order, the fulfillment by servicing or delivering of the merchandise. (2) The actions of the consumer after the initial order has been received. Through back-end analysis, the seller examines pay up, cancellation rates, and renewal or reorder rates.

back-end analysis. N. See *back end*.

backer card. N. A form of inexpensive advertising, poster space found on the back of a display; used to secure consumer awareness of an item or to encourage sales at point of purchase.

back-haul allowance. N. A price reduction to customers who make their own pickups at the seller's warehouse.

backing activities. N. Activities in a retail store that do not directly involve interfacing with customers.

backlighting. N. A full-color advertisement that has been printed on a translucent sheet instead of on paper stock in order for special lighting behind the sheet to turn it into a dramatic color slide.

back order. N. (1) A customer's request that is held up until the supplier has the capability to ship it. (2) Merchandise ordered but not available for delivery because the supplier does not have it in inventory.

back start. N. See *back dating*.

back-to-back commercials. N. Two commercials appearing in succession. Two competing products will not appear back-to-back; usually done when a firm buys time to sell two similar or companion items that it manufactures, e.g., curtains and curtain rods. See also *competitive separation, triple spotting*.

backup merchandise. N. Items held in reserve at a storage place removed from access to customers but available to employees for restocking purposes. See also *floor stock*. Synonymous with *reserve stock*.

backup space. N. Advertising space in a periodical that adjoins an insert, e.g., a coupon, reply card, etc. Should advertisers want to utilize an insert, they can purchase backup space. Periodicals and magazine do not sell inserts without backup space.

backward channel. N. A marketing channel running backward from the consumer to the middleperson, and, at times, as far back as the manufacturer or producer. Synonymous with *reverse distribution*.

backward integration. N. A firm's activities for increasing sales and profits by expanding its operations within its industry; usually

backward invention

involves acquiring firms that relate to the company's present business, e.g., a manufacturing company acquiring a supplier in order to lower costs of materials. See also *integration*.

backward invention. N. In international marketing, a product strategy where firms doing business in developing nations alter, and often simplify, their products in order for them to be more attractive in this new market.

backward market segmentation. N. Identifying segments of a population on the basis of a type of behavior. The principle is that groups having similar behaviors will at the same time share attitudes and beliefs and will react homogeneously to marketing promotions.

bad debt. N. (1) The amount due on an open account that has been proved to be uncollectible; any uncollectible receivable. (2) In sales, when the customer fails to pay for products or services received. Synonymous with *bad pay*. See also *bad pay list*.

bad faith. N. Acting to mislead or deceive. It does not include misleading by an honest, inadvertent, or uncalled-for misstatement. See also *fraud, mala fides, bona fide*.

bad pay. N. See *bad debt*.

bad pay file. N. See *bad pay list*.

bad pay list. N. People with a poor credit history are withdrawn from a list that includes individuals who would ordinarily receive promotions, advertisements, services, or future merchandise. They are purged as people who have a high probability of incurring bad debt expense. These lists can be purchased by advertisers and others. Synonymous with *bad pay file*.

bagman. N. *(slang)* The earliest salespeople who sold from bags of samples in the eighteenth century. Synonymous with *Manchester Man*.

bailment. N. In global marketing, the delivery of goods by one party to another, to be held according to the purpose of the delivery, to be returned or delivered when that purpose is accomplished.

bait advertising. N. Advertising exceptional prices or terms for a specified product to attract prospects to a store; potential customers find, however, that it is difficult to buy the product there as advertised. See also *bait and switch advertising*.

bait and switch advertising. N. (1) A pricing strategy in which a product is given a low price in order to lure customers into a store, where an attempt is made to persuade them to buy a more expensive model or product. (2) An unethical and illegal approach in which a retailer advertises a product at a particularly low price with the intention of inducing people who ask for the item to purchase a more costly one. Sometimes the switch is made by the salesperson telling the purchaser that the advertised item is not good or has been sold out. See also *switch selling*.

balanced product portfolio. N. Used in setting marketing strategies, the combination of old and new items maintained by a manufacturer.

balanced scale. N. In marketing research, an inquiry to provide an equal number of favorable and unfavorable category items.

balanced selling. N. The action of selling all products in a vendor's line in proportion to the sales potential found within a state area, or to the profit associated with the products.

balanced stock. N. A planned inventory available to customers in proportion to the request for all items they desire in every price range.

balanced tenancy. N. In retailing, where an area's type and number of stores correspond precisely to the mix proper to meet the needs of that community's population.

balance sheet

balance sheet. N. An itemized statement listing the total assets and total liabilities of an advertising firm to portray its net worth at a particular moment in time.

balance sheet close. N. A closing strategy when confronted with a prospect unable to make up his or her mind about a purchase. The salesperson prepares a list of advantages and disadvantages for both moving quickly or delaying a decision. If the salesperson has been creative, the pluses outweigh the minuses and hopefully become a major reason for the prospect to agree to a transaction.

ballooning. N. A deterrent to the successful sale of items and services; a price manipulation used to send prices beyond safe or real values.

ballpark pricing. N. A technique to determine the price for an item by examining the average price level for similar items, choosing a price in this range, and working backward to set the feasibility of yielding at the cost constraint disclosed.

banded pack. N. Items offered at retail that are secured by a tape, string, or plastic film strip and therefore sold as one unit. Synonymous with *factory pack*. See also *economy pack*.

bandwagon impact. N. When people purchase an item because others are doing the same thing. See also *law of demand*.

bangtail. N. A promotional envelope containing a perforated flap that is torn away and then used as an order form. Often used for placing exposed film to be returned for processing. See also *syndicator*.

bankruptcy. N. The conditions under which the financial position of an individual, corporation, or other legal entity is such as to cause actual or legal solvency.

banner. N. (1) In advertising, a large strip of fabric containing an advertisement, product image or slogan, or corporate logo. (2) In newspaper, in a layout, a headline running across, or nearly across, an entire page.

bannerhead. N. A newspaper headline announcing something very special.

bantam store. N. A community market that remains open in the late evening or on weekends or holidays when other markets are closed. See also *convenience goods, depot store, supermarket.* Synonymous with *superette, vest pocket supermarket.*

bar chart. N. The pictorial graph where bars of varying length are used to display the relative amounts of the variables or characteristics of interest.

bar code. N. (1) A series of vertical or horizontal parallel lines forming a code that is optically read and interpreted by a bar code scanner. Used on envelopes and forms for the rapid entry of data and for sorting. (2) In merchandising, package bar codes identify items, their prices, and manufacturers. Electronic cash registers scan the code to register price and prepare inventory figures. See also *electronic marketing, universal product code.*

bargain. N. An item bought at a low or advantageous price; a good buy. V. In sales, to arrive at an agreement on the price of goods to be sold.

bargain basement. N. The below-ground-level floor of a store, where special prices are offered on merchandise. The stock often contains lower-price merchandise or items not carried on the upper levels of the store.

bargain counter. N. An area for the sale of discounted merchandise.

bargain hunter. N. An individual who seeks out the store that is selling items at the lowest possible price.

bargain store. N. A store that sells merchandise at a submarket price. Assortments and sizes are often limited, and the merchandise is frequently damaged or seconds. See also *seconds*.

barnacle brand. N. A competitive brand that enters and attaches itself to the market in the later stages of the product life cycle.

barn-burner wizards. N. *(slang)* High-powered salespeople who skillfully push to achieve their stated goals or sales.

barometric price leader. N. Carefully watched by advertisers; a firm that usually interprets best the current economic trends within an industry and is often followed in the setting of prices for the industry.

barometric technique. N. A market forecasting technique that uses analyses of past trends to predict the future.

barriers to competition. N. Forces that limit market competition, usually economic or technological conditions that make the entry of more firms to a market more difficult, thereby creating a barrier to competition.

barriers to entry. N. Obstacles to creating a new company within a particular industry, resulting from legal or economic advantages enjoyed by existing firms. The greater the barriers to entry, the less competition there is for firms already functioning in the industry.

barter. N. (1) The direct exchange of one item for another without the transfer of money. (2) In advertising, trading merchandise or services for advertising time or advertising space; used more often during the earliest days of advertising as a means of promoting products and services, e.g., free hotel rooms in exchange for advertising. See also *exchange*.

barter broker. N. See *prize broker*.

basal skin resistance. N. The norm from which changes in emotional response to stimuli such as advertising messages are recorded by means of an electronic galvanometer. ABBRV. *BSR*.

basement store. N. Historically, the basement of a department store containing bargain items. Today, expanded to any place within the store for items sold at budget prices. Synonymous with *budget store*.

base period. N. A chosen date from the past used in measuring the price index.

base price. N. See *list price*.

base rate. N. (1) Under an incentive system, the amount guaranteed per hour or other time period. (2) In advertising, a one-time rate from an advertising medium prior to offering of discounts. See also *open rate*.

base record. N. A consumer's file maintained by a store, credit agency, etc., with critical information on the person, beginning with name and address.

basic market description. N. Market research done before or immediately after selecting an arena for product innovation charter focus; prepares the firm to innovate in that area.

basic network. N. The fewest grouping of stations that an advertiser needs to contract so as to use the facilities of a radio or television network.

basic price. N. (1) The standard published price of a magazine. Synonymous with *basic rate*. (2) In international sales, used in conjunction with price supports applying to fruits, vegetables, and pork. Once the average market price is below the basic price, or cost of production price, action is taken to support the market by buying in surplus output.

basic rate. N. See *basic price*.

basic station. N. A television station included in the list of network affiliates whose time an advertiser is contracted to buy if he or she uses the network.

basic stock. N. Merchandise that is in constant demand, thus requiring perpetual inventory throughout the year. See also *assortment plan, model stock*.

basing point pricing. N. (1) A geographic pricing policy in which the seller designates one or more geographic locations from which the rate that a buyer will be charged is calculated. (2) To be avoided in the promotion of goods and services, an approach used by an industry whose goal is for all sellers to charge identical prices. The basing point is frequently the location of a plant near the buyer. Such pricing has been declared to be price discrimination in violation of the Clayton Antitrust Act.

battleground map. N. A map used by the retailer to indicate the geographic location of the flagship and branch stores. Usually includes markings for competitor operations.

battle of the brands. N. The competitiveness between national brands and private brands in an attempt to split up the market. See also *brand*.

beachhead. N. The third phase of the launch cycle. It comes immediately after announcement, and ceases when the product is withdrawn or moves into the fourth (growth) stage. See also *launch*.

behavioral economics. N. An approach to economic research that uses behavioral sciences and findings in explaining and predicting economic behavior, including that of marketing and commerce. The pioneering work can be found in the *Handbook of Behavioral Economic*, edited by B. Gilad and S. Kaish (JAI Press, 1986).

behavioral researchers. N. Investigators and scientists who use findings from psychology, sociology, anthropology, political science, and other related areas of inquiry to develop concepts and theories pertaining to people, their environment, and their buying behavior.

behavioral segmentation. N. A market segment strategy resulting from how consumers utilize an item or service and the purchasing pattern they demonstrate; defines consumer groups as to when they make purchases, how frequently they do so, or what product characteristics they are most interested in. See also *benefit segmentation*.

behaviorism. N. In advertising; the application of the stimulus-response theory of learning where a stimulus—the advertising message—is repeated over and over again to yield the desired response, such as the purchase of the item.

behavior modification. N. The increase of desirable behavioral patterns or the decrease of undesirable behavior brought about by using rewards or punishments whose efficacy in promoting the desired change has been proved.

beliefs. N. How consumers feel or think about a product or service that will influence their behavior in making a purchase. Altering beliefs can be a major challenge in promoting a product or service. See also *brand awareness*.

believability. N. In advertising, the plausibility of an advertisement; all within the range of possibility. A believable advertisement is more effective in most cases than an unbelievable one that raises doubts in the mind of a prospective buyer.

bell cow. N. *(slang)* A frequently purchased item whose selling price far exceeds its manufacturing cost; a very profitable item. Synonymous with *blue chip*.

bell-ringer. N. *(slang)* A door-to-door salesperson.

belly-to-belly selling. N. A form of selling where the salesperson confronts the prospect or customer. Synonymous with *nose-to-nose selling*.

below par. N. At a discount; less than face amount.

below the market strategy. N. Pricing by the retailer according to a plan of offering items below usual levels. See also *discount house*.

benchmarking. N. (1) Comparing the performance of products and processes with those of world leaders. (2) In advertising, the creative role of an advertisement or commercial; the standard used for determining how well an advertiser represents a specific client.

benefit. N. (1) A gain or advantage received by an individual. (2) In advertising, that which fulfills a need.

benefit market segmentation. N. See *benefit segmentation*.

benefit segmentation. N. One of a four-way categorization of the strategies of segmentation; includes the benefits the market draws from products. Helps marketers in determining marketing mix decisions. See also *product usage segmentation, state-of-being segmentation, state-of-mind segmentation, behavioral segmentation*.

benefit strategy. N. A method salespeople use in the opening minutes of contact with a prospect. The salesperson attempts to focus on the rewards and benefits of the product. The benefit is usually specific and concrete, such as the saving of money.

best time available. N. An advertiser's instruction to his or her client to run a commercial in the best possible available time which is usually when the largest audience is going to watch or read the commercial.

beta error. N. In marketing research, failure to find an attitude, opinion, or probable reaction in the target market.

Beta test. N. The type of product use testing that follows Alpha testing and takes place on the premises of intended market users. The procedure may only concentrate on whether the product performs as expected or on whether the performance meets the needs of the user, as perceived by that user, in which case it is called a Gamma test. ABBRV. *BTA*.

Better Business Bureau. N. A voluntary agency of business executives created to improve business practices and to define fair standards and ethics in the conduct of business activity. The movement to improve conditions began in 1921, when vigilance committees for truth in advertising first appeared in local advertising clubs. Today, there are in excess of one hundred fifty local Better Business Bureaus in the United States. ABBRV. *three Bs*.

better offer complaint. N. The complaint of a customer who has found a special offer of a lower price that he or she already paid for the same item or service. Many retailers honor this complaint with a refund or store credit, although they are not legally required to do so.

bias. N. (1) An attitude that may influence an individual's feelings, resulting in a leaning toward or away from a particular idea, item, or person. See also *Hawthorne effect*. (2) In consumer research, the systematic error resulting from the wording of a questionnaire, an interviewer, etc., that suggests one answer over another. See also *interviewer bias*, *prejudice*.

bid. N. See *bidding*.

bidder's list. N. A list of firms believed to be qualified to supply a given item.

bidding. N. (1) The offering of money as an exchange for an item or service put up for sale. (2) In marketing, the making of an offer of price and other details as solicited by a prospective purchaser wishing to, or is required by law to, get competitive offers prior to placing an offer. Synonymous with *competitive bidding*.

bid pricing. N. When a supplier fixes the price for items or services to be provided, which covers all the costs incurred and makes a predetermined contribution to profit.

big-early, little-late technique. N. A method of evolving media advertising schedules where the beginning of the campaign is regarded as most significant and therefore allotted the largest amount of funds.

big ticket items. N. Frequently refers to merchandise that is large in size and high in price (furniture, appliances, etc.).

big ticket selling. N. See *megaselling*.

bilateral monopoly. N. A condition that exists when there is only one purchaser for an item or service and the creation of the supply is controlled by one seller.

billboard. N. (1) In advertising, a poster panel in outdoor advertising. Synonymous with *poster*. See also *billboard allowance*. (2) In broadcasting, the opening routine of a broadcast program, including identification, performer credits, producers, and similar information. See also *routine*.

billboard allowance. N. Funds in an advertising budget used for outdoor advertising. See also *billboard*.

billing. N (1) The process of submitting invoices or bills. (2) In advertising, the total amount of money charged to clients by an advertising agency. This includes production costs, expenses, media costs, and other service charges.

bill me order. N. See *credit order*.

bill of sale. N. A contract for the sale of goods.

bill to-ship to. N. Instructions to have the invoice sent to a different address than given for the merchandise.

bind-in. N. Promotional pieces, printed on heavy paper, that are bound into periodicals.

bingo card. N. A reply card for magazine users to indicate from which advertisers they are interested in receiving further information. Called a bingo card because it features a series of numbers corresponding to advertisements within the periodical and the reader is asked to circle the pertinent number for further information and return the card to the publisher, who then forwards the request to the appropriate advertiser.

biogenic needs. N. See *primary needs*.

bird dog. V. *(slang)* To seek data to assist in studying a firm's position and potential earnings. N. (1) In business law, an individual who is paid to spread fraudulent charges. (2) In sales, an individual who is paid to obtain business for a high-power salesperson. See also *airedale*.

black and white. N. An advertisement, appearing in black ink on white paper.

black box. N. In marketing research, a concept of the inner workings that take place between input and output. The black box, or the transformation process between input and output, is said to contain the answer. The black box contains these components: environmental factors (dealing with the marketing messages), personal characteristics (describing interpersonal forces motivating people to buy), and buyer's responses (how and when decisions to buy are made).

black list. N. In international marketing, a list of individuals and firms of another country with whom the domestic nation forbids commerce by its nationals.

black market. N. (1) Buying or selling products or engaging in the exchange of foreign currencies in violation of government restrictions. (2) In merchandising, a situation when goods are priced at a high level when scarce or unavailable from normal market channels.

blank-check buying. N. The practice of a retailer placing an open order with a supplier, with requests to be made throughout the season as needed.

blank dummy. N. The full-size, practical mock-up model of a display. Usually presented with art or lettering.

blanket contract. N. A negotiated agreement between an advertiser and a medium dealing with all products or services to be advertised. The contract supersedes any arrangements the advertiser may have with an advertising agency. Synonymous with *master contract*.

blanket order. N. A preseason order to meet expected buyer demand. See also *blanket pricing agreement, systems contracting*. Synonymous *with yearly order*.

blanket pricing agreement. N. A purchasing agreement where the purchaser's orders or anticipated time-period requirements are placed in advance; the seller agrees to make shipments as requested at the contract price throughout the contract's duration. See also *blanket order, incremental pricing agreement*.

blanket rate. N. The rate applicable from or to a group of points. Synonymous with *group rate*.

blanking paper. N. The paper, usually white, surrounding the perimeter of an outdoor poster. Internal to the border is an advertisement. See also *bleed*.

bleed. N. Technique resulting in the printed area of an advertisement extending to the very edge of a newspaper or magazine page, without the white margin. Serving as an attention-getter, the artist is usually given considerable freedom in communicating the advertiser's message. See also *blanking paper*.

bleed in the gutter. N. *(slang)* An advertisement whose artwork and copy flows without interruption through the center margin of a magazine across the two facing pages; appears without a central line.

blended family. N. Two families from prior marriages merged into a single household as spouses remarry.

blighted area. N. A factor considered by advertisers, the area in a community or neighborhood that is about to become a slum.

blind advertisement. N. A want advertisement where only the job is listed and the identity of the employer is hidden by utilizing a box number for replies. See also *open advertisement*.

blind goods. N. Unusual items that can carry a higher-than-normal margin because of unique and only occasionally appeals to customers who are more interested in filling their requirements than they are in the price.

blind offer. N. See *hidden offer*.

blind product test. N. In consumer research, where people from a sample test various items that are not identifiable to them by brand, hopefully reducing bias or prejudgment.

blind selling. N. *(slang)* Selling merchandise without the customer having a chance to examine the item prior to purchase.

blind testing. N. Consumer evaluations of intrinsic items' qualities taken in a controlled test condition with all brand identification characteristics, such as packaging, pricing, etc.

blister package. N. A type of plastic packaging that permits visual inspection of the merchandise. Synonymous with *bubble wrap*.

block. N. In broadcasting, a group of consecutive time slots, or the same time period from day to day.

blockbuster. N. In broadcasting, a program that exceeds estimated ratings and therefore can boast that its audience watched or heard more commercials than anticipated.

blocked-out time. N. Time periods during the broadcast schedule of a station or network that are not available for sale to sponsors. Such time may be used for the broadcast of public service programs.

blotter. N. A form of direct advertising consisting of a panel of flexible paper stock, one side of which is made of soft, ink-absorbent paper. The reverse (face) side is usually employed to bear a printed advertising message.

blow in. N. Placing promotional pieces in a periodical with a device that literally blows the pieces between pages. They are unattached and can easily fall out or be discarded by a disinterested reader.

blue chip. N. See *bell cow*.

bluefingers. N. (1) In advertising, considered by advertisers in planning strategies, people from one family who attain common goals with efficiency and team spirit; for example, relatives who successfully pursue their objectives while receiving pleasure from their togetherness. (2) In retailing, friends who spend considerable shopping time together and because of common interests and attitudes, purchase similar styles and items in a particular price range. (3) See *jebble*.

blue law. N. Any state or local law restricting business activity on Sunday. Blue laws have been contested as an infringement of individual and free enterprise rights.

blurb. N. *(slang)* A brief but highly laudatory statement (e.g., a quotation from a book review) used in further promotional activities. See also *testimonial*.

blurring gender roles. N. A consumer lifestyle in which more men are assuming the once-traditional roles of their wives, and visa versa.

body copy. N. The primary portions of verbal matter found in an advertisement, as contrasted with the headlines, subheadlines, etc. The length of the copy is determined by the item for sale, the copywriter's method, and the sales concept that is presented. Synonymous with *body text*, *text*.

body test. N. See *body copy*.

body text. N. See *body copy*.

body type. N. The typeface used for the major section of text in an advertisement.

bogey. N. In sales, a standard of performance, such as the volume of sales beyond which a bonus is given.

boilerplate copy. N. A series of sentences of copy that is standard in all print messages produced by the same advertiser, such as a firm having brochures for each of its products and services.

bona fide. N. *(Latin)* In good faith; with honest intent. See also *bad faith*.

bona fide sale. N. A transaction where the seller acts in good faith regarding the terms of the sale.

bonded items. N. In international sales and marketing, items stored in a bonded warehouse to guarantee the government that the tax or duty on the merchandise will be paid on withdrawal of the items.

bonded warehouse. N. A cost factor for global marketers; goods kept in a government-supervised storage facility where items are stored without payment of duties or taxes until they are removed. See also *warehouse*.

bonus circulation. N. The circulation of a magazine or periodical beyond the circulation number that was guaranteed by the publisher to advertisers. Advertisers benefit from this by having additional readers at no extra cost to them.

bonus goods. N. Merchandise given without extra charge by a manufacturer to a retailer who agrees to purchase a minimum quantity of units in a special deal.

bonus pack. N. A promotional package where the customer is offered more than the regular amount for the regular price; also used by manufacturers as an incentive to buy by affixing a sample size of an item to a full size of the same item. See also *twin pack*.

bonus plan. N. Used by continuity marketers to solicit multiple purchases, such as used by the Book of the Month Club, with one free book for every three books bought. Shipping and handling charges are even made on the free item. See also *continuity strategy*.

bonus station. N. A broadcast station carrying commercial network programs without extra cost to the sponsor.

bookends. N. Two fifteen-second commercials on television for the same item or service, separated by other advertisers' commercials. See also *piggyback (3)*.

booking. N. (1) Orders for merchandise accepted on hand at a given time. (2) Accepting an order for goods to be transported.

booklet. N. Bound printed pages containing an advertisement, instructions on an item's use, or a service policy. See also *brochure*.

boom. N. (1) A time when business expands and the value of commodities and securities increases. (2) A period of rapidly rising prices and increased demand for goods and services, usually accompanied by full employment.

boomerang. N. (1) In global marketing, an international program to minimize the practice of goods dumping by returning such items duty free and exempt of quantity restrictions. (2) In sales, a technique for dealing with objections. The salesperson uses the prospect's statement of reasons for not buying as the basis of the precise reason for purchasing. Synonymous with *conversion process, positive conversion*.

borax. N. *(slang)* Inexpensive items that are usually poorly designed and constructed.

border. N. The line or design surrounding an advertisement.

border barriers. N. In international marketing, the physical barriers encountered at borders between nations affect both goods and services. Reducing and eventually eliminating customs throughout an internal market enables the free flow of goods and services.

border tax adjustment. N. A rebate of sales, value-added, or other indirect taxes paid on merchandise prior to export.

borrow. V. To receive something from another, with the understanding that the item is to be returned.

Boston Consulting Group Matrix. N. Enables a firm to classify each of its strategic business units in terms of the unit's market share relative to major competitors and the annual industry growth rate. The matrix identifies four types of such units: star, cash cow, problem child (question mark), and dog, and suggests appropriate strategies for each.

bottle collar. N. The cardboard display around the neck of a bottle for carrying an advertisement. Synonymous with *bottle topper*.

bottleneck. N. Operation in production system whose output sets limits for the entire system's output.

bottle topper. N. See *bottle collar*.

bottom-up technique. N. (1) An approach to strategy making whereby the lower levels of the organization push ideas to the top and strategy is then made. (2) In retailing, a budget technique where the budgeter begins with an estimate of the spending needed to supply each classification, finally arriving at a total for the department, and eventually for the company. See also *top-down method*.

bounce-back. V. To increase total sales, an added offer sent with a self-liquidator.

bounty. N. In global marketing of goods, added payments offered by a government as an incentive for a specific industry or the export of certain items.

boutique. N. A shop or part of a store that specializes in merchandise that is new and different. See also *salon*.

boutique agency. N. A small, independent advertising agency that specializes in only one aspect of advertising, such as media purchasing, often on a fee basis.

boutique merchandising. N. A store organization where related items from a number of departments are brought together in one shop to meet special customer requirements.

box store. N. See *warehouse store*.

box-top offer. N. An offer of a premium based on return of the top of a package or other evidence of purchase. Synonymous with *continuity programs*.

boycott. N. Considered by global marketers; an attempt to prevent the carrying on of a business by urging people not to buy from the firm being boycotted; frequently used on the international scene for political or economic reasons; illustrated by appeals, threats, and so on, to secure redress of a grievance.

BPI. ABBRV. Brand potential index.

brainstorming. N. A process of generating creativity and useful concepts through team or group discussions for solving problems. In advertising, brainstorming aid in the rapid movement from idea to action that forms the basis of the promotional campaign. See also *synectics*, *new product planning process*.

brainwashing. N. In consumer psychology, a systematic and radical technique of indoctrinating, manipulating, and coercing a person to abandon loyalties, values, etc., and to adopt new ones.

branch house. N. A location away from headquarters that is maintained by a manufacturer and used almost exclusively for purposes of stocking, selling, shipping, and servicing the company's products.

branch office. N. An office or department of a company at a location away from headquarters. It is a part of the company and not a separate legal entity, as is a subsidiary, an affiliate, or a joint venture.

branch store. N. A store owned by a parent store. Usually the parent store is located in the center of the city, with branch stores located in suburban areas of the city or other cities. See also *regional store*.

brand. N. A name, sign, or symbol used to identify items or services of the seller(s) and to differentiate them from goods of competitors. A brand aids consumers in differentiating between items of different manufacturers. See also *trademark, battle of the brands, brand generic, manufacturer's brand*.

brand association. N. The degree to which a specific brand is associated with the general product category in the consumer's mind.

brand attitude. N. Consumer opinions toward a item determined by market research; finds what people believe concerning the item, whether it is fulfilling of a need, and to what degree the product is wanted by the consumer.

brand awareness. N. Realization by a buyer of the existence and availability of a branded product. See also *determinant attributes, differential advantages, family brands*.

brand category. N. A general classification of products and services. Competing items and services that are similar in nature are all defined within the same brand category.

brand choice. N. Selecting a particular brand of item from the variety of available brands with similar purpose and content.

brand competitor. N. An organization that competes with others to satisfy consumers' demand for a specific product.

brand decision process. N. Consists of nonrecognition, recognition, preference (or dislike), and insistence (or aversion) stages that consumers pass through.

brand development. N. A means of determining the penetration of an item's sales, traditionally per thousand population. See also *brand development index*.

brand development index. N. The percentage of a brand's sales in an area based on population in that location as contrasted with the sales throughout the country, related to the total U.S. population. See also *brand development*.

brand equity. N. A branding concept that recognizes the marketing and financial value associated with a brand apart from a product's tangible attributes.

brand extension. N. The competitive strategy involving the application of a market-accepted brand to other firm's products, providing doing so will not confuse present customers or lessen the original image of product or brand; traditionally targeted to a particular segment within the parent brand's general market. See also *line extension*.

brand familiarity. N. The customer's ability to recognize and accept a particular brand of products. Brand familiarity can be separated into: brand rejection, brand nonrecognition, brand recognition, brand preference, and brand insistence.

brand franchise. N. (1) Consumer loyalty toward a particular brand. See also *brand loyalty*. (2) An agreement between the wholesaler or retailer and a brand name manufacturer giving the former an exclusive right to sell the brand manufacturer's item in a carefully

brand generic

defined location. Permits the wholesaler or retailer to sell the item in a noncompetitive market and set price limitations as the traffic will permit.

brand generic. N. The second half of a product's identifying title (brand is the first) and identifies one seller's version, while the generic is the second half and identifies the general class of item. For example, Jello is a brand; gelatin dessert is generic. Not to be confused with generic brands where there is no individual brand. See also *generic brands*.

brand image. N. See *brand awareness*.

branding. N. The assignment of a brand name to an item or service, thus achieving product differentiation within the marketplace. See also *generic brands*.

brand insistence. N. The extreme of brand loyalty, where the consumer says he or she will accept no substitute item.

brand label. N. A label that indicates little more than the brand name of the item, the manufacturer, and other information fulfilling requirements of the law.

brand leader. N. An item that is considered best in its field or is marketed with that assumption.

brand loyalty. N. The strength of a buyer's preference for a particular brand, which suggests a refusal to purchase a substitute. Brand loyalty is usually measured in terms of repeat sales and is also reflected in purchases of other items produced by the same company.

brand manager. N. See *product manager*.

brand mark. N. That part of a brand identification that can be recognized but cannot be verbalized.

brand marketing. N. A technique where each company's items is marketed separately, usually under the direction of a brand manager.

brand name. N. (1) In business law, a registered name used to prevent copying. (2) In marketing, a word or term that is placed on an item for identification or to be communicated orally.

brand-name bias. N. A person's tendency to respond to a survey by naming widely advertised brands, often for purposes of giving a good impression, rather than naming the brands that are actually purchased.

brand nonrecognition. N. The inability of a customer to recognize a brand, even should he or she be able to recognize the product.

brand personality. N. (1) The image of an item from the manufacturer's point of view. (2) How the firm intends the item to be perceived by the target market.

brand position. N. The placing of an item in the marketplace. The ranking as compared to other products that compete together.

brand potential index. N. A means of predicting product sales in a given market as a relationship between the brand development index and the market development index. The former is the percentage of product sales, the latter is the relationship between the potential and actual item users; used for planning future advertisement budgets. ABBRV. *BPI*.

brand preference. N. When the consumer chooses a particular brand over its competitors, usually resulting from a favorable experience with the item. However, if the product proves to be unavailable, the consumer willingly shifts to a substitute.

brand proliferation. N. The expansion of similar products within a specific line.

brand recognition. N. The perception by buyers, when confronted with a product, that they have been exposed to that brand name previously.

brand share. N. See *market share, share of the market*.

brand standing. N. Bringing together of a brand with an event, concept, or event, such as testimonials in a specific sporting event year after year.

brand strategy. N. Plans and tactics relating to the use of brand names.

brand switching. N. When a consumer selects a product or service different from that purchased the last time around.

brand-switching model. N. A model that provides a manager with some idea of the behavior of consumers in terms of their loyalty and the likelihood that they will switch from one brand to another.

break. N. In advertising and marketing, a discount.

break-down approach. N. Allocating the advertising budget to the lines of offerings.

break-down method. N. An approach to sales force design in which the size of the sales force is determined by dividing the forecasted annual sales volume by the expected sales volume per sales person.

break-even model. N. A model that shows the basic relationships among units produced (output), dollars of sales revenue, and the levels of costs and profits for an entire firm or a product line.

break-even point. N. Used to assess the impact of an advertising campaign, the point of activity at which a company earns zero profit. It is reached when total revenue equals total expense. See also *margin of safety, break-even pricing.*

break-even pricing. N. (1) Pricing at a level that will enable a firm to break even. (2) An approach to pricing in which the price of a unit of the product is set high enough to cover the variable costs of producing that unit as well as the fixed costs of producing the product. See also *break-even point.*

breaking bulk. N. Splitting a large inventory of items into smaller quantities as the items move toward its target consumers.

breakthrough opportunity. N. A marketing situation that provides for a creative company to formulate a new marketing strategy, a new product, or even to evolve a new marketing mix. If effective, it may discourage other potential competitors from entering a similar market.

bribery. N. Unfortunately found with people or firms attempting to market and promote goods and services; the payment resulting in the payer receiving some right, benefit, or preference to which he or she has no legal right and that he or should would not have obtained except by paying the money. In the United States, a bribe is a criminal offense.

broadcaster. N. (1) A person who delivers or sponsors an announcement, commercials or program on a network, radio, or television station. (2) Owners and operators of radio or television station, and networks.

broad-line strategy. N. An offering by a firm of a large number of variations of the item. See also *limited-line strategy.*

broad market. N. A market situation where there are a large number of segments of widely different characteristics. See also *narrow market.*

broad price policy. N. Sets the overall direction and tone for a firm's pricing efforts and makes sure pricing decisions are coordinated with the firm's choices regarding a target market, an image, and other marketing-mix factors. It incorporates short- and long-term pricing goals.

broadside. N. A single sheet of advertising literature of comparatively large size printed in one or more colors on rather heavy white or colored stock, folded at least once, and designed to deliver a forceful impression by virtue of its size and bold display of type and illustrative matter.

brochure. N. In merchandising, a booklet that is printed on quality paper and features copy of the manufacturer's product, service, etc.

broker. N. (1) A person who prepares contracts with third parties, as with a freight broker and customs broker, on behalf of a principal. (2) A wholesaling intermediary whose primary function is to supply market information and establish contacts in order to facilitate sales for clients.

brokerage. N. (1) Found in global practices, the fee or commission charged by a broker. (2) In the United States, a brokerage firm.

brokerage allowance. N. The commission paid by the seller in a transaction to the broker who arranges the sale; usually a percentage of the selling price.

brood hen and chick method. N. Where branch retail stores are looked upon as part of chains, but with tighter merchandising controls. See also *brood hen concept*.

brood hen concept. N. When the retail buyer at the parent store maintains close communications with his or her branches, receiving requests for items and responds at the buyer's discretion. See also *brood hen and chick method*.

brown goods. N. What retailers often call television sets and radios. See also *orange goods, red goods, yellow goods*.

BSR. ABBRV. Basal skin resistance.

BTA. ABBRV. Best times available.

bubble wrap. N. See *blister pack*.

buckeye. N. *(slang)* A crude-appearing advertisement that is sloppy, lacking both balance and clarity.

budget. N. A critical factor in the successful organization of an advertising agency, or any other venture; an itemized listing, and frequently the allotment, of all estimated revenues a business anticipates receiving and a listing, and frequently the segregation of all estimated costs and expenses that will be incurred in obtaining those revenues during a stated period of time.

budget-book sale. N. Where the customer contracts for a specific amount to be paid back on a regular basis with a small carrying charge. A book with coupons is used as cash within the store.

budgeting. N. The process of determining and assigning the resources required to reach market and advertising objectives.

buffer stock. N. Merchandise kept on hand to prevent a shortage resulting from an unexpected increase in demand for the items. Synonymous with *reserve stock*.

build strategy. N. Increasing promotional funding to increase a product's market share; impacts the future of the product.

build-up method. N. A method for arriving at national forecasts for individual regions and then aggregating the regional forecasts.

bulk discount. N. A reduced charge for quantity or multiple purchases. See also *discount*. Synonymous with *volume discount*.

bulk mail. N. Second-, third-, and fourth-class mail, including parcel post, ordinary papers, and circulars.

bulk sales. N. Substantial quantities of a publication bought for redistribution.

bulk warehouse. N. See *warehouse, bulk*.

bullpen. N. The art department located within an advertising agency where creative artwork and related matters are attended to. Although more expensive than using freelancers, it provides for reliability, continuity for a firm's products or services, and consistency.

bundle. N. See *bundled pricing*.

bundled pricing. N. An offering of a basic product, options, and customer service for one total price.

bundle of benefits. N. A concept that consumer or industrial users do not purchase things as such, but instead purchase the benefits that those items are expected to offer. See also *bundle of services*.

bundle of services. N. A concept favoring leasing rather than owning of equipment based on the point that the purchase of a machine can be thought of as the purchase of the number of yearly services that the equipment is expected to last. See also *bundle of benefits*.

bundling. N. The practice of marketing two or more product or service items in a single package with one price.

burden. N. See *overhead*.

buried offer. N. See *hidden offer*.

buried position. N. The place on a publication page where the advertisement is bordered by other advertisements or is a bottom corner inside of a page with advertisements at the top and side. It is usually considered an inferior place for an advertisement.

burst advertising. N. Where the advertisement appears for only a short time, such as a week, with a "burst" of exposures. Used to accompany new item introductions or to coincide with special promotions. See also *saturation*.

business advisory services. N. Industrial services that include management consulting, advertising agency services, accounting services, and legal services.

business analysis. N. The stage in the new-product planning process that considers such criteria as demand projections, cost projections, competition, required investment, and profitability for new products.

business cycle. N. Frequently considered during an advertising campaign, any interval embracing alternating periods of economic prosperity and depression.

business domain. N. The sector of a market that a company targets as its business environment; often defined in terms of a line of products.

business ethics. N. Applied in the preparation of commercials, socially accepted rules of behavior that place pressure on business executives to maintain a high sense of values and to be honest and fair in their dealings with the public.

business marketing. N. The marketing of goods and services to commercial enterprises, governments, and other profit and not-for-profit organizations for use in the creation of goods and services

business publication

that they then produce and market to other business customers as well as individuals and ultimate consumers.

business publication. N. See *trade magazine*.

business-to-business advertising. N. Advertising directed at purchasing officials and other decision makers instead of the general consumer. Businesses advertise in their own trade publications. See also *consumer advertising, trade advertising*.

business unit goal. N. A performance target the business unit seeks to reach to achieve its mission.

business unit level. N. The level at which business unit managers set directions for their products and markets.

business unit mission. N. A statement specifying the markets and product lines in which a business unit will compete.

busy. N. *(slang)* A print layout where the elements are excessive and resist each other, thereby detracting from the advertiser's intent.

buy at best. V. To bid higher and higher prices without any limit until the required quantity is bought.

buy-back agreement. N. A provision in a sales contract stating that the seller will repurchase items within a specified time period, usually for the selling price, if the purchaser is transferred from the area. Synonymous with *product buy-back agreement*.

buy classes. N. Groups of three specific buying situations organizations face—new buy, straight rebuy, and modified rebuy.

buyer. N. (1) An individual who acquires goods for purposes of making a profit, usually as the result of a resale. (2) In retailing, an executive responsible for purchasing merchandise to be sold in a store.

buyer for export. N. In international marketing, a middleperson responsible for purchasing goods in the domestic market outright and then attempting to sell them globally.

buyer readiness stages. N. In purchasing a product, a consumer passes stages, ranging from awareness to completion and purchase.

buyer-seller dyad. N. The rapport developed between the customer and the salesperson, often based on close and detailed communication.

buyers' market. N. A market characterized by low or falling prices, occurring when supply is greater than demand and buyers tend to set the prices and terms of sale. See also *seller's market*. Synonymous with *loose market*, *soft market*.

buyer's over. N. A situation of more buyers than sellers.

buyer's surplus. N. The difference between what a buyer pays for an item and the amount more he or she would be willing to paid for it.

buyer turnover. N. The frequency with which new buyers enter the market to buy a product.

buying allowance. N. A lowering of price on given items offered by a producer to a purchaser as an incentive to buy the goods.

buying by description. N. The purchase from a verbal or visual presentation of an item. Usually, to be satisfactory, the customer has strong feelings of confidence in the business under consideration.

buying by inspection. N. Buying following the examination of the actual items to be purchased.

buying by sample. N. Buying following the examination of a representative sample or portion of the item.

buying by specification. N. A store submitting specific requests for delivery rather than purchasing standard merchandise available from the manufacturer.

buying center. N. All the individuals and groups participating in the buying process that have interdependent goals and share common risks.

buying committee. N. A group of buyers, often chain stores, who decide by committee on the items that will and will not be purchased.

buying criteria. N. The requirements of a firm evaluating suppliers of a product or service.

buying decision. N. Choices made by a consumer before making a purchase; begins once the consumer has established a willingness to purchase.

buying direct. N. The purchase of goods from the manufacturer, bypassing any middleperson.

buying distribution. N. A concept related to channels of distribution emphasizing that the price paid to gain channel support must reflect not only the marketing job expected of the channel, but also the competitive environment that the channel services.

buying error. N. The failure to match purchases with demand; often leading to a markdown so as to move the merchandise out of the store. See also *selling error*.

buying incentive. N. A premium of additional items, a discount, or a gift, available to prospects should they purchase an item or service.

buying income method. N. A method of projecting the results of a test marketing program to national performance, based on income.

buying intent. N. The measurement of a prospect's intention to buy an item or service.

buying loader. N. A manufacturer's gift, either a discount, premium, etc., to a retailer as a bonus for buying the manufacturer's item. See also *dealer loader*.

buying off the peg. N. The purchase of ready-to-wear merchandise, to be taken home or delivered immediately thus involving no adjustments or alterations.

buying power. N. See *purchasing power*.

buying signals. N. Verbal and nonverbal cues from a prospective customer that he or she is ready to make a purchase. See also *close*.

buying specialists. N. Employees of organizational consumers who have technical backgrounds and are trained in supplier analysis and negotiating.

buying structure of the organization. N. The level of formality and specialization used in the purchase process. It depends on the organization's size, resources, diversity, and level of specialization.

buy national. N. A growing appeal to restrain imports from other nations, especially when public procurement practices are at stake. The concept resists the international marketing of goods and services because each competing country claims that the other nations discriminate against foreign competition.

buy-or-die message. N. Promotional material focused on inactive direct-mail customers telling them that unless they make a purchase they will be purged from the mailing list.

buyout. V. (1) To purchase all the assets, stock, and so on, of an ongoing organization. (2) To purchase the interest in a firm that is owned by another. N. In broadcasting, a one-time payment to talent appearing on radio or television, which buys all rights to the performance in that commercial. Tends to be quite economical for the advertiser.

buy phases. N. Stages that people or groups go through when making purchasing decisions.

by-line. N. (1) A printed article, often in a newspaper or magazine, where the author's name is given. (2) An endorser who is a celebrity or other well-known individual.

C

CAD

CAD. ABBRV. Cash against documents.

call. V. To demand payment of a loan secured by collateral because of failure by a borrower to comply with the terms of the loan.

callback. N. The technique used by a sales representative on a second or subsequent effort to induce a potential customer to buy. See also *user calls*.

call bird. V. To increase store traffic, incorporating lower prices on items not usually bought in large quantities that are shown in windows or advertisements of the retailer.

call-blockage. N. In telemarketing, failure to receive a call made to an inbound telephone center because the caller received a busy signal.

call credit. N. Credit given for the price of an item when merchandise is picked up from a customer and returned to the store.

call planning. N. A telephone sales planning method used by salespeople; involves defining the goal of the call and devising a selling strategy.

call report. N. A salesperson's record for his or her supervisor identifying calls made to potential or real customers during a stated time period or within a specified market. Tells when a meeting occurred and what was talked about. See also *activity quota*. Synonymous with *conference report, contact report*.

call station. N. An area at which a pickup and delivery service is available, although there are no warehouse facilities.

call system. N. In retailing, when the salesperson receives compensation based at least in some aspects on the amount of business he or she finishes.

call to action. N. That portion of an advertising message directing the consumer what to do as a result of receiving the advertiser's message, such as to call an 800-telephone number to place an order, return a coupon, etc.

campaign. N. In advertising, a series of advertising communications or promotions, scheduled for a given time period, and connected by a central theme, common goals, etc. In principle, each step along the campaign adds a new, constructive element. See also *advertising campaign*.

campaign basis. N. Moving forward toward a marketing goal without concern for its relationship with the total business system.

campaign plan. N. See *advertising campaign, campaign*.

canalization. N. The building by an advertiser or salesperson on an association, a perfection, an anxiety, or data possessed by a prospective or real customer. It results in a major shift in behavior.

cancel. N. In merchandising, a customer's request to cancel an order or stop service. Synonymous with *kill, kill bad pay*. V. To terminate an advertisement or contract.

canned presentation. N. A prewritten and usually memorized presentation by a sales representative, spoken sentence for sentence, with little or no deviation.

cannibalization. N. See *cannibalizing the market*.

cannibalizing the market. N. The result of introducing a new product that, instead of creating greater sales, cuts into existing sales of the item it is intended to replace. See also *enhancement*.

canvass. V. (1) To count or examine. (2) In sales, to call on prospective customers in person or by telephone to sell merchandise or services, to determine interest, or to gather information.

capability survey

See also *cold canvassing, preapproach*. Synonymous with *territory screening*.

capability survey. N. In purchasing, inspecting a prospective vendor's operation to secure answers to issues dealing with quality control, capacity to finance and manage, quality of technology, etc.

capacity. N. (1) One of the three elements of credit. (2) In packaging, the volume of space within a container or other space, expressed in units. (3) In marketing, the ability of a factory or firm to produce results at a given level.

capital. N. (1) The amount invested in a venture. (2) A long-term debt plus owners' equity. (3) The net assets of a firm, partnership, and the like, including the original investment, all gains and profits.

capital account. N. (1) An account maintained in the name of the owner or owners of a retail business and indicating the equity in that business—usually at the close of the last accounting period. (2) Balance of payment items not included in a current account.

capital consumption allowance. N. See *depreciation*.

capital goods. N. Items ordinarily treated as long-term investment (capitalized) because of substantial value and life (e.g., industrial machinery). Synonymous with *durable merchandise*.

capital intensive. N. (1) Characterized by the need to utilize additional capital to increase productivity or profits. (2) Processes that require a high concentration of capital relative to labor per unit of output and products produced by such processes.

capitalize. V. (1) To include in an investment account expenditures for purchase or construction of property. (2) To divide income by a rate of interest to obtain principal.

caption. N. (1) The explanatory text accompanying a drawing or photograph. (2) In advertising, a word, phrase, or sentence describing the visual element of a print advertisement. Synonymous with *cutlines*.

captive audience. N. People exposed to commercial messages while passengers on carriers whose use of media they cannot control.

captive market. N. Purchasers who have little latitude in choosing the vendor of a product or service. Consumers purchase these items available through vendors in a particular location.

captive product pricing. N. A pricing technique of product manufacturers who require supplies, accessories, or additional devices for operation. The major product is moderately priced to attract customers while the supplies, etc., are given significant markups, i.e., camera film prices are kept low, while processing prices are high.

captive rotary. N. A set of outdoor advertising locations used primarily for one advertiser with differing items to expose to the marketplace.

captive warehouse. N. See *warehouse, private*.

carbon-copy concept. N. In sales, the training of new salespeople is best carried out by their emulating and memorizing the methods of proven salespeople.

car card. N. Advertising poster displayed in buses, trains, and subway cars.

card rate. N. The cost for advertising in a publication or a broadcast network or station as published on the rate card for that publication or network.

carload. N. Applied in global marketing, the amount of a commodity or product that can fill a freight car, or the amount that is sufficient to be treated as a full car.

carnet. N. In international marketing, a document of international customs that permits temporary duty-free importation of specific items into certain nations. See also *covered under carnet*.

carriage trade. N. *(Term is historic, and rarely used today)* The class of rich customers who expected and received superior services for their willingness to pay higher prices for merchandise and services.

carrier. N. In international marketing, an individual or organization, usually without a permit of public franchise, that is engaged in transporting products or people.

carrying charge. N. In merchandising, a charge added to the price of merchandise to compensate for deferred payment.

carryouts. N. Items bought in a store that are not shipped but are taken from the store by the customer. Synonymous with *take-withs*.

carryover effects. N. The influence exerted on the sales of future periods by present-day marketing expenditures.

cartage. N. The charge for pickup and delivery of a shipment.

cartel. N. A group of separate business organizations that have agreed to institute approaches to altering competition by influencing prices, production, or marketing; rarely as effective as a monopoly.

cart wrap. N. The printed advertising message composed of paper that is designed to wrap about the cart in a store. See also *case wraparound*.

case. N. A container used for goods sold at wholesale rates, e.g., a case of canned tuna.

case allowance. N. The discount that a wholesaler or manufacturer gives to a retailer when items are bought by the case. Usually, the larger the number of cases bought, the greater the discount.

case wraparound. N. A sales promotion item created to be placed around the case of merchandise. See also *cart wrap*.

cash acknowledgment. N. A notice sent to a cash buyer mentioning the receipt of an order. Often, cash acknowledgements are accompanied with new information about merchandise and prices, substitutes for out-of-stock items. Used primarily when a delivery is delayed.

cash against documents. N. In global marketing, the payment for goods on presentation of documents evidencing shipments. ABBRV. *CAD*.

cash and carry wholesaler. N. A wholesaler who demands that the buyer must pay when he or she picks up merchandise, without credit, or the wholesaler will not make delivery. Cash and carry wholesalers frequently deal in fast-moving, i.e., perishable, items, such as bakery goods. See also *truck jobber*.

cash before delivery. N. A requirement to pay prior to delivery of goods. Synonymous with *cash in advance*. ABBRV. *CBD*.

cash budget. N. A schedule of expected cash receipts and disbursements.

cash buyer. N. A customer who pays by forwarding cash, check, or money order with his or her order.

cash cancellation. N. Canceling a cash order; requiring a refund. Traditionally such cancellations occur because of customer dissatisfaction with the item or service.

cash card. N. A card given by a retailer or store owner to a customer to guarantee a discount for cash payment. It is a substitute for credit cards. Some merchants give cash-paying customers up to an 8% discount.

cash cow. N. Products that enjoy comfortable profits and whose excess earnings are used (milked) to support other divisions, or weaker selling products.

cash discount. N. A percentage deduction from the selling price permitted by the seller for merchandise sold on credit, to encourage prompt payment of the invoice covering the goods or services purchased. Synonymous with *sales discount*.

cash flow. N. The reported net income of an advertising agency, plus amounts charged off for depreciation, depletion, amortization, and extraordinary charges to reserves, which are bookkeeping deductions and are not actually paid out in cash. Knowledge of these factors results in a better understanding of a firm's ability to pay dividends.

cash in advance. N. See *cash before delivery*.

cash incentive. N. Any promotional method to encourage customers to pay when they order in return for a free, complementary gift. The gift usually is less expensive than the cost of sending another bill and waiting for payment.

cash on delivery. N. Describing any purchase made with the expectation that the item(s) will be paid for on delivery. Synonymous with collection on delivery. ABBRV. *COD*.

cash order. N. An order accompanied by the required payment. See also *cash buyer, cash with order, credit order*.

cash position. N. (1) A measure of the financial viability of an advertising agency, the percentage of cash to the total net assets;

the net amount after the deduction of current liabilities. (2) The ratio of cash and related assets to liabilities.

cash refund offer. N. A rebate offered by the manufacturer of an item to the customer. Once merchandise is bought the manufacturer returns a portion of the purchase price in exchange for a label or other proof that a purchase has been made. Cash refunds are used for low-cost packaged items as well as for expensive goods such as cars or refrigerators.

cash-register tape redemption plan. N. See *tape plan*.

cash sale. N. The surrender of cash at the time of sale.

cash terms. N. An agreement to pay cash for bought items, often within a given time period.

cash with order. N. Payment for goods in which the buyer pays when ordering and in which the transaction is binding on both parties. See also *cash order*. ABBRV. *CWO*.

catalog(ue). N. Printed material that identifies items for sale. In most cases, the merchandise is described and prices are given; sometimes, a photograph or drawing accompanies an entry. See also *mail-order wholesaler*.

catalog buyer. N. A person who makes a purchase from a particular catalog.

catalog merchandising. N. The promotion of items for sale in a catalog.

catalog plan. N. See *price agreement plan*.

catalog showroom. N. A discount store at which customers review catalogs and then place orders and wait for delivery.

categorical technique. N. A marketing strategy for evaluating the sources of supply. The purchaser maintains a record of all vendors and their products based on a list of characteristics to which performance evaluations are assigned as more experience with the supplier is acquired. This technique leads to a more efficient operation and usually lowers costs.

causal research. N. Marketing that zeroes in on cause and effect relationships within the marketplace, for example, the impact of advertising in the selling of a product or service. The value of casual research is that it illustrates the interrelationship of variables in a given marketing situation. See also *cause-related marketing*.

cause-related marketing. N. (1) A promotional campaign devoted to raising the awareness of or the generating funds for an event or social cause. (2) Where a specific product or brand is associated with a particular event, cause, or activity, thus producing increased sales in combination with good will. See also *causal research*.

caveat emptor. N. (*Latin*) Let the buyer beware; when merchandise is sold without a warranty by the vendor, the purchaser takes the risk of loss due to defects. See also *warranty, without recourse, caveat subscriptor (venditor)*.

caveat subscriptor (venditor). N. (*Latin*). Let the seller beware; unless the seller states no responsibility, he or she is liable to the purchaser for any alterations from the written contract. See also *caveat emptor*.

CBD. ABBRV. Cash before delivery.

cease and desist order. N. (1) A demand by a court or governmental agency that a person or firm cease an activity. (2) In advertising, an order from the Federal Trade Commission (FTC) to stop a particular advertising activity or unfair method of competing that violates an FTC or other federal regulation.

celebrity testimonial. N. Found in advertising, utilizing the recognition of a celebrity to promote a product or service. Usually serves as a promotion of both the celebrity and his or her cause or product being promoted. See also *spokesperson, testimonial*.

CE mark. N. Used to promote and sell goods from the European Union; a method to create a system for marking goods. Member states agreed on governing principles for the CE mark—the mark that indicates a product's compliance with technical regulations. The CE stamp, important to exporters, signifies a product's conformity to community rules on technical harmonization.

centerfold. N. See *center spread*.

centers of influence. N. People of high social or business standing through whom a salesperson seeks to find qualified buyers. Centers of influence are people who exert power or authority over others, for example, bankers and lawyers.

center spread. N. (1) In newspapers and other printed magazines, the center pages, providing an unbroken surface to the printing of an advertisement. Synonymous with *centerfold*. See also *spread*. (2) In outdoor advertising, synonymous with *double-page spread*.

central buying. N. A popular approach in chain stores whereby all purchasing is done through a central or main office. Shipments of merchandise, however, are usually made directly to the branch stores of the chain.

centralized purchasing. N. A system by which a department or unit is authorized to procure, handle, or store all supplies, materials, and equipment required by some or all of the other departments or units of a company.

centralized sales organization. N. An organization possessing the overall sales function that is concentrated at the highest levels of management. See also *decentralized sales organization*.

central market. N. (1) The geographical area with a significant concentration of suppliers, where both buyers and sellers can meet to interact more efficiently. (2) The location where a large number of the major suppliers or manufacturers of a given item or service may be found.

cents-off-coupon. N. A coupon that entitles the holder to a discount on merchandise at the time of purchase. The coupon is received by the retailer from the buyer, who submits it to the manufacturer, wholesaler, or clearing house. As many as one hundred fifty billion coupons are distributed each year in the United States See also *coupon*.

certificate. N. Any written or printed document of truth that can be used as proof of a fact.

certificate of inspection. N. A document certifying that merchandise (such as perishable goods) was in good condition immediately prior to shipment.

certificate of manufacture. N. Of importance to international marketers, a statement signed by an exporter that goods ordered by the importer have been finished and set aside for shipment. This document is used with a letter of credit for the benefit of the exporter.

certificate of origin. N. In international manufacturing, a certificate declaring that goods purchased from a foreign country have indeed been produced in that country and not in another. Under most multilateral trade accords, traders are required to submit duly completed certificates of origin to their international counterparts to claim full or partial exemption from customs duties.

certification. N. An administrative task that awards a product a certificate if it satisfies special tests.

certification mark. N. Used in marketing European goods, a symbol, word, or other imprint to designate a product or service as meeting the highest standards, safety, or certification of the sponsoring organization, e.g. the "E" found on items cleared by the European Union.

chain discount. N. A series of discounts based on an earlier discount for the same item, e.g., a chain discount of 40%, 5%, and 5% is the same as one discount of 45.85%, from the list price of the item.

chain markup pricing. N. A form of demand-based pricing in which final selling price is determined, markups for each channel member are examined, and the maximum acceptable costs to each member are computed; extends demand-minus calculations all the way from channel members back to their suppliers.

chain prospecting. N. Prospecting by the salesperson who wants the names of one or more prospects from each one that has been approached. See also *endless chain*.

chain ratio method. N. A method of sales forecasting in which a firm starts with general market information and then computes a series of more specific information. These combined data yield a sales forecast.

chain store. N. (1) Two or more stores, usually in different locations, being operated by the same organization. (2) A retail organization that consists of two or more units under a single ownership.

chain store law. N. See *Robinson-Patman Act of 1936*.

chamber of commerce. N. Traditionally, a national trade-promoting organization servicing its members with information and reports on increasing international sales and trade. Complaints by consumers relating to advertising are often brought to this institution.

channel. N. (1) In the communication process, the style of transmission. It can take the form of oral or written communication. (2) In marketing, a channel of distribution. See also *channel of distribution*.

channel behavior. N. Activities of cooperation and conflict between people and firms that make up a manufacturer's channels of distribution.

channel captain. N. (1) A channel member that is able to influence the behavior of the other members of the channel. (2) The manufacturer, retailer, or wholesaler who dominates and controls a channel of distribution, usually setting distribution policy that others follow.

channel change. N. The relationship between channel of distribution members in conflict.

channel competition. N. When marketers establish dominance over others.

channel fit. N. The degree to which a newly introduced item can be distributed through a channel of distribution already in use by the manufacturer of the new product.

channel functions. N. The functions completed by some member of a channel: marketing research, buying, promotion, customer services, product planning, pricing, and distribution.

channel interdependency. N. The members' relationship where each decision and activity impacts the decisions and activities of other channels of distribution members.

channel leader. N. A channel member that dominates the market and may influence or control decisions.

channel length. N. The levels of independent members along a channel.

channel management. N. The activities involved in anticipating and understanding the sources of channel conflict and trying to eliminate or minimize them.

channel members. N. Those participating in the distribution process.

channel number. N. The number of different marketing channels used by one marketer. Influenced by geographical areas and the size of purchasers.

channel of distribution. N. (1) The interrelated network of people and firms for delivering goods from the manufacturer to the consumer. Intermediaries assist as merchant middlepeople who take title to goods and then resell it, and as agent middlepeople who do not take title to goods, but serve as brokers. (2) The route a product follows from an original grower, producer, or importer to the last consumer. Often a middleperson is used (e.g., automobile manufacturers sell to car dealers, who then sell to consumers). See also *channel behavior, channel fit, distribution*. Synonymous with *market channel, trade channel*.

channel partnering. N. Agreements and procedures among channel members for ordering and physically distributing a producer's product through the channel to the ultimate consumer.

channel power. N. The influence of one member of a channel of distribution over another.

channel width. N. The different outlets or individual companies employed at each level of the channel of distribution, where

charge. v. In sales, to purchase for credit without making an immediate payment; usually to pay following billing.

charge account. N. A means of making sales on credit to retail customers. The various types are as follows: (a) open (thirty-day) account: an account in which the store accepts the customer's promise to pay for items bought, usually within thirty days of purchase; (b) revolving account: an account in which the store sets the maximum amount of money the customer may owe at any one time. The amount is determined at the time the account is opened and is based on individual income and credit rating; (c) budget (flexible) account: an account in which monthly installment payments are based on the size of the customer's account balance, and interest is charged on the unpaid amount; and, (d) coupon credit plan: an account in which the customer is given credit coupons that may be used in the store as cash. Payment for the coupons is made over a period of time, usually six months. This plan eliminates the need for a monthly billing.

charge buyer. N. A person who makes a purchase on credit to be billed at a later time. Synonymous with *credit buyer*. See also *credit order*.

charges forward. N. A system whereby the purchaser pays for merchandise and shipping charges only upon receipt of the goods or, following receipt of goods, when a bill arrives.

charging the top of the rate card. N. The ability to attract new advertisers to a medium at a one-time rate resulting from the demand that exceeds the capacity of the medium to accommodate.

charging what the traffic can bear. N. An expression suggesting that the seller ask the highest price that he or she believes the market will bear (i.e., people will pay).

cheap jack. N. *(slang)* An individual who sells merchandise rapidly by unorthodox approaches, including using unoccupied stores to set up his or her goods.

checkerboard. N. The direction provided for space utilization for placing advertising in a periodical or magazine. Space is usually sold at the half-page rate.

checking copy. N. A copy of a publication delivered to an agency or advertiser to verify the inclusion of an advertisement as requested. See also *tear sheet*.

checkout counter. N. The location where items bought are checked and paid for; frequently used by an advertiser for displays.

check question. N. In sales, a carefully phrased question that purports to elicit an answer from a potential customer to provide some clue as to the progress being made toward a buying decision. See also *trial close*.

cherry picking. N. Buyer selection of only a few items from a vendor's line, rather than buying a complete line or classification of merchandise from any one source. Synonymous with *hi-spotting*.

Child On-Line Protection Act. N. U.S. legislation of February 2, 1999, barring marketers from collecting personal information from children under the age of 12 via the Internet, unless parental approval is given. ABBRV. *COPA*.

China eggs. N. *(slang)* People who at first appear to be good prospects to purchase an item or service, but who fail to become customers.

chi-square test. N. Used in marketing research, a means of estimating whether a given set of data differs from expected values to such a degree as to be evidence of the operation of nonchance factors. It is the sum of the quotients obtained by dividing the square of each difference between an actual and an expected frequency by the expected frequency.

choice criteria. N. Critical characteristics used by the firms' purchaser when evaluating merchandise offered for sale.

cinema advertising. N. Commercials that appear on a movie screen in theaters prior to the presentation of the feature film.

circ. ABBRV. Circular.

circular. N. (1) Regular or small sheets of printed paper to be sent in the mail or delivered by hand. (2) An advertisement printed on one sheet of paper and distributed by third-class mail or by hand. Often contains technical and mechanical information that is important to the consumer. ABBRV. *Circ.* See also *flier.*

circular flow. N. A process that shows the exchange between households and firms in the interaction of the flow of real sources and commodities, and money income and expenditures.

circulation. N. (1) In advertising, the number of copies of a publication that are distributed. Advertising rates for publications are traditionally based on circulation figures. See also *readership.* (2) In broadcasting, the number of homes regularly tuned to a specific station.

circulation rate base. N. Circulation that a print media guarantees as a minimum. Should circulation fall below this on a regular basis, the publisher often makes a pro rate refund.

claim. N. (1) A demand for payment, reimbursement, or compensation for damages or injury as identified in a contract or under law.

(2) In advertising, a statement employed in advertising of a product or service that points to a positive aspect of the item or service benefit or value to be gain by its use.

claims-paid complaint. N. A customer complaint dealing with a bill, after the payment for the merchandise or service has been sent to the seller.

class-action suit. N. A law suit filed on behalf of many affected consumers.

class consciousness. N. The extent to which social status is desired and pursued by a person.

classification. N. In merchandising, an assortment of items, all of which are substitutable for one another to the customer.

classification data. N. Information by which an audience, a location, or broadcast and print media is to be organized into useful research data, e.g., by age, education, or occupations.

classification merchandising. N. A system of record keeping that assists inventory control and results in categorization of merchandise.

classified advertising. N. Advertising identified by product or service; usually appears in a particular section of the publication. Rates for classified advertising are determined by the size of the advertisement, either by word count or by line count. See also *display advertisement, classified display advertising*. Synonymous with *undisplay advertising*.

classified display advertising. N. Special sections in newspapers, at times called supplements, devoted to one product, service, or cause.

class magazine. N. A magazine designed to be bought by a special interest group, to those sharing a common interest. Class magazine

class rate. N. (1) An insurance rate applicable to risks that are so similar in character that it is unnecessary to go to the expense of differentiating among them as to varying factors of hazards. (2) In distribution, a special shipping rate for certain classes of commodities, expressed as a percentage of the base rate. (3) In broadcasting, a charge made for radio or television time according to the desirability of the time slot.

Clayton Antitrust Act of 1914. N. See *tie-in sales*.

clean bill of lading. N. Used in international sales and marketing; a bill of lading accepted by the carrier for goods received in appropriate condition (no damages or missing items).

clean draft. N. A draft to which no documents have been attached.

clean report of findings. N. In international marketing, a document from a recognized inspection agency certifying that certain items were examined and found to be in order.

clear. V. In retailing, to reduce inventory (e.g., clearing out merchandise.)

clearance. N. (1) An act of clearing. (2) In retailing, a reduction on the price of items; a special sale that is often used to clear inventory and/or off-season goods. See also *markdown*.

clear time. N. Time periods reserved by a station for the messages of an advertiser; a check by a network on the availability of time slots with station affiliates.

clerking activities. N. Retail store activities where there is direct customer contact.

click-through rates. N. Viewers of an Internet advertisement who click on the ad to access the advertiser's website.

client. N. (1) A person, firm, or other organization who uses the professional services of other people. (2) In advertising, what the agency calls an advertiser whose advertising it handles. The client is the customer for whom the advertising agency works. Frequently referred to as an account, but not always synonymous. See also *advertiser*.

client list. N. The list of clients belonging to a specific advertising agency.

client organization. N. A business firm that produces products and/or services and retains advertising agencies and other suppliers for special services.

Clio Award. N. In broadcasting commercials, an international prize for creative excellence; judged by a panel of advertising creative executives and specialists from countries around the globe.

close. V. In sales, to secure the customer's written or spoken agreement to purchase the item or service being offered. See also *buying signals*. N. In advertising, that section of the copy containing the idea of interest to an advertiser. Synonymous with *urge line*.

closed assortment. N. An assortment where the structure of items needed by the consumer is present and complete. See also *open assortment*.

closed display. N. Items placed under glass, requiring a salesperson to open a case in order for the customer to see the item closely. See also *open display*.

closed door membership. N. A retail store in which customers belong based on a common employee, such as government employees. Usually discounts are provided.

closed sales territory. N. Used by market researchers, a geographically defined area where the manufacturer allows only one middle person to handle his or her certain merchandise. See also *exclusive distribution*.

closed stock. N. Merchandise sold only in sets (e.g., glassware, china.) Individual items from a set cannot be purchased, and there is no certainty that replacements will be available at a future time.

close out. N. An offer by a manufacturer or retailer to clear away his or her inventory.

close rate. N. In assessing salespeople, the individual's number of successful closings divided by that salesperson's number of sales calls.

closing. N. See *close*.

closing clue. N. A verbal comment or body language movement which indicates that the potential buyer is on the verge of placing an order.

closing date/closing hour. N. (1) In advertising, the last day on which advertisements can be accepted for publication in a magazine or other periodical. Copy must be in the publisher's hands if the advertisement is to be included in a specific issue. Synonymous with *forms close*. (2) In broadcasting, the deadline for all broadcast materials to be delivered to the station or network if the commercial is to be included in the broadcast schedule for a specific time period.

closure. N. See *close*.

clucking hens. N. New or unusual concerns for a store's senior management that demand time and attention.

cluster. N. A grouping of specialty stores located within a high-density populated area.

clustered demand. N. A demand pattern in which consumer needs and desires for a good or service category can be classified into two or more identifiable clusters (segments), each having distinct purchase criteria.

cluster marketing. N. Featuring a number of related items in various advertisements as one unit that can be interchanged. The result is to position them to a specific target market.

cluster sample. N. (1) A random sample using groups of people rather than individuals as the respondent unit. See also *cluster sampling.* (2) A sample used when no total listing of the statistical universe is available. Groups are established and then a sample of these groups is drawn to represent the population. See also *sampling.*

cluster sampling. N. A means of evolving a probability sample by randomly choosing the elements in groups rather than by individuals. See *also cluster sample, sampling.* Synonymous with *single-stage sampling.*

cluster selection. N. A means of choosing names from a list by assigning each name to a group with common characteristics and choosing only those clusters that can be predicted will buy.

clutter. N. Having too many advertisements or broadcast commercials that broadcasters and advertisers claim obstruct a customer from making a decision. At times advertisers run clutter tests to measure the ability of their commercials to get the listener's or viewer's attention in this clutter situation.

clutter awareness. N. The percentage of people who recalled a brand was advertised when exposed in a clutter of seven ads in a test.

clutter test. N. See *clutter*.

C.O.D. ABBRV. (1) Cash on delivery. (2) Collection on delivery.

conative component (of an attitude). N. In consumer research, the intention or tendency to act that results from a person's evaluation of an object.

conative judgement. N. In marketing, a purchaser's decision to move on a certain belief or feeling, to use a product or service.

concealed damage. N. As it affects profits in marketing, damage to the contents of a package that is in good order externally.

concealed discount. N. Where items, whether price fixed or not, are identified on the same purchase order at a common discount, which is subsequently shown on the invoice.

concentrated marketing. N. A form of marketing segmentation in which the marketer concentrates on a single segment of a large market. See also *niche marketing*.

concentric diversification. N. A firm's strategy for expansion by acquiring another firm that provides for them new product lines that are similar to theirs, which hopefully will appeal to a different set of consumers. See also *conglomerate diversification, horizontal diversification*.

concept. N. An idea or its presentation as used in an advertising campaign, advertisement, commercial, or other promotional program.

concept generation. N. (1) The act by which new concepts, or ideas, are created. (2) The second phase of the overall product innovation process, during which the concepts are created.

concept statement. N. A verbal or pictorial statement of a concept (for a product or for an advertisement) that is prepared for presentation to potential buyers or users to get their reaction prior to its being implemented. Product concepts are followed by prototypes, advertising concepts by one of several forms of semifinished production.

concept statement commercialized. N. Used in distinguishing two types of product concept statements. A commercialized product concept statement is prepared in an advertising format, as a persuasive statement. A noncommercialized product concept statement is prepared in a neutral, nonpersuasive format.

concept testing. N. A marketing strategy whereby members of a psychological test panel conclude whether an idea is acceptable, as contrasted with market research that attempts to determine if an appropriate market exists. See also *market research, advertising effectiveness*.

concession. N. (1) Any deviation from regular terms or previous conditions. (2) In merchandising, a right granted to a company to sell its product or services (e.g., to rent chairs at an outdoor party; to check coats and hats in a theater). (3) In international marketing, a tariff reduction or other agreement to reduce import restrictions; usually accorded pursuant to negotiations in return for concessions by other parties.

conclusive stage. N. The stage of the research process in which the researchers develop a plan for collecting data, implementing the plan, and providing the resulting information to decision makers.

concurrence. N. The duplication of the structure stemming from the joining of marketing elements.

concurrent validity. N. A method of assessing validity that involves correlating two different measurements of the same marketing phenomena, which have been administered at the same point in time.

condition. N. (1) A contractual clause, implied or expressed, that has the effect of investing or divesting with rights and duties for members of the contract. (2) In advertising, anticipating and preparing the marketplace for a forthcoming advertising campaign, advertisement, or other promotional presentation to the public.

conditional sale. N. See *conditional sales contract*.

conditional sales contract. N. A sales contract in which ownership of sold items remains with the seller until the goods are paid for in full or until other conditions are met.

conference report. N. See *call report*.

confined goods. N. Merchandise sold by a producer or distributor to a limited number of stores so that each retailer can claim exclusive resale rights in his or her trading area.

confirmation. N. (1) In merchandising, a statement from a supplier that he or she will accept a buyer's purchase request. (2) In advertising, a written affirmation by a broadcaster to an advertising agency confirming spoken statements dealing with the availability of commercial time on a specific network or station.

confiscation. N. A fear of international marketers; the seizure of private property, without compensation, usually by a governmental agency.

conformance testing. N. A technical task of testing products to determine whether or not they meet the requirements defined in a standard.

confusion of items. N. The intermingling of the items of two or more different owners where, once combined, the items are difficult or even impossible to separate again.

conglomerate. N. Often mentioned in advertising to suggest profitability or competitiveness, the result of a merging of organizations that produce different items and services to secure a large economic base, to acquire sounder management, and to gain greater potential profit.

conglomerate diversification. N. A firm's strategy for expansion where new acquisitions have no direct relationship to theirs. In retailing, the store then proceeds to set up this additional service. See also *concentric diversification*.

conglomerate market competition. N. Sale of the identical item by different dealers and distributors; leads to multiplying channels of distribution.

conglomerchant. N. See *merchandising conglomerate*.

congruent innovation. N. One of a four-way classification of new items as to degrees of newness. It does not result in any shift to established consumption patterns. The other three are continuous, discontinuous, and dynamically continuous.

congruent production diversification. N. More items or lines of items that are added to a company's offering based on management decisions. Synonymous with *production-oriented diversification*. See also *operational diversification*.

conjoint analysis. N. A method for presenting the framework of consumer preferences, and predicting consumer's attitudes towards new stimuli. See also *product design model*.

conmanship

conmanship. N. Persuading consumers to part with their purchasing power for something that will not provide benefits, or even for nothing. The opposite of *salesmanship*.

conscious parallel action. N. Identical pricing behavior among competing organizations. It has been declared illegal by the courts in antitrust cases. See also *price fixing*.

consign. N. In international marketing, the act or ordering, via a bill of lading, of a carrier to deliver a lot of merchandise from a given point to a given destination.

consignee. N. The ultimate recipient of goods.

consignee marks. N. In international marketing, a symbol placed on packages for export, generally consisting of a square, triangle, diamond, circle, cross, etc., with designed letters and/or numbers for the purpose of identification.

consignment. N. In international marketing, the act of entrusting goods to a dealer for sale but retaining ownership of them until sold. The dealer pays only when and if the goods are sold. Merchandise can be consigned by manufacturers to wholesalers or by wholesalers to retailers. See also *on consignment*.

consignment note. N. In international marketing, an instrument given when goods are dispatched, providing details of the item, the sender, and the individual to whom they are sent. The latter signs it upon arrival, providing proof of delivery.

consignor. N. The originator of a shipment; a person who delivers goods to an agent.

consistency of a product mix. N. The relationship among product lines in terms of their sharing a common end-use, distribution outlet, consumer group(s), and price range.

conspicuous consumption. N. The purchase and use of items and services primarily for improving an individual's social prestige, rather than for the satisfaction of material needs.

constant costs. N. The difference between the out-of-pocket, or variable costs, and the total costs. Those costs that, within the limits of the range of output under study, are unaffected by increases or decreases in production.

constructed price. N. As it affect global profits on goods; a value for customs purposes that ignores the invoice price of the goods but is derived by computing the cost inputs of the item, to which are added the normal costs associated with preparing the goods for export.

consultative selling. N. A sales method where the seller positions him- or herself as a customer's consultant, and applies low-pressure sales, hoping to fulfill the prospect's particular needs.

consumatory purpose. N. As measured by consumer and market researchers, the goal of a message is fulfilled when it is consumed upon being received.

consumed consumers. N. Those people who are used or exploited, whether willingly or not, for commercial gain in the marketplace.

consumer. N. Any person who uses or consumes goods and services. A consumer need not be the purchaser of an item or service, e.g., the consumer would be the child who eats the baby food purchased by the mother. Synonymous with *end-user*. See also *ultimate consumer*.

consumer advertising. N. Advertising pointed to the final user of a service or item in contrast to advertising directed at business or industry. The biggest users of consumer advertising are radio,

consumer behavior. N. Based on behavioral science research, manifestations of the decision processes and the search activities in purchasing and using merchandise and services. See also *buying behavior patterns, selective perception*.

consumer behavior research. N. A technique used to determine what satisfaction people want out of life, how they use products and services to achieve is satisfaction, how they perceive items and various brands, what forms of promotional activities will lead to successful marketing, and how to access the effects of these activities. See also *marketing concept*.

Consumer Bill of Rights. N. See *consumerism*.

consumer convenience goods. N. Low-priced, frequently bought consumer items.

consumer cooperative. N. A group of consumers who band together to gain buying power; user-owned retail outlets. Such organizations act for the benefit of their consumer-owners.

Consumer Credit Protection Act of 1968. N. See *Truth in Lending Act of 1968*.

consumer deal. N. A price reduction to a consumer.

consumer demand. N. The characteristics and needs of final consumers, industrial consumers, wholesalers and retailers, government institutions, international markets, and nonprofit institutions.

consumer demographic profile. N. A composite description of a consumer group based upon the most important demographics.

consumer demographics. N. Objective and quantifiable population characteristics that are relatively easy to identify, collect, measure, and analyze.

consumer durables. N. See *consumer goods*.

consumer education. N. The formalized teaching efforts to provide consumers with the skills and knowledge to allocate their resources wisely in the marketplace.

consumer equilibrium. N. A situation in which no retaliation of a person's income will improve his or her economic situation.

consumer ethnocentrism. N. The tendency to believe that it is inappropriate, indeed immoral, to purchase foreign-made products.

consumer goods. N. Items bought and used by the final consumer for personal or household purposes, such as automobiles, food, and clothing. Synonymous with *consumer products*.

consumerism. N. The organized demand that businesses increase their concern for the public in both manufacture and sale of merchandise. Consumerism grew in importance when President Kennedy signed the Consumer Bill of Rights legislation in 1962 stating that consumers have the right to be safe (from faulty merchandise), to be informed (of a product's negative attributes or inherent dangers), to choose (sustaining market competition absent of monopolies), and to be heard (to be able to make complaints and have legitimate grievances acted upon.) See also *consumer protection legislation*.

consumerist. N. An individual or representative who takes a leading position to protect the interests and needs of the consumer. See also *consumerism, Naderism*.

consumer jury. N. Pretesting items or advertisements by seeking the reactions of potential buyers or users.

consumer list. N. People on a list who have inquired about or actually bought items or services who can be contacted in the future.

consumer magazines. N. Magazines directed to the public-at-large; used extensively in promoting merchandise and services.

consumer market. N. (1) Buyers who purchase for personal needs or family consumption. (2) A market in which goods and services are actually used up. Synonymous with *product market*. See also *organizational market*.

consumer motivation. N. The driving force in a person that compels him or her to act in the marketplace.

consumer panel. N. A group of selected people who serve over a period of time as a sample group for marketing research studies.

Consumer Price Index. N. Used by marketers and advertisers in planning their strategies; a measurement of the cost of living, determined by the Bureau of Labor Statistics; also indicates price trends of more than four hundred different items and services. Synonymous with *Cost of Living Index*. ABBRV. *CPI*.

consumer products. N. See *consumer goods*.

Consumer Product Safety Act. N. From 1972, legislation providing for control of the processing, manufacturing, and distribution of products that may cause unreasonable risk of personal injury. ABBRV. *CPSA*.

consumer profile. N. A market research factor; a description of the personal, demographic, and psychological characteristics of a specific item or service user. Includes age, sex, marital status, income, education, occupation, home location, previous buying patterns, and credit ratings.

consumer promotion. N. Sales promotion methods purporting to offer short-term incentives to prospects to stimulate product sales.

consumer protection legislation. N. A variety of federal, state, and local laws to protect the rights of consumers. See also *antitrust acts, consumerism, Federal Trade Commission, product liability*.

Consumer Protection Telemarketing Act. N. U.S. legislation passed in 1993 to strengthen the Federal Trade Commission's ability to protect consumers from telemarketing fraud, deception, and harassment; to require delivery of goods bought by telephone; and, to provide a cooling-off period during which the customer may cancel an order.

consumer research. N. Marketing research to predict the behavior of the consumer in the market; provides data about a consumer's needs, motivation, perceptions, and attitudes regarding advertising, reasons for purchasing a service or product; and, what influences their choices. Consumer research is of value in determining the target market and setting strategy for advertising campaigns and other promotions. See also *consumer survey*.

consumer sale disclosure statement. N. A form presented by a dealer giving essential details on financing charges relative to a purchase on an installment plan. This is required under the Consumer Credit Protection (Truth in Lending) Act.

consumer's cooperative. N. A voluntary association of consumers, organized to help fulfill members' needs for goods and services, e.g., a credit union.

consumer sovereignty. N. That the consumer is supreme in the market.

consumer stimulants. N. Promotions and incentives that purport to attract consumers and to stimulate interest and demand for a product or service.

consumer surplus. N. The difference, as perceived by a customer, between the price he or she pays for the item, and the value of the purchase.

consumer survey. N. A consumer research approach using a questionnaire to collect information from a sample of consumers, either by mail, telephone conversation, or personal interview. See also *consumer research*.

consumption. N. The utilization of goods and services for the satisfaction of human needs.

consumption patterns. N. The patterns of whether consumers use, or do not use, a product or service.

contact report. N. See *call report*.

container. N. In merchandising, a nonspecific term for a receptacle capable of closure.

content motivation theories. N. Consumer-buying theories that focus on the factors within the person that start, arouse, energize, or stop behavior.

contest. N. A sales promotion technique in which consumers are offered prizes for performing a task such as making up a slogan. See also *sweepstake*.

contiguity. N. (1) In advertising, commercial advertising time slots of equal cost value. See also *contiguity rate*. (2) In broadcasting, two programs, one flowing into the other without any commercial interruption or announcement. Used mostly on radio.

contiguity rate. N. (1) A special discount rate given by broadcasters to advertisers who sponsor contiguous program. (2) A special discount rate given for contiguous commercial time slots. See also *contiguity*.

contingency plan. N. That portion of a marketing plan that develops strategies for countering adverse developments that may occur during implementation.

contingency pricing. N. Where a service organization does not receive payment for services performed until the consumer's satisfaction has been assured.

continuing discount. N. The reduced rate given an advertiser by an advertising medium in a contract for a stated time slot; continues to be in effect when the contract terminates and a new one is released.

continuity in advertising. N. The extended utilization of advertising; in particular, repetition of theme, layout, or commercial format.

continuity programs. N. See *box-top offer*.

continuity series. N. In direct marketing, a multipart product such as a set of books, which is sent one part at a time to the user.

continuity strategy. N. A media scheduling strategy in which advertisements are spread out over the entire period of the campaign. See also *bonus plan*.

continuous improvement. N. Frequent incremental improvements driven primarily by customer requirements and competitor actions; requires active organizational learning.

continuous innovation. N. (1) A modification of an existing item instead of a new concept. (2) One of a four-way classification of new products as to degrees of newness; requires alteration of a product but does not cause major disruption in set purchasing patterns. See also *congruent, innovation, discontinuous innovation, dynamically continuous innovation.*

continuous-loop video. N. Advertising means where a two- to three-minute commercial message is displayed repeatedly on a video terminal.

contract account. N. A retailer's customer with whom there is agreement that periodic payments will be made on the basis of a fixed percent of the amount owing as shown by a statement issued regularly.

contract carrier. N. Used by marketers to determine added costs, a transportation firm that contracts with shippers to transport their goods. The price is negotiated between the carrier and the shipper. The contract carrier cannot accept shipments from the general public.

contract manufacturing. N. (1) A joint venture where the foreign firm contracts with local manufacturers in the host nation to produce a product. (2) A business arrangement where one manufacturer produces items for another manufacturer.

contract price. N. In overseas marketing, the sale price negotiated between a U.S. exporter of merchandise and the foreign buyer, payable in the United States for the export from the United States of U.S. goods and services. This price may include, among other things, freight and marine insurance, but it excludes any charges payable for non-U.S. goods and services unless otherwise permitted, certain engineering services, import duties or levies of a similar nature, charges for local costs, and any other charges not legally payable in the United States.

contract purchasing. N. A form of purchasing defined in a contract for orders and deliveries, covering a specific time period, usually one year.

contractual channels. N. A channel system based on a contractual agreement between a producer and other members of the channel of distribution.

contractual vertical marketing system. N. A vertical marketing system in which channel members draw up a legal agreement that specifies the rights and responsibilities of each party.

contracyclical pricing. N. A pricing technique that runs counter to traditional economic policy. During periods of prosperity the company increases output and lowers prices; during economic downturn, it lowers production and raises prices.

contribution margin technique. N. An approach to cost analysis that ignores nontraceable common costs.

control. N. In marketing, the monitoring and reviewing of overall and specific marketing performance.

controllable factors. N. Decision elements internally directed by an organization and its marketers. Some of these factors are directed by top management; others are directed by marketers.

controllable marketing activities. N. Those marketing activities over which a firm has control, such as the product itself, the product name, packaging, advertising, pricing, sales promotion, and method of distribution.

controlled brand. N. A brand of merchandise owned by its manufacturer whose distribution is restricted to a small number of distributors.

controlled circulation. N. See *total paid circulation*.

controlled distribution minimarkets. N. Test markets run in smaller test areas that electronically monitor product purchases at checkout counters for more careful testing at reduced costs.

controlled sale. N. A category of market testing techniques in which the ability of the firm to obtain distribution is not tested. Distribution is forced, for example, by giving the outlets free product.

control over use. N. A dimension of product-use tests; the degree to which the product developers maintain control over how the user uses the new item.

convenience goods. N. Products that the public wishes to purchase with a minimum of effort or time (toothpaste, sodas, paper, etc.). See also *bantam store, shopping goods*.

convenience sampling. N. A nonprobability sample in which respondents are selected to suit the convenience of the researchers. See also *nonprobability sampling, sampling*. Synonymous with *opportunistic sampling*.

convenience store. N. A small retail outlet that carries a limited line of high-turnover convenience goods and usually operates for extended hours.

conventional channel. N. A channel of distribution loosely organized, where members are traditionally autonomous.

conventional duty. N. A customs duty, or rate of duty, arising out of a treaty or other international agreement, as contrasted with an autonomous duty unilaterally imposed by a government absent of any international agreement.

convergent marketing. N. An efficient means of organizing the marketing activity within a company so that the same resources are employed to sell all the items made.

conversional marketing. N. Activities dealing with negative demand to urge the market's reaction to the product up to a positive level adequate to absorb a reasonable quantity of the available supply.

conversion process. N. See *boomerang*.

conversion renewal percentage. N. The proportion of new magazine subscribers who have renewed their subscription; often sold for more than the original price paid.

code number. N. The designation for identifying the source from which sales and marketing materials evolve, e.g., used on cents-off coupons to determine where people obtained them.

code price. N. The price resulting when a trade discount is deducted from a list price.

coding. N. See *code*.

coefficient of correlation. N. In marketing research, the statistical measure of the relationship between two variables, where one impacts the other. The correlation indicates both the magnitude and direction of that relationship.

coefficient of cross-elasticity. N. In marketing research, the arithmetic relationship between a percentage change in the price of an item and the actual percentage change in the sales of a substitute or competitive item.

COG. ABBRV. Customer-owned goods.

cognitive component (of an attitude). N. Utilized by consumer researchers, a person's evaluation of the characteristics of an object.

cognitive dissonance. N. (1) A mental state that occurs when there is a lack of consistency or balance among an individual's various

cognitive judgment

cognitions after a decision has been made. Two cognitions are in a dissonant state if they disagree with each other (e.g., when a commercial indicates that a cigarette is mild, but the consumer finds, through experience, that it is strong and irritating). (2) In merchandising, the state of anxiety or uneasiness that follows a purchase decision and creates a need for reassurance that the decision was the best one. See also *dissonance reduction*.

cognitive judgment. N. For the consumer, the result of his or her perceptions, or communications received from others.

coincidental telephone method. N. A procedure used by C. E. Hooper in the mid-1930s for ascertaining to what radio programs and commercials people tuned in. Respondents were called on the telephone and asked whether they were listening to the radio and, if so, to name the programs. See also *Hooperating, Trendex, audimeter, diary method*.

cold call. N. Contacting a potential customer without prior notice in order to make a sale or arrange for an appointment. It is used to obtain a meeting or to give a demonstration; a form of prospecting in order to identify qualified prospects for an item or service. Frequently conducted during a downtime period when the salesperson has some free time. See also *cold canvassing*.

cold canvassing. N. Determining potential customers without assistance from others or from references (e.g., selecting every tenth name in the telephone directory within a given location and having a salesperson call on these persons.) See also *canvass, cold call, territory screening*.

cold list. N. A list of people's names not previously used in promoting a service or item to a prospect.

cold mail promotion. N. A promotion sent by a mailer to prospects who presently are not listed customers.

collateral businesses. N. Support business in the advertising industry, such as package design houses, sales promotion firms, premium shops, media buying services, marketing research organizations, printing companies, and so forth.

collateral materials. N. Related materials used to enhance, support ,or reinforce an advertising promotion, e.g., film strips, catalogs, brochures, annual reports; used to prepare materials for advertising campaigns and promotions, as sales and informational materials about a firm and its products, or for special events that it sponsors.

collectible. N. See *liquid*.

collection. N. (1) The presentation for payment of an obligation and the payment thereof. (2) In retailing, an organized gathering of related items.

collection agent. N. An agency chosen by a seller to attempt to collect on credit orders that have not been paid in response to the seller's own attempts. The fee can run as high as 30%, and therefore these services are used as a means of last resort.

collection on delivery N. See *cash on delivery*. ABBRV. *COD*.

collective mark. N. Considered in the marketing of goods; a trademark, service mark, or other symbol used by members of an association or group of organizations to indicate membership within their group.

collusion. N. A secret agreement to defraud.

colorable imitation. N. Any mark or symbol resembling a registered mark that may confuse the customer; a form of deception.

column inch. N. Print advertising space is sold based on the dimension of one inch by one inch. Should a column be three inches wide and an advertisement four inches long, the total column inches to be bought is twelve. Rates for advertising are set by the number of column inches the advertisement occupies. See also *standard advertising unit*.

COM. ABBRV. Customer's own merchandise. Synonymous with *customer-owned goods*.

combination compensation plan. N. A sales compensation plan that uses elements of both salary and commission methods. Such plans balance company control, flexibility, and employee incentives.

combination house. N. A merchant middleperson acting as the wholesaler in the industrial market in addition to the retail and institutional market.

combination offer. N. A type of consumer fraud involving the sale of an item at a low price tied to the purchase of a continuing service.

combination pricing. N. A pricing approach whereby aspects of cost-, demand-, and competition-based pricing methods are integrated.

combination rate. N. A special rate for advertising in two or more publications owned by a single organization. To take advantage of this rate, the advertisement must be identical for all publications, in size, copy, and content, and each publication must be purchased at the same time or within one day.

combination sale. N. An item of merchandise that is combined with a premium at one price. It lowers the cost of promotion per dollar of revenue.

combination store. N. A type of superstore that places emphasis on nonfood items and services.

combo promotion. N. A promotion that offers two or more items together.

command headline. N. A headline that encourages a reader to use or purchase a product or service.

commercial. N. The advertiser's message presented on any radio or television program. A commercial is produced on film or videotape, then duplicated with copies going to subscribing networks for future airing. Commercials are filmed or taped and copies are then distributed. See also *advertisement, commercial time*.

commercial advertising. N. See *product reputation advertising*.

commercial audience. N. People who view or listen to a specific radio or television commercial.

commercial break. N. The schedule time break in radio or television programming allowing for the insertion of commercials.

commercial counterfeiting. N. A practice involving the manufacturer or sale of goods that defraud the purchaser by falsely implying that the products are produced by a reputable manufacturer.

commercial databases. N. Databases that contain information on population characteristics, the business environment, economic forecasts, industry and companies' performance, specialized bibliographies, and other material.

commercial delivery. N. (1) The full audience that has been "delivered" to a commercial, or received delivery of the commercial. (2) The portion of an audience exposed to a particular commercial.

commercial exposure potential. N. The number of prospective recipients of a commercial, determined by comparing the number of television sets in the receiving area with the number of television sets that are tuned in to the commercial in a particular receiving area.

commercial integration charge. N. The cost to an advertiser by a broadcast media to cover clerical costs for incorporating a commercial in their broadcast schedule.

commercialization. N. The stage a product is in when following testing and changing as deemed necessary; it is to be brought to the market with a full promotional campaign, either grand or small, regional or national.

commercial minute. N. Sixty seconds of broadcast time used for the airing of a commercial, or commercials.

commercial pool. N. A combined group of previously prepared commercial tapes that the advertiser can choose for showing.

commercial protection. N. See *product protection*.

commercial set. N. In overseas merchandising, the four major documents covering a shipment: the invoice, the bill of lading, the certificate of insurance, and the bill of exchange or draft.

commercial time. N. The permitted time per hour of programming that can be used by a broadcasting media for commercials. For example, during prime time (8:00 p.m.–11:00 p.m.) a station can have no more than nine minutes and thirty seconds of commercials in one hour. Advertisers can buy sixty seconds of commercial time and divide it into three twenty-second spots, or purchase thirty seconds and break it into two fifteen-second spots. See also *day parts*.

commissary store. N. A small retail store that sells usually to the workers of the firm who own it.

commission. N. The amount paid to an agent, which may be an individual, a broker, or an agency, for consummating a transaction involving the sale or purchase of goods or services. Salespeople receive salaries based on straight commission (compensation solely based on commission income) or a combination compensation plan, which offers a fixed-based salary plus a commission or incentives. Most salespeople prefer the latter as it provides immediate income. See also *agency commission*.

commissionable. N. An advertising agency's services to his or her client for which the agency receives money from another source, e.g., advertising space that is bought by an agency on behalf of a client, which is subject to a commission.

commission agent. N. A functional middleperson who receives the shipment of goods, mainly perishables, to sell for a principal.

commission house. N. An agent who negotiates the sales of merchandise that he or she handles, with control over prices and terms of sale.

commission merchant. N. An agent that performs selling functions for manufacturers, normally on a one-time basis.

commission rebating. N. Income earned by advertising agencies on the value of the orders they place with media owners, rather than being paid a fee by their clients.

commission with draw. N. A form of compensation for salespeople where payments are based on a percentage of sales in which regular payments are made from an account set aside for the purpose.

committee purchasing. N. The decision to buy by a group of people within a company who are charged with the responsibility of studying and recommending products.

commodity products. N. See *staple stock*.

commodity rate. N. In overseas marketing and sales, an allowable deviation from the class rate charged by shippers to customers.

commodity warehouse. N. See *warehouse, commodity*.

common carrier. N. (1) Used by international marketers to set consumer prices, a carrier that moves people or goods for a price and without partiality. (2) A transportation company that transports products on a specified schedule and according to regulations and standards established by government regulatory agencies.

common market. N. Impacts on global marketing profits; a trade interaction among nations that maintains a common external tariff and no internal customs. The European Union is one of the most famous common markets.

communication channels. N. (1) The paths that are used for delivery of messages. (2) In marketing, the means by which promotional communications are offered to the target market.

Community Trademark. N. Of importance to the selling of merchandise in the European Union; in November 1980 legislation was set, harmonizing national laws on trademarks, and for the establishment of a Community Trademark and a Community Trade Mark Office. It ensures that trademarks enjoy uniform protection under the laws of all member nations and indicates regulations governing registration of trademarks directly affecting the movement of goods and services within the Community.

company-controlled price environment. N. Characterized by moderate competition, well-differentiated goods and services, and strong control over price by individual firms.

company demand. N. The company's share of market demand.

company sales forecast. N. The expected level of company sales based on a chosen marketing plan and an assumed environment.

company sales potential. N. The limit approached by company demand as company marketing effort increases relative to competitors.

company-specific buying factors. N. Company-based variables that lead to either autonomous (independent) or joint decision making by organizational consumers. These variables are a firm's basic orientation, size, and level of decision-making centralization.

company warehouse. N. See *warehouse, private*.

comparative advantage. N. A determinant in global marketing of goods; a country's or area's advantage in the manufacture of a particular item when its social cost of production for that item is less than the social cost experienced by other countries or areas for the same item. See also *competitive advantage, social cost*.

comparative advertising. N. Promotional material in which competitor's products are named. Synonymous with *comparison advertising*.

comparative marketing. N. In international marketing, methods for differentiating similarities and differences of how consumers throughout the world are induced to purchase items and services, and how demand is set.

comparative messages. N. Implicitly or explicitly contrast a firm's offerings with those of competitors.

comparison advertising. N. See *comparative advertising*.

comparison department. N. A unit within a retail operation responsible for comparing the store's quality, service, prices, etc., with competitors.

comparison shopper. N. (1) an individual sent to competitors' outlets to determine goods carried and relative prices charged as part of information-gathering activity. (2) An industrial purchasing executive's review of competitors' marketing strategies such as new products offered, competitors' pricing concepts, and promotional initiatives.

comparison shopping. N. See *comparison shopper*.

compatibility. N. The degree that a consumer perceives that a new item is consistent with his or her current requirements, self-image, and attitude.

compensating product. N. An input or product secured by a manufacturer in a domestic market to substitute for an imported input or product used to produce items for export.

compensation. N. (1) Payment for any services or items. See also *compensation*. (2) In marketing, an attempt to disguise an undesirable characteristic by exaggerating a desirable one.

compensation deal. N. A semi-barter arrangement in which goods are bought partially in cash and with other goods; a common practice in merchandising worldwide.

compensation trading. N. In global marketing, when an exporter agrees to accept part-payment in items from the purchaser's nation in lieu of cash.

compensatory trade. N. Any transaction that involves asset transfer as a condition of purchase.

competition. N. (1) Any rivalry. (2) The situation in which a large number of manufacturers serve a large number of consumers, when no manufacturer can demand or offer a quantity sufficiently large to affect the market price. There are three forms of marketing competition: (a) brand competition: competition by producers offering a similar item; (b) generic competition: when items in totally separate categories perform the identical function; and, (c) form competition: merchandise that performs the same function but are structured differently.

competition-based pricing. N. A pricing strategy approach whereby a firm uses competitors' prices rather than demand or cost considerations as its primary pricing guideposts. A firm can set prices below the market, at the market, or above the market.

competitive advantage. N. Applied by international marketers, the position of superiority one company achieves over its competitors in the marketplace. A firm's competitive advantage can be based on its ability to provide superior output, or to have prices that are lower than a competitor's prices. Often used in comparing the export of merchandise from another country. See also *comparative advantage, unique selling proposition.*

competitive alliance. N. The cooperation between competitors for specific purposes; a practice in international manufacturing of goods.

competitive analysis. N. Determining a firm's or a product's performance in comparison with its competitors, based on product sales, profit, price, quality, delivery, customer service, etc.

competitive bidding. N. See *bidding.*

competitive institutional advertisements. N. Institutional advertisements that promote the advantages of one product class over another, which are used in markets where different product classes compete for the same buyer.

competitive intelligence. N. Data on a firm's competitors and marketing activities; used in developing new strategies. Involves a variety of research activities including studying of trade periodicals, obtaining information from a host of sources, and gathering data internally. Professor B. Gilad has been a leading advocate and pioneer of competitive intelligence.

competitive market. N. A price determined in the market by the bargaining of a number of buyers and sellers, each acting separately and without sufficient power to manipulate the market.

competitive parity. N. The budget allocation for advertising that is based on expenditures of competitors; based on the concept that one should defend against competition by spending at least as much (or as little) as one's competitor spends on advertising. Synonymous with *defensive budgeting*, *defensive spending*, *competitive parity technique*.

competitive parity technique. N. A method for setting an advertising budget wherein an advertiser determines advertising money to be spent on the basis of the spending by a competitor. Since objectives differ this method can be a poor predictor. See also *competitive party*.

competitive position. N. The place within the market that allows an item or service to compete on a level with other competitive items or services. At the time the item or service reaches a noticeable percentage share of the entire market, it is declared to be in a competitive position.

competitive price. N. The price determined in the market by the bargaining of a number of buyers and sellers, each acting separately and without sufficient power to manipulate the market.

competitive separation. N. (1) In advertising, usually, set in a contract, the space that is used for separating competitive advertisements from one another. See also *exclusivity*. (2) In broadcasting, the time span, traditionally ten minutes between competing commercials. See also *back-to-back commercials*, *commercial protection*.

competitive stage. N. The advertising stage a product achieves when its general usefulness is recognized, but its superiority over similar brands requires promotion to stay competitive. Advertisements in this stage often emphasize the item's differences. Synonymous with *selective stage*. See also *spiral stage*.

competitive strategy. N. A promotional approach found in an advertising campaign that is set to compete with competitive brands, such as discrediting the cereal of a rival manufacturer.

competitor. N. (1) The seller or maker of an item or service that is sold in the same market as that of other producers. (2) The provider of a service or item whose service or item fulfills a consumer need in the market where others offer item and services that may also fulfill the same need.

competitor analysis. N. The process of identifying the performance and marketing strategy of competitive brands or products within the marketplace.

competitor intelligence system. N. See *competitive intelligence*.

competitor orientation. N. A firm's plans in response to a competitor's activities. The company prepares a competitor response based on market share of a product. See also *competitive intelligence*, *customer oriented*.

compiled list. N. Names and addresses of people and organizations that represent a particular target market.

complaint management. N. Providing quality customer service by quickly requesting and responding to customer complaints; involves securing information on how best to provide customer services and how to resolve existing customer problems. See also *customer relations*.

complementary products. N. Items that tend to round out a line of products (e.g., shoes and shoelaces). See also *allied products, suggestive selling*.

complementation agreement. N. Impacting on global merchandising and sales, an accord between a commercial entity and two or more governments to lower or eliminate duties among themselves on given items produced by the firm in one or more of the signatory states, thus inducing a manufacturer to place a factory in one of the signatory nations to supply that nation and others with the output of the plant.

completed cancel. N. A consumer who fulfills his or her commitment to the seller prior to cancellation.

complete segmentation. N. A type of market segmentation where each potential consumer is treated as an individual instead of as part of a mass group.

complexity. N. (1) The measure of the relative difficulty of a new item to be understood by the consuming public. (2) How difficult an innovation is perceived by the public.

complex sales force. N. An organizational structure uniting three basic sales force types: product-structured, territory-structured, and market-structures sales forces.

component life-style. N. A living pattern whereby the attitudes and behavior of people depend on particular situations rather than an overall lifestyle philosophy.

component materials. N. Semimanufactured industrial goods that undergo further changes in form; these are considered as an expense rather than as a capital item.

component testing. N. The testing of various parts of the marketing program, separately. Marketing testing tests them in unison, but during the development process each item in the marketing mix may be put through separate testing. Copy testing is the most common form of component testing.

composite demand. N. The sum of demands for an item or service, beginning with any number of needs, all of which can be fulfilled by that particular item or service.

composition. N. The spread on a page of the visual characteristics of a print advertisement. See also *layout*.

composition house. N. A firm in the printing business that sets type, among other activities, for advertisers and advertising agencies.

compound duty. N. Impacting on the profit in global sales; a duty, tax, or tariff expressed or calculated as a combination of an ad valorem and a specified duty. Synonymous with *mixed tariff*.

comprehensive. N. A layout prepared to resemble a completed advertisement as nearly as possible. Once approved by the client, the layout becomes the basis for a final plate or print.

comprehensive layout. N. See *comprehensive*.

computerized-checkout (electronic point of sale) system. N. A system in which a cashier manually rings up a sale or passes an item over or past an optical scanner; then a computerized register instantly records and displays a sale.

cooling-off period. N. To protect consumers, there are laws permitting them to reconsider a purchase, and if they so desire, to cancel any commitment. Three days is the typical time frame used.

co-op advertising. N. See *cooperative advertising*.

cooperative. N. An outlet owned and run by the final consumers for purposes of buying and selling items to the members.

cooperative advertising. N. (1) In advertising, advertising paid for jointly by the advertiser and its wholesalers or retailers. ABBRV. *Co-op advertising.* (2) In retailing, an arrangement between the manufacturer and retailer where the producer reimburses the retailer in part or in full for advertising costs. Synonymous with *manufacturer's cooperative advertising, vertical cooperative advertising.*

cooperative exporters. N. Used by international marketers, established international manufacturers who export other manufacturers' goods as well as their own.

cooperative mailing. N. Where several messages from different advertisers are placed in the same mailing envelope. The goal of cooperative mailing is to lower the advertisers' individual mailing and production costs. ABBRV. *Co-op mailing.* Synonymous with *group mailing.*

cooperative marketing. N. Wholesalers, retailers, or any combination of them working collectively to buy, sell, or do both.

cooperative organization. N. A retail organization that consists of a set of independent retailers that combine their resources to maintain their own wholesaling operation.

co-op mailing. ABBRV. Cooperative mailing.

copy. N. (1) All components to be included in a completed advertisement or direct-mailing piece. (2) In print news media, the text in a newspaper or magazine article.

copy approach. N. The way the text of an advertisement opens. It may be informative of human interest, or imaginative.

copy date. N. The date by which all elements of the advertisement have to be delivered to the publisher, contracting firm, etc.

copy platform. N. The primary, critical concept behind any advertising campaign, with instructions on how best to discharge the program.

copy research. N. The study of an advertising message; includes both the pretesting and posttesting of commercials and advertisements in print and broadcast. Pretesting examines the product claims, technical components, and target audience prior to an advertising campaign. Posttesting examines the effectiveness of the copy in communicating the advertising message and its intent at the end of the advertising campaign.

copyright. N. An exclusive right, guaranteed by federal statute, to reproduce, publish, and sell the matter and form of literary, musical, or artistic work. Any attempt by another person or group to deprive the copyright holder of his or her property is cause for the latter to seek damages.

Copyright Act of 1976. N. Federal legislation revising the copyright laws for the first time in sixty-seven years. The act extends the length of copyright protection to the duration of the creator's life plus fifty years. Previously the protection ran twenty-eight years from the date of publication and was renewable for another twenty-eight years. The act also sets standards for fair use and reproduction of copyrighted material and a new system of compulsory licensing for cable television and jukeboxes. It also preempts state laws governing copyrighted materials that come within the scope of the federal act.

copy slant. N. The way in which a selling point is presented in an advertisement.

copy strategy. N. A brief statement that guides the preparation of advertising copy.

copy testing. N. Measuring the effectiveness of an advertising campaign. Its objective is to identify and eventually eliminate the negative components of an advertisement or an advertising campaign in order to obtain maximum effectiveness from the advertising. See also *aided recall, component testing, hidden offer, inquiry test, keying an advertisement, split run.*

copy thrust. N. The message communicated by the written copy and the accompanying illustration, starting with the objectives of the promotion in an attempt to convince the consumer that the item is useful.

copywriter. N. The individual who writes the copy for advertisement. He or she may also play a primary role in the advertising campaign.

core benefit. N. See *core product*.

core product. N. The central benefit or purpose for which a consumer buys a product. Varies from purchaser to purchaser. The core product or core benefit may come either from the physical good or service performance, or it may come from the augmented dimensions of the product. See also *augmented product*.

core services. N. The basic services that companies should provide to their customers to remain competitive.

corporate advertising. N. Advertising program that promotes a firm, instead of its products or services; often used in the image building of a company; used extensively by public corporations to increase their attractiveness to the public and to encourage investing in their company. See also *European Union, institutional barriers*.

corporate culture. N. Assessed by advertisers; a set of values that create a distinct pattern that is reflected in all of an organization's activities.

corporate licensing. N. The use of a company's name to enhance the saleability of a product.

corporate mission. N. Used by advertisers in promoting the firm's goods; a statement of an organization's overall goals, usually broadly defined and difficult to measure objectively.

corporate responsibility research. N. Market research created to assist firms to better understand the legal, political, or social environments in which they function, so as to better communicate their societal obligations to the general public.

corporate symbols. N. A firm's name (or divisional names), logo(s), and trade characters. They are significant parts of the overall company image.

corporate vertical marketing system. N. The system where a large organization controls two or more levels of a marketing channel.

corrective advertising. N. A Federal Trade Commission law requires that an advertiser found guilty of placing a deceptive advertisement devote space or time in future announcements with disclosure of the earlier deception.

correlation. N. In market research, a relationship or dependence reflecting the principle that two things or variables are so related that change in one is accompanied by a corresponding or parallel change in the other.

correlation coefficient. N. In market research, the quotient of the sum of the products of algebraic deviations of the corresponding numbers of two sets of data and the square root of the product of the sum of the squares of the deviations of each set.

cosponsoring. N. (1) Joining together in a mutual effort or activity. (2) In advertising, sharing by two or more advertisers of the cost of a single broadcast program.

cost. N. (1) The value given up by an entity in order to receive goods or services. (2) The value given up to obtain an item in the volume needed, shipped to the desired location. All expenses are costs, but not all costs are expenses.

cost analysis. N. A sales manager's measurement of the cost of sales activities; measures the levels of profitability of individual items and types of customers. See also *sales analysis*.

cost-based pricing. N. A pricing strategy approach whereby a firm determines prices by computing merchandise, service, and overhead costs, and then adding an amount to cover the firm's profit goal. Demand is not analyzed.

cost complement. N. See *cost multiplier*.

cost efficiency. N. The cost of reaching members of the target audience for a specific item or service as contrasted with the cost of reaching the entire audience of the medium; expressed in cost per thousand.

cost multiplier. N. In retailing, the average relationship of the cost of merchandise to the actual retail value of the items handled in an accounting period. Synonymous with *cost complement, cost percent*.

cost of credit. N. An advertising variable; the cost, in addition to the cash price, for the opportunity of purchasing something with an obligation to pay in the future.

cost of goods sold. N. The purchase price of goods sold during a specified period, including transportation costs.

cost of living. N. The average of the retail prices of all goods and services required for a reasonable living standard.

Cost of Living Index. N. See *Consumer Price Index*.

cost percent. N. See *cost multiplier*.

cost per inquiry. N. The statistical determination of the promotion costs divided by the number of inquiries received. See also *cost per order*.

cost per order. N. A statistical determination of the costs incurred in selling merchandise divided by the number of orders that are received. See also *cost per inquiry*.

cost per sale. N. In direct mailing, the cost of making one sale as compared to the cost of mailing.

cost per thousand. N. In advertising, the expense in reaching one thousand potential customers with a particular advertisement or advertising campaign. See also *cost efficiency, efficiency rating, selective index*.

cost plus pricing. N. The practice of adding a percentage of the costs of goods to the cost before the selling price is established.

cost trade-off. N. Spending more on one aspect of marketing so as to lower the cost of another aspect even more.

count and recount. V. To determine the results of a sale, to count the merchandise, run the sale, then recount the merchandise.

count certificate. N. A document confirming the count of merchandise at the time of shipment or delivery.

counteradvertising. N. Advertising carried out by groups in the public interest to convince them against the purchase of a product or service they believe harmful.

counter-cyclical advertising. N. Planning the advertising campaign so that the majority of advertisements appear when sales do not normally occur, and little is run during normally large-volume times.

counterfeiting. N. The illegal use of a well-known manufacturer's brand name on copies of the firm's merchandise.

countermand. N. In sales, to cancel an order that has not yet been carried out.

countermarketing. N. Activities that attempt to eliminate the demand for a product, especially by those who find fault with the item, or claim it to be unsafe.

counterpurchasing. N. Placing an order with a manufacturer in one country with the expectation that merchandise of equal value or quantity will be sold in the opposite direction to the other nation.

countersegmentation. N. Where the number of market segments targeted by a firm are lowered, by eliminating items that have been serving narrow segments of the population.

countertrade. N. (1) In global sales, the sale of goods or services that are paid for in whole or in part by the transfer of goods or services from a foreign country. (2) In international sales, where an export sale is contingent upon a reciprocal purchase or undertaking by the exporter. (3) A practice whereby a supplier commits contractually, as a condition of sale, to reciprocate and undertake certain specified commercial initiatives that compensate and benefit the buyer.

coupling. N. The joining of efforts between the firm innovating on new products and other firms or persons; can be upstream (with vendors), downstream (with customers), or sideways (with competitors).

coupon. N. (1) A certificate that entitles a consumer to a price reduction or a cash refund. (2) In advertising, a part of an advertisement that can be used for ordering items or redeeming premiums. See also *cents-off coupon, couponing, direct-response advertising, premium*.

couponing. N. With the use of a coupon, offering consumers a special, but temporary, price reduction on merchandise without actually changing the regular market price. May be mailed or placed in a package of another item, or published in an advertisement. See also *cross-couponing*.

coupon pad. N. Promotional coupons attached to a card often hung on a wall or affixed to a counter.

coupon research. N. Using coupons returned by consumers to analyze or compare the impact of promotions or advertisements in relation to where the coupons were distributed or published.

cover ad position. N. An advertisement placed on a cover of a periodical or magazine.

coverage. N. (1) The appearance of a news story in print or broadcast news media. (2) In advertising, the number of homes or persons exposed to a specific advertising medium in a controlled location. See also *reach*.

coverage map. N. A map showing the prime area of a medium's reach within a market.

covered under carnet. N. A strategy of marketers; export items making temporary trips to overseas nations, then reexported from them, and ultimately being reimported to their originating nation, under the authority of an International Chamber of Commerce carnet. See also *carnet*.

cow catcher. N. *(slang)* A brief announcement preceding a television or radio broadcast that features a product of the advertiser other than the ones associated with the program being shown or heard. See also *hitchhike*.

CPI. ABBRV. Consumer Price Index.

CPM. ABBRV. Critical path method.

CPSA. ABBRV. Consumer Product Safety Act.

creaming a list. N. (1) Choosing from a list only key prospects, i.e., those who are most likely to purchase an item or service, based on a variety of selection criteria. (2) An offer that cannot be turned down. It usually is made at a loss.

creative black book. N. A directory of people and firms that supply products and services for advertisers, marketers, and agencies. Advertisers in the book include photographers, producers, illustrators, etc. See also *Green Book*.

creative boutiques. N. Advertising agencies that specialize in developing advertising and provide no marketing services.

creative demarketing. N. See *demarketing*.

creative director. N. The person who manages the creative department in an advertising agency. He or she is responsible for all creative aspects of advertising, advertising campaigns, and commercials, starting with ideas and ending with production.

creative selling. N. In sales, applying techniques and strategies that elicit consumer demand, by proving the benefits of an offering to those who have never purchased the merchandise from that salesperson before.

creative stimuli. N. A method of ideation whereby one thinks of a problem or a product and then studies a set of words or phrases that research has shown to be stimulating. See also *ideation*.

creative strategy. N. The outlining of an advertising or commercial message; traditionally discharged by members of the creative unit of the agency.

credit. N. Sales or purchases that are accompanied by a promise to pay later.

credit bureau. N. An agency that holds central files of data on consumers in a given trade area. These bureaus collect personal data, data on paying habits, and so on, and make impartial reports for credit grants. Some national credit bureaus have been accused of invading personal privacy. See also *Fair Credit Reporting Act of 1971*.

credit buyer. N. See *charge buyer*.

credit cancellation. N. The cancellation of an unpaid credit order. Synonymous with *kill, kill bad pay*.

credit card. N. A card issued by an organization that entitles the bearer to credit at its establishments, restaurants, stores, etc.

credit card order. N. Paying for merchandise by using a credit card.

credit order. N. An order received without any payment and that requires billing at a future time. See also *cash order, charge buyer*. Synonymous with *bill me order*.

credit prescreening. N. List purge to remove names matching those on a list of customers with a nonpayment history.

credit rating. N. The amount, type, and form of credit, if any, that a bank estimates can be extended to an applicant for credit.

credit suspension. N. Placing the names of people with unpaid credit accounts on an inactive status list so that they will not receive merchandise or services. At the same time, these people continue receiving bills.

credit union. N. A cooperative financial organization established within and listed to a specific group of people.

crescendo method. N. See *snowballing method*.

critical path method. N. In planning and scheduling a complex series of marketing and sales operations, the sequence of events that are most critical as to timing; the longest path of activities in a system. The critical path method is based on the network analog principle and was first used in 1957 by E. I. du Pont de Nemours and Co. to improve the planning, scheduling, and coordination of its new-plant construction effort. ABBRV. *CPM*.

cross-branding. N. Brand promotion purporting to enhance a given item by utilizing the brand strength of one or more of its ingredients or constituents.

cross-classification matrix. N. A grid technique, used to identify specific subdivisions in a market for purposes of segmentation.

cross-couponing. N. A coupon given with merchandise. It carries the price reduction offer of another item and may involve more than one seller. See also *couponing*.

cross-elasticity. N. The impact on the demand for one product of price changes in a related product. For example, when the price of butter goes up, the price of margarine, sometimes used as a substitute, usually rises as well. See also *elastic demand, elasticity*.

cross-elasticity of demand. N. See *cross-elasticity*.

cross merchandising. N. Placing displays of complementary items in positions facing each other, with the hope that when customers see the displays they will cross over from one product to another. Synonymous with *related item display*.

cross plug. N. In a continuing broadcast program of alternating sponsorship, a commercial broadcast during the current program promoting the alternating sponsor for the purpose of providing continuity of advertising for both sponsors.

cross promote. V. To promote an item to purchasers of another item sold by the same firm. See also *tie-in advertisement, tie-in promotion*.

cross-promotion. N. See *tie-in promotion*.

cross-ruff advertisement. N. An advertisement or campaign involving cents-off deals, couponing, product sampling, and premiums, where several firms combine to link brands. Firms that participate in this program deal directly with each other and each continues to promote its own brands.

cross-selling. N. Where the salesperson is allowed to work in more than one department within the store, helping the customers with a variety of purchases.

cross-subsidization. N. A marketing method where a firm employs earnings in one foreign market to support its marketing activities in another foreign market.

cues. N. Weak stimuli that are not powerful enough to arouse consumer action but capable of providing direction to motivated behavior.

culture. N. In marketing, the way in which consumers behave in the marketplace.

cume. ABBRV. Cumulative audience.

cumulative audience. N. The number of unduplicated people contacts by a given schedule over a state time frame. The higher the cumulative audience, the larger the audience. ABBRV. *Cume*. Synonymous with *unduplicated audience*. See also *cumulative reach, reach*.

cumulative cost curve. N. The shape of a line that depicts a firm's cumulative costs of developing and marketing a new product. It is plotted against the cumulation of time, so it runs from zero (start of project) to 100% of time (launch). The curve necessarily runs from low left to upper right.

cumulative mark on. N. The difference between total delivered cost and total original retail value of merchandise handled within a stated time frame, inclusive of the accumulated inventory.

cumulative quantity discount. N. A type of rebate given to a store when the total price of all goods purchased is identified. The objective is to encourage the dealer to give the seller all his or her business in that line of trade.

cumulative reach. N. The same as cumulative audience, but usually indicates the total number of households reached by a medium during a stated time period.

curiosity headline. N. The headline purporting to encourage readers to read on into the advertisement resulting from heightened curiosity.

current account. N. In advertising, customer names taken from a list and ranked in order of past business and potential activity.

current assets. N. Helps to determine an advertising agency's profitability; includes cash and those assets that are readily convertible into cash or are held for current use in operations, current claims against others, and amounts accruing to the carrier, which are subject to current settlement. See also *current liabilities*.

current issue. N. Any printed material presently available, or on the newstand for sale.

current liabilities. N. Amounts payable within a comparatively brief period, usually not exceeding one year from the date of the balance sheet. See also *current assets*.

cushion. N. Adding inventory to a basic amount to provide for unexpected increases in demand, delays of delivery, a purchase in great quantity, etc. See also *cushioning, safety stock*.

cushioning. N. The protection of an item from physical damage by placing about its outer surfaces materials that have been designed to absorb the impact of external forces. See also *floatation, cushion*.

customary price. N. The price of some items become fixed, not because of the seller's decision, but as a result from having prevailed on the market for so long that consumers develop a habit of correlating that price to the item. Altering the package may be a significant way of changing this situation.

customary pricing. N. See *customary price*.

customer. N. An individual or organization that makes a purchase.

customer characteristics. N. Distinctive, unique, typical features that help distinguish one consumer or group of consumers from others; becomes the basis for market segmentation.

customer database. N. A computer-based system housing information about customers' history of purchases and other buying patterns; used to encourage repeat sales and to test new merchandise.

customer departmentation. N. The grouping of jobs into subunits based on the customers to be served, a common practice in retail organizations.

customer franchise. N. A loyal item-following by a group of consumers with repeat sales anticipated.

customer holdover. N. See *new-buyer holdover effect*.

customer market. N. Purchasers of a firm's items in any or all of its markets, i.e., consumers, industrial, organizational.

customer market focus. N. The decision of a firm acknowledging that purchasers can accept or reject the firm's merchandise. See also *market concept*.

customer orientation. N. See *customer-oriented*.

customer-oriented. ADJ. Describing the effort to comprehend the reasons, desires, and problems of the customer with the intent to use this information in fulfilling the customer's needs, while at the same time increasing sales and profits. See also *competitor orientation*.

customer-owned goods. N. For example, uits left at a store after purchase for alterations. Synonymous with *customer's own merchandise*. ABBRV. *COG*.

customer profile. N. The demographic breakdown of the consumers who purchase a brand; includes their purchasing behavior. Provides salespeople with data on buyer traits and behavior patterns and becomes useful in choosing the best prospects for a given item or for preparing selling strategies. See also *audience composition*.

customer relations. N. A salesperson's activities that attempt to ensure that consumers' needs are not neglected. Complaints are to be handled swiftly. See also *customer service*.

customer satisfaction. N. The measure of the degree to which a customer's expectations of an item or service matches the item or service's actual usefulness to the customer.

customer service. N. The department or special unit of an organization that responds to inquiries and consumer/customer complaints about their product or service, either by telephone or mail. Quality customer service usually leads to increased sales and customer attitudes. See also *customer relations, query*.

customer's own merchandise. N. See *customer-owned goods*.

customized marketing. N. Designing goods and services to fulfill each buyer's unique requirements, e.g., building customized bookshelves or customized dishes.

custom marketing. N. Marketing where the target consumers are totally segmented, i.e., each person is so unique from all others that he or she is treated as an individual.

custom marketing research firm. N. A firm retained by a client to conduct research to collect information for the client, which ultimately becomes the property, usually confidential and proprietary, of the client.

customs. N. Relevant to international marketers, taxes imposed by a government on the import or export of items.

custom selling. N. Creative selling where at least a portion of an item or service is designed for a specific prospect.

customs harmonization. N. Of relevance to global marketers, the continuing activity to standardize customs procedures and nomenclatures worldwide.

cut back. N. (1) The curtailment of production or expenditures provided for in a budget that has been or is about to be adjusted. (2) In manufacturing, a reduction to a form level (e.g., in production). (3) In advertising, interrupting the chronological sequence of an event by a scene recalling an event from an earlier time. Synonymous with *flashback*.

cut-in. N. Where a broadcast medium substitutes in one station a commercial that is different from the one that is employed in the network.

cutlines. N. See *caption*.

CWO. ABBRV. Cash with order.

cycle. N. The unit of time identified in a contract, when the contract is for a longer time period; e.g., an advertiser has a radio broadcast media purchase contract for a period of one year. Within that year-contract, there could be specified four thirteen-week periods of television programming. Each thirteen-week period is then considered a cycle. Advertisers can change or cancel a contract at the end of a cycle.

cycle billing. N. Matching of alphabetical breakdowns to specific days to assist in customer billing. Each breakdown is a cycle and occurs on the same day every month.

cyclical demand. N. See *cyclical forecast*.

dailies

dailies. N. Newspapers that are published at least five times a week, Monday through Friday. See also *daily rate, weekly.*

daily effective circulation. N. In outdoor advertising, the number of people who can be expected to observe a message; traditionally measured as one-half of all people passing the display in cars and trucks, plus one-quarter of total mass-transit passengers.

daily rate. N. The cost of daily advertising space, usually used in dailies.

DAR. ABBRV. Day after recall.

data. N. (1) A representation of facts, concepts, or instructions in a formalized manner, suitable for communication. (2) A collective mass of factual material used as a basis for inference of conclusions. (The plural "data" is often incorrectly construed as singular. "Data" is the plural of "datum.")

data analysis. N. The coding, tabulation, and analysis of marketing research data.

data bank. N. In market research, a comprehensive collection of information on a principal subject and related areas.

database. N. A collection of information specific to an operation, business, or enterprise. In marketing situations, information on customers is retrievable for each application from a shared file that is not dependent on the applications programs for its structure. See also *database marketing.*

database marketing. N. Utilizing computers to store data on consumers' characteristics and purchasing habits for use in future direct-marketing activities.

data capture. N. The act of collecting marketing and advertising data into a form that can be directly processed by a computer

data reduction. N. The process of transforming large masses of marketing data into useful, condensed, or simplified intelligence.

data storage. N. The stage in a marketing information system involving the retention of all types of relevant company records (such as sales, costs, personnel performance, etc.), as well as the information collected through marketing research and continuous monitoring.

date for value determination. N. Critical in setting duties for merchandise shipped overseas; the date when imported goods were exported from their country of origin. The value of the merchandise in effect on that date is used in setting duties.

date line. N. In advertising, the payment-due line on an order blank or a contract.

dating. N. A technique of extending credit beyond the time it was originally given; often used as an inducement to dealers to place orders far in advance of the coming retailing season.

datum. N. See *data*.

dawn raids. N. In sales, a means of dealing with price fixing; the right to raid firms for evidence of alleged price fixing.

day after recall. N. A post-test method for assessing advertising effectiveness. Information is obtained over the telephone, with interviewees provided with the name of the item or brand and then asked what information they can recall. ABBRV. *DAR*.

day parts. N. The means where a broadcast medium divides its on-the-air time. Usually it is: morning, afternoon, early evening, night, and late night. Radio day parts are: morning drive (6:00 a.m.–10:00 a.m.), daytime (10:00 a.m.–3:00 p.m.), afternoon drive (3:00 p.m.– 7:00 p.m.), nighttime (7:00 p.m.– 12:00 a.m.), and all night (12:00 a.m. to 6:00 a.m.). Television dayparts are: morning (7:00 a.m.–9:00 a.m., Monday–Friday), daytime (9:00 a.m.–4:30 p.m., Monday–Friday), early fringe (4:30 p.m.–7:30 p.m., Monday–Friday), access (7:30 p.m.–8:00 p.m., Sunday–Saturday), prime time (8:00 p.m.–11:00 p.m., Monday–Saturday), late news (7:00 p.m.–11:00 p.m., Sunday; 11:00 p.m.–11:30 p.m., Monday–Friday), late fringe (11:30 p.m.–1:00 a.m., Monday–Friday), and late night (1:00 a.m.–7:00 a.m., Sunday–Saturday). See also *afternoon drive, commercial time.*

days per outstanding. N. The ratio of accounts receivable to credit sales per day.

days purchases outstanding. N. A measure of how promptly a marketing firm pays its bills; calculated as accounts payable divided by purchases per day.

deadbeat. N. (1) A person who tries to avoid paying for things. (2) A customer who fails to pay his or her entire charge every billing period, thus incurring revolving credit charges. Often their names are ultimately purged from lists for future promotional items or services.

dead corner. N. The area in a retail store that is either empty or is used for nonretailing activities in order to affect the drawing power of the area for retailing purposes, or tends to stop the flow of shopper traffic between multiple shopping areas.

deadline. N. (1)The time, day, or other period on which something is due. (2) In advertising, the hour or day after which the advertising material will not be accepted to appear in a publication or specific broadcast time period.

dead stock. N. Merchandise that cannot be sold.

deal. N. (1) *(slang)* A large transaction involving a change in ownership. (2) *(slang)* In marketing, a sales promotion enabling a customer to save money on the purchase of a product or service, often with special discounts. By law, such arrangements must be offered on an equal basis to all dealers or retailers having business with a particular manufacturer. Synonymous with *trade deal*.

dealer. N. (1) A retailer of goods. (2) An individual or firm that divides quantity goods or services into smaller units for resale to customers.

dealer brand. N. A brand that is created and owned by an intermediary.

dealer imprint. N. A dealer's name, address, or other identification, put on material created by an advertiser.

dealer incentive. N. A point-of-purchase display incorporating as one of its parts a desirable unit for the dealer to bring home.

dealer listing. N. A list of local dealers appearing on a nationally presented advertisement in a local or regional magazine. The advertisement remains the same in all regional issues, but the dealer list changes by region. See also *ad-slick*.

dealer loader. N. A retail point-of-purchase fixture provided by the manufacturer or supplier; usually placed next to a cash register or checkout counter to display items. Synonymous with *display loader*. See also *buying loader, trade promotion*.

dealer's privilege. N. A card or similar display unit carrying an advertisement on one side, which also provides for the retailer's message on the reverse side.

dealer tag. N. At the conclusion of a nationally broadcast commercial, the local dealer is tagged on at the end of the commercial.

dealer tie-in. N. A manufacturer's advertisement given at a countrywide rate with a list of local dealers to be included in the advertisement.

deal pack. N. An item of merchandise with an attached premium. Usually handlers (wholesalers or retailers) expect payment for handling these because regular items must be withdrawn during the promotional period.

debit system. N. Transfer arrangement in which, when a purchase is made, the amount is immediately charged against the buyer's account; no delayed billing is permitted without an interest charge.

debt. N. Money, services, or materials owed to another person as the result of a previous agreement.

debt capital. N. Funds borrowed to finance the operations of a business, e.g., an advertising firm.

debtee. N. A creditor.

debtor. N. One who owes money to another.

decay curve. N. The curve representing death of concepts during the development stage. Begins on the left with 100% of concepts and ends up on the right with the percent actually marketed successfully. Usually declines rapidly. Synonymous with *mortality curve*.

decay rate. N. The number or proportion of customers lost within a time period, usually one year; shows the amount of weakening of the effects of earlier marketing activities. Indicates a need to continue marketing an item, even if presumed to be successful.

deceit. N. Conduct in business whereby one person, through fraudulent representations, misleads another person who has the right to rely on such representations as the truth or is unable to detect the fraud. See also *false advertising, advertising fraud, fraud.*

decentralization. N. (1) Placing the decision-making point at the lowest managerial level, involving delegation of decision-making authority. (2) The redistribution of population and business from a city to its suburban areas.

decentralized sales organization. N. A firm whose sales management responsibility is delegated to lower levels within the hierarchy. Primary decisions are made, not at the highest levels, but with separate divisions, with sales management duties handled by the divisions' sales forces. See also *centralized sales organization.*

deceptive advertising. N. Advertising that gives false claims or misleading information, in addition to creating a false impression. Should retailers, on a regular basis, advertise goods and services at low prices to lure people into their outlets and then fail to have the merchandise or services, they are guilty of deceptive advertising. Jurisdiction for regulating and enforcing laws in this area is with the Federal Trade Commission. See also *consumer protection legislation.*

deceptive packaging. N. Utilizing packages of differing sizes and shapes that may give the impression that they contain more of the item than is actually enclosed, or that the item is significantly bigger than it actually is. See also *deceptive advertising, Fair Packaging and Labeling Act of 1966.*

deceptive practice. N. See *deceptive advertising, deceptive packaging, deceptive pricing.*

deceptive pricing. N. Pricing methods that are determined to deceive or confuse consumers; includes misrepresentation of credit procedures. See also *deceptive advertising.*

decider. N. In the exchange process, the person who chooses an alternative that will satisfy a want or need.

decision making. N. In marketing and advertising, the process of resolving differing options into one opinion or course of action so that, when supported by authority, the decision becomes a policy of the organization.

decision rule. N. The conditions determined following a marketing research activity that urges a particular course of action within a company.

decision tree. N. In marketing research, a description of the sequence of decision choices and the possible occurrence of chance events.

deck panels. N. In outdoor advertising, panels that are placed one above the other.

declared value. N. The value of merchandise stated by the owner when the goods are delivered to a carrier.

decline stage. N. The period in a product's life cycle between saturation and abandonment. Since sales are dropping, costs are carefully controlled to minimize added losses. Synonymous with *market termination stage*.

deep stock. N. Frequently used merchandise kept in large quantities and in many sizes and colors.

defend-and-hold strategy. N. Investment and marketing efforts designed to maintain sales and profit levels for a particular service or product.

defensive budgeting. N. See *competitive parity*.

defensive pricing. N. A firm's strategy where its products are priced so as to protect or defend well-known items or market share. For example, introducing a new product at a higher price than other items of the firm so as not to upset their success.

defensive spending. N. See *competitive parity*.

deferred billing. N. Delaying invoicing of a credit order buyer at the request of the seller. Traditionally used to promote a product to send it without obligation to pay.

deferred discount. N. See *patronage discount*.

deferred payment sale. N. (1) In retailing, buying on installment. See also *layaway plan*. (2) In sales, a sale that is extended beyond a customary credit period.

degree of freedom. N. A concept describing a person's exemption or liberation from the control of some other person or power. Often, within a tightly controlled company where the president dominates, employees are allowed a minimal degree of freedom. Used also to appeal via advertisements to people aspiring to become independent and possess great control of their destiny. ABBRV. *DOF*.

delay card. N. A postcard with information that is sent to a customer advising of an expected delay in the delivery of ordered goods.

delayed broadcast. N. A repeat broadcast of a program, often used to compensate for time differentials between station locations of a network. Used especially in rural communities where the different networks share the same local station at differing times.

delayed response impact. N. Where the lags that occur between the time a marketing expenditure is made and the time purchase induced thereby takes place.

delinquent. N. See *deadbeat*.

deliverability. N. The extent to which an organization is viewed as being capable of actually delivering to the customer and adequately servicing a particular new product concept. The measure is an attribute of the concept, much as manufacturability is. See also *manufacturability*.

delivered at frontier. N. In global selling, when the seller is required to supply items that conform with the contract, at his or her own risk and expense, the seller must place the items at the disposal of the purchaser at the named place of delivery at the border at the specified time. The purchaser is responsible for complying with import formalities and duty payments.

delivered cost: N. The price at which goods are billed to a store, including transportation charges.

delivered duty exempt. N. In global selling, an obligation of the seller to pay the costs of the goods, insurance against loss, the freight charges to get them to the named port of destination, and any duties, surcharges, or taxes levied on the items by the importing nation.

delivered price. N. The price to the purchaser's store, which also includes transportation costs.

delivery. N. The transfer of possession of an item from one person to another.

delivery date. N. The date by which a vendor must ship purchases to a store in order to comply with the agreed-upon terms. Failure by the store to meet this deadline is considered reason for cancellation of the order.

Delphi technique. N. In market research, a forecasting approach whereby, at intervals, the organization polls experts who predict

deluxe items. N. Higher-priced, unique goods maintained for sale to wealthier customers.

demand. N. (1) A request to call for payment or for the carrying out of an obligation. (2) In marketing, the willingness and capability to purchase goods or services. (3) In consumer behavior, the composite desire for particular products and services as measured by how consumers choose to allocate their resources among different products and services in a given market.

demand-backward prices. N. See *market-minus prices*.

demand-based pricing. N. A pricing technique based on determining consumers' or distributors' attitudes toward the fair cost of goods and services. Ultimately the prices are determined by market analysis that provides consumer needs and the range of prices that are acceptable to them.

demand creation. N. See *sales promotion*.

demand curve. N. (1) The graphic representation of the quantity of goods demanded in relation to price. On each point of the curve, the consumer is in equilibrium and the value of the item equals its price. (2) The amounts of the goods or services buyers are prepared to purchase at different prices during a specified time period.

demand elasticity. N. See *elasticity of demand*.

demand expansibility. N. See *expansibility of demand*.

demand-oriented pricing. N. Determining the price of an item, taking into account the nature and quality of market demand for the offering.

demand patterns

demand patterns. N. Indicates the uniformity or diversity of consumer needs and desires for particular categories of goods and services.

demand price. N. The maximum price a purchaser is willing to pay for a stated quantity of a commodity or service.

demand-pulled innovation. N. Innovation caused or at least stimulated by the needs, wants, or desires of customers.

demand sensitivity. N. The speed of movement for merchandise in a retail store. See also *turnover*.

demand states. N. Varying demands that are acknowledged by marketing planners in order to relate marketing mix elements to target market needs. The eight demand states are: (a) negative demand: when most consumers dislike a product or service and avoid it; (b) no demand: where consumers are casual and indifferential toward the item or service; (c) latent demand: where consumers search for a product benefit not offered by items already available; (d) falling demand: trends that lower the size of the market; (e) irregular demand: where time factors, including season, time of day, etc., lead to fluctuations in product usage; (f) full demand, when a firm has the full market share that it had sought; (g) overfull demand: where market demand is in excess of the firm's ability to provide sufficient supplies of the service or good; and, (h) unwholesome demand: where the demand for unhealthy products or services (e.g., cigarettes, alcohol) spawn organized efforts to lower market consumption. See also *falling demand state, seasonability, supply and demand, wholesale demand state, latent demand, overall demand, overfull demand*.

demand stimulation. N. See *sales promotion*.

demarketing. N. Term coined by Philip Kotler and Sidney J. Levy for the concept that part of marketing attempts to discourage customers, either individually or collectively, from desiring a good or service. Synonymous with *creative demarketing*.

demo. ABBRV. Demonstration.

demographics. N. (1) The statistical breakdown of the population within a given area. (2) A market containing characteristics that can be used for making consumer predictions. See also *demographic segmentation, market demography, vital statistics*.

demographic segmentation. N. The most popular segmentation method, a market segmentation approach where the market is separated into groups based on age, sex, education, nationality, religion, etc. See also *psychographic market segmentation*.

demonstration. N. See *sales demonstration*.

demonstration advertising. N. Advertising where the attributes of the item are displayed or communicated to consumers; usually the items' attributes are emphasized. See also *demonstration commercial*.

demonstration commercial. N. A broadcast commercial used by a producer, advertising agency, technical representative, etc., to demonstrate talent and to obtain new or repeat work. See also *demonstration advertising*.

de novo basis. N. Commencing a new business as contrasted with acquiring an existing one.

density. N. In direct marketing, the proportion of target customers in a particular geographical location in contrast to the total population within that area.

denying method. N. See *direct denial technique*.

departmentalization. N. The manner in which a store is structurally divided; for example, by function, territory, product, customer, or task.

departmentized specialty store. N. A specialty shop that has grown in size and now contains a variety of items carried that accounted separately for profit knowledge and for general decision making by its executives.

department manager. N. An executive charged with the operation of a selling department of a store. Often this individual is the buyer, but he or she may also be involved with stock and sales.

department store. N. A retail organization that employs twenty-five or more people and sells merchandise in the following categories: home furnishings; apparel for men, women, and children; and, home linens and dry goods. See also *store, traditional department store*.

dependent variable. N. In market and consumer research, the variable in an experiment that the research tries to predict or explain, usually by altering the independent variables. By shifting independent variables, changes in attitudes can be determined. Only one independent variable at a time is altered so that its impact can be determined. See also *experiment, variable, independent variable*. Synonymous with *response variable*.

deposit plan. N. See *layaway plan*.

depot store. N. A store carrying popular items that customers purchased because of the store's convenient location. In most cases, the customer is charged higher prices for the items than in supermarkets, discount stores, and other nondepot outlets.

depreciable value. N. In marketing goods and services, the cost of an asset minus the expected salvage value.

depreciation. N. Charges against earnings to write off the cost, less salvage value, of an asset over its estimated useful life. It is a bookkeeping entry and does not represent any cash outlay, nor are

depth. N. The number of distinct items within a product line.

depth interview. N. A method, based primarily on the use of open-ended questions, to elicit from the person interviewed natural and lengthy statements about a predetermined subject. Depth interviews are critical in the assessment of consumer reaction to a product or service. See also *motivation research*.

depth of assortment. N. The variations available within a product line, such as the variety of colors of a specific dress.

depth of exposure. N. The degree of penetration of the advertising message into the marketplace. The greater the frequency of repetition of the advertiser's message, the greater the depth of exposure. Usually this results in the consumer being more likely to buy the item or service when he or she has seen or heard the advertisement most often.

depth of market. N. The extent of business that can be done in a market without causing a price disturbance.

depth of product mix. N. The number of product items within each product line.

depth of space. N. Advertising space dimensions, usually in reference to a printed column.

derived demand. N. The demand for an item that grows out of the wish to fulfill the demand for another item (e.g., when a demand for community tennis courts is filled, it leads to increased sales of supplies for the courts and tennis equipment). See also *suggestive selling, whiplash impact*.

descriptive approach. N. See *institutional approach*.

descriptive billing. N. A billing system in which an account statement is not accompanied by copies of original invoices. Instead, the statement contains sufficient detail to permit the customer to identify the nature, date, and amount of each transaction processed during the statement period.

descriptive labeling. N. (1) Labeling that explains the important characteristics or benefits of a product. (2) The labeling of merchandise by characteristic, but without considering grades or accepted standards. See also *grade labeling*.

descriptive model. N. An analytical model that attempts to explain or predict factors relating to a marketing issue or problem, e.g., the impact of advertising expenditures on sales.

descriptive research. N. (1) Research concerned with determining the nature of something. (2) In marketing, research that focuses on demographic information about markets and their composition.

descriptive studies. N. See *descriptive research*.

design. N. The full sequence of activities for a marketing research effort.

designated market area. N. Established by the A.C. Nielsen Company, a geographic area making up a specific television market. Areas do not overlap, and every county in the United States belongs to only one designated market area.

design-for-response. N. Introduction of a new product or campaign with a flexible design that is readily adjusted in response to consumer reaction.

desire set. N. The benefits a consumer wishes or expects to receive from using an item. Used by advertisers in the planning and buying of media.

desk jobber. N. A merchant wholesaler who usually becomes a middleperson and rarely takes possession of merchandise. Instead, he or she sends items directly to the customer from the manufacturer. The desk jobber traditionally is responsible for billing the customer he or she services.

desktop publishing. N. Special programs from personal computers to design and print professional quality documents, advertisements, etc.

detailer. N. A salesperson who places vendor displays and insures that they are stocked with merchandise.

detail person. N. (1) A salesperson who visits a manufacturer's customs and is responsible for most of the service details that encourage future sales. (2) A salesperson whose major task is to increase business from existing and future customers by offering them current product information and other personal selling assistance. Synonymous with *missionary salesperson*.

determinant attributes. N. Product characteristics that help consumers discriminate among products and that influence product preferences. See also *brand awareness*, *differential advantages*.

determinant gap map. N. A two-dimensional map that uses two determinant attributes to plot all brands in a product category. The plotting is done by an experienced analyst, not by the consumers themselves.

determining behavioral variables. N. See *determining factors*.

determining dimensions. N. See *determining factors*.

determining factors. N. (1) Characteristics traditionally identified with a purchasing decision. Used often in setting marketing strategies. See also *qualifying factors*. (2) A set of variables that

determining behavioral variables 178

determine whether or not a consumer is a member of a particular market segment. Synonymous with *determining dimensions*.

determining behavioral variables. N. See *determining factors*.

development expense. N. The cost of developing products, processes, or other commercial activities to make them functional.

diagnostic information. N. Information obtained from any of the evaluative steps of a product's development that goes beyond the current evaluation to give guidance to later steps. A product-use test, for example, rates the product's usefulness but also gives suggestions on packaging, positioning, and pricing.

diary method. N. A technique used to determine brands purchased and the frequency of buying. The user makes arrangements with households to keep a continuous log of brands purchased day by day over a specified period; also used to follow consumers' product buying. See also *Videodex, aided recall*.

difference threshold. N. The smallest change in the intensity of a stimulus that can be noticed.

differential. N. See *differential advantages*.

differential advantages. N. Selling characteristics that provide an advantage over competitors. These include price, product features, location, method of delivery, advertising skills, packaging, and brand name. Synonymous with *differential*. See also *brand awareness, competitive advantage*.

differential oligopoly. N. An industry composed of a small number of sellers manufacturing products that are only slightly different. See also *oligopoly*.

differentiated marketing. N. A form of market segmentation in which the marketer employs different products and/or different marketing programs to reach two or more market segments.

differentiation. N. (1) The process by which subunits in an organization develop particular attributes in response to the requirements imposed by their subenvironments. The greater the differences among the subunits' attributes, the greater the differentiation. (2) In marketing, a marketing method used by the manufacturer to create close identity in a particular market. The manufacturer will introduce different varieties of the same basic item under the same name into a particular item category and thereby cover the range of items available in that category. (3) In marketing, positioning a brand in order to differentiate it from its competition and thereby create a unique image. Synonymous with *product differentiation*, *segmentation strategy*.

differentiation strategy. N. See *differentiation*.

diffused demand. N. A demand pattern in which consumer needs and desires for a good or service category are so diverse that clear clusters (segments) cannot be identified.

diffusion model. N. A method for forecasting the flow of an innovation through the population; assisting decision makers in setting the timing with which an innovation can spread through the target population. See also *innovation diffusion*.

diffusion of innovation. N. See *innovation diffusion*.

diffusion process. N. The manner in which a new concept evolves in a product or service, going from idea to consumer usage. See also *diffusion rate*.

diffusion rate. N. The speed in which the diffusion process makes. See also *diffusion process*.

dimensional analysis. N. A technique of attribute analysis, whereby new concepts are generated from an exhaustive listing of the dimensions of products in a given category.

dimensional marketing. N. In direct-mailing, where the promotional package's contents have dimensions, consisting of more than printed papers. A costly marketing method, these packages are usually sent to a limited list of prospects who are chosen by the advertiser's salespeople.

diminishing marginal utility law. N. The concept that, in a specified period, the consumption of an item while tastes stay the same can lead to increasing marginal utilities per unit of the item consumed, but a point will be reached when additional units of consumption of the item will lead to decreasing marginal utilities per unit of the item consumed.

diminishing relative values. N. Used in consumer and market research, the concept that the value to a person of item A in terms of item B declines if there is a greater consumption of item A and less of item B, resulting in a condition under which the person is no better or worse off.

diminishing returns. N. May occur in a firm with high sales penetration if the firm attempts to attract nonconsumers because the costs of attracting additional consumers may outweigh the revenues. See also *point of indifference*.

diorama. N. In point-of-purchase advertising, a fancy display with scenery that is usually lighted and in three- dimensions.

direct accounts. N. A list of the firm's customers who are serviced by home-office salespeople or executives. These accounts are rarely assigned to regular sales personnel within a territory since they are perceived as the firm's major, large buying clients. Synonymous with *house accounts*, *national accounts*.

direct-action advertising. N. A goal of an advertisement to have the targeted audience react immediately, with little time to make a decision. See also *indirect-action advertising*.

direct advertising. N. (1) Print advertising sent by mail to prospects, salespeople, and dealers, in contrast to advertising presented by other media. Synonymous with *direct-mail advertising*. (2) Advertising that uses person-to-person communication instead of the mass media. Nearly 10% of all advertising is direct advertising, with a positive response rate hovering around 30%.

direct buying. N. Bypassing the middleperson, the process of buying directly from the manufacturer. See also *direct channel*.

direct cancel. N. A subscriber's request to a publisher to cancel his or her subscription.

direct channel. N. A channel of distribution free of a middleperson. The manufacturer sells directly to the consumer. See also *direct buying, direct distribution, indirect channel*.

direct close. N. Frequently employed after the seller receives positive buying signals from a prospect, a closing method of the salesperson where the seller just asks the prospect for a favorable purchase decision free of persuasive manipulations.

direct competitor. N. A company running competitively with another, offering possible customers similar or identical items or services.

direct cost. N. The cost of any good or service that contributes to the production of an item or service, e.g., labor or material. See also *indirect costs*. Synonymous with *direct expense*.

direct costing. N. A technique for implementing the economic theory of marginal analysis to assist a firm in making short-term

direct denial method

promotional and/or advertising decisions. See also *marginal analysis*.

direct denial method. N. Where the salesperson, to offset resistance to a product or service, presents reasons why the consumer is incorrect. Synonymous with *denying method*.

direct distribution. N. Where the manufacturer sells directly to industrial consumers through his or her own salesperson and/or warehouses. See also *direct channel, indirect distribution*.

direct expense. N. See *direct cost*.

direct-mail advertising. N. See *direct advertising*.

direct-mail list. N. Names and addresses of potential customers, purchased by or given without charge to an organization.

direct marketer. N. See *direct marketing*.

direct marketing. N. (1) A more personal type of promotion than advertising, the process of selling to consumers, personal or industrial, free of a middleperson. The direct marketer chooses the people who will receive his or her promotion, and is the direct recipient of the response, if any. See also *direct media, direct response agency, direct sales*. (2) Similar to retail mail-order, but in addition the advertisement is usually delivered by multiple media instead of only a local advertisement or direct mail piece. (3) See *direct selling*.

direct material. N. All raw material that is an integral part of the finished good and can be conveniently assigned to specific physical units.

direct media. N. Communication channels, e.g., direct mail or telephone, used in direct marketing to bring the promotion communication to the prospect, as contrasted with

directory advertising. N. Advertising that appears in printed directories (e.g., telephone books and city directories); is usually less costly than other forms of advertising and offers advertisers the chance to call attention to their merchandise or services at a time when the prospect is actively seeking and ready to purchase. See also *yellow page advertising*.

direct ownership. N. A form of international marketing company organization in which a firm owns production, marketing, and other facilities in one or more foreign countries without any partners. The firm has full control over its international operations in those countries.

direct package. N. A bundle of letters tied together, all addressed to the same office.

direct premium. N. Merchandise given without cost with the purchase at the time of the purchase. A form of premium-giving.

direct promotion. N. An effort for delivering promotional communications directly to consumers without using communications media, e.g., television or radio. See also *indirect promotion*.

direct response. N. See *direct response advertising*.

direct-response advertising. N. Similar to direct-mail advertising, except that the message is not limited to be delivered by a particular medium. Its impact is directly correlated with the volume of sales. See also *direct-response agency*.

direct-response agency. N. A unit of an advertising agency, or an advertising agency that specializes in the creation of direct marketing promotions. See also *direct-response advertising*.

direct retailing. N. Selling items to consumers without the involvement of middlepersons.

direct sales. N. Sources of periodical or magazine subscriptions sold by a publisher without the use of a subscription agent. They utilize other approaches including direct mail advertising, insert cards, and space advertising. Synonymous with *direct-to-publisher sales*.

direct selling. N. See *direct marketing*.

direct-selling house. N. A relatively new field where the firm creates its own items and sells them directly to the advertiser through its own sales force. See also *specialty distributor*.

direct-to-publisher sales. N. See *direct sales*.

disaggregated market. N. A market where buyers are so significantly different from each other that no aggregates can be formed. These markets are completely segmented.

discontinuous innovation. N. One of a four-way classification of new items as to degrees of uniqueness; involves the establishment of previously unknown merchandise and the formation of new usage patterns based on a concept or new behavior pattern. The other three are: congruent, continuous, and dynamically continuous.

discotetic. N. The chaos resulting from continuous shifts and changes within an organization that fails to yield constructive results in attaining a primary objective or goal.

discount. N. (1) A deduction from the list price in the form of cash or something else of value. Often used as a strategy to counter competitors' initiatives. (2) In sales, the selling of an item or service at a price below the normal list price. Discounts are often given in reaction to competitive advertising; other discounts are given when customers pay for their services or products in cash instead of using credit cards. See also *bulk discount, suggested retail price, rebate*.

discount house. N. A retail operation, usually a no-frills store, in which prices are lower than at other stores selling the same merchandise. Synonymous with *discount store*. See also *below the market strategy*.

discount loading. N. In retailing, where all inventory and purchase figures are compared on a comparable basis by predetermining all invoice prices to reflect the assumed desirable cash discount percent. Should a purchaser be unable to secure that size discount from a supplier, the item is costed in as though he or she has been successful. The higher-cost base figure traditionally results in setting higher retail prices on the item.

discount store. N. See *discount house*.

discrepancy letter of credit. N. In international marketing, when documents presented do not conform to the letter of credit.

discrepancy of assortment. N. The difference between the extent of choice among goods that are usually interchangeable that is expected by the purchaser and the choice that is available from a given source.

discrepancy of quantity. N. The difference between the quantity a seller should purchase at a specific time from the manufacturer and the quantity a purchaser chooses to purchase at one time from the seller.

discrepancy of variety. N. The difference between the number of distinct types of merchandise that the purchaser would like a given source to have available and the number actually in stock.

discretionary costs. N. Fixed costs arising from periodic, usually yearly, appropriation decisions that directly reflect

discretionary fund

top-management policies, as with, for example, an advertising campaign.

discretionary fund. N. Discretionary income enlarged by the amount of new credit extensions, which also may be deemed spendable as a result of consumer decisions relatively free of prior commitment or pressure of need.

discretionary income. N. The amount of disposable income that is left over after spending on essentials such as food, shelter, and clothing. Marketers of items compete with these essentials to obtain purchases. During a weak economy people concentrate on necessities and often have less for advertised goods and services. See also *disposable income*.

discretionary spending power. N. Money available to consumers after necessities have been purchased. See also *disposable income*.

discriminatory pricing. N. The sale of merchandise at different prices to different customers, thus giving one party an advantage over another. See also *Robinson-Patman Act*.

diseconomies of scale. N. Considered by market researchers, situations that occur when costs increase as a business grows in size. For all firms, there is a point at which, as the company becomes larger, costs also increase. See also *point of indifference*.

disequilibrium. N. A condition in which incentives to change exist; usually used in reference to markets in which either purchasers or producers, or both, have not yet adjusted prices and quantities to their satisfaction.

dispatcher. N. An agent responsible for efficiently routing and sending merchandise to its destined location.

display. N. A visual presentation of data or merchandise. Displays differ based on their placement and type, e.g., window displays, floor displays, and point-of-purchase advertising displays.

display advertisement. N. (1) An advertisement that uses attention-attracting features, such as illustrations, white spaces, or colors. See also *classified advertising*. (2) Free-standing advertisement created for exhibition in heavy traffic locations, such as public buildings, railroad stations, department stores. See also *classified advertisement*.

display advertiser. N. See *display advertisement*.

display allowance. N. See *retail display allowance*.

display card. N. A tear-off card containing an advertisement that is affixed to a store display.

display case. N. (1) In merchandising, a carrying case used by salespeople for displaying their merchandise contained, as with a door-to-door costume jewelry salesperson. (2) In point-of-purchase advertising, a display where the item is in a closed container of sturdy material. To be used, a prospective customer requests that the often locked case be opened.

display loader. N. See *dealer loader, trade promotion*.

disposable income. N. Of particular interest to market and consumer behavior researchers, personal income minus income taxes and other taxes paid by an individual, the balance being available for consumption or savings. See also *discretionary income*. Synonymous with *personal disposable income*.

dissociative group. N. Of importance to market analysts, a reference group to which a person does not choose to belong.

dissonance-reduction. N. A postpurchase behavior occurring when the customer becomes agitated in thinking that he or she has made the wrong purchase decision; often compensated by seeking new reinforcing information on the item or service, or ultimately by returning the item or service. Marketers in anticipation of dissonance-reduction suggest using thank you letters to purchasers and forwarding additional information on the product. See also *cognitive dissonance.*

distinctive competencies. N. Used by advertisers to promote an organization, activities that a firm can perform better than other firms.

distress merchandise. N. Goods that must be sold at reduced prices.

distribution. N. (1) The separation of merchandise into different categories and group levels. (2) The process of making sure that a product is available when and where it is desired. Different forms are: (a) intensive distribution: where the firm makes the item available in as many stores as possible; (b) exclusive distribution: where one store carries the item in a given market; and, (c) selective distribution: where the item is available in a select few stores in a market area. See also *channel of distribution, physical distribution.*

distribution allowance. N. Frequently used with new items, a price reduction from the manufacturer to a distributor, retailer, or wholesaler allowing for the cost of distributing products.

distribution center. N. (1) A warehouse in which the emphasis is on processing and moving goods rather than on simple storage. (2) A storage facility that takes orders and delivers products.

distribution cost analysis. N. When marketing an item in a particular location, the breaking down of all direct and indirect costs.

distribution intensity. N. The measure of the exposure a product receives at the wholesale or retail level. With more outlets, the distribution is more intense.

distribution intermediaries. N. Wholesalers, retailers, and marketing specialists, such as transportation firms, that are acting in their roles as facilitators between manufacturers and service providers and their consumers.

distribution model. N. A statistical model used to assist management in choosing and assessing the values of various distribution channels; can also help in determining store and warehouse locations and logistics for inventory purposes.

distribution planning. N. The systematic decision making regarding the physical movement of goods and services from producer to consumer, as well as the related transfer of ownership (or rental) of them. It encompasses transportation, inventory management, and customers' transactions.

distribution shipment. N. A truckload of small goods that are transported at a truckload rate to a specified destination.

distribution standards. N. Customer service standards of performance.

distribution strategy. N. The conclusion that marketing items through a specific channel will achieve the most economic or cost-effective results. See also *channel of distribution*.

distribution structure. N. The sum of all the distribution channels existing within a given industry.

distributor. N. See *wholesaler*.

distributor brand. N. A brand name that is owned by the retailer, wholesaler, or other distributor instead of the producer. A private label item is sold as a distributor brand.

diversifiable. N. (1) A project-specific risk in marketing, such as that deriving from uncertainty over entry of competitors, strikes, or technological advances. (2) The part of total risk in marketing that is unique to the firm or asset and is, therefore, the risk that can be eliminated by diversification. See also *diversification*.

diversification. N. The manufacture or sale of unrelated products. Major diversification strategies include: (a) concentric diversification: securing items with technical similarities to its existing product line; (b) horizontal diversification: where the acquired items appeal to the firm's current customers but are not directly related to the present item line; and, (c) conglomerate diversification: where the acquiring items are completely unrelated to the firm's product line and require reaching new market segments. See also *concentric diversification, diversifiable, horizontal diversification, simplification*.

diversionary pricing. N. In order to give the impression that all prices are low within a store, some of the items are priced very low. This is considered a deceptive practice when most of the merchandise is found to be higher than the usual pricing for the items.

diversion in transit. N. In the distribution process, a service of rail carriers that permits a shipper to reroute merchandise to a destination other than the original while the items are in transit.

divest-and-exit strategy. N. When an item or service fails to sell well and their overall market growth rate is slowing, in order to avoid or minimize losses, efforts designed to eliminate a product or service line by selling or discontinuing it. See also *product life cycle*.

divest strategy. N. See *divest-and-exit strategy*.

dock warrant. N. Impact on overseas sales and merchandising, where items are imported but immediate delivery is not required, and may be deposited in a warehouse, owned either by the dock authority or by the public warehouse people.

dodger. N. An advertising brochure brought from house to house.

DOF. ABBRV. Degree of freedom.

dog. N. (1) *(slang)* An advertised item having proved unprofitable with a dismal future potential. (2) *(slang)* A small business unit that has a low relative market share and is in a low-growth market.

dollar merchandise plan. N. An estimate of anticipated sales, frequently over a six-month period, integrated with inventory estimates and purchases in harmony with sales and profit goals.

dollar value per order. N. The relative measure of the performance of a promotion or mailing list, determined by dividing the total gross revenue generated by the number of orders received.

domestic-based export agent. N. In international marketing, the independent middleperson used in indirect export, who negotiates foreign purchases for the domestic manufacturer and receives payment in the form of a commission. See also *domestic-based export department, indirect exporting.*

domestic-based export department. N. In direct exporting, the part of a domestic company whose activities are directed toward selling merchandise overseas. A self-contained unit of the manufacturer, it does not make use of an independent international marketing middleperson. See also *domestic-based export agent.*

domestic-based export merchant. N. An independent international marketing middleperson used in indirect export who purchases the manufacturer's items and sells it overseas. See also *domestic-based export agent, indirect exporting.*

domestic-exchange ratio. N. The relative costs of producing two goods domestically. The exchange ratio is the opportunity cost of one good in terms of the other. See also *opportunity cost*.

domestic marketing. N. Encompasses an organization's efforts in its home country.

domestic-only orientation. N. A marketing approach that excludes all foreign sales, both imports and exports.

domestics. N. Yard goods from which sheets, linens, towels, and so on, are cut. Today, the term is more popularly identified with finished products.

domestic value-added. N. The market price of a final item, less the cost of the imported inputs that were used in the production of the item. See also *value-added tax*.

domicile. N. A dwelling; a place of permanent residence. See also *legal residence*.

dominant company. N. A firm within a market that has the largest market share.

domination. N. Achieving objectives by direct command; utilizing power or influence to impose one's will on others.

don't wants. N. *(slang)* Cash-on-delivery packages refused by the customer.

donut. N. A prerecorded commercial with a blank time span in its center where a special advertising message is to be placed; produced by a production firm and used by advertisers to advertise on a regular basis and whose message is basically the same, but whose product differs from time to time, e.g., a retail store will feature a different item for sale every week, although the theme of each sales promotion is to be the same.

door opener. N. (1) In sales, an inexpensive item, given as a premium by the salesperson (usually house to house) as a means to get the customer to listen longer to the sales representative. (2) In direct marketing, any service or item offered free by mail, or with a solicitation reprinted from the publication being sold or that consists of materials related to the publication, which is used to increase response to a promotion.

door-to-door selling. N. Selling of a product or service directly from the manufacturer by the manufacturer's employee to potential customers in their homes or offices. This process eliminates the middleman, with the expectation of cutting costs. See also *Green River ordinance, house-to-house selling.*

dormant account. N. An account that has had little or no activity for a period of time. Synonymous with *inactive account*.

double-decker. N. Two outdoor advertising panels built one above the other. Traditionally placed in high-volume traffic locations.

double-page spread. N. A very costly process, used mostly with the introduction of a new product, in which an advertisement appears on two facing pages. When featured in the center of the periodical or newspaper, it is referred to as a center spread. See double truck. Synonymous with *center spread (2)*. ABBRV. *DPS*.

double search. N. Where consumers seeking products they wish and simultaneously manufacturers are seeking customers, i.e. each party searches for the other.

double spotting. N. Placing two broadcast commercials back to back with no program material intervening.

double spread. N. (1) Two pages facing each other in a publication and bought as a unit for a single advertisement. (2) An advertisement occupying two facing pages in a publication.

double top. N. In marketing goods, when a price twice reaches a high point, only to fall back. The likelihood is that the price will continue to fall.

double truck. N. An advertisement on a double-page spread. See also *double-page spread*.

doubling day. N. The moment in a direct-mail promotion life cycle when half the expected returns are received.

downscale. N. Used by consumer and marketing researchers, a derogatory term for the low-income segment of the population; often, but not always, having less formal education than most. See also *upscale*.

downstream dumping. N. Of concern to international marketers, the condition that occurs when foreign producers sell at below cost to a producer in its domestic market and the product is then further processed and shipped to another country.

DPS. ABBRV. Double-page spread.

dramatic strategy. N. A sales approach in the opening minutes of consumer contact where the salesperson demonstrates how the product functions. Frequently the item or service is shown in the context of a real-life highly emotional situation, e.g., replacing a tire on a wintery night because the tire was defective. See also *slice-of-life*.

draw. N. See *drawing account*.

drawing account. N. A regular allowance made available to salespeople employed on a straight commission basis. The commission earned is balanced against the drawing account at various intervals. Synonymous with *draw*.

drive. N. See *drive theory*.

drive stimulus. N. A sales promotion offered in the form of a deal to retailers, sales prospects, and consumers to stimulate sales for the duration of the campaign, when the item or service is being actively advertised.

drive theory. N. (1) The psychological concept that attributes action to primary (biological) and secondary (learned) motives. (2) A strong motivating tendency that arouses an organism toward a particular type of behavior. See also *motive*.

drive time. N. In radio broadcasting, the local commercial placed within the time period of a nationally sponsored network program. Drive time is the equivalent of television's prime time, which also commands the highest audience figures and the most costly advertising rates. See also *day parts*, *prime time*.

drop. V. In manufacturing, to discontinue an item from production. N. In direct marketing, direct-mail promotion that enters the direct mail system; frequently done for a specific holiday, event, or season, e.g., advertising fur coats in early fall. Enables prospective buyers to receive promotional information before the actual buying season for such items. Synonymous with *mail date*.

drop date. N. See *drop*.

drop-in. N. A local television commercial that is shown during a network broadcast, e.g., a network film has drop-in commercials by retailers. Stations can sell a prescribed amount of time for drop-in commercial per hour of programming.

drop-out percent. N. A relative proportion of prospects who stop making purchases or stop renewing subscriptions of magazines each year.

drop shipment. N. In merchandising, items shipped directly from manufacturer to retailer; usually involves large items, such as

drop shipper 196

ovens and refrigerators that are considered expensive to retain in inventory. Suppliers of drop shipments charge a premium to retailers, who, in turn, charge such costs to consumers. The wholesaler receives only the invoice and then bills the retailer. See also *drop shipper*.

drop shipper. N. A wholesaler who performs most wholesaling activities except storage and handling. He or she sends requests to the manufacturer, who ships directly to the customer. The customer pays the drop shipper, who has already paid the bill to the manufacturer. See also *desk jobber, drop shipment, jobber, shipment*.

drumming. N. A traditional American-style salesperson who calls on retailers of soft goods or meets them at buying centers.

dry goods. N. Specifically, fabrics made from cotton, wool, rayon, silk, and other textile materials; includes ready-to-wear clothing, bed linens, and so on.

dry testing. N. Promoting an item that is not yet available for delivery to the purchaser so as to test response to the item prior to production or delivery of the merchandise. Failure to continue production requires the maker to make a refund.

dual adaptation. N. A technique in international marketing where the offered item for export is different from the domestic merchandise and is promoted differently in the overseas market.

dual billing and posting. N. Posting a customer's purchases to ledger independently from the preparation of a bill for the customer.

dual brand loyalty. N. When a consumer purchases either of two brands most of the time without exhibiting a consistent preference for one over the other.

dual channel market. N. A geographic location that receives at least two television stations.

dual distribution. N. The sale of a product through more than one distributive system.

dual drive. N. The strategic combination of technology and market as sources for product innovation. Innovations are based on at least one specific technical strength of the firm and at least one specific market opportunity. See also *market-driven economy, technology driven*.

dual marketing. N. See *dual merchandising*.

dual merchandising. N. Offering for sale by a particular company of items made by other firms as well as itself.

dual offer. N. An "either-or" promotional method; increases response because customers can select from two items, and because the offer enhances the perceived value of the items.

dual pricing. N. See *unit pricing*.

dummy. N. A model indicating the size, shape, and layout of a finished printed product. A dummy shows clients how the printed piece should look like upon its completion and is traditionally made for client approval before developing the mechanical art.

dummy invoice. N. A statement prepared by a retailer as a temporary replacement for a vendor's invoice if the latter is not available when the goods are to be received, marked, and put in inventory.

dump bind. N. A container to hold items as they are dumped into it from the shipping case. Only the one item is displayed in it. See also *jumble basket*.

dumping. N. (1) The selling of goods abroad at prices below those that the exporter charges for comparable sales in his or her own country, often involving a subsidy. (2) In the United States, selling imported items at prices less than the cost of manufacture. (3) Selling items to other countries below cost for purposes of eliminating surplus or to hurt foreign competition. See also *persistent dumping, predatory dumping, rules of origin, sporadic dumping, third country dumping, unloading.*

dumping margin. N. In international marketing and sales, a margin determined once a product is declared to have been dumped. It represents the difference between the home market price and the price at which the items are sold abroad less incidental charges, such as export packaging, peculiar to foreign sales. See also *dumping.*

duopoly. N. An industry containing two businesses that sell the identical items. In a duopoly, both firms exercise control.

duopsony. N. A market situation in which only two buyers are seeking an item. See also *monopsony, oligopsony.*

duplicated audience. N. Readers, viewers, or listeners who are reached more than once by the same commercial or advertisement appearing in different media.

duplication. N. In advertising, reaching the same person or household by two or more media.

durability. N. The lasting quality of an item.

durable goods. N. See *capital goods, hard goods.*

durable merchandise. N. See *capital goods, hard goods.*

Dutch auction. N. An auction sale in which the prices on items are continuously lowered until a bidder responds favorably and buys.

dutiable list. N. Of importance to international marketers, a nation's tariff law giving those items that will be subject to duty and the applicable rate.

duty. N. (1) An actual tax collected; impacts international sales volume. (2) A tax imposed on the importation, exportation, or consumption of goods.

duty-free. ADJ. Items that are not affected by any customs duty. See also *free list*.

duty-free port. N. See *free-trade zone*.

dwelling units. N. Places of residence where a person, family, or group of unrelated people live, in either single-family homes, townhouses, apartments, etc. Marketers and advertisers use this information since residents of these dwelling units tend to purchase items and services in common.

dyad. N. See *buyer-seller dyad*.

dynamically continuous innovation. N. One of a four-way classification of new items as to degrees of their newness, intended to fulfill new consumer needs, often brought about by changes in lifestyle or fashion. The other three types are: congruent, continuous, and discontinuous.

dynamic economy. N. An economy of growth and change.

dynamic models. N. In consumer research, models that identify the behavior of variables over a given period.

dynamic research. N. Research that emphasizes the reaction of consumers to one another instead of how they react as individuals.

E

E

E. N. The European Union stamp placed on products indicating that the items have met with the standards established by the European Union.

ear. N. The space adjacent to the masthead on either corner at the top of the front page of a newspaper. In only a few newspapers are ears sold for advertising space, which is traditionally reserved for weather forecasts, newspaper logos, newspaper slogans, etc.

early acceptors. N. See *innovators*.

early adopters. N. Consumers who buy a product early in its life cycle and influence other people to buy it. See also *innovators*.

early followers. N. See *early majority*.

early fringe. N. In television broadcasting, the time period from 4:30 p.m. to 7:30 p.m. It precedes prime time and is on the early side, or fringe, of prime time. The cost of commercials in this slot is less than prime time, but still costly compared with other time periods. The hope is that television watchers will tune into programs prior to prime time programs.

early majority. N. (1) Consumers who wait and watch others before adopting a new product. (2) Early adopters in the innovation diffusion process. A new product or concept is considered after numerous early adopters have used it and found it fulfilling. Consequently the time required between trial and adoption may be long. Synonymous with *early followers*.

earmuff problem. N. A condition when a salesperson becomes so involved in monopolizing the interest that incoming communications from the prospective consumer are interfered with, thus destroying the value of listening.

earned rate. N. The amount an advertiser pays for media space or time actually used.

E Award. N. The president of the United States' prestigious award for excellence to firms and individuals in the U.S. exporting of goods and services; at times used in an advertising campaign.

EBI. ABBRV. Effective buying income.

EC. ABBRV. European Community.

eco-audit. N. Impacts international marketing procedures; an eco-audit applies to a company's production method and sites anywhere in a trade or regional community. Within the European Union, any company that submits its production facilities to an eco-audit by independent environmental monitors, covering areas such as energy efficiency, waste reduction, and accident prevention, would receive an environmental logo it could use for public relations purposes. Without an eco-audit system, there would be considerable risk that widely varying national standards would develop, leading to uneven environmental controls. See also *eco-label, sociolecological view of marketing.*

eco-label. N. Impacts international marketing procedures; use of this European Union (EU) label helps consumers identify environmentally sound products and protects them from choosing the often misleading "green labels" that businesses are increasingly using to market their products in response to green consumerism. Products will be examined and graded for their impact on the environment throughout their life span by national competent officials using criteria agreed at the EU level. Only products genuinely less damaging to the environment will receive the eco-label logo. The eco-label signals consumers that the product with the EU sticker will be less damaging to the environment than others without such a label. This label is a sign that the EU is willing to use market forces as well as the law to protect the environment, and intended to counter the plethora of dubious, unregulated advertisements of products claiming to be ecologically friendly. These standards required for such labeling would be strict and based on an analysis of a product's impact throughout its life cycle—from the raw materials employed to produce it, through distribution, packaging, use, and ultimately, disposal. See also *eco-audit, sociolecological view of marketing.*

e-commerce. N. Business transactions by electronic methods; usually Internet-based relationships. Synonymous with *Internet marketing.*

economic. N. Any action having to do with the evolution of goods and services that are purported to satisfy a human condition.

economic analysis. N. In marketing and advertising, the process of gathering and evaluating quantitative information about the costs and benefits of a project.

economic environment. N. The interaction of all the phases of the economy in which a marketer conducts business.

economic forecasting. N. Used by market researchers, the employing of behavioral relations (equations) linking many variables in the economy to obtain short-term projections of the future.

economic growth rate. N. Used by advertisers to identify markets, the percentage rate at which total annual output grows; an increase in real per capita income.

economic indicators. N. Government or commercial indices reflecting economic activity and general business conditions. Marketers and advertisers analyze such measures when planning strategies and decisions and when projecting the demand for items and services.

economic lot technique. N. Of interest to marketers and retailers, an approach that describes the amount of an item that should be made or sold at one time to reduce the total costs involved.

economic man theory. N. In consumer behavior, where price is the primary motivating feature in consumer-buying decisions.

economic needs. N. Consumer needs that are related to making the best usage of limited resources.

economic order quantity model. N. (1) The optimum quantity of a product to order at a given time; used by marketers in setting strategies. (2) An inventory decision-making approach used to create a formula for determining when to order supplies and in what quantity. ABBRV. *EOQ*.

economic profit. N. The residual profit after explicit and implicit costs have been paid. Synonymous with *pure profit*.

economic shoppers. N. One of a four-way sociological classification of consumers who are interested primarily in price, quality, variety, and ease in forming conclusions. They are the largest group of the four, which also include apathetic shoppers, ethical shoppers, and personalizing shoppers.

economic system. N. A general concept of economics and marketing principles; the way in which society organizes its resources to produce goods and services that will satisfy its members' wants and needs.

economic value. N. A general concept of economics and marketing principles; the value given to an item as a function of its usefulness and its scarcity.

economies of scale. N. (1) The savings that result when fixed costs are spread over more units of a product; applied in marketing strategies. (2) The result of production functions showing that an equal percentage increase in all inputs leads output to increase by a large percentage. See also *economies of scope*.

economies of scope. N. Of importance to marketers, the ability of a manufacturer to offer a wide product variety while at the same time significantly limiting the costs for manufacturing and then distributing. See also *economies of scale*.

economy pack. N. In merchandising, its appeal derives from the savings when several items are included in one wrapping; a form of repackaging. "Two for the price of one," is an example of a price pack, or when featured as two related items packaged together and priced at a reasonable rate, e.g., a toothbrush and toothpaste, it is a banded pack.

economy size. N. A large quantity of an item, sold in a single very large package to provide the customer with a lower per-unit price.

E.D. ABBRV. The abbreviation for a newspaper insertion order indicating that a particular advertisement be run every day. See also *E.D.D.*, *E.D.D.T.F.*

E.D.D. ABBRV. The abbreviation for a newspaper insertion order indicating that a particular advertisement be run every other day. See also *E.D.*, *E.D.D.T.F.*

E.D.D.T.F. ABBRV. The abbreviation for a newspaper insertion order indicating that a particular advertisement be run every other day until forbidden. See also *E.D.*, *E.D.D.*

editing. N. (1) Preparing an author's work for publication. (2) In marketing, in research data analysis, the step that precedes coding and involves checking collected data for errors, omissions, irrelevancies.

editorial. N. See *editorial copy*.

editorial calendar. N. Articles that are included in a periodical's upcoming publications that are circulated to advertisers who use the calendars in planning their periodical media buys and publicity strategies. Closing dates are indicated on editorial calendars.

editorial copy. N. Reading material found in a publication that is not advertising; prepared by the staff or contributing staff of the publication, while advertising copy is prepared by an advertiser or advertising agency. Synonymous with *editorial*.

editorial credit. N. Identification of a specific retail operation as a source for a fashion item features editorially (i.e., not in an advertisement) in a consumer magazine or newspaper.

editorial environment. N. The philosophical concept for which an editorial concept of a medium is formed. Advertisers impact advertising, and it is used in selecting an appropriate media for promoting a product or service.

editorial matter. N. News, information, and entertainment portions of a publication or broadcast, as distinguished from the portion given to advertising.

editorial mention. N. Promotional copy about goods that is inserted without charge in a magazine because an editor believes it has value for readers. Editorial mentions are prepared by the seller and presented to publications with the hope that they will be accepted.

EDM. ABBRV. Electronic direct marketing.

effective buying income. N. The measure of purchasing power that is equivalent to after-tax income. It demonstrates actual consumer purchasing power. See also *disposable income*. ABBRV. *EBI*.

effective circulation. N. The least number of persons comprising the traffic passing by an outdoor advertising display who have a reasonable physical opportunity to see the poster, painted bulletin, or spectacular.

effective date. N. (1) The starting date. (2) The date on which an agreement or contract goes into effect, e.g., the beginning of an advertising campaign.

effective demand. N. (1) The combination of the desire to buy and the ability to buy. (2) The demand by a particular market to purchase, combined with the capacity to pay.

effective protection. N. In international marketing of goods, indicates that the real rate of protection afforded goods by a tariff depends not only on the nominal tariff rate on that good, but also on the nominal tariff rates on all goods used as inputs in its production.

effective rate of protection. N. In global sales, the annual percentage of domestic prices of items that are attributed to tariffs that raise costs to consumers, in order to dissuade them from buying imported items.

efficiency. N. A criterion used to judge whether a market research study produces the maximum amount and quality of information for the minimum expenditure of time and money.

efficiency rating. N. The measurement of efficiency of advertising money in terms of how many dollars are spent on media to reach how many consumers. See also *cost per thousand*.

effort. N. A mailing in a series of promotional mailings with a common goal, such as renewing a subscription.

effort scale. N. A system for charting the amount of effort a buyer will expend to purchase a specified item.

ego-involved items. N. Merchandise that consumers feel has an emotional or psychological stake.

eighty-twenty principle. N. The concept that a business gets 80% of its activity from 20% of its product line, while spending 80% of its energy to get the remaining 20% of volume. This indicates a misdirected marketing effort.

elastic demand. N. Used in setting marketing goals; demand that changes in relatively large volume as prices increase or decrease. When a small change in price results in a greater change in the quantity people buy, the demand for the items is said to be elastic. The demand for jewelry, furs, and second homes is considered to be elastic. See also *cross-elasticity, elasticity, price elasticity.*

elasticity. N. Used in setting marketing goals; the impact on the demand for an item created by changes in prices, promotion, or other factors affecting demand. See also *cross-elasticity, elastic demand, negative elasticity.*

elasticity of demand. N. A theory relating quantities of merchandise sold to change in price. Usually, demand for merchandise varies inversely to price with other factors remaining constant. Synonymous with *demand elasticity.* See also *expansibility of demand, expansionist price.*

elasticity of expectations. N. A ratio of importance to marketers; the ratio of the future expected percent change in price to the recent percent change of the price.

elastic supply. N. Supply that changes in relatively large volume with a minor change in price.

electronic catalog. N. A relatively new means of marketing, electronically showing goods to consumers on a television screen on a preset basis. Can be scattered throughout, in public buildings, shopping malls, or via a consumer's own television set. Electronic catalogs are now becoming interactive, thus permitting viewers to respond electronically, while most remain noninteractive, requiring the use of another means to respond, such as calling in on the telephone. See also *electronic direct marketing, electronic retailing.*

electronic direct marketing. N. An interactive unit, where the ideas of direct marketing are united with television, radio, and/or the telephone; purports to secure a direct response on the part of potential customers. See also *electronic catalog, electronic marketing, marketing.* ABBRV. *EDM.*

electronic marketing. N. Utilizing electronically generated consumer purchase information in marketing and sales promotion activities; used in supermarkets and other stores where information is received by having customers use computer-readable cards, such as bar codes, that log data on their product purchases. See also *bar code, electronic retailing, electronic direct marketing.*

electronic point-of-sale system. N. See *computerized-checkout system.*

electronic retailing. N. Utilizing electronically transmitted data to facilitate customer shopping without having to enter the grounds of the store. A form of direct marketing with telephones hooked directly to home computers, television screens, etc. The manufacturer usually bypasses the retailer and sells directly to the consumer. See also *electronic marketing, electronic catalog.*

electronic shopping. N. See *electronic marketing, electronic retailing.*

eligible exporter. N. In overseas marketing of goods, any of the following entities that sells products or services to a foreign buyer: (a) a corporation, partnership, or other business entity organized and existing under U.S. or state law or under the law of the District of Columbia; (b) an individual residing in the United States; or, (c) a foreign corporation, partnership, individual, or other business entity that certifies to a participating commercial bank that is doing business in the United States.

embellishment. N. A device for giving a larger surface area to an advertising display by fitting over the frame and extending its borders.

emergency items N. (1) Goods that numerous consumers do not purchase until needed, e.g., tires for their car and plumbing repairs. (2) Goods that are needed to solve an immediate crisis.

emergency products. N. See *emergency items*.

emergency rate. N. The rate established to meet some immediate and pressing need, and without due regard to the usual rate factors.

emotional appeal. N. A form of advertising where the copy is prepared to stimulate a person's emotions, rather than one's sense of the practical. Such copy arouses fear, love, hate, humor, etc. See also *fear appeal*.

emotional buying motives. N. Subjective, irrational motivation that affects consumer purchasing.

empathy. N. The ability to perceive how potential customers feel and what their attitudes, needs, and expectations are.

emporium. N. A major place of trade; a large store. The term is rarely used today.

empowering employees. N. When companies give their workers broad latitude to satisfy customer requests. Employees are encouraged and rewarded for showing initiative and imagination.

emulative product. N. A new offering by a competitor of a similar product. See also *adaptive product*.

enabling characteristics. N. Elements of a company that indirectly impact the success of the company's efforts to satisfy a target market at a profit. Includes financial resources, management experience, etc.

enclosure. N. Material, including an advertisement, promotional brochure, etc., put in an envelope along with the primary reason for the mailing.

encode. V. (1) To convert data by the use of a code or a coded character set in such a manner that reconversion to the original form is possible. (2) To translate a message into words and signs that can be transmitted, received, and understood by the receiver; used by advertisers in their visual campaigns.

encoding. N. See *encode*.

end-aisle display. N. A point-of-purchase display of goods that is placed at the end of a row of shelving. Found most frequently in discount stores and supermarkets, they are created to attract the consumer's attention in order to increases sales of the featured item.

end display. N. A display with a considerable amount of goods set up at the end of a store aisle. It can be readily dismantled.

endless chain. N. A prospecting method where sellers solicit referrals from consumers, and then obtain other names from the people to whom they were originally referred. In order, each individual is encouraged to offer additional names, thus evolving a chain of referrals, going on and on. See also *chain prospecting, lead generation*.

endorsement advertising. N. A strategy of employing endorsers in advertisements so as to try and convince prospects of the increased creditability of the item or service. See also *celebrity endorsement*.

end-product advertising. N. See *subordinate product advertising*.

end rate. N. The lowest rate at which a broadcast station will offer time.

end run. N. The competitive strategy where a company determines a new approach to securing sales, which avoids a direct collision with a market leader who is well-known and established with consumers.

end sizes. N. The large and small sizes that set the range in the line carried by stores. Synonymous with *outsizes*.

end-use application segmentation. N. In industrial marketing, the subdivision of a market based on how the item is to be used by the buyer.

end-user. N. See *consumer*.

Engel's laws. N. (1) An economic theory claiming that the lower a person's income is, the greater the percentage of it that is spent for food; of value to marketers and advertisers. (2) A set of statements concerning the proportional changes in expenditures that accompany increases in family income.

engineering design. N. A function of interest to marketers in the product creation process where a good is configured. Specific form is decided. The activity is sometimes seen as a late step in the R&D process and sometimes as an early step in the manufacturing process. The design engineering department is therefore often independent of both.

engrossing. N. Purchasing and holding away from the market large quantities of merchandise until the time arrives when it is believed they can be sold at a higher price.

enhancement. N. When a new item is introduced to the public, it tends to increase the sales rates of one or more other items in the firm's line. Opposite of cannibalizing the market.

en route. ADV. On the way.

ensemble display. N. In retailing, an interior display for showing all items which it is suggested be used simultaneously. These articles are referred to as coordinates.

enterprise. N. Any entity constituted or organized under applicable law, whether or not for profit, and whether privately owned or governmentally owned, including any corporation, trust, partnership, sole proprietorship, joint venture, or other association.

entireties doctrine. N. In marketing equipment parts overseas, the principle of customs law permitting components, in some situations, to be entered for duty purposes under the tariff item applicable to the finished item.

entrapment method. N. A method in marketing research where the goal of the study is not revealed to the participant.

entrepreneur. N. One who assumes the financial risk of the initiation, operation, and management of a given business or undertaking.

entrepreneuring. N. *(slang)* The taking of risk in the running of an organization and an advertising agency, usually a small business enterprise.

entropy model. N. Mathematical model of brand loyalty estimating the probability that a brand can be bought based on market forces such as the total number of available brands and the distribution of market share across brands.

entry evaluation. N. The first evaluation done after a concept emerges. It may be the person creating it, but usually involves others in the immediate vicinity. Judgmental, experience-based; not with creation of new data or opinions.

envelope stuffer. N. Direct-mail advertising placed in mailings of statements.

environment. N. A set of forces external to the organization that the marketer may be able to influence but cannot control.

environmental analysis. N. As part of the situational analysis portion of a marketing plan, assessing a firm's external environment for marketing planning and strategy purposes. See also *macroenvironment*.

environmental forecasting. N. Projecting future events by marketers and advertisers, in order to prepare strategy programs by adjusting existing strategies to the altering environment.

environmental scanning. N. A set of procedures for monitoring the organization's external environment; of particular importance to marketing specialists.

environmental selling. N. Displaying items for sale in a setting that simulates a buyer's home.

EOQ. ABBRV. Economic order quantity model.

E.O.W.T.F. N. A newspaper insertion order directing that an advertisement be run every other week until forbidden. See also *E.D., E.D.D., E.D.D.T.F.*

ephemeralization. N. Buckminister Fuller's concept for increasing the rate of obsolescence of products in order to increase the rate of recycling of their elements.

Equal Credit Opportunity Act. N. Federal legislation prohibiting creditors from discriminating against credit applicants on the basis of sex or marital status. After March 1977, discrimination in credit on the basis of race, color, religion, national origin, age, and receipt of public assistance was prohibited. Compliance with the law comes under the jurisdiction of the Federal Trade Commission.

equal-store concept. N. A growing trend in retailing, a multi-store retailing agreement where, in place of a flagship store and branch stores, all downtown and suburban outlets are given equal status. Synonymous with *sister-store concept*.

equation price. N. A price attained by the adjusting action of competition in any market at any time, or a unit of time, such that the demand and supply become equal at that price.

equilibrium. N. In consumer and marketing research, any condition that, once reached, continues unless one of the variables is altered or the change of one variable is not offset by an equivalent change in another variable.

equilibrium price. N. (1) The quantity that maximizes a firm's profitability. (2) In manufacturing, the quantity of goods determined in the market by the intersection of a supply and demand curve.

equilibrium quantity. N. The quantity of goods determined in the market by the intersection of a supply and demand curve.

erratic demand. N. The desire for goods and services that is unstable and unpredictable over a given time period. See also *seasonality*.

erratic fluctuations. N. Short-term changes that are difficult to measure and predict because they tend to be unexpected; of critical importance to marketers and advertisers who seek ways of saving money.

escalator clause. N. In purchasing, a clause permitting adjustments of price or profit in a purchase contract under specified conditions.

esquisse. N. A reduced, rapidly sketched approximation of the layout of an advertisement, providing the artist with a basic idea of the advertisement's look and tone. Synonymous with *thumbnail*.

established trends. N. Patterns of increased demand for particular items by color, style, price, etc., as shown by consumer preference reflected in either sales or consumer research.

establishment. N. (1) A factory, store, or other place of business, under the ownership of one management, located usually in one geographic area, and producing related goods. (2) More recently, those in power, and the system under which such power is exercised, maintained, and extended.

establish the differential. V. Publicity and sales campaigns a company uses within its budgetary capacity to take advantage of a possible differential advantage. At times the item makes a strong impact with such ease that the differential becomes established without much effort.

estimating. N. Computing the cost of an advertising media schedule based on rate cards. Such work is usually performed in a large advertising agency.

estimator. N. The person in a large advertising agency whose major responsibility is to calculate the cost of the advertising media schedules.

ethical advertising. N. (1) Advertising directed to doctors and medical practitioners. (2) Advertising that is determined to meet standards of fairness, honesty, and equitable content.

ethical pricing. N. Consciously holding back from charging all that the traffic will bear; not overcharging customers.

ethical shoppers. N. One of a four-way classification of consumers who feel obligated to support local and small retainers because they desire their availability and because it ensures viability to the community. See also *apathetic shoppers, economic shoppers, personalizing shoppers.*

ethics. N. A system of moral principles and their application to particular problems of conduct.

ethnic buying habits. N. The ways a particular ethnic group conducts its buying activities. Market strategies are often targeted to fulfill needs of differing ethnic groups.

ethnicity. N. A marketing approach to attracting buyers by emphasizing the satisfactions and fulfillment of needs in acquiring ethnic goods or services.

ethnic marketing. N. Approach of marketing toward members of a specific minority or nationality group that is part of the larger community.

ethnic media. N. Media directed toward a particular ethnic group and often broadcast or written in a language known to the group, e.g., a Chinese radio station. Some items or services are best targeted through ethnic media.

ethnocentricity. N. One of a three-way classification of the policies of companies engaged in international marketing; dealing with the exploitation of a domestic manufacturing base in order that foreign business carried out is considered marginal and incrementally accomplished via the exportation of standard items. See also *geocentricity, polycentricity.*

EU. ABBRV. European Union.

Euro-Ad. ABBRV. Euro-Advertisement.

Euro-Advertisement. N. Advertising prepared to consumers in member states of the European Community. They are usually similar in concept, execution, and production standards, and different only in language, and they purport to overcome differences in culture and traditions of the people in western Europe. ABBRV. *Euro-Ad.*

Eurobrand. N. Consumer items that carry the same brand name throughout the European Community, thereby involving cross-cultural advertising that attract prospective consumers in all member nations of the community.

Eurocard. N. A European credit card developed by the German banking system that is accepted in most western European nations for the purchase of goods and services.

Eurocheque. N. A credit card for purchasing goods and services in several western European countries.

European Common Market. N. See *European Community.*

European Community. With a huge consumer market, and of great interest to marketers, its aims are to break down trade barriers within a common market, and create a political union among the peoples of Europe. It has its own budget raised from its own resources (e.g., customs duties, agricultural levies, a proportion of value added tax) and offers loans, subsidies, or grants through a variety of financial instruments. Increasingly used since 1993. Synonymous with *Common Market, European Union.* See also *European Union.* ABBRV. *EC.*

European Journal of Marketing. N. A British journal, formerly the *British Journal of Marketing*, published every other month.

European Union. N. Effective November 1, 1993, with the passage and signing of the Maastricht Treaty, the new name for the old European Community with two additions: a common foreign and security policy and cooperation between the member governments

evaluation

in justice and police matters. The rest remains with the original European Community. Often wrongly considered synonymous with the *European Community*. ABBRV. *EU*.

evaluation. N. A step in the adoption process; a consumer's estimate of the value, quality, and reaction to a product or service.

evaluation rights. N. In purchasing, the authority granted executives to evaluate performance and to reward or punish on the basis of these assessments.

evaluator. N. In the exchange process, an individual who provides feedback on a chosen product's ability to satisfy.

even-line pricing. N. A strategy of giving whole number selling prices to goods to give the impression of high-end retailing.

even pricing. N. See *even-line pricing*.

events marketing. N. A marketing strategy where events are used as a sales promotion and/or public relations activity, e.g., sponsoring sporting events, film festivals, and street concerts. See also *sports marketing*.

evoked set. N. A specific group of brands to which a consumer limits the considerations of choice for purchase. See also *span of recall*.

evolving product. N. Where a product begins as a concept, or even just an opportunity, then goes through various stages, such as protocol, prototype, pilot plan product, and marketed product.

ex-. PREFIX. The point from which merchandise is shipped, not necessarily its point of origin. For example, a machine made in New York and exported through the port of Elizabeth, New Jersey, is said to have been shipped "ex-Elizabeth."

excess. N. See *scrap*.

excess demand curve. N. A graphic representation of the quantity of goods demanded less the quantity offered at each price. See also *excess supply curve*.

excess supply curve. N. A graphic representation of the quantity of goods offered less the quantity asked at each price. See also *excess demand curve, supply curve*.

exchange. N. An exchange occurs when two or more individuals, groups, or organizations give to each other something of value in order to receive something else of value. Each party to the exchange must want to exchange, must believe that what is received is more valuable than what is given up, and must be able to communicate with the other parties. V. (1) In retailing, to return an item to a store to substitute another item. (2) In marketing, when two or more parties trade item for item, or money for item, or item for money. An exchange is finalized when parties mutually agree to conditions of the sales, when and where it shall occur, and, usually, a preparation of a contract governing the agreement. See also *barter, swap, transaction*.

exchange commercial. N. The last advertisement on a program when the time is used by the alternate series sponsor.

exchange efficiency. N. An aspect of marketing efficiency, the completion of the trading process at the lowest possible cost with existing information on markets and technology.

exchange flow. N. Activities within organizations that connect manufacturers and consumers or industrial users, that in turn creates demand and consummates exchanges of title.

exchange functions. N. The buying and selling activities in the market process resulting in the exchange of title to merchandise or services. Exchange is one of the basic marketing activities.

exchange permit. N. In international marketing of goods, a government permit required by the importer's government to enable the importer to convert his or her own country's currency into foreign currency with which to pay a seller in another country.

exclusive. N. (1) Goods obtainable from a limited number of stores or dealers. (2) Sales of merchandise limited to a single retailer in a given location. See also *exclusive outlet selling*.

exclusive agency selling. N. That form of selective selling whereby sales of an article or service or brand of an article to any one type of buyer are confined to one dealer or distributor in each area, usually on a contractual basis.

exclusive dealing. N. See *exclusive dealing contract*.

exclusive dealing contract. N. (1) An agreement that a buyer will make all purchases of a specific item from only one seller and will refrain from carrying competing goods. (2) A method of control over distribution in which the manufacturer forbids dealers to carry competitors' products.

exclusive distribution. N. (1) A manufacturer's protection of a dealer against the location of the dealers in the same area, often giving the right to sell an item to the exclusion of other sellers. (2) An approach to distribution in which the number of intermediaries is limited to one for each geographic territory. See also *intensive distribution, open distribution, selective distribution, closed sales territory*.

exclusive merchandise. N. Items not available in other retail outlets in a particular market. See also *exclusive outlet selling, exclusives*.

exclusive outlet selling. N. One retailer or wholesaler in a location having exclusive control over the sale or an article or service, usually determined by contract. See also *exclusive merchandise*.

exclusives. N. See *exclusive merchandise*.

exclusive selling. N. Where a supplier or manufacturer agree with a wholesaler or retailer not to sell to other wholesalers or retailers within the same market. Can be illegal if found to be in restraint of trade.

exclusivity. N. (1) When a public relations person offers only one news medium for a specific story. (2) In advertising, an arrangement between the medium and advertiser to have no competing items or services advertised in the same show or issue as the advertiser's items or services. Usually requires that the advertiser buy a large amount of space or time. See also *competitive separation*.

execution. N. An approach in an advertisement to direct attention to and involve the public with the merchandise. Sometimes the execution is looked upon as being more critical than the message and some copywriters of advertisements apply this in their approach.

execution delay. N. A delayed response effect created by the making of a market expenditure in the current time period for a presentation to be made to the market at some future time.

exempt commodity. N. Merchandise shipped in interstate commerce to which published rates do not apply.

exogenous demand. N. A demand for goods determined by factors outside the present economy and including exports and government expenditures.

expansibility of demand. N. (1) A concept that the use of salesmanship or advertising, or perhaps both, in the promotion of an item or service brings about an increase in the total demand for the item or service. (2) The degree to which the demand curve for a product shifts to the right by some method or because of natural forces. This implies that the market accepted more product volume at the same price. See also *elasticity of demand*. Synonymous with *demand expansibility*.

expansionist price. N. Similar to the penetration price, but also anticipates the cost savings projected possible by increased scale of production. It assumes a high price elasticity of demand.

expectation. N. The benefits or satisfaction that the customer anticipates following the purchase of goods and services.

expectation impact. N. Rising prices can increase the demand for merchandise as purchasers rush to secure the item before the price rises further. The opposite may also take place when buyers put off purchasing in a falling price situation.

expected effects matrix. N. Used by market researchers, a matrix of two dimensions—damage and probability. Used to classify negative events that might take place during the launch of a new item. A high score on both dimensions increases the need for action.

expected price. N. The level at which a customer expects an item or service to be priced.

expected product. N. A generic product plus a set of features that meet additional expectations of consumers.

expected profit concept. N. Used by market researchers, a mathematical calculation applied to competitive bidding, which states that as the bid price increases, the profit to a firm increases, but the probability of its winning the contract decreases. The long-run average expected profit (loss) at each bid amount equals a firm's profit (loss) times its probability of obtaining the contract at this bid amount.

expected return. N. The profit that is anticipated from a business venture.

expected value. N. A weighted average of all the conditional values of an act. Each conditional value is weighted by its probability.

expenditure multiplier. N. The amount resulting from an increase in sales because of the induced spending created thereby.

expense. N. (1) The cost of resources used to create revenue. (2) The amount shown on the income statement as a deduction from revenue. Should not be confused with cost. All expenses are costs, but not all costs are expenses.

expense-to-sales ratio. N. Indicator of the economic efficiency of a marketing organization, such as the ratio of advertising expense to product sales.

experience curves. N. (1) Graphic representations of the effect of experience on the per-unit cost of producing a product. (2) A phenomenon in which costs of production decrease arithmetically as experience increases geometrically; of concern to marketers in setting profit objectives.

experience items. N. Merchandise that a consumer tries prior to purchase to be able to assess the claims made for the item. See also *search goods*.

experiment. N. (1) An investigation that involves two elements: manipulation of some variable (independent variable) and observation of the results (dependent variables). See also *dependent variable, independent variable*. (2) In market research, the activity of testing a hypothesis so that the results will be objectively measurable and can be differentiated from extraneous variables.

expert channel. N. Where independent experts offer statements regarding specific items or services to target customers.

expert power. N. The capacity to influence based on some expertise or knowledge. It is a function of the judgment of those

expire

less powerful that the expert has ability exceeding their own; often utilized by advertisers.

expire. v. To arrive at the termination period of an agreement, contract, or other instrument; included in signed papers between advertising agencies and clients.

expire file. N. A list of expired customer records used primarily for promotional activities. Marketers use these files for a few years and then the names and addresses are purged because they are no longer considered useful.

explicit costs. N. Costs of a company that involve cash outlays to individuals, other businesses, or the government. Explicit costs include the purchase of resources, land, labor, and capital needed in a firm's production process and indirect business taxes.

exploration state. N. When developing new products, the first stage where ideas for such items are either searched out or internally generated by the company.

exploratory research. N. Within marketing research, the collecting of preliminary information to suggest the nature of a marketing situation and to provide ideas and useful concepts.

exploratory stage. N. The stage of the research process in which the problem is defined, objectives are set, and possible solutions are explored.

exponential diffusion. N. See *exponential growth*.

exponential growth. N. Following the introduction of a new product, the slow, initial growth of sales as the item becomes better known and accepted. It then slows down as the market becomes saturated and the purchase becomes a repeat or replacement decision.

export. v. (1) To ship an item away from a country for sale to another country. (2) To send an item or service out of one sovereign domain to another for purposes of sale. N. An item or service sent from one sovereign domain to another for purposes of sale.

export agents. N. Brokers and others in the domestic market who sell to or buy for foreign agents or customers.

export broker. N. A person or firm that brings together buyers and sellers for a fee but does not take part in actual sales transactions. See also *export jobber*.

export credit. N. (1) Financing for a domestic supplier to generate goods and services that can be exported. (2) Deferred payment terms, loans, or other financial facilities, provided to overseas buyers/importers of goods and services; impacts the marketer's profitability.

export duty. N. A tax or tariff on a nation's exports; impacts the marketer's profitability.

Export Enhancement Program. N. A U.S. program of 1985 permitting exporters to sell and market American products to foreign customers at world market prices. The U.S. Agriculture Department subsidized the difference in the world price and the higher domestic price, which exporters have to pay for the product in the form of commodities.

export finance lease. N. In international marketing of goods, a lease, the intent of which is to transfer the benefits and risks of ownership to the lessee; title to the asset is expected to pass to the lessee at the end of the contract.

export incentives. N. Applied by global marketers, subsidies or tax rebates paid by governments to firms to encourage them to export goods and services.

export jobber. N. A nationally based intermediary who purchases items domestically and resells them to foreign buyers, without ever taking physical possession of them.

export license. N. A government document that permits the licensee to engage in the export of designated goods to certain destinations. See also *validated export license*.

export management company. N. Used primarily by small firms in marketing and selling abroad, a private firm that serves as the export department for several manufacturers, soliciting and transacting export business on behalf of its clients in return for a commission, salary, or retainer plus commission. An export management company helps to establish an overseas market for the firm's products, usually on an exclusive basis, and maintains close contact with its clients.

export quotas. N. See *quantitative restrictions*.

export restraints. N. Restriction by an exporting country of the quantity of exports to a specified importing country. Usually, this is a result of a request (formal or informal) of the importing country.

exports. N. A general principle in global selling; items produced in one country and sold to another.

export subsidies. N. (1) Payments made by a government to companies that export specific goods in order to encourage them to compete in foreign markets; impacts marketing profitability. (2) Government benefits made available to domestic producers of goods contingent on their exporting those items to which the benefits received apply. These include support prices, tax incentives, etc. See also *export support efforts*.

export support efforts. N. Of particular importance to overseas sales efforts, a program, usually maintained by governmental agencies, to assist domestic exporters, and usually located in the country where the import of goods will occur. See also *export subsidies*.

export tariff. N. A tax or duty on goods exported from a country.

export value. N. The price at which an overseas manufacturer offers for sale a given item for export to the United States in the usual wholesale quantities, less export discounts, packing, and costs of preparing the goods for export.

ex post facto. ADJ. *(Latin)* In marketing research, the seeking of a cause after the observation were made. ADV. *ex post facto*.

exposure. N. (1) The condition of being open to loss from a specific hazard, event, or contingency. (2) In advertising, how often and how well an advertisement is read in a print media, especially a magazine. For example, if a tennis club advertisement is exposed to one thousand tennis players, it has greater value than if it is exposed to one million non–tennis players. See also *media reach, reach*.

expressed warranty. N. See *express warranty*.

express warranty. N. (1) A statement that specifies the exact conditions under which a manufacturer is responsible for a product's performance. (2) A seller's position statement concerning the quality, benefit, or value to a consumer of his or her goods, intended to convince an individual to make a purchase. The consumer has the right to expect the seller to back up these statements based on the seller's express warranty. See also *implied warranty, warranty*.

extend. V. To prolong a contractual obligation beyond the originally stated date of maturity or termination, as with a magazine subscription.

extended consumer decision making. N. Occurs when considerable effort is spent on information search and evaluation of alternatives before a purchase is made. Expensive, complex items with which a person has had little or no experience require this form of decision making.

extended family. N. A nuclear family plus aunts, uncles, grandparents, and in-laws.

extended item. N. An element that is both tangible and intangible that follows merchandise or service, such as a warranty, service contract, or ownership prestige.

extended terms. N. (1) A contractual obligation that has been prolonged beyond the originally stated date of maturity or termination. (2) In retailing, where a customer has been given an additional period in which to pay for merchandise.

extensible market. N. A market with room for growth, either by securing more new customers, or by increasing per capita consumption.

extension. N. See *extend*.

extensive distribution. N. An approach to distribution that seeks the widest possible geographic coverage.

extensive market challenges. N. Challenges for new expansion beyond the traditional marketing and advertising campaign. For example, creating a new product line to attract existing consumers.

extensive problem solving. N. In consumer behavior, the time and effort taken to comprehend people's needs and determine how best to satisfy them.

externalities. N. The external benefits or costs of activities for which no compensation is offered. Synonymous with *spillovers*. See also *market failure*.

external source. N. A marketing data source found outside of the organization.

external stimuli. N. External forces that influence the attitudes or behavior of buyers in the market, such as trends and economic opportunities.

extinction price. N. The price established to eliminate as much of the competition as possible, with variable costs used as the base. See also *predatory pricing*.

extraction rate. N. The proportion by weight of a processed product to its raw material.

extra dating. N. Adding days beyond the regular date for invoice payment. Extensions are usually for thirty- or sixty-day periods.

extraneous items. N. Charges for gift wrapping, special mailing, and so on, which must be removed when auditing sales to arrive at true net sales totals.

extrapolation. N. The estimate of an unknown value beyond the range of a series of identifiable values (e.g., projecting the world's population in AD 2500). Advertisers extrapolate data from audience and copy testing information in order to project trends when creating future advertising.

extrinsic cues. N. Cues that can influence a consumer's perception of a product or service, as factors separate from the item or service itself.

eyeball control. N. The visual examination of inventory to determine whether there is sufficient stock on hand until requested by the wholesaler, retailer, or consumer. See also *inventory control.*

eye camera. N. An instrument for measuring and observing eye movements of people reading advertising copy; used by researchers to determine which part of the copy attracts the greatest attention, as well as how strong the holding power of the sales message is. See also *advertising testing.*

fabricated parts. N. Industrial goods used in manufacturing without further changes in form; considered as an expense rather than a capital item. See also *raw material*. Synonymous with *semi-finished items*, *semi-manufactured items*.

fabrication. N. The process of converting materials into units, parts, or items. See also *fabricated parts*.

facilitating activities. N. The marketing functions of standardization and grading; risk taking, financing, and market information are typically included.

facilitating agency. N. (1) An organization that services other institutions but does not take title to goods. (2) An agency that aids in the performance of some marketing function but does not own the items and is not involved in buying or selling.

facing. N. (1) In retailing, the appearance of a display on shelves. Each unit of an item is one facing wide, because its face occupies one space. The overall shelf display is measured by the number of facings per item. (2) In advertising, the surface of an outdoor billboard used for advertisements. When two billboards are next to each other and visible from the same direction, they have a double facing.

facing text matter. N. The position in a magazine of an advertisement opposite editorial materials.

facsimile. N. See *facsimile broadcasting*.

facsimile broadcasting. N. Transmission of words or pictures by radio. ABBRV. *fax*.

fact finding. N. Investigating, collecting, and making known to a specified organization the facts regarding a specific situation.

factor. N. (1) An individual who carries on business transactions for another. (2) In merchandising, an agent for the sale of goods who is authorized to sell and receive payment for the merchandise.

factorage. N. The commission collected by a factor.

factor analysis. N. A statistical method for interpreting scores and correlations of scores from a number of tests. It searches for factors that can be multiplied to give all the correlation coefficients of a test with other tests. The most usual restriction is that the factors be as few as possible to yield all the correlations.

factoring. N. Selling accounts before their due date, usually at a discount.

factors. N. Ingredients needed for the production of any good or service. The primary factors are land, labor, capital, and enterprise.

factor's lien. N. A factor's right to retain the merchandise consigned to him or her as reimbursement for all advances previously made to the consignor.

factory outlet. N. Historically, a manufacturer-owned store located at the factory where merchandise is sold at greatly reduced prices. Today, also includes the selling of top-graded merchandise, often of more than one manufacturer. Synonymous with *outlet store*.

factory outlet mall. N. A shopping center that focuses on quality, name brand items offered at lower-than-usual prices.

factory pack. N. See *banded pack*.

factory position warehouse. N. A facility where merchandise is stored, usually close to the manufacturer.

fact sheet. N. An informational document included in a package of sales material, providing data on the firm manufacturing the item and the item itself.

factual approach. N. A copy approach where technical information about merchandise or a service is emphasized to indicate the logic of the benefits for which the market should purchase the merchandise or service. Synonymous with *reason-why approach.*

fad item. N. (1) A short-lived fashion, usually limited to a small portion of the population. (2) A demand pattern for merchandise or services that rapidly achieves considerable popularity but loses it just as quickly. Such goods or services have extremely short product life cycles as they rarely satisfy major consumer needs.

failure rate. N. The percentage of a firm's marketed new products that fail to achieve the objectives set for them. Should only be used on products that go to the full intended market target, not a trial or roll-out subset.

Fair Credit Billing Act. N. An amendment to the Federal Truth in Lending Act that protects charge account customers against billing errors by permitting credit car customers to use the same legal defenses against banks or other third-party credit card companies that they previously could use against merchants. See also *Truth Act of 1968 in Lending.*

Fair Credit Reporting Act of 1971. N. Federal legislation giving the user of credit, the buyer of insurance, or the job applicant the right to learn the contents of his or her file at any credit bureau.

Fair Debt Collection Practices Act of 1978. N. Federal legislation prohibiting the use of abusive, deceptive, and unfair debt collection practices.

fair market value. N. The value an imported item would command, under similar circumstances of sale, were the goods sold in the country of origin.

Fair Packaging and Labeling Act of 1966. N. Federal legislation requiring manufacturers of many consumer items to state clearly the net quantity of contents on the principal display panel of a package. The act is of importance to manufacturers since they are required to meet all government labeling requirements prior to introducing an new product. Synonymous with *Truth in Packaging Act*.

fair trade. N. See *fair trade acts*.

fair trade acts. N. Laws passed by various states by which retailers are obliged to maintain specified prices on select goods. In recent years, fair trade pricing has been withdrawn by a great number of retailers and manufacturers. The Consumer Goods Pricing Act of 1975 is federal legislation that prohibits the use of resale price maintenance laws in interstate commerce, resulting in the near elimination of fair trade arrangements. See also *Miller-Tydings Resale Act of 1937, Price Maintenance Act, unfair practices acts*.

fair trade price. N. The retail price fixed by the manufacturer of a branded item below which the retailer is prohibited by law from making sales. Increasingly, states are removing this form of pricing. See also *price control price, resale maintenance, retail price maintenance, list price*.

fairy money. N. *(slang)* In advertising, coupons used by a consumer, thereby reducing the cost of the item for the consumer, with the difference paid by the manufacturer.

falling demand state. N. A market situation where goods or services lose demand because of increasing social or environmental factors.

Faced with this issue, marketers often attempt to restimulate sales by targeting different people and adding new promotional strategies. See also *demand states*.

false advertising. N. Advertising that is misleading in a material respect, including not only false representation of the benefits or results of using the advertised commodity or its contents, but also failure to reveal any potentially damaging consequences that are likely to follow from its use. See also *deceit*.

faltering demand. N. That time in a product life cycle when demand for the item or service begins to decline.

family brands. N. Brands that appear on two or more products of a company (e.g., Hershey Company using the Hershey name for both candy bars and cocoa; Lipton Corporation using its name for both soups and teas). See also *brand awareness*. Synonymous with *family packaging, umbrella brands*.

family life cycle. N. The identified consumer marketing stages: (a) bachelor stage: young, single person; (b) newly married couples: young married couple with no children; (c) full nest I: married couple where the youngest child is under age 6; (d) full nest II: married couple where the youngest child is over age 6; (e) full nest III: older married couples with dependent children; (f) empty nest I: older married couples with no children at home and the head of the household still earns income at work; (g) empty nest II: older married couples with no children at home and the head of the household is retired; and, (h) solidarity survivors: older people living alone, either retired or still working.

family of orientation. N. The family into which a person is born.

family of procreation. N. The family that a person establishes through marriage.

family packaging. N. See *family brands*.

fantasy commercial. N. A media commercial using special effects or caricatures to form a framework of fantasy about an item, such as elves who make bread, or the Jolly Green Giant on a can of peas. Fantasy commercials stress the fantasy rather than the message or the actual item or service.

farm out. V. To subcontract.

FAS. ABBRV. Free alongside ship.

fashion. N. The style that is popular within a major part of the market at any given time period.

fashion coordination. N. In retailing, continuous monitoring of fashion trends to assure that store merchandise is in keeping with updated style, quality, and appeal.

fashion cycle. N. A variation of the product life cycle reflecting the sales history of the prevailing style of consumer items such as clothing, car design, etc. Its cycles are: (a) distinctiveness: when the fashion is first sought; (b) emulation: where followers seek it out; and, (c) economic stage: when the style enters the mass market.

fast evening persons report. N. From the A.C. Nielsen Company, a document giving audience estimates and composition information for network evening television programming. See also *day parts*.

fat budget items. N. Merchandise approved by buyers in the hope that the goods will substantially increase sales potential.

fax. ABBRV. Facsimile broadcasting.

FCC. ABBRV. Federal Communications Commission.

fear appeal. N. Advertising purporting to evolve anxiety within the consumer based on fear so that he or she would overcome this anxiety by purchasing a particular item or service, as often done with mouthwashes and deodorants, and selling fire insurance by depicting a burned-out house. See also *emotional appeal*.

feature. N. (1) In marketing, a characteristic of a product or service. (2) In sales, the components of an item or service that yields a benefit. (3) In sales, a product given special sales promotion. (4) In advertising, promoting a brand at a reduced price. (5) In retailing, giving a dominant display and space to an item.

features/benefits approach. N. In salesmanship, assumes that a product's characteristics mean little to the consumer unless he or she can be convinced that it is a benefit to them. It results in the salesperson seeking a way to incorporate this message into his or her presentation.

Federal Cigarette Labeling and Advertising Act of 1967. N. Federal legislation intended to protect consumers from the hazards of cigarette smoking; requires that cigarette packaging and advertising bear appropriate and specific health warnings.

Federal Communications Commission. N. A federal agency established in 1934 to regulate interstate and foreign commerce in communications by both wire and radio activity. Its jurisdiction now includes radio, television, wire, cable, microwave, and satellite. The Federal Communications Commission consults with other government agencies on matters involving radio communications and with state regulatory commissions on telegraph and telephone matters; it also reviews applications for construction permits and relevant licenses. ABBRV. *FCC*.

Federal Equal Credit Opportunity Act of 1977. N. Federal legislation prohibiting discrimination, when responding to credit requests, on the basis of race, color, religion, national origin, sex, marital status, or age; because all or part of a person's income derives from any public assistance program; or, because a person has exercised in good faith any right under the Truth in Lending Law. It gives married persons the right to have credit information included in credit reports in the name of both the wife and the husband if both use or are responsible for the account. This right was created, in part, to ensure that credit histories will be available to women who are later divorced or widowed.

Federal Hazardous Substances Labeling Act of 1960. N. Federal law establishing a list of hazardous household substances subject to stringent labeling standards. As a result, the words "danger," "warning," and "caution" now appear more often in labeling.

Federal Trade Commission. N. A federal agency established in 1914 to enforce antitrust laws by seeking voluntary compliance or civil remedies. The enabling legislation, which also declared unfair methods of competition illegal, was amended by the Wheeler-Lea Act of 1930. The Federal Trade Commission (FTC) is empowered to investigate interstate and foreign commerce as well as to take legal action to enforce the laws that fall under its jurisdiction. In the advertising industry, the FTC attempts to prevent fraudulent or deceptive advertising and unfair trade practices. See also *consumer protection legislation, grade labeling.* ABBRV. *FTC.*

Federal Trade Commission Improvement Act. N. U.S. legislation from 1975 to protect consumers; requires full warranties on products to meet every specific minimum standard; reduces manufacturers from using warranties as marketing tools.

fee. N. A remuneration for services.

fee basis. N. The agreement with an advertising agency where the agency accepts a fixed fee for specific services to be provided. See also *agency commission, fifteen and two (15 and 2).*

feed. V. To transmit a program to stations, particularly those included in the network whose key station originates the broadcast.

feedback. N. (1) Market data collected in the field from surveys, polls, or interviews. (2) Information that tells an organization's managers about the performance of each marketing program. See also *advertising testing*.

fee system. N. A compensation method for the involved advertising agency. Under this approach the agency estimates the total cost of its services for the entire year, and projects its hourly costs for creative media, and other services. The firm will add another 25% to cover overhead costs and to realize a profit. Materials and other expenses incurred from employing outside vendors are to be billed at cost.

field. N. In marketing, the geographic location where goods or services are sold. Consumer research is carried out via interviews with people, and is accomplished by sending interviewers into the field. See also *field testing*.

field agency. N. Agency that sells subscriptions via personal contact, such as telephone sales and door sales.

field-intensity map. N. A geographic map prepared by a radio or television station as a means of plotting the location of those areas in which the station can be heard.

field person. N. An employee, such as a salesperson, who travels in a certain territory, developing new agencies and servicing agencies that already represent the company.

field salesperson. N. A salesperson who travels about and visits prospects and customers in their office, factory, or residence.

field testing. N. Describes product-use testing. Field separates this type of testing from in-house, laboratory-type testing. See also *field*.

field warehousing. N. A method for receiving collateral pledged in business loans. The warehouseperson usually leases part of the borrower's facility and appoints a custodian to care for the items.

FIFO (first in-first out). N. Relating to inventory valuations; (the balance sheet figures for inventory should be qualified accordingly. That means that the cost shown for the first shipment of an item is used for valuations. This could inflate or deflate profits.

fifteen and two (15 and 2). N. The usual discount to advertising agencies permitted by most media, whereby 15% of the gross bill is the commission retained by the agency and 2% of the net bill is a cash discount given to the advertiser. See also *advertising agency*, *basis*, *net rate*.

fifty-fifty plan. N. In cooperative advertising, where 50% of the advertising costs are paid by the manufacturer and the other 50% by the retailer. See also *cooperative advertising*.

fighting brand. N. The brand presented to the consumer that is intended to engage in price competition without harming the prices of its regular products. May be a one-run offer and rarely finds a permanent place in the firm's lines.

file proof. N. A copy of an advertisement found in a publication for record purposes instead of for corrections.

file segment. N. (1) A group of records in a file. (2) In marketing, extracting customer records from a file to establish a promotion test segment that is to be representative of the entire file.

filler. N. A short item of less than five hundred words, found in the print media to fill in spaces between editorial material or advertisements.

fill-ins

fill-ins. N. Merchandise secured during a period of demand to replace that already sold to avoid lost sales of merchandise that is moving well. See also *running*.

final consumer. N. See *ultimate consumer*.

final consumer's decision process. N. The procedure by which consumers collect and analyze information and make choices among alternative goods, services, organizations, people, places, and ideas. It consists of six basic stages: stimulus, problem awareness, information search, evaluation of alternatives, purchase, and postpurchase behavior. Demographics, social factors, and psychological factors affect this process.

final sales. N. The total of net sales to consumers, governments, and foreigners. Final sales exclude sales made to producers, except sales of durable plant and machinery.

financial advertising. N. Advertising directed to the world of investing and finance. The Security and Exchange Commission enforces strict legal rules in regard to this form of advertising. Much of financial advertising deals with promoting and building the image of financial institutions, such as banks, insurance firms, and investment houses.

financial distress. N. When an advertising or marketing firm has difficulty in meeting contractual obligations to its creditors.

financial documents. N. Bills of exchange, promissory notes, checks, payment receipts, or other similar instruments used for obtaining the payment of money.

financial intermediaries. N. Organizations that operate in money markets to permit buyers and sellers, borrowers, and lenders to meet easily.

financial position. N. The status of a company, indicated by combining the assets and liabilities as listed on a balance sheet.

financial ratios. N. The relationship that exists between various items appearing on balance sheets, income accounts, and occasionally other items. These ratios are used to measure and evaluate the economic condition and operating effectiveness of a firm.

financial statement. N. Any statement made by an individual, a proprietorship, a partnership, a corporation, an organization, or an association regarding the financial status of the legal entity.

financing. N. A marketing activity that includes the management of money and credit needed to obtain the goods and services desired by consumers. It excludes manufacturing activities.

finder's fee. N. (1) A payment to an individual for bringing together a buyer and seller. The finder serves as an intermediary until the deal is concluded. The fee is based on either a percentage of the profit or the value of the deal, but it may also be a flat rate paid. (2) In advertising, the paid fee by an advertising agency to a person or firm responsible for bringing a large account into the agency.

fines. N. A consumer-protection legal concept in which dollar penalties are levied on a firm for deceptive promotion.

finished art. N. The advertising artwork that is completed and camera-ready.

finished goods. N. Completed products awaiting sale.

finished-goods inventory. N. All items a manufacturer has made for sale to customers. See also *work-in-process inventory*.

fire sale. N. Goods sold at reduced prices because they have been damaged or water-soiled in a fire.

firm. ADJ. Describing the full acceptance of an obligation to perform, deliver, or accept (e.g., a firm bid, a firm offer). N. (1) Any business, corporation, proprietorship, or partnership. (2) An unincorporated business or a partnership. Unlike a corporation, a firm is not recognized as a separate person apart from those managing it (i.e., it is not an entity).

firm bidding. N. A policy as requesting bids for merchandise in which prospective vendors are informed that original bids are to be final, and that changes cannot be accepted under any circumstances.

firm market. N. A condition of stable prices.

firm order. N. A definite order that cannot be canceled. It may be written or oral. See also *firm order date*.

firm order date. N. The time after which an order for advertising space or time is no longer cancelable. Following the firm order date, found in the original contract, the advertising will run no matter what the appeal.

firm price. N. An obligation to the maker of a stated price that must be met if accepted within a specified time period.

first in-first out. N. See *FIFO*.

first time buyer. N. A customer who purchased an item or service from a seller for the very first time. They are considered sound future prospects and are often recipients of promotional materials.

first-to-market. N. The first product that creates a new product category or a substantial subdivision of one. Distinguishes the pioneering product from those that follow.

fiscal period. N. A twelve-month accounting period for which business activities are reported.

fiscal policy. N. A planned course of action on budgetary issues.

fishyback service. N. The transportation of loaded truck trailers onto ships. See also *piggyback*.

fix. V. To set the cost of an item or service.

fixed assets. N. Permanent assets required for the normal conduct of a business, which usually are not converted into cash during the period after they were declared fixed (e.g., furniture, land, buildings).

fixed charges. N. Business expenses that are not related to the level of operations.

fixed cost. N. A cost for a fixed period and range of activity that does not change in total but becomes progressively smaller per unit as the volume increases. Synonymous with *period cost*. See also *variable cost*.

fixed cost contribution. N. The portion of a selling price that is left over after variable costs have been accounted for.

fixed factors of production. N. Those productive resources that a company cannot alter in the short run (e.g., basic plant facilities).

fixed location/position. N. (1) In advertising, space in a periodical carrying an advertisement by the same advertiser in two or more consecutive issues. (2) In broadcasting, the time period on television or radio for which an advertiser's commercial has been held for future playing. See also *preferred position*.

fixed-order period model. N. A method for determining the number of items to be ordered at fixed time intervals up to a predetermined maximum level.

fixed-order quantity model. N. A method for determining the standard number of items to be ordered when the inventory reaches a predetermined level.

fixed position. N. In broadcasting, the commercial delivered at a given time agreed to in advance.

fixed routing. N. Calling on customers on a regular basis. See also *irregular routing*.

flag. N. (1) A character that signals the occurrence of some condition, such as the end of a word. (2) In outdoor advertising, a strip of poster paper hanging loose.

flagging an account. N. Temporarily suspending activity on an account until it is brought up to date or for other relevant reasons.

flagship station. N. The main station of a broadcasting network.

flagship store. N. A downtown or home office store where executive, merchandising, and sales personnel are located. To qualify, the store must have one or more branches. See also *main store*.

flame rate. N. Receiving a percentage of angry or negative emails from consumers.

Flammable Fabrics Act of 1953. N. Federal legislation banning the sale of certain items of clothes and household furnishings that present an "unreasonable risk of death, personal injury, or significant property damage" due to fire.

flanker brand. N. See *flanker product*.

flanker product. N. (1) A new product similar to an already existing companion product, with the same brand name. (2) A new product introduced into a product category by a firm that already markets an existing brand in that category. The flanker can be of a different shape and size, but basically the same product.

flanking. N. See *flanker product*.

flash-count. N. Count of direct-mail promotion replies to a survey or study.

flash sales report. N. An unaudited report of a previous day's sales.

flat. ADJ. With no interest.

flat rate. N. (1) A uniformly charged rate for each unit of goods and services, irrespective of quantity, frequency of purchase, and so on. (2) In advertising, a standard rate for advertising space or time, with no discounts given for volume or repeat times. (3) In direct marketing, the fixed cost for a list rental irregardless of the number of names remaining following a purge is performed. See also *variable pricing*.

flexform. N. Where an advertisement can be presented in a media in a nontraditional form; shaped in any manner.

flexible charge account. N. Synonymous with *all-purpose revolving account*.

flexible price policy. N. Synonymous with *variable pricing*.

flexible pricing. N. A pricing strategy based on the study by the manufacturer of all market forces, as contrasted to an approach of a rigid adherence to a set ratio of profit to sales. Synonymous with *variable pricing*.

flier. N. (1) A handout used to promote an idea, product, or person (e.g., a political candidate). (2) In advertising, an advertising medium that is traditionally a single, standard-size page print

flight

on one or two sides with an advertising message. Also used in direct-mail advertising and as handbill given out by retailers. Although relatively inexpensive, fliers have a high throw-away rate. Synonymous with *flyer*. See also *circular, handbill*.

flight. N. (1) In advertising, the length of the advertising period; usually for a set number of weeks, followed by a period of inactivity, which is often reactivated. Each activity period is called a flight. See also *flight saturation*. (2) In broadcasting, the time in a broadcast media when the advertiser runs spots when the total period is less than fifty-two weeks, as in a fall flight or November flight.

flighting strategy. N. A media scheduling strategy in which there is heavy advertising during some parts of the campaign and no advertising in between.

flight saturation. N. (1) Maximum concentration of spot advertising in a relatively short period. (2) A heavy concentration of advertising during a flight, when the media has become saturated with an advertising message and therefore additional advertising will not only have no positive impact, but may have a negative effect on the marketplace. See also *flight, saturation, spot advertising*.

float. N. (1) The amount of funds in the process of collection. (2) In retailing, variations in the placement of a label on a form. (3) In advertising, placing of a space advertisement in an area larger than needed to accommodate the dimensions of the advertisement. (4) In advertising, funds given to an advertising agency by an advertiser that may be invested or otherwise used, prior to its delivery to the media owners for which it is targeted.

floation. N. A method of interior packaging to protect a packed item from shock and vibration by wrapping it in a cushioning substance thick enough that the wrapped shape of the item conforms to the dimensions of the container. Synonymous with *flotation*.

floor limit. N. The largest amount for which a merchant may accept non cash payment (check or credit card) without obtaining an authorization. A zero floor limit calls for authorization for every transaction, and this is becoming more feasible as the time and cost of obtaining authorization decline. See also *negative authorization*.

floor plan financing. N. Short-term financing of big ticket items, where the retailer borrows funds and pays the vendor for the goods at time of receipt. The lending institution that has loaned the money retains title to the items as collateral and is repaid by the retailer once the merchandise is sold.

floor price. N. In the marketing of goods and services, the minimum price that normally cannot be further reduced, due to economic, political, or trade reasons.

floor pyramid. N. In retailing, a point-of-purchase advertising display where products for sale are piled in the shape of a step pyramid, usually within arm's reach.

floor stand. N. A rack, frame, or mounting used by retailers for goods in a point-of-purchase advertising display.

floor stock. N. Items accessible to customers within the store. See also *back-up merchandise, shelf stock*.

floorwalker. N. A person who moves about a store through various selling departments and assists customers in ways not handled by sales personnel.

flop. N. *(slang)* A failed effort, such as an unsuccessful advertising program or a broadcast that has disappointed its audience.

flotation. N. See *floation*.

flow chart. N. See *flow process chart*.

flow process chart. N. Used by consumer and marketing researchers, a graphic approach used for the classification and analysis of organizational activities in terms of the various individual operations, transfers, inspection points, and storages, so as to make these activities as feasible, economical, and efficient as possible.

fluctuating demand. N. In industrial marketing, the haphazard demand for goods and services; usually less stable than demand for consumer goods and services.

fluff. N. In broadcasting, a minor error while on the airwaves.

flyer. N. See *flier*.

flying squad. N. Seasoned salespeople able to freely move to work throughout a store's system; going from branch to branch.

FOB. ABBRV. Free (freight) on board. Identifying the point from which a store is to pay transportation on incoming shipments. When the terms are FOB shipping point, the store must pay all charges from the vendor's shipping point. When the terms are FOB store, the vendor must pay all charges up to the store's receiving dock. See also *FOB pricing*.

FOB pricing. N. A geographic pricing policy in which buyers pay transportation costs from the point at which they take title to the product. See also *FOB*.

focus. N. A subject, concept, or issue that is the center of attention; of value to advertisers in setting strategies.

focused market unit. N. A market-oriented division that services potential customers regardless of their location.

focus group. N. A form of personal interview in which a group of eight to twelve people are brought together, usually in a studio where they can be properly monitored and often videotaped for future study, to offer their views on an issue, idea, or product.

focus of sale. N. A benefit or claim about an item or service that is emphasized in the advertising and toward which a prospect is directed by the advertising agency.

folder. N. A large, direct-mail advertisement, folded more than once, forming a leaflet. It is usually a self-mailer. Synonymous with *leaflet*.

follower. N. A marketer whose product fails to get to market first, or who does not maintain a major market share. See also *leader*.

following, next to reading matter. N. An order for placement of advertisements in a periodical; indicates a position that is either totally flanked by reading matter or located at the top of the page and alongside reading matter.

follow up. N. A step in a marketing strategy that appears after the implementation of an advertising campaign or promotion or the introduction of a new item, in order to evaluate the results.

follow up letter. N. A letter that is never mass mailed; a sales communication sent to someone who has made an inquiry inviting the prospect to make a purchase; generally reserved for expensive merchandise.

Food and Drug Administration. N. A U.S. agency established in 1930 by federal legislation (now part of the Department of Health and Human Services) to develop standards and conduct research with respect to reliability and safety of drugs. It evaluates new drug applications and claims for drugs, conducts clinical studies on the safety of drugs, operates an adverse drug reaction reporting program, maintains a nationwide network of poison control centers, and advises the Justice Department on the results of its research. See also *Food, Drug, and Cosmetic Act of 1938*.

food brokers. N. People who introduce buyers and sellers of foods and related general-merchandise items to one another and bring them together to complete a sale.

Food, Drug, and Cosmetic Act of 1938. N. Federal legislation that strengthened food labeling requirements and extended strict requirements to advertising and labeling of cosmetics. The act requires that drug advertising and labels include "all material facts" about a drug. See also *Food and Drug Administration.*

forced relationships. N. In marketing research, a concept generation technique whereby creativity is stimulated when two or more separate things are brought together. The items are unrelated, and the mere combining of them shows new and unexpected patterns.

forced saving. N. The situation that occurs when consumers are prevented from spending a portion of their income on consumption.

forcing style. N. Of critical importance to consumer analysts, the tendency to be coercive and reward power to dominate another person by suppressing differences and requiring the adoption of one's own position.

forecasting. N. Of critical importance to market researchers for goal setting, projecting events of the future utilizing current data. See also *predictive research, sales forecast.* Synonymous with *projection.*

forecasting model. N. A model for predicting the sale of goods or services, market share levels, and other related variables.

foreign. ADJ. Outside the country, such as an advertisement placed in a medium outside the advertiser's nation. N. A newspaper advertisement placed by an advertiser located outside the area in which the paper is usually sold.

foreign national pricing. N. Local pricing in another nation.

foreign sales agent. N. An individual or firm that services the foreign representative of a domestic supplier and seeks sales abroad for the supplier. ABBRV. *FSA*.

foreign trade zone. N. See *free trade zone*. ABBRV. *FTZ*.

forestalling. N. (1) Dominating the supply by purchasing up items on the way to the market, thus allowing the merchant to obtain a higher price. (2) Anticipating resistance from the prospect, thereby permitting a reply in the presentation dealing with the buyer's concern.

forfaiting. N. The purchase, without recourse committing, of receivables from the export sales of items.

forfeiture. N. The automatic loss of cash, property, or rights, as punishment for failure to comply with legal provisions and as compensation for the resulting losses or damages.

forgetting rate. N. The rate at which memory of an advertisement is lost from one advertising period to another without prolonged reinforcement. The forgetting rate plays a large role in developing advertising strategies. Ideally an effective strategy contains minimal or no forgetting.

form. N. In marketing, the physical state of goods, as with liquid, solid, and gas.

formal balance. N. Advertisements having all the elements in it of equal optical weight at all point vertically pairs on opposite sides of a line drawn from top to bottom through the center of the advertisement. Synonymous with *symmetrical balance*.

form analysis. N. The method and practice of examining and analyzing organizational forms, charts, documents, and other records to discover the most appropriate way of facilitating procedures.

format. N. (1) An arrangement of data. (2) In broadcasting, the style or content of material used by a radio or television program, such as musical, talk-show, etc. Synonymous with *personality*.

former purchaser. N. A customer who has not bought additional goods within a specified time period, traditionally one year. In general, they represent future potential sales in that they have shown an ability to buy merchandise.

forms close. N. See *closing date*.

formula pricing. N. A pricing technique where the final price is set using a formula.

form utility. N. The characteristic of merchandise that makes it possible to fulfill a consumer's needs when processing is altered to put it into a more useful form. See also *utility*.

fortuitous scan. N. A class of concept-generating techniques not based on the problem find/solve route. The techniques are many, usually logical, and tend to make variations in products currently on the market.

forward buying. N. Bought items to provide for needs during a time period longer than is needed for immediate gratification.

forward integration. N. A marketing system where the producer owns or controls the distribution channels through which his or her goods pass as it approaches prospects. See also *integration*.

forward invention. N. The development of new goods for overseas markets.

forward market segmentation. N. Identifying segments of a population using race, age, education, psychological characteristics, etc.

forward order. N. A commitment to accept merchandise to be delivered at a later time.

forward stock. N. Stock that is brought into the selling department. See also *inventory, shelf stock*.

foul-weather pricing. N. Selling an item without profit, at times not even covering costs of production and advertising; used to keep a firm in operation during recession.

fourchette. N. In international sales of farm items, the higher and lower price levels between which member nations must operate their agricultural prices. It was first introduced for cereals.

four Os. N. Primary characteristics of a market. They are: objects (what was purchased), objectives (why the item or services was purchased), organization (who the buyer was), and operations (how the buyer operated). See also *four Ps*.

four Ps. N. Primary characteristics of a marketing mix. They are: product (the right one for the target market), place (all considerations and institutions involved in getting the correct item to the target market), promotion (communicating to the target market about the merchandise), and price (determinating the price which will best attract buyers so as to make a profit). See also *four Os*.

fourth cover. N. See *back cover*.

fractional page advertisement. N. A print advertisement that occupies only a part of the page—one-eighth, one-quarter, or one-half—as distinguished from a full-page advertisement.

fragmentation. N. When marketers identify and then divide the total market into units with common characteristics, interests and needs. See also *segmentation*.

frame of reference. N. A sociological-psychological interpretation of how a person perceives his or her external environment. A significant portion of consumer behavior is based on an individual's frame of reference.

franchise. N. (1) A privilege granted to a dealer for distribution of a manufacturer's product. (2) A legal contractual relationship between a supplier and one or more independent retailers. The franchisee gains an established brand name and operating assistance, while the franchisor gains financial remuneration as well as some control over how the business is run. (3) Specific territory or outlet involved in such a right. See also *refusal to sell*.

franchised dealer. N. A retail dealer who, under terms of a franchise agreement, carries a supplier's products.

franchisee. N. See *franchise*.

franchise extension. N. A new product that capitalizes on a firm's market strength. A franchise is a strength of relationship with customers and may be based on a brand, a sales force relationship, a favorable trade relationship, etc. The new item is often not unique but sells based on the favorable franchise.

franchiser. N. An individual or company that licenses others to sell its products or services.

franchise store. N. An independently owned store that sells branded items produced by a franchise holder. The store pays the franchiser a percentage of sales for the use of the name.

franchise wholesaling. N. A full-service merchant wholesaling format whereby independent retailers affiliate with an existing wholesaler to use a standardized storefront design, business format, name, and purchase system.

franchising. N. See *franchise*.

franchisor. N. See *franchise*.

fraud. N. Intentional misrepresentation of the truth in order to deceive another person. Aspects of fraud include the false representation of fact intentionally made, with the intent that the deceived person act thereon; knowledge that the statement would deceive; and, knowledge that the person deceived acted, leading to his or her injury. See also *bad faith, deceit, voidable contract*.

free and open market. N. A market in which the supply and demand are freely expressed in terms of price as contrasted to a controlled market, in which supply, demand, and price may all be regulated.

free association. N. Used by some creators of advertising, the first thought entering a person's mind when presented with a given word. Used in advertising research to determine a person's awareness of and attitude toward a given item, service, concept, or firm. Synonymous with *word association*.

free carrier. N. Similar to free on board, except that the seller fulfills his or her obligations when the merchandise is delivered into the custody of the carrier at the named point. See also *F.O.B.*

free examination offer. N. See *trial offer*.

free goods. N. Items that are so abundant that it is not profitable to attempt to charge for them (e.g., sunlight).

free goods offer. N. Merchandise received by a buyer at no cost for having purchased some unit of goods. See also *giveaway*.

freelance. N. An independent person, including one who does advertising and who receives assignments from a firm, but is not their employee.

freelancer. N. See *freelance*.

freely offered. N. The concept where merchandise will be offered in the normal course of trade to all buying on essentially the same basis.

free on board. N. See *FOB*.

free on rail. N. The price of goods that includes the cost of moving them to a railhead for shipment and loading onto a rail wagon.

free on truck. N. The price of goods that includes the cost of moving them to a truck for shipment and loading onto a truck.

free samples. N. The easiest way to get a prospect to try an item. It is expensive and usually used with high-volume merchandise; a popular sales promotional method for new product introductions.

free standing stuffer. N. See *newspaper stuffer*.

free trade. N. A preferred ideology of marketers, trade among countries in the absence of policy restrictions that may interfere with its flow. See also *managed trade*.

free trade agreement. N. Of importance to marketers; a means for lowering tariffs of exported merchandise; a comprehensive agreement design to remove barriers to substantially expand all trade through eliminating tariffs and quotas, enhancing market access, and improving standards for treatment of investors. Free trade agreements cover virtually every aspect of trade between signatories. They purport to remove all significant barriers to trade in goods and services. Under free trade agreements, firms will be able to make decisions based on their market advantage, rather than on arbitrary tariff and nontariff barriers. See also *free trade zone*. ABBRV. *FTA*.

free trade zone. N. Of importance to global marketers, a port designated by the government of a country for duty-free entry of any nonprohibited goods. Merchandise may be stored, displayed, used for manufacturing, and so on within the zone and reexported without duties being paid. Duties are imposed on the merchandise (or items manufactured from the merchandise) only when the

freight paid to

goods pass from the zone into an area of the country subject to the customs authority. Synonymous with *foreign-trade zone*.

free trial offer. N. See *trial offer*.

freight. N. All merchandise, goods, products, or commodities shipped by rail, air, road, or water, other than baggage, express mail, or regular mail.

freight absorption. N. (1) Where the seller is not charging a customer for freight outward. (2) A geographic pricing policy in which the seller charges the same freight rate as the competitor located nearest to the buyer. See also *mill net return*.

freight allowed. N. An agreement whereby a store pays the transportation charges on incoming goods but is permitted to charge back all or part of that cost to the vendor. Synonymous with *postage stamp pricing*.

freight equalization. N. See *unsystematic freight equalization*.

freight forwarder. N. (1) A transportation company that pools many small shipments to take advantage of lower rates, passing some of the savings on to the shippers. (2) An organization that consolidates the less-than-carload or less-than-truckload shipments of manufacturers into carload or truckload shipments. Synonymous with *make-bulk center, package consolidating agency, packing house*.

freight inward. N. Freight paid on shipments received.

freight on board. N. See *FOB*.

freight outward. N. Freight paid by a seller on outgoing customer shipments. See also *freight absorption*.

freight paid to. N. Where a seller must forward the goods at his or her own expense to the agreed destination and is responsible for all risks of the goods until they are delivered to the first carrier.

frequency. N. (1) The number of cases in a class or other subdivision of a group. (2) In advertising, the number of times an advertisement is delivered within a set time period. (3) In advertising, the average number of times that the average prospect will be exposed to a specific advertisement in a specified period. See also *reach*.

frequency discount. N. A reduction in advertising rates based on the number of insertions or broadcasts used in a given time period.

frequency distribution. N. Used by market researchers, the categorization of statistical information according to size or magnitude, with the number of items (frequency) applicable to each interval.

friend-of-a-friend promotion. N. A promotional method where established customers are presented with incentives, e.g., a free gift, for referring to the seller names of people who might be interested in securing the product or service. See also *member-get-member promotion*.

fringe area. N. In broadcasting, the outer listening or viewing area. Within miles close to the fringe area, reception is lost or becomes static.

fringe market. N. That segment of a firm's customers who are outside the firm's core market; i.e., who frequent the firm on an occasional basis.

fringe time. N. Time slots when there are relatively few people in the audience to receive an advertisement. See also *prime time*. Synonymous with *transition time*.

front. N. In retailing, the selling area of the store.

front end. N. In retailing, where store buyers pay for their merchandise.

front load. N. Scheduling the bulk of an advertising budget for a given time period in the early days or weeks of an advertising campaign.

FSA. ABBRV. Foreign sales agent.

FTA. ABBRV. Free trade agreement.

FTC. ABBRV. Federal Trade Commission.

FTC rule. N. See *thirty day delayed delivery rule*.

FTZ. ABBRV. Foreign trade zone. See *free trade zone*.

fulfillment. N. Processes for receiving, servicing, and tracking orders sold via direct marketing. They include: subscriptions, book club orders, catalog items, and fund raising. Fulfillment systems purport to fill orders rapidly, maintain customer files, send invoices and record payments, react to customer complaints and other inquiries, and to produce purchase and payment information to be used in future marketing programs. See also *customer service*.

fulfillment system. N. See *fulfillment*.

full cost approach. N. Used by advertising agencies in setting pricing policies; an approach to cost analysis that takes both direct and common costs into consideration. See also *full cost pricing*.

full cost pricing. N. The practice that includes all appropriate manufacturing costs in determining inventory. See also *full cost approach*.

full demand. N. Where buyers want and are willing to pay for all the items that are being manufactured.

full disclosure. N. Providing total information to consumers regarding merchandise and services. In products, found on labels and in advertisements.

full-function wholesaler. N. See *full-service wholesaler*.

full line. N. Goods found in a store having all styles, sizes, colors, etc., that a customer can expect to find.

full-line discount store. N. A department store with lower prices, a broad merchandise assortment, a lower-rent location, more emphasis on self-service, brand-name merchandise, wide aisles, shopping carts, and more merchandise displayed on the selling floor. Synonymous with *promotional department store*.

full line forcing. N. Urging the customer to purchase the least desirable item of a seller's line in order to secure the more desirable goods. See also *cherry picking*.

full mark. N. A 100% markup in goods.

full position. N. On a newspaper page, the space occupied by an advertisement, which is so placed that it appears at the top of the column with editorial matter along one side or placed so that editorial matter appears directly above it and along one side.

full run. N. A request for advertising to be inserted in all editions of a newspaper that are put out on any one day. To advertise on a full run is to advertise in all editions of a newspaper, even those of different regional editions. See also *full showing*.

full sale. N. A class of market-testing techniques where the marketing is complete and in the mode that would be used to launch. No limitations on distribution, advertising, etc., unless planned in launch.

full screen. N. A screening stage where all preliminary work is finished, a scoring model is usually used, and a favorable assessment is followed by a preliminary business analysis that releases the concept to development.

full-service agency. N. An advertising agency that will handle all the needs of his or her client in regard to advertising, such as developing, production, and placement of an advertisement. Such agencies offer total service in both advertising and non advertising activities, from preparation and placement, to dealing in production and preparation of annual reports, exhibits at trade shows, and useful sales training materials. See also *advertising agency*.

full service wholesaler. N. A wholesaling middleperson who takes title to goods that are resold and frequently takes physical possession of the items. Such people often operate warehouses, extend credit, and assist customers with accounting and marketing data. Synonymous with *service wholesaler*. See also *limited-service wholesaler*.

full showing. N. (1) A 100% (full) display of outdoor advertising. (2) The purchase of all the outdoor advertising positions in a particular area for an advertising display for a specific time period, usually thirty days. Suggests that 100% of the population in a community pass by the advertising at least once on any day.

full warranty. N. A statement of liability by a manufacturer that has no limit of noncoverage.

functional costing. N. Classifying costs by allocating them to the various functions performed (warehousing, delivery, billing, etc).

functional discount. N. A deduction taken to effect different prices for different customers (e.g., retailers get 40% off the list price, wholesalers 40%–50% off) See also *price discrimination*. Synonymous with *trade discount*.

functional manager. N. A manager who is responsible for a specialized area of operations, such as marketing.

functional matrix. N. An organization option in which the matrix leans toward the functions. Participants have dual reporting relationships, but the functional reporting is intended to dominate thinking and action.

functional middleperson. N. An independent business that purports to assist in the passing of title to merchandise without taking title to the items in the process. Synonymous with *agent middleperson*.

functional obsolescence. N. Considered in preparing an advertising campaign; obsolescence created by structural defects that reduce a property's value or market ability. See also *weakest link theory*, *planned obsolescence*, *product development*.

functional satisfaction. N. The satisfaction received from the tangible or functional features of a product.

functional spin-off. N. When a market channel relationship has become established, each member agrees to fulfill specific activities based on expected cost structures.

functional standards. N. Standards that provide needed selections from the range of options in the use of international standards, and do so in a harmonized way.

functions of exchange. N. The marketing functions of buying and seller.

functions of physical supply. N. The marketing function of distribution, transportation, and warehousing.

Fur Products Labeling Act of 1951. N. Federal legislation protecting the public against false labeling and advertising of furs.

further processing method. N. See *superdeductive*.

future shock. N. Considered in advertising efforts, especially targeted for senior citizens, coined by Alvin Toffler to describe people's problems in dealing with rapid changes in society, including fads found in lifestyles.

G

GAFF

GAFF. ABBRV. Abbreviations for a store category including the general merchandise, apparel and accessory, and furniture and home furnishings and appliances stores. Synonymous with *GAFFO*.

GAFFO. ABBRV. See *GAFF*.

gain opportunity. N. The difference between a company's goal in a market and its actual achieved sales.

galvanometer. N. One of numerous measuring instruments used to determine advertising effectiveness. Perspiration on the palm can be measured as emotional reactions to advertisements.

game plan. N. Any strategy designed to achieve organizational goals.

game theory. N. Used by advertisers, a mathematical process for choosing an optimum strategy when faced by an opponent who has a strategy of his or her own.

Gamma test. N. A type of product-use test wherein the developers measure the extent to which the item meets the needs of the target customers, solves the problem(s) targeted during the development, and leaves the customer satisfied. See also *Alpha test*, *Beta test*.

gap analysis. N. A category of techniques based on the idea that if one can position all of a market's products onto one two-dimensional chart, they will not be spread around. Instead they will clump in some places and be void in others. Any void (gap) thus offers an opportunity for a new product. The charting uses x- and y-axes and plots against such attributes as price, strength, speed, and ease of use.

gatefold. N. A magazine or periodical page of extended size that is folded over and reinserted. Gatefolds are expensive and are primarily used for introducing new products.

gathering. N. The collation of promotional package components prior to inserting into an outer envelope.

gender analysis. N. Separating names on a mailing list into male and female categories; especially useful to marketers when promoting products and services meant for one sex more than another, such as shaving cream or cosmetics.

general acceptors. N. See *late majority*.

general advertising. N. National or nonlocal newspaper advertising.

general export license. N. Any of various U.S. export licenses covering export commodities for which validated export licenses are not required. No formal application or written authorization is needed to ship exports under this license.

general line distributor. N. An industrial distributor called a general line wholesaler. Synonymous with *general line house*. See also *general line wholesaler*.

general line house. N. See *general line distributor*.

general line retailer. N. A retailer that carries a wide range of products.

general line wholesaler. N. (1) A merchant wholesaler who carries merchandise in a host of unrelated lines. (2) A full-service wholesaler that carries a wide variety of product lines.

general merchandise retailer. N. See *general line retailer*.

general merchandise store. N. A retail operation with a wide variety of items.

general merchandise wholesaler. N. See *general line wholesaler*.

general rate. N. See *one-time rate*.

general sales manager. N. The sales executive responsible for complete coordination of the firm or division's sales force. Although he or she will not traditionally set policy, developing strategies and methods to fulfill the firm's marketing plan is a major responsibility, along with supervisory involvement.

general sales tax. N. A tax on most items, collected at the time of purchase. In many states purchases of food and medicine are excluded from this tax.

general store. N. A small retailing operation, not departmentalized, often found in country areas, where a wide variety of items can be bought, including food, clothing, and supplies.

generation X. N. The generation of children born between 1966 and 1976.

generic advertising. N. See *primary advertising*.

generic appeal. N. Advertising appeal on behalf of a product category where no mention is made of a particular brand name; for example, the advertising that encourages the use of plastics. Its primary purpose is to make the public aware of the product category.

generic brands. N. Unadvertised, plain label grocery items that often sell for 30%–40% less than advertised brands. Packaging tends to be sparse, with only the generic product name and required governmental labeling information given. See also *branding*, *generic product*.

generic competitor. N. An organization that competes with others to satisfy consumers' wants or needs within a general category of products or services.

generic market. N. A market where vendors offer substitute items that are different perceptually and physically.

generic name. N. A brand name that has become associated with a product category rather than with a particular brand.

generic product. N. (1) An item sold under a common name rather than a brand name. (2) Not the product itself, but a concept incorporates the hopes the purchaser has with regard to the item. (3) A set of tangible or intangible attributes that are assembled into an identifiable form. See also *generic brands*.

geocentricity. N. One of the three-way categories of the policies of firms' activities in international marketing; focuses on the techniques of understanding the economic, cultural, and legal condition among nations that are included in the global target, and the means by which they can be managed. See also *ethnocentricity, polycentricity, regiocentrism*.

geodemographics. N. Techniques that combine consumer demographic information with geographic consumption patterns to permit precise targeting of consumers with specific characteristics.

geographical hole. N. The absence of a global corporation from a place in one of the regional areas of the world that is considered important. Such an absence is harmful to the globalization of the firm's market offerings.

geographic demographics. N. The basic identifiable characteristics of towns, cities, states, regions, and countries.

geographic pricing. N. Outlines the responsibility for transportation charges. The basic forms of geographic pricing are free on board (FOB) mill pricing, uniform delivered pricing, zone pricing, and base-point pricing.

geographic segmentation. N. Where the target market is divided by world regions, population density, city size, etc. By doing this, a firm takes into account the varying consumer preferences in different locations.

geographic skew. N. Where the advertiser, resulting from inadequate knowledge of the market, significantly overspends in one area and underspends in another.

getting by. N. A frugal consumer lifestyle that is usually pursued by people because of their economic circumstances.

giant insert. N. See *newspaper stuffer*.

Giffen good. N. See *inferior goods*.

gift card. N. A card received for a gift by a seller or sent directly by a donor.

gift close. N. A salesperson's closing method purporting to provide the prospect with an added incentive to buy the item or service immediately. Usually a service is rendered, such as shipping the same day, and not a "gift" as suggested in the term, since no hard item is involved. See also *close, gift with purchase offer*.

gift with purchase offer. N. An advertising incentive program where a premium is given away with the buying of a service or good; frequently used in direct-response promotions as with direct-mail advertising. See also *gift close*.

gimmick. N. (1) Any clever idea or device. (2) In advertising, an attention-getting device used to promote an item or service; can be clever wording in the copy, a different type of display, or any other unusual form of promotion for an item or service. See also *hook, giveaway*.

giveaway. N. (1) A premium available without charge. See also *free goods offer*. (2) The award of prizes to studio contestants, radio listeners, or television viewers. See also *gimmick*.

global approach. N. See *standardized approach*.

global firm. N. A firm that markets a standardized item worldwide and permits only minimum adaptations to local conditions and tastes from one country to another. Its marketing and advertising strategies are global with little differentiation among nations or areas as to product.

globalization. N. The tendency for markets to expand across national boundaries, leading to increasing competition among firms from different nations and a growing dependence on diverse, multinational, and multicultural customer bases.

global marketing. N. (1) Where a multinational firm seeks to achieve long-run, large-scale production efficiencies by producing standardized products of sound value and long-term reliability in every segment of the market. (2) The marketing of a standardized product worldwide with little allowance for, or acceptance of, regional or local differences. See also *international advertising, Euro-ad, Eurobrand.*

global quotas. N. Explicit limits set by one country on the value or quantity of merchandise that may be imported or exported through its borders during a given period on a global basis.

glut. V. To oversupply.

goal. N. An objective or something specific to be achieved.

godown. N. In the Far East, a commercial storage warehouse. See also *warehouse, commodity.*

going rate pricing. N. Applying the average price level charged by the industry to determine the price charged by the firm. Synonymous with *imitative pricing.*

golden circle. N. A group of brands in a particular product field, all of which are equally acceptable to consumers.

gondola. N. In retailing, a merchandise display stand; a bank of freestanding shelves open on all sides.

good. N. See *goods*.

Good Housekeeping Seal. N. A seal of approval of a product that meets the standards of the *Good Housekeeping* magazine. The magazine, to protect consumers, will license use of the seal by an advertiser but will set limits for the ways the seal can be used. Since the public recognizes and trusts this seal, its use provides a seemingly independent endorsement of a product's safety and quality, leading to the belief that using the seal in advertising will enhance sales of the product.

goods. N. (1) The result of industrial work, equaling the gross national product for one year. (2) Any movable personal property, excluding livestock and intangible property such as leases. See also *merchandise, product*.

goods in free circulation. N. Merchandise not subject to customs restrictions.

goods marketing. N. Entails the sale of physical products.

goods on approval. N. Items obtained when a potential buyer requests and receives from a seller the right to examine them for a stated time period before deciding whether to purchase the goods.

goods-services continuum. N. Visualizing the distribution between objectives and services. The continuum is shown graphically as a spectrum with pure goods at one extreme (for example, a bottle of hair conditioner) and a pure service at the other extreme (for example, a haircut). The continuum shifts gradually from the tangible to the intangible.

good 'til canceled order. N. An order to buy or sell that remains in effect until it is either executed or canceled. Synonymous with *open order*. ABBRV. *GTC*.

good will. N. The intangible possession that enables a business to continue to earn a profit in excess of the normal or basic rate of profit earned by other businesses of similar type.

gouge. V. *(slang)* To acquire an excessive profit by either overcharging or defrauding.

government-controlled price environment. N. Characterized by prices being set or strongly influenced by some level of government.

government market. N. (1) That portion of the industrial market within the public sector, including all levels of government. (2) A set of federal, state, country, or local agencies that buy goods and services for use in meeting social needs.

government procurement policies and practices. N. The means and mechanisms through which official government agencies purchase goods and services.

grade label. N. (1) The product's label indicating its quality. (2) A label that identifies the quality of a product by a letter, number, or word.

grade labeling. N. As authorized by government agencies, the labeling of certain consumer items as specified by standards (e.g., the grading of meat). See also *Federal Trade Commission, Food and Drug Administration, standardization, descriptive labeling*.

grading. N. (1) The classification of major commodities into well-defined grades. (2) The standardization of quality differences of staple commodities for purposes of identification during

graduation 276

trading periods. When combined with standardization, one of the marketing functions.

graduation. N. As applied in international marketing of goods and services, the presumption that individual developing countries are capable of assuming greater responsibilities and obligations in the international communication; within the General Agreement on Tariffs and Trade, for example, as their economies advance, as through industrialization, export development, and rising living standards.

grand strategy. N. The long-term set of goals and the means for achieving them used for setting tactics over a given time period.

graphic design. N. The creation of the visual element of a printed communication, such as an advertisement, product packaging.

graphics. N. All visual elements of communication affiliated with the presentation of an item or service to the market. It includes art, color effects, photographs, and copy.

grassroots method. N. A sales forecasting method that relies on input from salespeople in the field.

gravure. N. The printing process that transfers an image to paper by means of the ink retained in plate depressions.

gray market. N. (1) Sources of supply from which scarce items are bought for quick delivery at a premium well above the usual market price. (2) Commodities that are either mimics or counterfeits of genuine items.

gray trade. N. In international marketing of goods between nations that do not officially recognize one another; often by transshipment through third-country ports.

Green Book. N. An international directory, published by the American Marketing Association's New York chapter. Lists marketing research firms and research service providers. See also *creative black book*.

green label. N. A label that is awarded to consumer products considered friendly to the environment, hoping that the initiative will increase the pressure on industry to develop products that reduce pollution levels.

green marketing. N. Promoting items that are biodegradable (that will rapidly disintegrate when exposed to the air) and attempt to further protect the environment.

Green River ordinance. N. A municipal law regulating house-to-house selling, unless the resident has invited the salesperson. See also *door-to-door selling*.

greige goods. N. Unfinished fabric as it comes from the loom before bleaching, dyeing, printing, or the application of particular finishes.

grid card. N. A station's rate card in which the commercial times are priced separately, spot by spot. See also *day parts*.

gross. N. In merchandising, twelve dozen.

gross amount. N. (1) The total before deductions. The gross amount minus deductions equals the net amount. See also *gross profit*. (2) In advertising, the total amount owed by the advertiser to an advertising medium for advertising time and space bought prior to the deduction of the advertising agency's commission. See also *gross audience, gross billing, gross night hour, gross rating point*. (3) In direct mail, responses from a promotion, including prepaid order and credit orders.

gross audience. N. The total number of people or households in a listening, viewing, or reading audience without concern for the duplication of audience members, e.g., a person is counted twice should he or she appear in the audience of two of the television programs in the broadcast schedule being counted. See also *gross rating point*.

gross billing. N. (1) In advertising, the cost of advertising with a communications medium, including the advertising agency commission. (2) In broadcasting, the cost of a one-time insertion in a communications medium.

gross circulation. N. The maximum amount of people who walk past an outdoor advertising display and have a good chance of viewing the message; determined for a particular display over a given period of time, usually thirty days.

gross domestic product. N. (1) The total of goods and services produced in a nation over a given time period, usually a year. See also *gross national product*. (2) The market value of a country's output attributable to factors of production located in the country's territory. ABBRV. *GDP*.

gross margin. N. (1) In sales, the amount, determined by subtracting the cost of goods sold from net sales, that covers operating and financial expenses and provides net income. Synonymous with *gross profit*. (2) In retailing, the dollar difference between net sales and the net cost of goods sold during a stated time frame. Gross margining percentage is calculated by dividing net sales into this figure.

gross national product. N. The total retail market value of all items and services produced in a country during a specified period, usually one year. Distribution is presented in terms of consumer and government purchases, gross private national and foreign investments, and exports. See also *gross domestic product*. ABBRV. *GNP*.

gross night hour. N. In television, a one-time cost to sponsor one hour of prime time programming.

gross processing margin. N. The difference between the cost of existing raw materials and the sales revenue from the finished items.

gross profit. N. See *gross margin*.

gross rating point N. (1) In broadcasting, the number of advertisements required in a medium to achieve the percent of exposure desired of the message to the consumer. (2) In outdoor advertising, the number of panels used for delivering in one day the desired percent of exposure opportunities. ABBRV. *GRP*.

gross response. N. See *gross amount*.

gross sales. N. Total sales over a specified period, before the customer returns and allowances have been deducted.

gross savings. N. The sum of capital consumption (depreciation) and personal and corporate savings.

gross state product. N. The total monetary value of all final goods and services produced and marketed in a state during one year.

gross weight. N. The full weight of a shipment, including goods and packaging. See also *tare*.

groupage. N. A service that consolidates small shipments into containers for movement.

group discounting. N. (1) In broadcasting, a special discount for the use of a group of broadcasting stations simultaneously. (2) In merchandising, a special discount for the purchase of large quantities of an item or service (e.g., group discounts on air fares).

group mailing. N. See *cooperative mailing*.

group norms. N. Standards of behavior established by a group that describe the acceptable behavior of members.

group plan. N. See *party selling*.

group purchase plan. N. A selling where the retailer offers purchase incentives to a group. An identity card is frequently distributed to users.

group rate. N. See *blanket rate*.

group selling. N. The presentation for sale of goods or services to two or more people simultaneously.

grow-and-penetrate strategy. N. Active marketing efforts designed to increase the size and sales of a firm.

growth-share matrix. N. A display matrix showing market growth on the vertical axis and relative market share on the horizontal axis, used in analyzing the cash flow and marketing requirements of a firm's products. See also *harvesting strategy*.

growth stage. N. The second phase in a product's life cycle, characterized by a rise in sales and profit and the appearance of competitors in the market. See also *product life cycle*.

growth strategy. N. The strategy used by a firm that wants to expand its product's market share at the expense of a short-term profit, either by targeting users of a competitor's item to get them to switch, or by targeting people who have never used the item before.

GRP. ABBRV. Gross rating point.

GTC. ABBRV. Good 'til canceled order.

guarantee. N. A written statement assuring that something is of stated quantity, quality, content, or benefit, or that it will perform as advertised for a stated period. In some cases all or part of the purchaser's money will be refunded if the item fails to meet the terms of a guarantee. See also *guaranty, product reliability, warranty.*

guaranteed draw. N. A means of compensating salespeople by permitting them a draw that is not repayable if the commissions earned in a stated time period is less than the draw.

guarantor. N. See *guaranty.*

guaranty. N. A contract, agreement, or undertaking involving three parties. The first party (the guarantor) agrees to see that the performance of a second party (the guarantee) is fulfilled according to the terms of the contract, agreement, or undertaking. The third party is the creditor, or the party to benefit by the performance.

guaranty against price decline. N. Synonymous with *price guaranty.*

guerilla warfare. N. A marketing warfare technique used by small firms in trying to compete with large firms. A tightly bounded or well-defined small market is chosen to defend, and let the remaining portion go to the larger firm. Two additional concepts are: (a) guerillas do not accept the marketing or organizational practices of brand leaders, no matter how successful the former become; and, (b) guerilla firms respond firmly and quickly to market changes by exiting the market when situations call for it.

gutter position. N. The position of an advertisement that adjoins the inside margin or gutter of a newspaper, magazine, or other publication. Many advertisers think that when a message is placed in such a position, its effectiveness is adversely affected because of decreased readership.

HABA. ABBRV. Health and beauty aids.

habitual purchasing. N. A person's repeated buying of an item or service, done out of habit as contrasted with brand loyalty, especially when the consumer concludes there is little difference between products or services. A marketer's dream, to have repeat sales with habitual purchasers. See also *brand loyalty*.

haggling. N. See *higgling*.

half-page double spread. N. A magazine advertisement placed on either the bottom half or the upper half of two facing pages. Usually, this layout is as expensive as a full-page advertisement, but is selected by advertisers over a full-page when the copy more readily lends itself to this format, i.e., gives a continuous flow of material.

halo effect. N. (1) A bias whereby one favorable characteristic influences an overall judgment of an individual. Ratings of consumers are sometimes inaccurate because of the frequency with which a single or general impression tends to permeate the rater's application of evaluation criteria. (2) A subjective evaluation by consumers when analyzing consumer attitudes and their relationship to the market structure, especially when dealing with advertising or brand evaluation. This effect makes it difficult to assess brands based on strengths and weaknesses. At times, when a brand name has a positive reputation, the halo effect serves the brand advantage, especially when the manufacturer introduces a new product.

handbill. N. A form of direct advertising, usually a single sheet or a small pamphlet, distributed by hand. Handbills are frequently placed on a counter in the store or entranceway for customers to pick up while shopping. They are also distributed by hand for placement on car windows. Handbills provide an inexpensive form of advertising and are easy to produce. Synonymous with *throwaways*. See also *flier*.

handling allowance. N. (1) A special price or discount given by the manufacturer to a wholesaler, distributor, or retailer when a manufacturer's goods demand special handling. (2) An incentive given to the retailer for handling a particular promotional program that demands extra effort on the retailer's part.

hand-to-mouth purchasing. N. Purchasing that satisfies needs of the moment only, neglecting long-range requirements of the individual or entity.

hard copy. N. (1) A record that can be read by the human eye. It has the advantage of being accessible to everyone, anywhere. (2) Information printed on paper in contrast to being electronically shown, usually on a computer screen.

hard goods. N. See *capital goods*. See also *soft goods*.

hard offer. N. A promotion, especially in direct marketing, that requests payment at the time an order is placed, which includes an option to review the merchandise first and then pay or return the items as desired by the customer. No matter what the offer, the right of the purchaser to return unwanted items for a refund or prior to payment will be honored by most marketers.

hard sell. N. A dynamic, determined, and insistent approach to sales, where the seller attempts to control the sales situation by creating a level of tension. See also *soft sell*. Synonymous with *high-pressure selling*.

hardship point. N. In sales, the territory of a prospective customer who lives in a difficult area to reach or in a part of the community that is isolated.

harmonization. N. See *standardization*.

harmony. N. The impact of an advertisement on a desired product image and the goals of the message.

harvesting strategy. N. In response to an anticipated deterioration of the market or when the firm is deciding whether or not to withdraw its product from the market, a method for maximizing a product's short-term cash flow. The strategy requires lowering the investment in the product to cut costs and improve cash flow that, if and when created, is used for other needs of the organization. See also *growth-share matrix*.

harvest strategy. N. See *harvesting strategy*.

Hawthorne effect. N. (1) The tendency of people who are being observed to react differently than they would otherwise. An outgrowth of the Hawthorne studies undertaken at the Hawthorne, Chicago Plant of Western Electric between 1924 and 1933. These investigations showed the importance of the social system of an organization and became the foundation of human relations theory. (2) In consumer research, a factor taken into consideration, by disguising or concealing the true purpose or reason of the research, so as not to impact the interviewee's true feelings or attitudes. See also *bias*.

Hazardous Substances Labeling Act of 1960. N. See *Federal Hazardous Substances Labeling Act of 1960*.

HBA. ABBRV. Health and beauty aids.

header. N. A sign or marking at the top of a display, merchandiser, or exhibit.

headline. N. The beginning statement in a print advertisement where the advertiser anticipates what will attract the reader's attention. Its goal is to encourage the reading of the copy. In print advertising, it is considered to be a critical element, as it maneuvers the reader into the advertisement. Consequently, to be effective, it should stimulate interest and curiosity from the reader.

head of household. N. Of target importance to market researchers, the individual who is responsible for managing the household and is the major source of financial support; may be married or unmarried, male or female.

head of stock. N. In a large retail store, a major sales key clerk or other specialist responsible for maintaining front stocks and for advising the buyer of shortfalls and other related problems.

head-on position. N. An outdoor advertising location that faces the flow of traffic, rather than being placed on an angle or parallel to the traffic.

head-to-head positioning. N. Competing directly with competitors on similar product attributes in the same target market.

health and beauty aids. N. Include: (a) merchandise of over-the-counter medicines and remedies; (b) personal care products, e.g., toothpastes and mouthwashes; (c) hair care products, e.g., shampoos and setting lotions; (d) body care products, e.g., body lotion and skin moisturizers; and, (e) cosmetic products, e.g., perfume and face makups. ABBRV. *HABA, HBA*.

healthcare marketing. N. Public service marketing carried out for hospitals, clinics, medical associations, etc., to promote the health benefits of a product or service.

heartland. N. See *primary market area*.

heavy buyers. N. People in the market for an item who account for more than half of the total volume of sales of the merchandise. They represent less than half the number of users of the item. Synonymous with *heavy-half users, heavy users*.

heavy-half users. N. See *heavy buyers*.

heavying up. N. In advertising, an increase in the use of a medium by an existing long-time user. Should an advertiser's item be actively used at a given time over another, the advertiser often chooses to heavy-up the advertising for that time period, as with promoting the sale of Christmas ornaments in early December.

heavy market. N. A declining market created when buying exceeds the demand for orders.

heavy users. N. See *heavy buyers*.

hedging clause. N. A caution to customers attached to circulars, brochures, advertisements, and so on; a protective statement of warning for customers that typically reads: "The information furnished herein has been obtained from sources believed to be reliable, but its accuracy is not guaranteed."

hedonic items. N. Consumer products whose attractiveness is that they offer the user considerable pleasure.

heterogeneous shopping items. N. Merchandise perceived by the customer as different in quality and suitability.

heuristic. N. A concept used by advertisers; any method used to assist a person in discovering or learning something for himself or herself.

hidden offer. N. A special offer buried in the copy of an advertisement as a test of readership. Synonymous with *blind offer, buried offer*. See also *copy testing*.

hidden persuaders. N. A term popularized by Vance Packard in 1957 in connection with the motivational and manipulative techniques used by advertising agencies in their campaign programs. See also *motivational research, subliminal advertising*.

hidden service sector. N. Encompasses the delivery, installation, maintenance, training, repair, and other services provided by firms that emphasize goods sales.

hierarchy of effects models. N. Models of advertising communications that conceptualize communications as proceeding through a succession of stages from awareness to purchase.

hierarchy of needs. N. See *motivational needs, primary needs*.

hi-fi. N. *(slang)* A color advertisement preprinted on one side of a continuous roll of smooth coated paper, so that the advertisement appears to look like a wallpaper pattern, which is then fed into a newspaper's printing press.

higgling. N. The procedure whereby, when the buyer offers a low price and the seller asks a high price, a third price is arrived at through bargaining to satisfy both parties. Synonymous with *haggling*.

high-end. N. The most expensive items in a classification.

high involvement. N. An advertising medium demanding involvement on the part of the buyer. For example, print media are high involvement, as people are active participants in that they must read in order to obtain information. See also *low involvement, merchandise*.

high pressure selling. N. See *hard sell*.

high spot. N. In outdoor advertising, the location of significantly heavy traffic at which a showing is feasible.

hire purchase. N. Purchasing by installment payment where title does not pass to the buyer until final payment is made.

hi-spotting. N. See *cherry picking*.

historical design. N. In marketing research, a design using information recorded from the past. The design can be statistical or more descriptive, as in a report.

hitchhike. N. An end of a program commercial, within the sponsor's time, featuring the sponsor's product not shown in the program's other commercials. See also *cowcatcher*.

hitlist. N. A salesperson's list of prospective customers he or she plans to pursue; includes both weak and strong prospects, with the stronger ones receiving the greatest attention. See also *prospecting*.

HMS. ABBRV. Horizontal marketing system.

hoarding. N. (1) Collecting for the sake of accumulating. (2) A planned effort by persons to accumulate items beyond normal need (e.g., purchasing dozens of cartons of socks in anticipation of a price hike).

holding fee. N. An additional payment given to talent in a commercial; gives the advertiser the right to hold the commercial after its initial airing and use it again without having to renegotiate any payment.

holding power. N. The ability of a product, program, or entity to retain an audience over time.

holdover audience. N. In broadcasting, an audience that remains behind to watch at least the commencement of a succeeding program over the same network or station.

hold strategy. N. A firm's decision to retain a product's existing market share, with a continuance of levels of production and promotion needed to do so.

holism. N. A tool of marketing, the concept according to which economic knowledge can be gained from totals or aggregates rather than the action of individuals.

home audit. N. Determining consumer patterns in a product field by the recruitment of a sample of homes that will represent the larger target market.

home country orientation. N. A marketing approach where the firm gives domestic business the highest priority, making little or no effort to build up global markets.

homogeneous demand. N. A demand pattern in which consumers have relatively uniform needs and desires for a good or service category.

homogenization. N. Mixing together response data from consumers so that any variation in response by advertising campaign components cannot be identified because the components have been poorly key coded.

hook. N. (1) In advertising, items in copy that attract the reader's, viewer's, or listener's attention. (2) In retailing, a free offer given along with the purchase of a product. (3) In broadcasting, a giveaway offer, e.g., a free tape to the next fifteen callers.

Hooperating (Hooper rating). N. The percentage of individuals who are listening to radio stations, ascertained by using the telephone coincidental method of data gathering. These data are supplied by C.E. Hooper, Inc. See also *coincidental telephone method, share of audience, Nielsen rating.*

horizontal audit. N. Studies the overall marketing performance of a firm, with particular emphasis on the interrelationship of variables and their relative importance.

horizontal buying. N. (1) An advertising schedule using periodicals and magazines with varying audience appeals for the widest coverage of people. (2) Any use of many units of the same medium.

horizontal conflict. N. Conflict that occurs between channel members at the same level of the distribution channel.

horizontal cooperative advertising. N. Advertising in which marketers at the same level in the distribution system advertise jointly.

horizontal diversification. N. Using unrelated products, added to existing line items, to enhance total sales. New items are technologically different from existing product lines and have a different manufacturing process. See also *concentric diversification, diversification.*

horizontal half-page. N. Space, usually in periodicals, offered for advertisements; either the upper or lower half of a page.

horizontal industrial market. N. The broad market for industrial items, one which includes a number of industries.

horizontal integration. N. A strategy for a firm's expansion where the organization attempts to increase sales and profitability by expanding within its own industry, e.g., acquiring a competitor that markets the same item.

horizontal market. N. (1) A market that is made up of a broad spectrum of industries. (2) The condition of a market where the manufacturer's item is sold to buyers in several industries. See also *vertical market.*

horizontal marketing system. N. Joining of two or more firms on the same level for purposes of pursuing a new marketing or reinvented marketing challenge. ABBRV. *HMS.*

horizontal price fixing. N. (1) An agreement on price among competitors at similar levels of distribution. (2) A form of price fixing in which marketers at the same level of the distribution system get together and decide the price at which all of them will sell the product.

horizontal publication. N. A trade periodical whose content is directed to businesspeople in general as contrasted with a specific industry or professions. See also *vertical publication*.

horizontal sales company. N. A sales force company employing both company and external salespeople who are assigned sales responsibility based on geography, form of merchandise, type of customer, or specific selling activity.

horizontal saturation. N. See *saturation*.

hot items. N. *(slang)* Any goods that show quick salability.

house. N. An internal product or possession, controled by customers or owners, or a house advertising agency owned by an advertisers. See also *house agency*.

house accounts. N. See *direct accounts*.

house agency. N. An advertising agency that has only one client. Not very popular today. Synonymous with *house shop*.

household. N. A person or group of persons occupying a housing unit, whether related or unrelated.

household life cycle. N. Incorporates the life stages of both family and nonfamily households.

household saving. N. Household disposable income less existing household consumption.

house list

house list. N. A mailing list of existing customers and those who are not yet customers, but have made inquiries about the product or service.

house shop. N. See *house agency*.

house-to-house salesperson. N. A sales representative who visits homes in an attempt to make direct sales; made with or without an appointment. See also *door-to-door selling*.

house-to-house sampling. N. The distribution of a product sample to homes in a market location as a way of introducing people to the merchandise; a promotional strategy to stimulate word-of-mouth advertising.

house-to-house selling. N. See *door-to-door selling*.

housewife time. N. The portion of the day, between 10:00 a.m. and 3:00 p.m., when most viewers and listeners are women. With women returning to the workplace in great numbers, the percentage of women viewers and listeners during this time period is declining, but still they represent the largest number. See also *day parts*.

huckster. N. A peddler or petty retailer who will attempt to sell anything profit-making.

huckstering. N. See *huckster*.

human interest approach. N. See *imaginative approach*.

humorous sell. N. An advertising message that jokes about the merchandise being sold.

hurdle rate. N. Any criterion or test figure that a new product must meet or exceed as it goes through development.

hybrid technologies. N. A technique for industrializing services that combines both hard and soft technologies, such as computer-based truck routing and specialized low-priced repair facilities.

hype. N. (1) *(slang)* In advertising, an activity that attempts to encourage consumer interest and sales (e.g., advertising). (2) In broadcasting, special promotional activities in programming presented by a network to attract a significant audience and to generate higher audience ratings for a specific time period. Synonymous with *hypo*.

hypermarche. N. A large operation, combining the features of a supermarket and a discount house. Synonymous with *hypermarket*.

hypermarket. N. See *hypermarche*.

hyperreality. N. A phenomenon associated with modern advertising in which what is initially simulation or hype becomes real.

hypo. N. See *hype*.

hypothecated deposit. N. The aggregation of periodic payments on an installment contract received by a reporting institution in a state in which, under law, such payments are not immediately used to reduce the unpaid balance of the installment note, but are accumulated until the sum of the payments equals the entire amount of principal and interest on the contract, at which time the loan in considered paid in full.

hypothesis. N. (1) Used by market researchers, a tentative statement of an apparent relationship among facts that can be observed and therefore measured. (2) Used by market researchers, a theory imagined or assumed to account for what is not understood; a model for testing.

iceberg principle. N. A concept that 10% of required data are apparent and the other 90% are not seen. Used in sales predictions to indicate that gross numbers can hide the bulk of the critical data that would be determined upon closer examination.

ID. N. Broadcast station's call letters and location.

idea advertising. N. Advertising whose objective is to communicate a position or platform on a public concern.

idea generation. N. Developing concepts to be used for promoting new products and their promotional campaigns. See also *synectics*.

ideal marketing exposure. N. Degree to which an item receives exposure to its potential market so as to be available to meet customer's needs without exceeding them.

ideal other. N. Concept of how a person wishes others to perceive him or her; impacts on buying behavior and advertising promotions. See also *ideal self image*.

ideal points. N. Combination of attributes that consumers would like products to possess.

ideal self image. N. The way an individual would like to be. See also *ideal other, self-image*.

identity disclosure. N. Issue of whether to release to the user the name of the firm making the product being tested.

illegal. ADJ. Behavior that is contrary to the basic principles of law. An illegal act is forbidden by law, whereas an unlawful act, though not forbidden by law, is not given the protection of law.

illegal merchandise. N. Unlawful sale of items, e.g., stolen goods.

illth. N. Consumer items that are harmful to people who consume them and to the general welfare.

illustration. N. Visual element found in an advertisement; helpful in making copy believable. In order to maximize its effectiveness as a communication's tool, the illustration should complement and reinforce the advertisement's other elements of copy and headline.

illustrator. N. In advertising, the artist who creates, by hand, and develops pictures to be used in an advertisement. Cameras, computers, and other mechanical devices are not used by the illustrator.

image. N. (1) What people believe to be true about something. (2) In marketing, a buyer's mental picture of himself or herself; how an individual sees a product. (3) In merchandising, the feelings of customers toward a store.

image advertising. N. See *institutional advertising*.

image builder pricing. N. In retailing, where one item within the line is offered at a significantly higher price than the other line products so as to upgrade their image in the consumer's perception.

image building. N. Marketing relations approach to advancing, upgrading, or generally improving the customer's attitude toward an item, service, organization, or person.

image liner. N. See *pop-in*.

image sell. N. An advertising message that focuses on creating and sending a specific image for an item or service being advertised.

imaginative approach. N. A copy approach where the concentration is on ways to enrich life by using the product or service. Synonymous with *human interest approach*.

imaginative segmenter. N. Segmenter that attempts to offer an improved marketing mix to fulfill the requirements of a target market that has already been identified by an innovative segmenter. Merchandise developed this way often resembles or at times copies the innovator's item. See also *segmenter, innovative segmenter*.

imbricative marketing. N. Where implementation of the marketing strategy demands an understanding of the company's capabilities, the true needs of the market, the determination of that market, an awareness of the total system within which the firm functions, and the commitment to fulfilling in an orderly way all aspects of the company's marketing activities.

imitative innovation. N. Strategy of copying the creativity of others, but modifying each copy enough to give it originality and, hopefully, market value.

imitative pricing. N. See *going-rate pricing*.

immediate objectives. N. Objectives that the organization can accomplish now without obtaining more resources or doing additional research.

impact. N. The way in which an advertisement or a medium affects the audience receiving it. See also *impact advertising, motivational research*.

impact advertising. N. Sstrategy of placing advertising messages in the media where they are expected to have the greatest impact, where more consumers are exposed to it, recall it, and are motivated to purchase the advertised item or service. Some advertisements are best in one medium instead of another.

imperfect competition. N. Circumstances under which prices are usually altered by one or more competitors. This occurs because of unusual conditions in the market or advantages secured by some buyers or sellers. See also *perfect competition, pure competition*.

implementation. N. (1) Planning or putting an idea, schedule, method, or proposal into actual practice. (2) The actual execution of a strategic plan.

implicit costs. N. Costs originating within the business that are the responsibility of the owner (e.g., time, money).

implied warranty. N. Legal promise that a product will serve the purpose for which it is intended, whether stated by the manufacturer or not. See also *express warranty*.

import. V. (1) To receive goods and services from abroad. (2) To bring goods and services from abroad. N. An imported item.

importance of a purchase. N. Degree of decision making, level of perceived risk, and amount of money to be spent or invested. The level of importance of a purchase affects the time and effort a consumer will spend shopping for a product as well as the amount of money allocated.

import quota. N. Protective ruling establishing limits on the quantity of a particular product that can be imported. See also *quantitative restrictions*.

import quota auctioning. N. Process of allocating the right to import a good that is subject to an import quota by auctioning the quota, in whole or part, to future importers.

import restrictions. N. Scheme for reducing or controlling imports through a variety of measures including import deposits, licenses, or quotas.

imports. N. See *import*.

import surcharge. N. Charge on imports over and above regular tariffs or customs fees.

impost. N. Tax, usually an import duty.

impressions. N. (1) In advertising, the total number of exposures to a specific advertisement in a specified period. (2) In broadcasting, the reaction to a single exposure from a broadcast commercial in a specified period.

imprint. N. Identification printed on a container during the process of manufacture. It may give the brand, container capacity, material quality, freight classification, and similar data.

impulse buying. N. Purchasing by the customer without any prior planning, usually determined by a rapid appeal of the item or service; a spontaneous purchase made in response to an unexpected urge or external stimulus. Synonymous with *impulse purchasing*. See also *impulse merchandising, planned impulse buying*.

impulse merchandising. N. Items susceptible to spontaneous rather than purposeful purchasing. These goods benefit from display in store locations that have a considerable flow of customers; they are a specific category of convenience goods and tend to be low-cost items, e.g., candies and candles. See also *impulse buying*.

impulse products. N. Convenience items that the consumer does not plan to buy on a specific trip to a store.

impulse purchasing. N. See *impulse buying*.

imputed cost. N. Cost that is not specified but is implied to exist by the policies of the organization (e.g., interest that would have been earned on cash spent to purchase inventories).

inactive. N. Customer that has not bought something over a set time period, usually twelve months.

inactive account. N. See *dormant account*.

in-ad coupon. N. Coupon placed along with an advertisement; used mostly by stores as a means of getting people into their outlet. This coupon can only be used in the store sponsoring the advertisement.

in bond. N. Items shipped by a producer several months before a store's usual selling season. The items are held in bond in the store's warehouse until the selling season.

in-bound telemarketing. N. In direct marketing, where the sales representative handles incoming telephone calls from customers who place orders, make inquiries, or voice annoyances. Traditionally, an 800-number is used in in-bound telemarketing systems. See also *out-bound telemarketing*.

incentive. N. Motivational force that stimulates people to greater activity or increased efficiency. Customer sales promotions often involve incentives such as coupons, rebates, and discounts.

incentive agency. N. Company providing a variety of incentive products, usually representing a number of manufacturers. Serving as middlepeople, they often assist in preparing promotional materials.

incentive plan. N. Reward scheme that attempts to tie pay directly to job performance, e.g., a piece rate or a sales commisisons.

incentive rate. N. Salary increment given after the completion of a specified, usually probationary, period.

inchoate. ADJ. Newly begun or incomplete.

income. N. Money or its equivalent that is earned or accrued, arising from the sale of goods or services.

income distribution. N. Used by market researchers, the way in which personal income is dispensed throughout the various socioeconomic levels in a nation.

income effect. N. Used by market researchers, the change in the quantity of an item demanded because a person's purchasing power has been altered.

income elasticity of demand. N. Variables that remain constant; the percent change in quantity demanded that can be expected to follow from a percent change in one's income. See also *price elasticity*.

income segmentation. N. Dividing markets or customers on the basis of their earnings.

income statement. N. Profit and loss statement of a given concern for a particular period of time.

increasing-cost industry. N. An industry that experiences increases in resource prices or in manufacturing costs as it expands when new firms enter it.

incremental costs. N. Costs that increase or decrease as the direct result of a specific decision.

incrementalism. N. Decision-making approach whereby executives begin with a current situation, consider a limited number of changes in that situation based on a small number of alternatives, and test those changes by instituting them one at a time.

incremental pricing agreement. N. Pricing arrangement between a buyer and seller utilizing a schedule of price that shifts with the cumulative increment purchased. See also *blanket pricing agreement*.

incremental revenue. N. Increase or decrease in revenue that results from a subtraction or addition of a unit of sales or from the advance or decline in price.

incremental spending. N. Budget allocation permitting for more or less spending on media for advertising in direct proportion to sales.

incremental technique. N. Promotional budget method in which a company bases its new budget on previous expenditures. A percentage is either added to or subtracted from this year's budget to determine next year's budget.

incumbent agency. N. (1) An advertising agency under contract with a specified client. (2) The current tenured advertising agency for an advertiser's goods or services.

indebtedness. N. Debt that is owed; any form of liability.

indent. N. Request from a purchaser to an importer to import specific items at a stated price. The importer has a given time period in which to accept or refuse the offer.

independent. N. (1) An individual whose behavior is self-determined. (2) In retailing, a store that does not belong to an association of companies or chains.

independent distributors. N. Individuals and firms that buy from producers and other intermediaries and sell to other resellers and to end users.

independent media. N. Communication vehicles, such as newspapers and television, not controlled by a firm, yet they influence the government's, consumers' and public's perceptions of that firm's products and overall image.

independent network. N. Any broadcast system that is not affiliated with the three major networks, i.e., ABC, CBS, or NBC. Presently, with the increase in cable stations, the term has lost its critical status and influence. See also *independent station*.

independent retailer. N. Retailer that owns a single outlet that is not affiliated with any other retail outlet.

independent station. N. Broadcast station not owned or controlled by or affiliated with a network. See also *independent network*.

independent store. N. Retail operation that is controlled by individual ownership or management, not by outside management.

independent variable. N. (1) The factor that is not dependent for change on other factors. Synonymous with *predictor variable*. See also *experiment, variable*. (2) In advertising, an element that is subject to random change, in order to test the results. For example, an audience response is dependent on the stimulus provided and advertising copy can be considered the independent variable when it is time to chart results. See also *independent variable*.

index. N. Symbol or number used to identify a particular quantity in an array of similar quantities.

index number. N. Symbol or number used to identify a particular quantity in an array of similar quantities.

index of sales activity. N. Relative measure of a store's sales record within a given market.

indicia. N. Imprinted designations used on mail pieces to denote payment of postage.

indifference barrier. N. Created where purchases are made from habit to save time and effort, without regard to advertising. Advertising purports to neutralize this barrier with new products and approaches.

indirect-action advertising. N. Creating a positive attitude toward an item or service via long-range planning of frequent exposure over a time period, so that at a given moment when the potential consumer is ready, the impact already made will encourage a positive decision to buy. See aslo *direct-action advertising, indirect advertising.*

indirect advertising. N. Synonymous with *indirect-action advertising.*

indirect channel. N. Channel of distribution using numerous middlepeople. The opposite of *direct channel.* See also *indirect distribution, semi-direct channel.*

indirect competition. N. Where consumers for a product satisfy their needs by purchasing a different item or do not make a purchase at all, instead of securing the item or service of another company.

indirect costs. N. Important to marketers and advertisers in measuring profits; costs not usually identifiable with or incurred as the result of the manufacture of goods or services, but applicable to a productive activity generally. Included are costs from manufacturing operations (wages, maintenance, overhead, etc.). See also *direct cost.*

indirect damage. N. Consequential loss.

indirect distribution. N. Using middlepeople to sell a product. Traditionally manufacturers prefer indirect distribution when they have limited financing, few lines, require assistance at the customer level, and do not want to be involved in distribution matters. See also *direct distribution, direct channel, indirect channel.*

indirect exposure. N. Consumer purchase of a good or service resulting from the influence of another person who has been exposed to an advertisement.

indirect material costs. N. Costs of materials that are included as manufacturing overhead and assigned to products on some reasonable allocation basis.

indirect production. N. Producing an item needed for the manufacture of major goods or services (e.g., producing a machine designed specifically to produce a given consumer product).

indirect promotion. N. Sales promotion that is impersonal as contrasted with personal selling. Advertising, packaging, etc., are examples. It purports to make a service or item known to the market and to present it in the most favorable light. See also *direct promotion*.

indirect retail outlet. N. Retailer that purchases items via a wholesaler.

individual brand. N. Name applied to one product only (e.g., Crest, Tide). See also *family brand*.

individual change stimuli. N. Forces that determine a part of the activities of a purchasing unit in the market following changes in the characteristics of the purchasing unit, such as age, educational level, and income.

individual characteristics. N. Interests, values, attitudes, and needs that people possess.

induced consumption. N. Additional consumer buying caused by new capital formation.

induced investment. N. New capital formation caused by an upturn in consumer buying.

industrial advertising. N. Advertising goods or services for use in the manufacture or distribution of other goods and services. Advertised items include raw materials, components, or equipment required in the making and distribution of goods and services.

industrial buying behavior. N. Patterns and purchasing procedures of groups in the organizational market. These actions differ from

industrial marketing research

those of the consumer and are characterized by highly professional, detail-oriented purchasing activities. Items bought are usually large-scale acquisitions of raw materials or office supplies and equipment.

industrial classification. N. Analysis and synthesis of the factors pertinent to a business into a logical and systematic hierarchy, in which like things are combined in terms of their similarity and then categorized according to their essential differences.

industrial coding. N. Assigning identifying symbols to the permanent characteristics of items classified singly or in logical groupings, to ensure that characteristics contain the same identification.

industrial concentration. N. Factor reflecting the extent to which a large proportion of an industry's sales are produced by a few companies.

industrial consumer. N. User of industrial goods or services.

industrial distributor. N. (1) A full-service wholesaler representing industrial manufacturers and selling to industrial buyers. (2) An independently owned operation that buys, stocks, and sells industrial products.

industrial goods. N. Merchandise purchased for commercial reasons, instead of for personal or domestic needs.

industrial market. N. Producer market that consists of firms that engage in the manufacture of goods. See also *industrial buying behavior*.

industrial marketing. N. (1) The marketing of industrial goods and services. (2) The process of anticipating, discovering, and designing product and service specifications that will satisfy the requirements of industrial customers.

industrial marketing research. N. The systematic gathering, recording, and analyzing of data for use in solving problems related to the marketing of industrial goods and services. See also *industrial marketing*.

industrial products. N. See *industrial goods*.

industrial purchasing. N. Buying of goods and services at the business or institutional level.

industrial services. N. Includes maintenance and repair, and business advisory services.

industrial standardization. N. Orderly and systematic formulation, acception, usage, and revision of the given requirements to be achieved in order to attain a goal.

industrial store. N. See *commissary store*.

industrial supplies. N. Convenience goods that are necessary for the daily operation of a firm.

industrial user. N. An individual or company that purchases goods or services for commercial rather than personal or domestic reasons.

industry. N. (1) Trade, business, production, or manufacture. (2) As determined by the Standard Industrial Classification (SIC) of the U.S. Bureau of the Census, any commercial activity identified by this listing.

inelastic demand. N. Condition that exists when a price increase leads to a higher total sales revenue, or a price decrease leads to a lower sales revenue. A perfectly inelastic demand occurs when the demand for an item does not change with changes in price. See also *price out of the market, price elasticity of demand*.

inelastic supply. N. Condition in which the quantity of an item produced does not alter, or changes minimally, with a price change.

inelasticity. N. See *inelastic demand*.

inept set. N. In consumer behavior, those particular brands that a potential customer refuses to consider when seeking an item within the product category. See also *inert set*.

inertia. N. Any form of resistance to change; often considered a human and natural characteristic.

inert set. N. In consumer behavior, those particular brands that a potential customer remains indifferent toward when seeking an item within the product category. See also *inept set*.

inferential statistics. N. Statistical technique in marketing research of projecting the results of a sample to a larger group of people.

inferior goods. N. Any item for which demand decreases as income increases.

inflation. N. Of concern in setting market strategies; an increase in the price level, creating a decrease in the purchasing power of the monetary unit.

inflationary bias. N. Tendency toward a persistent upward trend in the price level.

inflationary spiral. N. Impacts marketing strategy; the situation in the time of rising prices when employees demand higher wages, which in turn increases costs, leading sellers and producers then to demand still higher prices.

influencer. N. (1) Any person who, though not directly involved in a purchase, affects the buying decision of another person. (2) In the exchange process, an individual who provides information about how a want or need may be satisfied.

infomercial. N. Program-length television commercial that is created to appear as a regular television show, thus making it difficult for the viewer to differentiate between a paid-for commercial and noncommercial programming.

informal balance. N. An advertisement layout that appears to appeal to a person's sense of balance, but is off-balance or uneven. Synonymous with *asymmetrical balance*.

informal buying group. N. See *pooled purchasing*.

informal economy. N. These businesses often pay no taxes, have no licenses, offer no Social Security, and sometimes deal in smuggled goods; represented by companies that are involved in legal activities, but are not registered with the government because of excessive red tape, which in some countries takes up to one year.

informal groups. N. Natural (i.e., unorganized) groups of people in a work situation, or market.

informal organization. N. Rather complicated and nebulous network of communication and interaction patterns of groups, or cliques within the formal organizational structure. Such a phenomenon usually arises spontaneously in order to: (a) augment, interpret, speed up, or change the formal communication system (or the lack of it); (b) regulate the flow, extent, manner, and enforcement of formal authority; (c) humanize the formal organization by trying to maintain a feeling of individuality among the members, while providing some security, unity, integrity, and feelings of belonging; and, (d) meet related psychological and social needs to such an extent as to give the impression of being the organization. See also *formal organization*.

informal selling. N. Type of market test in which one or a few salespeople make calls on intended market users and full presentations are made. There is actual request for the order. However, product has not been released to the full sales force.

information search. N. (1) In consumer buying, securing information about an item or different brands prior to making a purchasing decision. Often done by asking people, reading articles about the item or service, etc. (2) In industrial buying, where purchasing agents acquire information on vendors or suppliers when wishing to fulfill a given item or service wanted. See also *buy classes*.

informative institutional advertising. N. See *institutional advertising*.

informative label. N. (1) A message or affix to merchandise providing data about the item. (2) A label that advised consumers about the care, use, or preparation of a product.

informative product advertising. N. Advertising in its earliest stage. See also *pioneering stage*.

infrastructure. N. Used in international marketing, the basic structure of a nation's economy, including transportation, communications, and other public services on which the economic activity relies.

infringement. N. (1) In manufacturing, production of a machine that yields the same results by the same action as a patented machine. This is a patent infringement. (2) In merchandising, the reproduction of a registered trademark and its use on merchandise to mislead the public into believing that the items bearing the reproduced trademark are the product of the true owner of the trademark. This is a trademark infringement.

ingredient labeling. N. Information printed on a product package describing the contents.

inheritance audience. N. Segment of a broadcast audience that stays turned to a succeeding program. The percentage of a program's audience that is inherited may be a clue to the show's strength.

inherited audience. N. See *hold-over audience*.

in-home. N. Media seen, heard, or read in one's home. See also *out-of-home, alternative media*.

in-home retailing. N. Retailing where the sale occurs within the purchaser's house. See also *house-to-house retailing*.

in-house advertising agencies. N. Advertising agencies that are owned and controlled by client organizations.

initial margin. N. Amount a buyer is requested to deposit with a broker before commencing trading.

initial mark-on. N. Difference between the retail value of goods and the delivered costs when they are first priced and placed on display. See also *mark-on*.

initial mark-up. N. See *initial mark-on*.

initial purchase. N. (1) The first-time purchase of an item or service by a consumer. (2) The first-time purchase of a media vehicle for purposes of advertising.

initiator. N. In the exchange process, the person who first recognizes an unsatisfied want or need.

innate needs. N. See *primary needs*.

inner-directed. N. Used by market researchers, a consumer's purchase based on the satisfaction of an inner need that is consistent with his or her own values, such as being self-sufficient. See also *outer-directed, VALS*.

innocent purchaser. N. An individual who, in good faith, does not expect any hidden property defects to appear when he or she has purchased something.

innovation. N. Concept or approach in the production cycle, frequently involving the use of inventions in a practical task. The innovation theory suggests that waves of innovation are followed by lulls, which mean depression. See also *adopter categories*, *innovativeness*.

innovation diffusion. N. Concept that anything introduced into the market as new is quickly purchased for use by a group of people. See also *diffusion model*.

innovation dominated strategy. N. Focus of key managers on the creation or implementation of new technologies, products, or services.

innovative combiner. N. Marketing organization that applies the combined target market approach to identify a new combination of submarkets.

innovative efficiency. N. An aspect of the concept of marketing efficiency, the availability of items or services desired by and supplied to the market by activities that, together with the offerings, are the most appropriate that can be purchased into being under the existing knowledge of markets and technology. It usually demands the constant choice-making with given alternatives.

innovative maturity. N. Stage at the end of the product life cycle where the item is either altered to extend its lifespan or rejuvenated by identifying new or differing uses for the item.

innovativeness. N. (1) When applied to the seller; the degree to which the firm has the capability of, and follows the practice of, being innovative. (2) When applied to a buyer; the extent to which that person or firm is willing to accept the risks of early purchase on an innovation. See also *innovation*.

innovative segmenter. N. A segmenter who finds new submarkets, identifies unsatisfied needs of consumers, and evolves a marketing mix to fulfill sales to new customers. See also *imaginative segmenter, innovative segmenter*.

innovators. N. These are the people who are among the first to try or adopt an idea, service, or product. See also *innovation*. Synonymous with *early acceptors*.

inoculation strategy. N. Used in a comparative advertising campaign to create customer resistance to competitive merchandise or to resist the attractiveness of competitive advertising. A commercial that uses a portion of its length attacking the value of its competitor is an example.

INP. ABBRV. Information-need product; a traditional method of selling in which the sales presentation is made step by step.

in-pack. N. Direct premium found in a product package. With a high redemption rate, traditionally it offers the next purchase of the named item at a lowered price. Synonymous with *package enclosure*. See also *on-pack, with-pack premium*.

input-output strategy. N. Means for measuring and predicting fluctuations in supply and demand within the industrial market; based on the correlation between industries where the output of one is purchased by the other industries within the marketplace.

inquiry. N. Information requested about a particular item or service, either solicited or unsolicited. Inquiries can represent valuable sales leads since consumers have already indicated some interest in the item or service. Inquiries are frequently followed up by salespeople with telephone calls or letters. See also *inquiry and follow up, query*.

inquiry and follow up. N. Promotional method involving the offer of information about a product or service, with pressure to follow to purchase the item or service. To increase sales, follow up is important when such inquiries are made. See also *inquiry conversion, inquiry.*

inquiry conversion. N. Conversion of an inquirer to a customer. See also *inquiry and follow up.*

inquiry test. N. Technique for testing advertisements by noting the number of inquiries from listeners, viewers, or publication readers. See also *copy testing.*

insatiability concept. N. Concept that people are never fully satisfied and seek out new products and services. This leads to increased consumer sales and a further demand for more services and items to satisfy future needs.

inseparability of services. N. Inability of many services to be separated from the service provider. Customer contact is often considered an integral part of the service experience.

insert. N. (1) A special advertising page found within a newspaper or magazine. (2) Promotional material found within a mailing, such as merchandise coupons. Inserts are sold as advertising with the design and production handled by an advertiser. See also *insertion.*

insertion. N. The advertisement itself. See also *insert.*

insertion order. N. Written instructions for an advertisement to be placed in a particular issue of a publication at a stated rate. See also *insertion.*

insertion schedule. N. Schedule of insertions in the media for a specific advertising campaign.

inside back cover. N. In magazine advertising, a preferred place for advertisements. Synonymous with *third cover*. See also *inside front cover*.

inside front cover. N. In magazine advertising, a preferred place for advertisements. Synonymous with *second cover*. See also *inside back cover*.

inside-outside approach. N. Strategy approach whereby managers look first at the organization and then at the environment.

inside salespeople. N. Salespeople, usually involved in industrial and wholesaling, who take calls from customers within an office. See also *field salespeople*.

inspection purchasing. N. Buying an item only after each item has been thoroughly studied for imperfections. Found especially in industrial consumption, especially with goods not standardized.

inspirational strategy. N. Use of imitation, intuition, feelings, or creativity.

installations. N. Nonportable industrial capital goods used in the production process that involve a high degree of consumer decision making, are very expensive, last for many years, and do not change form. Synonymous with *process machinery*.

installed base. N. Volume of products of a specific product category and of a given brand currently in use in a market area.

installment buying. N. Acquiring goods or services with no down payment or a small down payment, to be followed by payments at regular intervals.

installment credit. N. Form of consumer credit involving regular payments, permitting the seller to reacquire the purchased item if the buyer fails to meet the payment schedule.

instantaneous audience rating. N. Size of a radio or television audience as measured during any specific instant or point in time expressed as a percentage of a specific base, such as total number of individuals or households able to receive the broadcast under study.

instantaneous reference recording. N. Recording of a radio program made at the time of its broadcast by the radio station for delivery to the program's sponsor, who may use it for reference purposes.

institutional advertising. N. An attempt to sell the image of a firm—its quality, services, role in community activities, merchandise, and so on—rather than specific items. Goodwill and position are foremost in the development of institutional advertising. Synonymous with *image advertising, informative institutional advertising*. See also *corporate advertising, institutional advertising*.

institutional approach. N. Way of examining marketing by considering the middlepeople and facilitating agencies that discharge the marketing functions. Synonymous with *descriptive approach*.

institutional decisions. N. Decisions that involve long-term planning and policy formulation aimed at assuring the organization's survival as a productive part of the economy and the society.

institutional market. N. Set of not-for-profit organizations that buy goods and services for use in achieving a particular goal or mission.

in stock. N. Describing merchandise on hand, available for shipment or sale.

in-store demonstration. N. When the item is demonstrated to increase store sales.

instrumental performance

instrumental performance. N. Performance of the physical product per se.

instrumental purpose. N. To encourage action at some future time; becomes critical in changing attitudes before any potential consumer can be convinced of the need to buy.

instrumented store. N. Retail outlet designed and organized based on computer analysis in the setting of efficiency, layout, and shelfspace, inventory control, ordering, etc.

intangibility of services. N. Inability of many services to be displayed, transported, stored, packaged, or inspected before buying.

intangible rewards. N. See *psychic income*.

integrated commercial. N. Broadcast commercial that appears or is heard as part of the program's entertainment.

integrated marketing. N. Where the firm's marketing efforts are handled by one organization, usually a large advertising agency that can provide appropriate services. Evolved as a popular strategic approach when advertisers became disenchanted with lessening media advertising effectiveness brought about by the spread of advertisements.

integrated marketing communications. N. Concept of marketing communications planning that recognizes the added value of a comprehensive plan that evaluates the strategic roles of a variety of communications disciplines—advertising, public relations, personal selling, and sales promotion—and combines these disciplines to provide clarity, consistency, and maximum communication impact.

integration. N. Centralization of authority in the hands of a top administrator or executive. There are three forms of integration:

(a) backward integration (the firm acquiring supplier to evolve greater control over materials procurement); (b) forward integration (securing retailers or wholesalers); and, (c) horizontal integration (the firm taking over one or more of its competitors, as long as it does not violate federal or state regulations). See also *backward integration, forward integration*.

integrative market opportunity. N. Potential within the marketplace for new expansion, based on new production and differing levels of distribution.

intellectual property. N. An intangible creation that is possessed; examples include patents, trademarks, copyrights, computer software, industrial designs, and trade secrets. Knowledge of this subject is critical in the avoidance by marketers and advertisers of violations. See also *intellectual property rights*.

intellectual property rights. N. Critical in international marketing and sales, accords that attempt to find adequate and effective protections for intellectual property rights. Needs of intellectual property include: (a) to create a trademark applicable throughout a regional trading area; (b) to ensure that registered trademarks enjoy the same protection under the legal system of all trading countries; and, (c) to specify the fees payable to a trademark office and its methods of payment. See also *intellectual property*. ABBRV. *IPRs*.

intensity. N. (1) The extent to which an advertiser's message is shown. (2) The number of posters found in a showing.

intensive distribution. N. (1) Placement of an item in all available outlets. Its shortcoming is that retailers have little commitment for promoting the item, as their competitors will also be offering the merchandise. (2) An approach to distribution that seeks the largest possible number of outlets in a given territory. See also *exclusive distribution, open distribution, selective distribution*.

interaction

interaction. N. In sales, the impact or relationship that exists between a salesperson and his or her potential customer.

interactive agency. N. Marketing firm specializing with advertisers who wish to advertise on the World Wide Web, and elsewhere.

interactive television. N. Relatively new concept in television where consumers shop, along with other activities. Merchandise is displayed before the consumer and can be ordered by pressing keys on a special keyboard or on a touch-tone telephone dial that is connected directly to the seller.

interest. N. Following the awareness stage in the adoption process, the consumer's curiosity in pursuing the value of a product or service. See also *activities, interests, opinions*.

interface. N. Point where different functions in a firm come together during the product innovation process. Usually applies to pairings of the major players: technical (R&D), operations (especially manufacturing), and marketing.

intermedia comparison. N. Comparisons of media classes based on their potential for inclusion in an advertising schedule. See also *intramedia comparison*.

intermediaries. N. See *middleperson*.

intermediary. N. See *middleperson*.

intermediate customer. N. Buyer who is not a consumer.

intermediate market. N. Set of wholesalers and retailers that buy goods from others and resell them.

intermediate sort. N. Assemblage from a host of sources of any large inventory of items and then separating them into smaller units for resale.

intermittent process. N. Any process designed to produce a variety of items.

internal economies scale. N. Utilized by advertising executives factors that bring about increases or decreases to an organization's long-run average costs or scale of operations resulting from size adjustments with the company as a product unit. They occur primarily because of physical economies or diseconomies. See also *diseconomies of scale*.

internal forecast. N. Forecast relating to a firm's output and its internal operations.

internal inventory transfer. N. Shifting of semi-finished goods through the plant's manufacturing process.

internal marketing. N. The notion that a service organization must focus on its employees, or internal market, before successful programs can be directed at customers.

internal reports system. N. That portion of a marketing information system providing up-to-date data on sales, costs, inventory levels, accounts receivable and payable, etc.

international advertising. N. With increased activity in global markets, this form of advertising carried out overseas. Differences in culture, language, tradition, government regulations, and consumer requirements suggests a different approach to advertising as contrasted with advertising in the United States, both nationally and locally. Often but incorrectly used synonymously with global advertising. Global advertising is worldwide while international advertising suggests advertising in a foreign market, which could be restricted to one nation. See also *international advertising*.

international division. N. Division in the organization that is at the same level as the domestic division in the firm and is responsible for all nondomestic country activities.

international forwarding agent. N. See *freight forwarder*.

international freight forwarder. N. See *freight forwarder*.

international marketing. N. (1) Operations within the home nation to produce merchandise and services for export, to be marketed overseas. (2) Activities in foreign nations that manufacture merchandise in that nation for sale there. Some overseas operations are wholly-owned subsidiaries of the parent firm while others may be joint or licensed ventures or contract manufacturing operations.

International Organization for Standardization. N. Geneva-based organization; sets worldwide technical standards in areas dealing with international commerce. ABBRV. *ISO*. See also *ISO 9000*.

international product life cycle. N. Product life cycle theory that aids in the explanation of trade flows and investment on the basis of a product's position in the four stages of: (a) exports of an industrialized country; (b) beginning of foreign production; (c) foreign competition in export markets; and, (d) import competition in the nation where the product was introduced originally.

international trade. N. Foreign trade measured by merchandise exports and imports of a country for a stated period, often one year.

Internet. N. Public network connecting millions of computers worldwide; transformed the way in which people communicate and conduct business. See also *Intranet*.

Internet marketing. N. See *e-commerce*.

interpretation. N. Step in the process of how a consumer gains awareness of advertising or a particular service or item; involves understanding of how advertising messages are received and comprehended by people.

interpretivision. N. A research perspective that produces a thick description of consumers' subjective experience and stresses the importance of the individual's social construction of reality.

interselling. N. Assigning sales personnel so that each is able to work in two or more related departments rather than being limited to one. See also *cross-selling*.

intertype competition. N. Competing for business using differing methods of distribution.

interurbia. N. (1) The urban-suburban sprawl. (2) A continuous population center composed of many communities with significant populations; for example, the entire coast of California.

interview. N. Conversation designed to yield information for purposes of research or assistance in attitudes, marketing, etc.

interview bias. N. See *interviewer bias*.

interviewer. N. Person who conducts an interview.

interviewer bias. N. Influence resulting from the presence of personal prejudice in the individual conducting the interview. See also *bias, halo effect*.

intrabrand competition. N. Competition, usually among resellers or between resellers and the direct sales force, for sales of same-brand products.

intramedia comparison. N. Comparisons of media vehicles within a media class, in terms of their potential for inclusion in an advertising schedule. See also *intermedia comparison*.

Intranet. N. Private network inside a firm that conforms to the same standards as the Internet but that is only for use inside the organization. See also *Internet*.

in transit. N. Items that have left the consignor's location and are en route to the destination.

intrapersonal variables. N. Utilized by market researchers; psychological determinants that influence a person's awareness, values, beliefs, and ideas.

intrapreneurship. N. An approach to new-product development in which a small team of employees is set apart from the rest of the organization and freed from ordinary bureaucratic requirements long enough to develop a particular product.

intrastore transfer. N. The purchase of goods from one selling department for use by another selling department.

intrinsic cues. N. Reasons for a buyer's feelings toward a product or service, as physical characteristics of the item itself. See also *extrinsic cues*.

intrinsic value. N. Market value of the material in something.

introduction stage of the product life cycle. N. Period during which only one or two firms have entered the market and competition is limited. Initial customers are innovators.

introductory offer. N. An offer, such as a free gift, premium, or discount given to prospects of a new product, or a reintroduced item that has been altered or improved upon.

introductory price dealing. N. When prices are temporarily lowered during the introduction phase of an item and raised at the end of the introductory period.

introductory stage of product life cycle. N. The first stage of the product life cycle. The new product is introduced to the market, sales are slow, promotion is usually heavy, costs are accumulated, and expectation is focused on determining when and if the product will soon enter the second (growth) stage of the cycle.

introductory technique. N. See *introductory price dealing*.

intrusiveness. N. Point at which an advertisement ceases to have a positive effect and becomes an irritant to consumers, thereby having a negative impact. Often leads to a complete reevaluation of the campaign.

invention. N. New device, process, etc., that has been created. Can be in either physical or conceptual form. Preexisting knowledge is combined in a new way to yield something that did not heretofore exist. Not to be confused with a product innovation, which is an invention that has been converted by further management and process development into a marketable product.

inventive creativity. N. Creativity required for product innovation. Is thought to combine artistic creativity and engineering creativity, either of which alone can be very strong but not productive of new product ideas.

inventory. N. Name given to an asset of a business. Inventories are of two general types, direct and indirect. Direct inventory in an industrial concern consists of raw materials, work in process, and finished goods. Direct inventories represent various stages of fabrication; in commercial and retail businesses, they are inventories purchased for resale. Indirect inventories, in general, are all supplies used to carry on the business and not purchased for resale. Indirect inventories are usually considered deferred assets. See also *forward stock*, *perpetual inventory*.

inventory carrying costs. N. Costs for conducting business related directly to the merchandise found in inventory, along with warehouse and insurance costs.

inventory change. N. Amount of increase or decrease in business inventories during a specified period.

inventory control. N. Control of merchandise on hand by accounting and physical methods. See also *eyeball control, periodic stock control.*

inventory cutoff. N. Determination of which inventory items are to be included in the year-end inventory balance.

inventory management. N. Involved with providing a continuous flow of goods and matching the quantity of goods in inventory with sales demand.

inventory model. N. Type of production control model that answers two questions relating to inventory management: "How much?" and "When?" An inventory model tells the manager when goods should be reordered and what quantity should be purchased.

inventory policy. N. Relationship desired between the quantity of stock on order and the quantity available, and the rate of usage.

inventory profit. N. Profit accrued on merchandise held in inventory during a period when the value of the items increased.

inventory risk. N. Financial risk of carrying items in inventory, as their value may decrease or because of reduced demand.

inventory shortage. N. Inventory reduced by theft, internal or external fraud, waste, sabotage, or careless operation. Synonymous with *inventory shrinkage.* See also *pilferage, shrinkage.*

inventory shrinkage. N. See *inventory shortage.*

inventory turnover. N. The number of times, on the average, that inventory is replaced during a period. It is calculated by dividing cost of goods sold by average inventory.

inverse demand pattern. N. Situation that exists when price and volume vary at the same time and more is sold at a higher price than at a lower one.

invisible supply. N. Uncounted stocks in the hands of middlepeople, manufacturers, and consumers. See also *visible supply*.

invoice. N. An instrument prepared by a seller of goods or services and rendered to the buyer. The instrument usually lists all items making up the bill for the convenience of the buyer; to prevent disagreements, the amount is stated on the instrument.

involvement. N. Importance made by a consumer to the purchase of a specific service or item; varies based on the degree of relevance the item or service has to the purchaser; for example, a high-involvement item is one that has a significant degree of emotional importance to the consumer.

I/PRO. ABBRV. For-profit corporation providing advertisers with verification and analysis of Internet website traffic.

IPRs. ABBRV. Intellectual property rights.

irregular demand. N. Fluctuations in demand for a product or service not attributed to seasonal changes or in the nation's economy. Marketers faced with an irregular demand state frequently attempt to alter the pattern of demand by establishing special promotions and incentives to increase demand during slow periods. See also *demand states, seasonal demand*.

irregular routing. N. Sales call pattern in which the sales representative determines the frequency of calls to be made. See also *fixed routing*.

irregulars. N. Items having defects that may affect appearance but not wear.

island display. N. Merchandise shown in a store's aisle or open space. Items are readily accessible from all sides and the display is often freestanding.

island position. N. Placement of newspaper advertising copy that is surrounded by editorial matter or page margin. An island position is enviable, in that no other advertising message is nearby to compete for consumer attention. See also *commercial protection, competitive separation.*

ISO. ABBRV. International Organization for Standardization.

ISO 9000. N. Critical for those marketing and selling overseas, a series of five international industrial standards for quality assurance. ISO 9000 aids a trading firm to devise a step-by-step guide on quality standard for each core process in almost every department. Development of a system that compiles with the external standards and leads to registration or certification and uniform standards that are acceptable universally. The five standards cover: (a) ISO 9000, an overview and introduction to the other standards in the series, including definitions of terms and concepts related to quality that are used in the other standards; (b) ISO 9001, which is a comprehensive general standard for quality assurance in design, development, manufacturing, installation, and servicing of products; (c) ISO 9002, which is a less comprehensive standard focusing specifically on manufacturing and installation of products; (d) ISO 9003, the lest comprehensive standard covering final inspection and testing of completed products; and, (e) ISO 9004, the guidelines for managing a quality control system.

isolated location. N. Store located alone within a residential area; usually a convenience store.

issue. N. (1) A hard copy. (2) One of a series of regularly published materials, such as newspapers, magazines, and newsletters.

issue definition. N. Statement of the topic to be investigated via market research. It directs the research process toward collecting and analyzing appropriate information for the purpose of decision making.

item. N. Singular for goods or merchandise.

itemized response. N. Unique response whereby one person hearing another person's new product idea is to (a) give a full statement of support by citing several advantages to the idea and (b) express any problems or concerns in positive (what's the best way to solve this) form.

item merchandising. N. Attempt to take advantage of sales opportunities presented by merchandise that is in the greatest demand by customers. Lost revenue is created when such demand cannot be filled because stock is not available.

item price removal. N. Practice whereby prices are marked only on store shelves or aisle signs and not on individual items.

items of trade. N. Merchandise or service that a country buys or sells in the world markets. Items include commodities, credit, and services.

iteration. N. Process of repeating a sequence of logical steps for purposes of improving or refining.

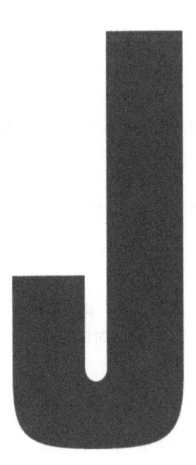

jacket

jacket. N. Extra-protection cover of a book, bearing the title, name of author, and other matter relating to the contents of the volume. Often designed to help promote the sale of the volume.

jam auction. N. *(slang)* A store that sells inexpensive jewelry, souvenirs, and the like. Synonymous with *jam pitch*.

jam pitch. N. See *jam auction*.

jebble. N. See *bluefingers*.

jingle. N. A musical commercial; usually part of a television or radio commercial.

JIT purchasing. ABBRV. Just-in-time purchasing.

JND. ABBRV. Just noticeable difference.

job. N. In merchandising, to purchase or sell merchandise in quantity, not in selected categories.

jobber. N. Middleperson who handles merchandise in odd or job lots. Some jobbers take possession of the title to the goods, which they resell to another jobber, to a retailer, or directly to the consumer. Others have a buying agreement with the manufacturer to drop-ship the merchandise on orders obtained by the jobber. See also *drop-shipper, limited-service wholesaler, premium jobber, rack jobber, truck jobber, wholesaler*. Synonymous with *reseller*.

job description. N. Statement, usually in writing, of the responsibilities, approaches, conditions, and other relevant factors built into a job.

job evaluation. N. Systematic rating of job content on such factors as skill, responsibility, and experience. The evaluation is primarily used to minimize wage inequities.

job lot. N. In merchandising, a miscellaneous grouping of items of various styles, sizes, colors, and so on, bought at a reduced price by a store or an individual middleperson.

job price protection. N. Guarantee of quoted prices on sufficient material to complete a specific task in which the purchase is engaged.

job specification. N. Carefully written description of a specific job, with duties and opportunities described. It identifies the requirements of the job and the desired qualifications needed for a worker to perform effectively. See also *specification*.

job ticket. N. Tag affixed to an order that provides details about the pertinent data about work to be done as well as the information about the person or firm for whom the job is being done. For advertising agencies, the job ticket gives the date, name of agency, name of client, and printing instructions to be carried out.

joint cost. N. (1) A cost that is common to all the segments in question and that can be assigned to the segments only by arbitrary allocation. (2) The costs of two or more items that must be manufactured together.

joint decision making. N. Process whereby two or more consumers have input into purchases.

joint demand. N. (1) Demand for two or more items that are usually used together because of necessity or consumer preference. Used primarily with industrial goods. (2) Demand for two products that are complementary.

joint mailing. N. Promotional mailing combining two or more complete mailing packages from two or more direct marketers.

joint production costs. N. Costs of two or more produced goods that are made by a single process and are not identifiable as individual products up to a certain stage of production, known as the split-off point.

joint promotion. N. Where a group of companies sponsor a sale.

joint venture. N. Commercial undertaking by two or more people, differing from a partnership in that it relates to the disposition of a single lot of goods or the termination of a specific project. See also *partnership*. Synonymous with *strategic alliance*.

judgment forecasting. N. Utilizing judgment in forecasting sales of both present and future merchandise. Methods used are the aggregate of individual sales representative forecasts, expert consensus, and the Delphi method. See also *Delphi technique*.

judgment sampling. N. Used by consumer and market researchers, nonprobability sampling in which respondents are selected on the basis of criteria that the researchers believe will result in a group that is representative of the population being surveyed. See also *nonprobability sampling, sampling*.

jumble basket. N. Merchandiser having a jumble display of a number of different items. See also *dump bind, jumble display*.

jumble display. N. Collection of items tossed together in a container or on a table counter. It is an open display that is primarily used in retail operations where customers can rummage through to find different items. See also *jumble basket*.

junior department store. N. Retail operation smaller than a traditional department store, which carries a wide variety of merchandise. Often large appliances, such as washing machines and television sets, are not sold in this store.

junior page. N. Space designation for periodical and magazine advertisements, where the space is the standard size of a page in small material. Synonymous with *junior unit*.

junior spread. N. See *pony spread*.

junior unit. N. See *junior page*.

junk mail. N. Promotional mail containing unsolicited material. See also *direct mail advertising*.

jury of executive opinion. N. Forecasting approach utilizing the opinions of senior executives as to their estimate of the market potential and sales. Following that, they attempt to reach a consensus.

jury of expert opinion. N. See *jury of executive opinion*.

jury test. N. A pretest in which a panel of customers is shown an advertisement and asked to rate its attractiveness, how much they like it, and how much it draws their attention.

just-in-time inventory system. N. See *just-in-time purchasing*.

just-in-time purchasing. N. An approach to inventory management in which products are bought in small quantities to reduce inventory carrying costs and obtain delivery just in time for use. ABBRV. *JIT purchasing*.

just noticeable difference. N. Small difference in an item that is apparent to consumers when the item's characteristics are modified, either to face competition or to save money. See also *Weber's Law*. ABBRV. *JND*.

K

KBI. ABBRV. Key buying influence.

KD. ABBRV. Knocked down.

keep out price. N. See *preemptive price*.

Kefauver-Harris Drug Amendment to the Food and Drug Act of 1962. N. Federal legislation requiring the manufacturer to test for both the safety and effectiveness of drug items before marketing them to the public. Also, the generic name of the item had to appear on the label of the product. See also *Food and Drug Administration*.

key. N. One or more numerals or letters or a combination of these, usually inserted as part of an advertiser's address appearing in an advertisement for the purpose of identifying the source of the inquiries or orders received in response to the sales message.

key account. N. (1) The crucial, important, or primary account. Synonymous with *major account*. (2) In advertising, any client who spends a considerable sum of money on advertising with one particular advertising agency.

key account marketing. N. See *national account marketing*.

key buying influence. N. Person in an organization who is the central figure in making buying decisions of specific merchandise or services. See also *multiple purchasing influence*. ABBRV. *KBI*.

key code. N. Either numeric or alphanumeric codes; a graphic designation found in an advertisement or print communication that is used in tracking responses to that communication.

keyed advertising. N. See *keying an advertisement*.

key industry. N. An industry that, because of a unique characteristic, holds major importance in the country's economy (e.g., steel or automobile).

keying an advertisement. N. Placing a code or letter in a coupon or in the advertiser's address so that the specific advertisement producing as inquiry can be noted. See also *copy testing*.

key items. N. (1) Those in greatest consumer acceptance. (2) Merchandise that determines the acceptance of a line of products.

keynote idea. N. Central or single concept to be shown in an advertisement that will be the most important for the potential buyer. Often, it becomes the continuing theme for a promotional campaign.

key resource. N. Vendor whose former activities with a specific retailer have been outstanding and from whom the retailer has consistently purchased a significant portion of its merchandise.

key station. N. The station that originates the principal program of a broadcast network.

keystone markup. N. See *keystoning*.

keystoning. N. Doubling of the maker's prices to determine retail prices. Synonymous with *keystone markup*.

kickback. N. (1) An illegal rebate given secretly by a seller for granting an order or contract (e.g., a payoff). (2) In advertising, an unethical practice where an advertising agency secretly offers to split the media commission with an advertiser or a person representing the advertiser so as to receive the advertiser's business.

kicker. N. In advertising, the subheadline in the writing of copy that appears above the headline for the copy.

kill. N. See *cancel, credit cancellation*.

kill bad pay. N. See *credit cancellation*.

Kimball tags. N. Prepunched tags affixed to goods, containing the size and style data that are utilized in speeding inventory control. See also *marking*.

kiosk. N. Originated in European cities, a freestanding display used to provide merchandise information. They are located on streets, in shopping malls, and in stores.

knocked down. ADJ. Applies to sales or shipments of equipment that is to be assembled by the receiver. See also *knocked down price*. ABBRV. *KD*.

knocked down price. N. In retailing, a seller's asking price that has been lowered for purposes of making the sale. See also *knocked down, upset price*.

knocker. N. *(slang)* A door-to-door salesperson.

knockoff. V. *(slang)* To cease working for a break, for a lunch period, or at the end of a working day. N. *(slang)* Imitation of a design of clothing or of a textile item, usually done so to sell at a lower price than the original.

know-how licensing. N. In international sales and marketing, agreement through which one firm possessing technical information covered by patents authorizes another to use it to produce goods or services; procompetitive in that it facilitates the transfer of technology and boost innovation, but it may, in particular circumstances, inhibit competition within the trading nations by imposing territorial restrictions.

knowledge stage. N. Beginning stage of an innovation decision process; commences when a customer receives physical or social stimuli that gives exposure and attention to the innovation's existence and a comprehension of how it functions or operates.

known loss. N. Loss discovered before or at the time of delivery of a shipment.

kurtosis. N. Measure of the concentration or clustering of cases around the mode of a frequency curve. A high concentration will result in a peak, and a low concentration results in a flatness. See also *skewness*.

label

label. N. (1) An identification record. (2) In advertising, the portion of an item that provides information about the item to the buyers. A tag that may be attached to the item or inserted with the package. (3) In advertising, classifying people according to a type, such as single parent, housewife, or divorced. (4) In merchandising, the brand name of a clothing manufacturer, retailer, fashion house, or recording company. (5) In direct mail, the small piece of paper or sticker on which a mailing address appears. (6) See *labeling*, *performance label*.

label copy. N. Advertising copy written primarily for the labels of goods.

labeling. N. All labels and other written, printed, or graphic matter appearing on any article or any of its containers or wrappers. See also *label*.

label panel. N. See *label set*.

label set. N. Records, categorized by name and address, that are printed in label form and separated from the total list before printing. Every record within the label set is given a code to identify it as a member of that particular set. Synonymous with *label panel, label split*.

label split. N. See *label set*.

laboratory test market. N. A procedure whereby shoppers are exposed to an ad for a new product and then taken on a stimulated shopping trip in a laboratory facility.

laggards. N. (1) Consumers who are strongly oriented toward the past and very suspicious of new concepts; they are the last to adopt a new product. They follow the late majority in the innovation diffusion process, and usually have the lowest economic and social status. See also *nonadopters*. (2) The fifth, and last, group of users to adopt an innovation.

lagged effects. N. See *carryover effects*.

lag indicators. N. Used by market researchers, a series of economic indicators that often follow changes in the economic cycle.

laissez faire. N. Doctrine that governments refrain from any form of trade regulation, leaving productivity and wealth distribution purely to market forces and individual industry.

Lanham Act of 1947. N. Officially the Landham Trade-Mark Act; federal legislation governing trademarks and other symbols for identifying goods sold in interstate commerce. As amended, it allows a manufacturer to protect his or her brand or trademark in the United States by having it recorded on a government register in the U.S. Patent Office, and provides for the legal right to register any distinctive mark. See also *trademark*.

large-scale production. N. See *mass production*.

last-in, first-out. N. See *LIFO*.

lasting distinctiveness. N. See *distinctive competencies*.

late fringe. N. In broadcasting, the 11:00 p.m.–1:00 a.m. segment designated by the television media for purposes of selling commercial time, which is usually charged at a significantly lower rate than prime time. See also *day parts*.

late majority. N. (1) Consumers who are committed to familiar ways of doing things and skeptical of new ideas. They follow the early majority in the innovation diffusion process, are below average in economic and social status, and usually have minimal use of mass media and salesforce. (2) The fourth group of users to adopt an innovation. Synonymous with *general acceptors*.

latent defect. N. (1) A defect in goods that is not visible to the naked eye. (2) A deficiency in merchandise offered for shipment not discernible by careful inspection.

latent demand. N. Market situation where a major segment of that particular market exhibits a preference for an item that is not being offered. The marketer's goal in dealing with a latent demand state is to measure the potential market's size and manufacture a product that will meet demand in the best possible fashion. See also *demand states*.

launch. N. Signifying the marketing of a new product. Can be either in a full-sale form of market testing or in the final marketing stage. See also *beachhead, launch control, launch style*.

launch control. N. Process by which a management plans for and supervises the introduction of a new product; the product's progress is monitored against pre-established norms, variances are detected, and corrections made such that the original goals set for the product are achieved.

launch cycle. N. Subphases of the innovation stage of a traditional product life cycle. The big step of innovation is broken into preparation (for marketing), announcement, beachhead, and early growth.

law of demand. N. Where the quantity demanded in a time period is negatively related to price; based on the assumption that the average potential customer is aware of alternative goods, has limited purchasing power, and a determination to maximize the utility accruing to him or her. See also *bandwagon impact, Veblen effect*.

law of increasing costs. N. Concept that the average total unit cost in a production process increases as the volume of a firm increases. See also *proportional law*.

lawyer. N. *(slang)* A friend who advises another in a store regarding whether or not to purchase an item, frequently resulting in the customer's not buying the item.

layaway plan. N. Method of deferring payments whereby goods are retained by the store until the customer has completed payments for them. See also *deferred payment sale*. Synonymous with *deposit plan*.

layout. N. (1) Sequence of printed matter, such as the pages of a brochure or booklet. (2) In advertising, plan or makeup of an advertisement. The job readied to typesetting showing the arrangement of the copy elements and style of print; usually required before the production of an advertisement can begin because it serves as a guide to those concerned with approving and executing the printed advertisement. See also *composition*.

L/C. ABBRV. Letter of credit.

lead. N. In sales, the name and address of a potential customer, either an individual or organization. See also *referral leads*.

leader. N. In marketing, a dealer offer conditioned by a unit volume-purchase. See also *follower*.

leader pricing. N. A method where prices of specific merchandise are set at levels so low that they yield minimal or no profit. Its purpose is to increase consumer traffic and to give the impression that the establishment offers items at low prices. See also *loss leader*.

lead generation. N. A salesperson's identification of the best possible prospects (leads) that he or she can approach using sales calls or personal visits, by either asking known customers for names of others believed to be candidates, joining associations; speaking before professional or community groups, etc. See also *endless chain*.

lead-in. N. (1) In sales, the part of the interaction that permits a sales representative to move toward a summing up or to close with a customer. (2) In broadcasting, a program immediately preceding another program on the same station. The lead-in program leads the audience to an advertiser's program on the same station. See also *lead-out*. (3) In advertising, the opening words in the copy text of the advertisement; used to lead the reader to the next text.

lead indicators. N. Applied by market researchers, a series of economic indicators that often precede changes in the economic cycle.

lead-out. N. In broadcasting, a program directly after another program on the same station that leads the audience out of the advertiser's program on the same station. See also *lead-in*.

leads. N. See *lead*.

lead time. N. In purchasing and marketing, see *order cycle*.

lead user. N. Those people or firms who most need the innovation being worked on and who will most likely participate in the innovation process. The idea itself often originates with a lead user and may even appear in prototype form in the lead user's firm.

leaf. N. A single section of paper constituting two pages of a book or other publication, one page being formed by either side of the paper.

leaflet. N. See *folder*.

learning. N. The process by which people's experiences produce changes in their behavior.

learning curve. N. A graphic representation of the measured changes at successive units of practice.

learning curve pricing. N. A pricing technique where the manufacturer lowers the price of an item as production increases and becomes more cost-efficient.

learning requirements. N. Various types of learning that new products often require from their purchasers. Without that learning, the purchase, trial use, or satisfaction will be threatened.

leaseback. N. A seller who remains in possession as a tenant after completing the sale and delivering the deed.

leased department. N. A department in a retail store, usually a department, discount, or specialty store, that is rented to an outside party.

least-effort concept. N. The belief by advertisers that consumers tend to make purchases based upon the least amount of effort possible and will buy what is readily available.

leave behind. N. See *leave piece*.

leave piece. N. Printed information that the salesperson uses and leaves with a prospect. This piece usually has the name and telephone number of the salesperson so the prospect, upon making a decision, will contact the salesperson and no one else. Synonymous with *leave behind*.

leftover matter. N. Copy that has been set in type but not used in the printing of an issue of a periodical or magazine.

legal lexicography. N. See *nationally advertised brand*.

legal residence. N. Where a person lives. The law does not require anyone to spend a majority of his or her time in a certain place for it to be categorized as a legal residence; however, federal law recognizes only one legal residence for an individual. See also *domicile*.

legal weight. N. Used in international marketing and sales; the weight of the goods and interior packing but not the container.

legitimization. N. With new merchandise, where early users serve as examples for future consumers who may be somewhat more conservative.

letter gadget. N. A three-dimensional article attached to or enclosed with direct-mail literature and used as a means of attracting attention and stimulating interest in the sales message.

letter of credit. N. An instrument or document issued on behalf of a buyer by a bank on another bank or banks or on itself. It gives the buyer the prestige and financial backing of the issuing bank. The acceptance by the bank of drafts drawn under the letter of credit satisfies the seller and the seller's bank in the handling of the transaction. The buyer and the accepting bank also have an agreement as to payment for the drafts as they are presented. ABBRV. *L/C*.

letter of indemnity. N. A document issued by a merchandise shipper to a steamship company as an inducement for the carrier to issue a clean bill of lading, where it might not otherwise do so; serves as a form of guarantee whereby the shipper agrees to settle a claim against the line by a holder of the bill of lading arising from the issuance of a clean bill.

level expenditure technique. N. A means of developing media advertising schedules where each segment of a campaign is treated equally.

leveling. N. A cognitive process in which the information retained becomes shorter and more concise.

leveraged creativity. N. Working a lesser creativity off the major creativity of others. A strategy of pioneering whereby the innovations are technically new and unique but considerably less significant than the original.

leveraged marketing. N. The process where companies making industrial items diversify into high-profit consumer goods by shifting the process to the needs of consumers; may be accomplished with minimal extra cost.

leveraging. N. The advantage (or disadvantage) obtained from using borrowed money to finance a business when the net interest rate of the borrowed funds is less (more) than the company's earnings rate.

levies. N. Varying duties applied to imports from another nation.

lexicographic model. N. Consumer attitude method that believes consumers assess products in some form of ranking order of acceptability; choices are then made based on top ratings.

liability. N. (1) An obligation an individual has by virtue of law, e.g., a debt or a responsibility. (2) In advertising, an amount owed by advertisers for space or purchased time.

liberal return policy. N. The practice of a store to accept goods returned for refund or exchange with a minimum of difficulty to the customer.

licensing. N. A business arrangement in which the manufacturer of a product (or a firm with proprietary rights over technology or trademarks) grants permission to a group or an individual to manufacture that product in return for specified royalties or other payments.

licensing agreement. N. Of importance to international marketers, the contracts between the exporter (a licensor) and an importer (a licensee) to make available to an importer some property of the exporter for a charge.

lien. N. A legal claim upon goods for the satisfaction of some debt or duty. See also *seller's lien, vendor's lien*.

life. N. In advertising, the length of time during which response may be felt from an insertion of an advertisement in a publication. When a message calling for an inquiry or an order is placed in a newspaper or magazine or other medium, requests are received soon after the appearance of the advertisement and continue for some time.

life cycle hypothesis. N. A theory of the saving decision stating that consumers save to be able to maintain a stable level of consumption in the future. See *marginal propensity to consume, marginal propensity to invest, marginal propensity to save*.

life cycle of product. N. The pattern of sales for an item as competition and new products evolve, bringing the item to its maturity, then decline, and eventual disappearance. The cycle time varies and is influenced by numerous variables; varies according to each product's progress through the stages of its life cycle. See also *saturation*.

life cycle purchasing. N. Where marketers promote consumer items to deemphasize acquisition cost as the major variable, and focus instead on four factors—acquisition, operating costs, servicing costs, and disposal.

lifestyle. N. The way in which a person lives and spends time and money. It is a function of the social and psychological factors that have been internalized by that person, as well as his or her demographic background.

lifestyle segmentation. N. Dividing a market into subunits based on the way the member of each group chooses to live, and a person's activities, interests, and opinions.

lifetime proceeds. N. Total profit or loss from a customer over the active life of the buyer's record. Synonymous with *lifetime value*.

lifetime value. N. See *lifetime proceeds*.

LIFO (last in-first out). N. In valuation of inventories, the system whereby the price shown on the last incoming shipment of a particular item is the one used for current valuations and cost. See also *next in, first out*.

lift. N. Material used in an advertisement that is taken from one advertisement and used in another, thus giving continuity, such as in a television soap opera.

lift letter. N. Letter inserted into a direct-mail promotional packet to encourage purchasing of the enclosed goods or services. Synonymous with *publisher letter*.

limen. N. See *subliminal advertising*.

limited assortment store. N. A convenience store carrying up to one thousand food items, usually private labels or packer labels. Usually the customer does his or her own packing of purchased items.

limited consumer decision making. N. Takes place when a person uses every step in the final consumer purchase process but does not spend a great deal of time on any of them. The person has previously bought a particular good or service, but makes some fresh decisions when that good or service comes under current purchase consideration.

limited distribution. N. See *selective distribution*.

limited-function wholesaler. N. See *limited service wholesaler*.

limited line stores. N. Smaller retail operations that carry most goods in a narrow line of items (e.g., a women's apparel shop that carries casual and formal ladies' garments, sportswear, and lingerie, but not baby clothes).

limited line strategy. N. The choice of a company to concentrate on only a small number of variations of an item. See also *broad-line strategy*.

limited-line wholesalers. N. See *specialty-merchandise wholesalers*.

limited marketing. N. A type of market testing that follows test marketing and precedes full-scale availability. Commitment has been made to full-scale marketing, but the marketing is tentative and based on limited geographic areas, specific firms, or specific applications.

limited order. N. An order in which the customer has set restrictions with respect to price.

limited service advertising agency. N. An advertising agency that specializes in a specific advertising function, i.e., having only copywriting services or art design services. See also *full-service agency, advertising agency*.

limited service wholesaler. N. A wholesale middleperson who takes title to merchandise he or she resells, but provides fewer services in an effort to lower costs. Synonymous with *limited-function wholesaler*. See also *jobber*.

limited time station. N. A broadcast station that is assigned a channel or frequency for broadcasting during a particular time period. At all other times, the channel or frequency is then shared by other stations, as found in numerous local television stations.

line. N. (1) In merchandising, the silhouette and description of any apparel style. (2) In retailing, items carried by a merchant. See also *product line*. (3) In advertising, a unit of space measure equal to one-fourteenth of a column inch.

linear programming. N. A means for indicating how materials should be combined to produce the highest profits, given a set of materials with specified characteristics and a set of prices for the finished product.

linear system. N. A marketing system adjunct to a plant. Should the merchandise not be correct for a market, they pile up at the factory.

line consistency. N. The lines of items closely related to each other as determined by usage and production requirements, or that are distributed through the same channel.

line extension. N. (1) A new variety of a basic product. (2) Adding of another variety of an item to an already established brand line of goods. See aslo *brand extension*.

line haul. N. The movement of cargo between cities and towns, as distinguished from pickup and delivery activities.

line of business. N. The general goods/service category, functions, geographic coverage, type of ownership, and specific business of a firm.

line positions. N. People, such as group marketing managers, who have the authority and responsibility to issue orders to the people who report to them, such as marketing managers.

line rate. N. The cost of advertising in a printed media based on a per-line basis.

line structure. N. The extension of a line of item by a manufacturer beyond the range currently produced.

linking phrase. N. In sales, the words that connect a feature with a benefit in a smooth, logical fashion. See also *objection*.

liquid assets. N. Assets that are easily converted into cash.

liquidity. N. The solvency of a business, with special reference to the speed with which assets can be converted into cash without loss.

list. N. (1) An ordered set of items. (2) In direct-mail advertising, the completed assembly of the names and addresses of people to whom an advertiser chooses to send his or her message. Synonymous with *mailing list*.

list broker. N. A commission agent who rents direct-mail lists to advertisers. A list broker also advises clients on which lists to rent and often evaluates list performance. See also *list supplier*.

list buyer. N. Direct markets that pay a fee for the one-time use of a mailing list.

listening area. N. The territory surrounding a radio or television station in which are to be found set-owning families who can hear the station satisfactorily or those families who actually listen to the station.

list house. N. An organization specializing in the sale of lists of names and addresses of individuals and firms of various business classifications used for circularization by direct-mail advertisers.

list manager. N. The person or organization responsible for marketing a list to list buyers. This manager places advertisements regarding lists in trade bulletins.

list marketing. N. See *list manager*.

list price. N. (1) The price of an item, subject to sale and cash discounts; any quoted price in excess of that obtained in the actual sale. Synonymous with *base price*. See also *phony list price*. (2) In retailing, the retail price suggested for fixed by the

local brand

manufacturer rather than the retailer. See also *fair trade price*, *unchanging list price*.

list supplier. N. The company that provides direct-mail advertisers with names and addresses of groups of people segmented by some common characteristic. See also *list broker*.

list trade. N. The major activity of direct marketing, the business of selling and purchasing lists.

list user. N. People who rent or use, frequently on a one-time basis, a list for promotional purposes.

live. N. In broadcasting, not prerecorded; said to be happening in "real time." See also *live time*.

live goods. N. Displayed items that are for sale that are in great demand.

live time. N. In broadcasting, time set aside for a live broadcast. See also *live*.

loader. N. A dealer offer tied to a single, volume purchase. A form of dealer premium.

load factor. N. The average number of passengers per automotive vehicles passing any outdoor advertising display.

loading. N. (1) The amount added to an installment agreement to cover selling and administrative overhead, interest, risk, and so on. (2) The addition of overhead to prime cost. See also *prime cost*.

local advertising. N. Advertising paid for by the retailer at a local rate. Often the advertisement suggests that the customer purchase the item "here." See also *retail advertising*.

local brand. N. A brand found in a limited geographic territory.

local broadcast. N. A program sent out by a local advertiser over a station within a community.

local channel station. N. A radio station operating by license of the Federal Communications Commission with a power of two hundred fifty watts or less with a coverage area that is limited because of interference from other stations in the vicinity.

local costs. N. Expenses incurred for goods or services purchased from suppliers in the buyer's country. The goods or services purchased must be needed to execute the exporter's contract or to complete the project of which the exporter's contract is a part.

local market. N. The area where the first steps are taken in assembling items from a number of farmers. Synonymous with *primary market*.

local media. N. Newspapers; magazines and periodicals; radio, television and cable stations that were established to service the communication needs of a particular community or urban area. Local advertisers are usually given a special discount rate to advertise in local media. See also *local rate*.

local plan. N. The media choice determined by an advertiser's limitation of sale of his or her products in one town and its immediate trading area.

local program. N. A broadcast program that originates from a local broadcast station, as contrasted with a network program.

local rate. N. (1) The advertising rate applied to regular advertisers in a newspaper as contrasted with transient rate. See also *local media, single-rate, one-time rate*. Synonymous with *retail rate*. (2) The transportation rate when a shipment is handled totally over the lines of a single carrier.

local wholesaler. N. A wholesaler who operates within a small circle from his or her operation, usually less than one hundred miles. See also *sectional wholesaler.*

location habit. N. The buyer's idea as to the type of marketing establishment he or she should use as a source of supply for certain goods.

logical appeal. N. An advertising strategy that purports to appeal to a consumer's sense of logic in promoting a product or service.

logistics. N. The science of planning, organizing, and arranging the most feasible combination of resources, areas, personnel, and time needed to carry out established objectives, policies, and procedures.

logistics manager. N. See *physical distribution manager.*

logo(type). N. Two or more letters, often making a short word, that represents the name or signature of an advertiser (e.g., NBC).

lollipop display. N. In outdoor advertising, a large round advertisement mounted onto a pole.

long-range plan. N. (1) A plan in which the organization's managers set goals for a period of more than one year. (2) In advertising, a systematic procedure for directing and controlling future activities of an advertising agency for periods longer than a year. It predicts the future and establishes a strategy of action and expected results.

long-run. N. An extensive time period that permits a firm to develop its capability to manufacture.

long-run planning capacity. N. The rate of activity needed to meet average sales demand over a period long enough to include seasonal and cyclical fluctuations.

long-term sales. N. Sales of goods and services on terms of five years or more.

looking glass self. N. Used by consumer psychologists, the way a person thinks he or she is perceived by other people.

loose market. N. See *buyers' market*.

loss leader. N. A retail merchandising strategy of advertising an item at a price below cost, to attract customers to the store in the expectation that they will purchase other items at full profit margins. See also *leader pricing, merchandising leader, pricing lining*.

low-baller. N. *(slang)* An executive who underestimated his or her expected financial situation.

low-ball price. N. The promotion, usually by telephone, of a product to lure the customer into the store, where the customer finds the salesperson unwilling to sell him or her the item at the previously announced price and attempts to pressure the customer to purchase a more expensive item.

lower-involvement model. N. Advertising media needing little or no active participation by consumers to receive the advertising message, such as radio and television.

low-involvement merchandise. N. Items that are bought routinely by the consumer without much thought, search, or purchase time. These people are usually indifferent to particular brands since there is minimal personal consequence to the purchase decision, nor does it relate to major objectives or values of the consumer. See also *high involvement*.

low-pressure selling. N. A strategy used by a relatively new salesperson where the potential buyer is lead to make the purchase by skillful questioning and apparent hesitation and reluctance on the part of the salesperson. Purports to give the customer the impression that he or she has been in full control of the situation throughout the conversation.

loyalty. N. See *brand loyalty*.

luxuries. N. Comforts and beauties of life that are in excess of what is needed for normal or standard living. See also *optional consumption*.

macroeconomics. N. The study of statistics (e.g., total consumption or total employment) of the economy as a whole, rather than as single economic units. Synonymous with *aggregate economics*. See also *microeconomics*.

macroenvironment. N. All external market forces that determine a firm's ability to sell its products and services. These include: (a) economic environment—economic forces that impact the consumer's ability and preparedness to buy items or services; (b) demographic environment—the examination of the population of target purchasers, with attention to their geographic dispersion, income levels and distribution; (c) social-cultural environment—those sociological variables that influence consumers' attitudes and behavior and that, consequently, impact demand patterns; (d) political-legal environment—monetary and fiscal factors, e.g., taxes, environmental legislation, or federal laws affecting advertising; (e) technological environment—new technologies that influence the market by altering the ways people use items and services, e.g., the introduction of VCRs and microwaves; and, (f) competitive environment—the process of evaluating competitors and the characteristics of their product and service offerings. See also *microenvironment, environmental analysis*.

macromarketing. N. (1) The study of the economic exchange process of a total economy. See also *micromarketing*. (2) Bringing about exchanges between individuals and/or groups so as to provide satisfaction of a society's wants and needs.

macrosales model. N. A way of illustrating the sales process by permitting sales to be presented by one variable consisting of units or dollars, and then examining this in relation to other pertinent variables. See also *microanalytic sales model*.

macrosegmentation. N. (1) Primarily used in industrial marketing where market potential is determined by studying broad segmentation variables, such as data from the U.S. Bureau of the Census. (2) A process in which an industrial market is divided into segments based on types of buying organizations.

MADA. ABBRV. Money, authority, desire, access.

Madison Avenue. N. A grouping of communications and advertising enterprises found along Madison Avenue in New York City. Today, many advertising firms have moved off of Madison Avenue and other major ones have moved out of New York City. The phrase is still used to refer to the advertising industry and its agencies.

magazine. N. A print publication, usually issued regularly, devoted to a specific category of editorial matter. The majority of the revenue generated comes from the sale of advertising space rather than from the sale of the magazine. Synonymous with *periodical*.

magazine coupons. N. Cents-off coupons printed within a magazine.

magazine group. N. Magazines are divided by their appeal to differing interest groups and are all published by one publisher, such as the magazines of Time, Inc., which publishes *Time, Life, People, Money, Fortune,* and *Sports Illustrated* magazines.

magazine impact technique. N. A means of recall testing to determine the communications effectiveness of periodical advertisements. With this method, respondents are asked to read the magazine and afterward describe the advertisements they recall from that issue.

magazine plan. N. A media strategy for placing advertisements solely in magazines within the target audience's area. For example, to reach people in the southwestern part of the United States, advertisers would primarily place advertisements in magazines that have a circulation in the southwest.

Magnuson-Moss Improvements Act of 1975. N. Federal legislation designed to broaden the powers of the Federal Trade Commission with respect to misleading packaging and the advertising of toys. Fines can result when violations are determined. See also *Magnuson-Moss Warranty Act of 1975*.

Magnuson-Moss Warranty Act of 1975. N. Federal legislation requiring that all consumer items distributed in interstate commerce and sold with a written warranty must have the warranty designated as "full" or "limited," as the only permitted designations. To be known as a "full warranty" it must promise to remedy any defect or malfunction within a given and reasonable time period, by refund or free repair or replacement with an equivalent or very similar product. The consumer need not do anything more than give notice of the defect or malfunction. See also *Magnuson-Moss Improvements Act of 1975*.

mail-ballot map. N. A form of coverage map prepared for a radio or television station showing the location of those areas in which set owners listen to the station with a specified degree of regularity.

mail date. N. See *drop*.

mailer. N. A business that uses the mail primarily as the source of contact with purchasers. See also *direct marketing*.

mail-in. N. A premium provided that is requested by mail, sometimes found free for boxtops or labels.

mailing list. N. See *list (2)*.

mail-in premium. N. A gift given as a special promotion by a manufacturer in exchange for appropriate representation of purchase of his or her goods that is mailed to the manufacturer.

mail interview. N. A survey technique in which questionnaires are mailed to potential respondents.

mail key. N. See *key code*.

mail-order. N. Direct marketing activities use the mail as its primary means for promoting and delivery goods and services, and to communicate with customers. Mail order is different from other forms of direct marketing in that the purchaser and seller do not have any direct contact with each other. See also *mail-order advertising*.

mail-order advertising. N. Advertising designed to yield orders directly from prospects by mail. Media of any form can be used to deliver the advertising message. Its primary characteristic is that there is no interaction between the consumer and the advertiser and that, except for telephones, the only other means of interaction between the two parties is via mail.

mail-order house. N. A commercial organization that receives its orders and makes its sales by mail. Some types of retail stores often conduct a mail-order business, usually through departments set up for that purpose, but this does not make them mail-order houses.

mail-order retailer. N. A reseller that enters and fulfills customer orders through the mail.

mail-order wholesaler. N. An individual who sells by mail and usually advertises goods and services in a catalog.

mail-survey map. N. A geographic map prepared by a radio or television station for the purpose of plotting the location of those areas in which the station may claim a listening audience.

main store. N. See *parent store*.

maintained mark-on. N. The difference between the cost for delivering goods and the price at which they are sold.

maintenance and repair services. N. Industrial services that include painting, machinery repair, and janitorial services.

maintenance, repair, and operating supply items. N. Consumable supplies used in the production of goods and services. ABBRV. *MRO*.

maintenance marketing. N. The monitoring of the market for shifts in customer demand.

major account. N. A firm's customers that are critical and therefore require special treatment and attention. Usually, such accounts are dealt with by senior personnel. Synonymous with *key account*.

major account marketing. N. See *national account marketing*.

major appliances. N. Large in size and price, electrical housewares, such as refrigerators, freezers, television sets, etc.

major innovation. N. An item that has never been sold by any other organization.

majority fallacy. N. The belief that the trust of a promotion is pitched to the majority of the market. See also *segmentation*.

major media. N. The principal advertising media—newspapers, television, posters, radio, and movies.

make bulk. N. In international marketing, the process of placing together large shipments from multiple or smaller shipments to take advantage of large-volume discounts from carriers.

make bulk center. N. See *freight forwarder*.

make good. V. (1) To discharge an obligation or debt. (2) In advertising, to repeat a message without additional charge or to refund space or time charges as compensation for an error or omission of an advertisement. Most of the time this credit given is in the form of a rerun of the advertisement, subject to negotiation between the advertiser and the medium. (3) In broadcasting, an offer in the form of an extra run of a commercial when the medium did not deliver the anticipated audience volume or composition promised for a previously contracted commercial. Also given when transmission is poor because of a failing on the part of the broadcasting firm, or should the commercial be run at a time not originally accepted by both parties.

make-or-buy decision. N. A firm's decision of whether to produce an item itself or purchase it elsewhere.

maker. N. (1) A manufacturer, processor, or producer of merchandise or products. (2) An individual, firm, or other legal entity that signs a note, check, or other negotiable form as a responsible party.

makers and shakers. N. *(slang)* Those who are in power.

make the cash. V. To decide whether the funds on hand, following receipts and payments, balance with the record of sales and payments of obligations.

make-up. N. The appearance of a page of the newspaper.

make-up restriction. N. A limitation imposed by a publication on the size and layout of an advertisement, to assure that the publication will not end up with an unusually shaped space on its pages, which tends to be unsuitable for editorial copy as well as being unsalable. See also *bad advertising space*.

mala fides. N. *(Latin)* Bad faith.

malfeasance. N. A wrongdoing; a criminal act. See also *misfeasance*.

mall

mall. N. (1) A shopping center of a few or numerous blocks closed off to car traffic. (2) A public promenade or concourse open only to pedestrian traffic. Synonymous with *plaza shopping mall*.

mall intercept interview. N. An interview conducted by a researcher in a shopping mall. The interviewer randomly chooses people walking around the mall, thus introducing a potential bias in how they are chosen.

managed obsolescence. N. See *planned obsolescence*.

managed trade. N. (1) Of concern to international marketers, where goods entering borders are primarily determined by the political and economic weight of more dominant economic nations, with others left very much on the margins. (2) Any international commercial transactions that are impacted by nonmarket factors such as nontrade measures and quantitative restrictions. See also *free trade*.

management. N. (1) The individual or group of individuals responsible for studying, analyzing, formulating decisions, and initiating appropriate actions for the benefit of an organization. (2) In advertising, the functions of planning, coordinating, and directing the activities of an advertising agency.

management by crisis. N. A leadership style that attempts to deal with shortcomings and failures by waiting until things get so bad that people will accept drastic measures. It is usually destructive and fails to attain stated organizational goals of marketing and advertising agencies.

management by exception. N. The practice by an advertising executive of focusing attention primarily on significant deviations from expected results. See also *variance (3)*.

management by objectives. N. A process whereby superiors and those who report to them jointly establish marketing or advertising objectives over a specified time frame, meeting periodically to evaluate their progress in meeting these goals. ABBRV. *MBO*.

management consulting. N. The service performed, for a fee, by independent and objective professionals, or by an organization, to assist managers in analyzing management problems, to recommend practical solutions, and, at times, to help in the implementation of the recommendations.

management functions. N. The basic activities required of advertising and marketing managers in the performance of their jobs. The major management functions are planning and decision making, organizing for effective performance, leading and motivating, and controlling performance.

management information system. N. A specific data-processing system that is designed to furnish management and supervisory personnel with current information in real time. In the communication process, data are recorded and processed for operational purposes. The problems are isolated for referral to upper management for higher-level decision making, and information is fed back to top management to reflect the progress in achieving major objectives. See also *marketing information system*. ABBRV. *MIS*.

management of demand. N. Includes stimulation, facilitation, and regulation tasks.

management science. N. Used by market researchers, the formulation of mathematical and statistical models applied to decision making and the practical application of these models through the use of digital computers.

managerial marketing. N. Marketing carried out in large firms. Involves planning, setting goals, developing strategies to achieve goals, etc.

Manchester Man. N. See *bagman*.

mandatory copy. N. The copy as required by law that appears in the advertisement or on a product's label, such as, "Warning: the Surgeon General has determined that cigarette smoking is dangerous to your health."

manifest. N. A statement itemizing the contents, value, point of origin, destination, and so on, of cargo that is shipped.

manit. N. One man-minute of production.

manpower planning. N. Used by consumer researchers; a forecast of the future manpower requirements of an organization and the establishment of a plan to meet these needs.

manufacturability. N. The extent to which a new product concept or prototype is figured to be capable of effective and efficient manufacturing by available resources; also used during the design process, particularly when using computer-aided design. See also *deliverability*.

manufacture. V. To produce, make, or fabricate something, by hand or using equipment.

manufacturers. N. Products for resale to other consumers.

manufacturer's agent. N. An agent (wholesale or middleperson) who takes neither title to nor possession of the merchandise he or she sells. The agent represents several noncompeting producers of goods that are purchased by one type of trade (e.g., a manufacturer's agent in women's apparel might sell dresses, blouses, belts, coats, stockings, and so on, for different manufacturers). Synonymous with *manufacturer's representative*.

manufacturer's brand. N. (1) Items licensed for sale by other firms outside the manufacturer's product category. For example, a clothing manufacturer licenses its name to a firm who use the name on jewelry. See also *brand*. (2) A brand name owned by

manufacturer's/service provider's sales office

the item's maker (e.g., Hershey's Chocolate Kisses). The primary goal of having such a brand is to attract people loyal to the manufacturer's name. Synonymous with *national brand*.

manufacturer's cooperative advertising. N. See *cooperative advertising*.

manufacturer/service provider wholesaling. N. Occurs when a producer undertakes all wholesaling functions itself. It may be carried out via sales offices and/or branch offices.

manufacturer's representative. N. See *manufacturer's agent, sales representative*.

manufacturer's sales branch. N. An operation owned and controlled by a manufacturer separate from his or her factories out of which his or her salespeople may work, and that contains stocks from which deliveries can be made to customers. See also *manufacturer's sales office*.

manufacturer's sales office. N. Similar to a manufacturer's sales branch, except no stock is housed within the office.

manufacturers'/service providers' agents. N. Agents who work for several manufacturers/service providers and carry noncompetitive, complementary products in exclusive territories. A manufacturer/service provider may employ many agents, each with a unique product-territorial mix.

manufacturer's/service provider's branch office. N. A form of manufacturer/service provider wholesaling. It includes facilities for warehousing goods, as well as for selling them.

manufacturer's/service provider's sales office. N. A form of manufacturer/service provider wholesaler. It is located at a company's production facilities or a site close to the market, and no inventory is carried there.

manufacturing. N. Converting raw materials into a completed product by a mechanical, electrical, or chemical (i.e., not manual) process. See also *production*.

manufacturing costs. N. Costs incurred in the manufacturing process to bring a product to completion, including direct materials, direct labor, and manufacturing overhead costs.

manufacturing-driven firm. N. A company that gives major emphasis on manufacturing requirements in lieu of marketing considerations. Special attention is given to smooth production scheduling, low costs of production, and high volume. See also *marketing-driven firm*.

manufacturing inventory. N. A general term covering all items of inventory for a manufacturing entity. Items included are usually raw materials, work in process, and completed goods.

manufacturing order. N. Instructions for directing production.

manufacturing overhead. N. All expenses arising from manufacturing activities except those of labor and materials.

margin. N. (1) The difference between the market value of collateral pledged to secure a loan and the face value of the loan itself. See also *gross margin*, *markup*. (2) The difference between the cost of sold items and the total net sales income.

marginal analysis. N. Analysis of economic information by examining the results of the value added when one variable is increased by a single unit of another variable. See also *direct costing*.

marginal borrower. N. A borrower who will reject an opportunity to borrow if the interest charge is increased.

marginal buyer. N. A buyer who will refuse to buy if the price is increased.

marginal cost. N. Increase in the total cost of production that results from manufacturing one more unit of output.

marginal cost pricing. N. The rule enforced by competitive markets that price should be equal to the cost of producing the final (marginal) unit.

marginal customer. N. A purchaser judged by the seller to be at the edge between providing a profit large enough to be continued as a customer by the seller and a profit so small that he or she may be dropped as a customer.

marginal producer. N. A producer who is just able to meet his or her costs of production, with little actual profit.

marginal product. N. The additional product derived by increasing a given factor of production by one further unit.

marginal profits. N. The increase in total profits that is obtained by producing an additional unit of output.

marginal propensity to consume. N. The percentage of increases in income that is spent for consumption purposes. See also *life cycle hypothesis*. ABBRV. *MPC*.

marginal propensity to invest. N. The percentage of increases in sales that is spent on investment items. See also *liquidity, quantity demanded, accelerator, life cycle hypothesis*. ABBRV. *MPI*.

marginal propensity to save. N. The percentage of increases in income that individuals save. See also *life cycle hypothesis, multiplier principle*. ABBRV. *MPS*.

marginal rate of factor substitution. N. The number of units of one factor of manufacturing needed to replace a unit of another factor of manufacturing to maintain the same level of output. See also *law of diminishing rate of factor substitution*.

marginal return. N. The amount of sales of goods that are generated by an increment in the cost of advertising.

marginal revenue. N. The added revenue a business receives from the sale of one additional unit. In the short run, under conditions of competition, this is the same as the market price.

marginal seller. N. A seller who refuses to sell if the price is lowered. See also *upset price*.

marginal utility. N. The increase in satisfaction one receives from adding or consuming one more unit of an item.

marginal worker. N. A worker value whose production equals his or her actual wage.

margin of preference. N. The difference between the duty that would be paid under a system of preferences and the duty payable on a most favored nation basis.

margin of profit. N. Operating income divided by sales. Income taxes are usually excluded and depreciation is usually included in the operating expenses.

margin of safety. N. (1) The balance of income left after payment of fixed charges. (2) In sales, the amount by which sales exceeds the break-even point, thus providing a cushion against a drop in sales or other unforeseeable forces. See also *break-even point*.

mark. N. See *trademark*.

markdown. N. A reduction of an originally established selling price; popular with domestic goods sold in overseas markets where incomes tend to be lower, where wholesalers require a large piece of the revenue, and/or where surplus items are discarded. See also *clearance, markup*.

markdown cancellation. N. The increase in the retail price of an item that has been reduced. The increase can be up to the retail price at which the item was originally placed for sale, but not higher. See also *retail method of inventory*.

market. N. (1) People who possess the ability and desire to purchase, or prospects for a product or service. See also *marketplace*. (2) In marketing, a geographical area that includes a significant number of potential customers. (3) In marketing, an estimated or realized demand for an item or service.

marketability. N. The rapidity and ease with which a given asset can be converted into cash. See also *liquid*.

marketable. N. That which can be sold.

market access. N. (1) The degree of difficulty of admittance to an overseas market by an exporting nation. (2) The ability of a domestic industry to penetrate a related market in a foreign country. The extent to which the foreign market is accessible generally depends on the existence and extent of trade barriers.

market aggregation. N. See *undifferentiated marketing*.

market analysis. N. An aspect of market research involving the measurement of the extent of a market and determination of its characteristics. See also *Delphi technique*.

market anticipation. N. Determination of how consumers will react in the marketplace at a given time.

market appeal. N. The attractiveness of a market based on its size or annual rate at which it is growing. This appeal is influenced by economic and technological forces, to competitive variables and to environmental considerations.

market atomization. N. A marketing strategy that treats each individual consumer as a unique market segment.

market attractiveness. N. See *market appeal*.

market audit. N. A method for studying the marketing activities and structure of a business. It is designed primarily to identify areas in which improvements are necessary to boost profits.

market-based groupings. N. Organizational groupings that assign responsibility for a specific type of customer to a unit.

market basket pricing. N. Setting a situation where the sale of one item encourages a buyer to purchase other items. Specials and tie-in sales are often used.

market beliefs. N. The specific beliefs or decision rules pertaining to marketplace phenomena.

market breakdown technique. N. A forecasting technique in which the sales forecast for a large unit is broken down into forecasts for smaller units.

market build-up technique. N. A forecasting method where data from a number of market segments is collected, analyzed separately, and then added together to yield a picture of the marketing environment for the purpose of sales forecasting.

market-by-market allocation. N. See *area-by-area allocation*.

market-by-market buy. N. A technique of buying commercial time on broadcast stations, where the time is purchased in one market at a time, as contrasted to a network purchase, where the time is purchased all at once on all the stations that are affiliated with the network throughout the nation or region. See also *network buy*.

market channel. N. The path of the direct or indirect transfer of ownership to a product as it goes from a manufacturer to industrial or retail customers.

marketcide. N. Self-inflicted and avoidable harm caused to an organization due to a lack of attention to and poor implementation of marketing concepts and principles.

market cleavage. N. See *segmentation*.

market concentration. N. (1) A form of market segmentation where the firm's efforts are concentrated on one segment of the potential population. (2) That portion of an item's sales volume that is determined by a small number of large firms, expressed in dollars, units sold, etc.

market controlled price environment. N. Characterized by a high level of competition, similar goods and services, and little control over price by individual companies.

market coverage. N. The measure of the degree of market exposure achieved. It is the total product sales of all the producer's retail customers expressed as a percentage of all retail sales for the product group or classification. The strategies used in determining what types of item to offer to which parts of a market include: (a) single market strategy, where the firm concentrates on one segment of the market only; (b) production specialization strategy, where the firm chooses to manufacture one item for all segments of the market; (c) market specialization strategy, where the firm develops all items for a particular market segment; (d) selective specialization, where the firm develops different merchandise for different market niches; and, (e) full coverage, where the firm makes different items for each individual customer (a rare approach).

market delineation. N. Determining who will be the customers and prospects for a product and what are their particular characteristics. See also *market segmentation*.

market demand. N. The total amount of an item that is wanted at a specified price at a specific time. Market demand is measured by: (a) product levels, determined by product type, form, sales (national, industry wide, etc); (b) space levels, determined by territory (region, nation, global); and, (c) time levels, determined by whether it is for a short, medium, or long-term period. See also *overall market capability*, *potential demand*, *total market potential*.

market demography. N. Demographics applied to a particular market. See also *demographics*.

market development. N. An approach where a firm develops new markets for its merchandise or services where the firm creates alternate uses for the same items with the hope that it will yield increased sales.

market disruption. N. Difficulties in a domestic market as a result of a sudden increase in imports into that market.

market driven economy. N. An economic system in which supply, demand, and price determine what products will be produced and who will receive those products. See also *dual drive*.

market-driven firm. N. See *marketing-driven firm*.

market entry. N. Effort to sell a new or existing product to a group of consumers not previously targeted by a marketer.

marketer. N. Those involved in the activity of attempting to sell something to someone.

market factor. N. A variable within the environment that can determine the call for a product or service.

market failure. N. A condition under which markets do not allocate resources efficiently, usually because of ignorance or externalities. See also *externalities*.

market fit. N. The likelihood that a new item will be purchased by the same people who buy a firm's other goods. See also *test marketing*.

market forecast. N. The level of market demand given an expected level of industry marketing effort and an assumed environment.

market growth rate. N. The yearly increase or decrease of a market, either presently or in the future; usually expressed as a percentage.

marketing. N. Activities that accelerate the movement of goods or services from the manufacturer to the consumer, including everything connected with advertising, distribution, merchandising, product planning, promotion, publicity, research and development, sales, transportation, and warehousing of goods or services. See also *merchandising, administered marketing, brand marketing, cause related marketing, comparative marketing, concentrated marketing, convergent marketing, conversional marketing, custom marketing, data base marketing, dimensional marketing, electronic direct marketing, electronic marketing, events marketing, global marketing, health care marketing, key account marketing, leveraged marketing, limited marketing, major account marketing, managerial marketing, mass marketing, metamarketing, mismarketing, multinational marketing, national account marketing, Pan-European marketing, pilot marketing, political marketing, pooled marketing, preemptive marketing, premarketing, retail marketing, service marketing, social marketing, societal marketing, sports marketing, stimulation marketing, symbiotic marketing, target marketing, telemarketing, undifferentiated marketing, value marketing*.

marketing audit. N. A careful study of the marketing system within a company to determine the value of the system's parts and how well the parts are performing their given tasks. To be successful,

marketing boards

these audits should be comprehensive (examining all critical components of the marketing program) and systematic (including appropriate diagnostic steps that deal with the marketing environment, resources, and existing marketing initiatives).

marketing boards. N. Agencies established to monopolize the sale of specified products, especially agricultural commodities. Marketing boards are similar to labor unions in that they organize large numbers of small producers to negotiate with a small number of purchasers.

marketing budget. N. A financial plan, based on projected sales of merchandise or services, that is used for allocating funds to cover marketing costs over a time period.

marketing channel. N. See *channel of distribution*.

marketing communications mix. N. Efforts to communicate product information to existing and future customers.

marketing company era. N. Recognition of the central role of marketing. The marketing department becomes the equal of others in the company. Company efforts are well-integrated and frequently re-evaluated.

marketing concept. N. (1) A strategy or idea for marketing products or services. (2) A business philosophy consisting of the notions that marketing strategy should be developed based on customer needs and desires and that all marketing functions should be structured within the firm, with one person having overall responsibility. See also *consumer behavior research, marketing management, market research*. Synonymous with *marketing philosophy*.

marketing control chart. N. A chart that combines trend analysis with the performance standards set by the organization.

marketing cost analysis. N. Examination of the costs incurred from the time items are produced to final delivery and payment, with a view toward providing useful quantitative financial data for the marketing firm.

marketing decision support system. N. A coordinated collection of data, models, analytic tools, and computing power by which an organization gathers information from the environment and turns it into a basis for action.

marketing department era. N. A stage during which the marketing department participated in company decisions but remains in a subordinate or conflicting position to the production, engineering, and sales departments.

marketing director. N. The individual who is responsible for overseeing all marketing activities.

marketing-dominated strategy. N. A focus of key managers on managing the consumer.

marketing-driven firm. N. A company that places its major effort in satisfying customers, such as shifting production schedules to accommodate customers' requirements, even if it incurs a loss to the manufacturer. See also *manufacturing-driven firm*.

marketing dynamics. N. Usually within the control of management, shifts in the marketing mix determined by changes in the external environment.

marketing environment. N. Contains controllable factors, uncontrollable factors, the organization's level of success or failure in reaching its objectives, feedback, and adaptation.

marketing ethics. N. The values and moral principles that should govern the marketer's behavior in the marketplace.

marketing function. N. An activity such as buying, selling, shipping, warehousing, grading and standardization, financing, assuming responsibility for taking the risk, or data accumulation.

marketing information. N. A marketing function characterized by the accumulation and dissemination of intelligence concerning market developments and other market information. See also *marketing research*.

marketing information system. N. The entire system employed by a firm to gather, analyze, store, and disseminate relevant marketing information to those who require these data. See also *marketing intelligence, management information system*. ABBRV. *MIS*.

marketing institutions. N. Includes manufacturers and producers, wholesalers, retailers, transporting firms, advertising agencies, etc.

marketing intelligence. N. The part of the marketing information system that includes the procedures a company routinely uses to keep abreast of developments in the external environment. See also *marketing information system*.

marketing management. N. The planning, directing, and controlling of the total marketing operation, including formulation of marketing goals, policies, programs, and strategy, and often embracing product development, organizing and staffing to discharge plans, supervising marketing operations, and monitoring performance. See also *product manager*.

marketing-manager system. N. A product management organizational format under which a company executive is directly responsible for overseeing a wide range of marketing functions and for coordinating with other departments that perform marketing-related activities.

marketingmanship. N. The measure of skill in marketing a product or service.

marketing mix. N. (1) The concept of Neil Borden that market strategy is based on the product, price, promotion, and channels in an integrated marketing program. (2) The combination of activities involving product, price, place, and promotion that a firm undertakes in order to provide satisfaction to consumers in a given market. See also *four Os, four Ps*.

marketing myopia. N. A short-sighted, narrow approach to the marketplace. For example, when the firm fails to emphasize the assets or services inherent in an item's design, and instead emphasizes only the product's physical attributes.

marketing objectives. N. More customer-oriented than the overall goals set by top management.

marketing opportunity analysis. N. A study of the marketing environment to determine what shifts may occur and when problems might develop. Important in setting strategies in dealing with competitors.

marketing organization. N. The organization of the marketing function by either: (a) functional units, where individual marketing functions are headed by managers; (b) product management units, where distinctive items are assigned to product managers who oversee the activities of functional specialists; (c) marketing management units, where major are assigned to marketing managers who supervise the activities of functional specialists; or, (d) division units, where a diversified firm has division marketing departments led by managers who report to a central corporate marketing department.

marketing orientation. N. When an organization focuses its efforts on (a) continuously collecting information about customers'

marketing performers

needs and competitors' capabilities; (b) sharing this information across departments; and, (c) using the information to create customer value.

marketing performers. N. Includes manufacturers and service providers, wholesalers, retailers, marketing specialists, and organizational and final consumers.

marketing philosophy. N. See *marketing concept*.

marketing plan. N. A carefully designed outline providing the firm's self-image, its objectives, all marketing programs to fulfill goals, and the means for assessing the effectiveness of such efforts. Also indicates responsibilities for discharging the plan, the strategies involved in the suggested development of the items, the definition of its target market(s), and the types of media and sales promotions to be incorporated. Synonymous with *action program*, *marketing strategy*.

marketing program. N. The coordination of the features of the marketing mix for a firm as a whole in reaching an objective.

marketing relativism. N. In international marketing, where decisions are based on experiences in selling people of differing backgrounds, traditions, and cultures. Synonymous with *principle of marketing relativism*.

marketing research. N. (1) A systematic, objective approach to the development and provision of information for decision making regarding a specific marketing problem. Its results provides facts required to make marketing decisions and will determine the extent and location of the market for a product or service. (2) The process of gathering, recording, and analyzing information pertaining to the marketing of goods and services. See also *market research*.

marketing risks. N. Possible losses of the marketer, including waste, obsolescence, damage, physical deterioration, stealing of items, credit, discontinuity of supply, shifts in demand affecting pricing, and acts of God. See also *risk*.

marketing strategy. N. See *marketing plan*.

marketing tactics. N. The detailed day-to-day operational decisions essential to the overall success of marketing strategies.

market leader. N. The firm that controls the market share of products or services.

market level analysis. N. Measurement of the degree to which a product or service has penetrated the market.

market-mapping inquiry. N. A study for identifying consumer attitudes, product comparisons, or marketing evaluations, where results are charted on a graph to show a correspondence among variables.

market maven. N. A person who often serves as a source of information about marketplace activities.

market minimum. N. The rate of sales for an item or service that would be accomplished without any demand-stimulating costs such as promotional campaigns or advertisements.

market-minus prices. N. Trying to price similar items for less than the competition. See also *at-the-market prices*, *market-plus pricing*, *variable pricing*. Synonymous with *demand-backward prices*.

market modification. N. Attempts to increase product usage by creating new-use situations or finding new customers.

market news. N. Information regarding the condition of the marketplace.

market niche. N. Usually a strategy of small firms; a narrow market segment that a firm targets because the segment lacks competitors yet offers a sizeable sales potential. See also *niche marketing*.

market order. N. An order to buy or sell something at the price prevailing when the order reaches the market.

market-oriented production. N. Production of a product or products in a foreign country that uses the product.

market outline. N. A summary of the relative place of a type of brand or item in the total market. See also *positioning, market structure analysis*.

market penetration. N. (1) The degree to which a product captures a percentage of the total market for that item. This includes the absence of competition for the item. (2) A marketing strategy of the manufacturer to increase his or her sales within an existing market through using more aggressive marketing methods, such as greater concentration of commercial advertising or special promotional methods. See also *penetration strategies*.

market period. N. The period from when an item is made until the moment it has been purchased.

marketplace. N. A general term identifying business and trade activities. See also *market*.

market planning. N. The process of identifying a firm's potential customers and their needs. Impacts the entire promotional campaign. See also *planning*.

market-plus pricing. N. The price at which an item is exchanged in the market from day to day. Synonymous with *above the market strategy*.

market-position analysis. N. See *attribute mapping*.

market-positioned warehouse. N. A storage facility where merchandise is kept that is owned by the manufacturer, distributor, or retailer and is used to consolidate shipments and position items near their ultimate destinations.

market positioning. N. See *positioning*.

market potential. N. The maximum sales potential for all sellers of a product or service over a fixed period. See also *sales potential*.

market power. N. The ability of a purchaser or seller to control price and quantity of an item.

market presence. N. In advertising, being present in the marketplace; having a reputation or identity with competitors or consumers.

market price. N. (1) The price established in the market where buyers and sellers meet to buy and sell similar products. (2) A price determined by factors of supply and demand rather than by management decisions.

market-product grid. N. Framework for relating market segments to products offered or potential marketing actions by a firm.

market profile. N. (1) A description of the characteristics of a market or market component. (2) Data about potential customers or an analysis by individual background (sex, age, etc.) of people who make up the market for a particular item or service. See also *market segmentation, market target, market structure analysis*.

market rate. N. The interest rate charged by a firm in order to borrow funds.

market ratio. N. The strength of one item or service to command another in exchange for itself in the open market.

market redefinition. N. Changes in the offering demanded by buyers or promoted by competitors.

market representative. N. The executive of a firm's buying office who gives his or her time and effort to a particular grouping of goods and makes data about it available to buyers of owned or operated stores.

market research. N. The part of marketing research that deals with the pattern of a market, measuring the extent and nature of the market and identifying its characteristics. Market research precedes marketing research. See also *product planning, concept testing, marketing research.*

market review. N. See *situational analysis.*

market sales potential. N. The maximum level of sales that might be available to all organizations serving a defined market in a specific time period given the marketing-mix activities and efforts of all organizations, and a set of environmental conditions.

market segment. N. A subdivision of the population, the people sharing similar characteristics. The firm often develops different marketing programs for each segment of its target market. See also *market segmentation.*

market segmentation. N. Separating the market for an item into categories of location, personality, or other characteristics for each division; evolves as a result of the observations that all potential users of goods or services are different and that the same general appeal will not appeal to all prospects. Once the market has been segmented by a firm, it then engages in one of the following marketing strategies: differentiated marketing, undifferentiated marketing, or concentrated marketing. See also *market profile, market target, segment, segmentation, subculture, whole market approach, zoning price, market segment.*

market share. N. (1) A firm's percentage of its industry's total sales. (2) The total number of units of a product (or their dollar value) expressed as a percentage of the total number of units sold by all competitors in a given market. Synonymous with *brand share, share of market*.

market share analysis. N. A forecasting technique in which it is assumed that the firm's market share will remain constant and sales forecasts for the firm are based on forecasts for the industry.

market share goal. N. A benchmark representing that portion of a market a firm wishes to capture.

market size. N. The total demand for a given item or service in terms of the volume or value of that demand.

market skimming. N. An introductory pricing strategy of charging a high price in order to recover investment quickly.

market strategy. N. A marketing approach designed to enable a product to fulfill the objectives set for it by management. See also *strategy*.

market stretching. N. A competitive strategy involving narrow segmentation where competitors aim on a wide basis, or the simplification where a market has been unduly fragmented.

market structure analysis. N. The study of competitive product offerings and buyer product preferences that account for the design features of items and the item preference characteristics of purchaser/consumer segments. See also *market outline*.

market-structured sales force. N. A sales force structure where sellers specialize in particular market segments, and where individual sales forces are created for different industries or for major customers within those industries. See also *product-structured sales force, sales force*.

market target. N. The people or groups for whom an item and its program or marketing are intended. A strategy and a meaningful approach to fulfilling a stated goal must be established with respect to a market target. See also *market profile, positioning, target audience.*

market temper. N. A consumer's attitude of his or her future.

market termination stage. N. See *decline stage.*

market testing. N. A marketing method where the new item or service, once introduced, is tested to predict its success in the marketplace. Also permits the firm to adjust production schedules. See also *product testing, test marketing.*

market value. N. The prevailing price at which a product can be expected to sell within a given market.

marking. N. Placing the correct tag on new goods, usually containing price, size, and style data. See also *Kimball tags.*

marking duties. N. A special duty, in addition to ordinary duties, imposed on merchandise not properly marked so as to indicate to the ultimate purchaser the country of origin.

mark-on. N. The difference between the billed-cost price and the original retail price of an item. See also *initial mark-on.*

Markov chain. N. Used by market analysts, a probabilistic model of events in which the probability of an event is dependent only on the event that precedes it. See also *Monte Carlo method.*

marks of origin. N. In overseas sales, the physical markings on a product that indicate where the article was produced. Most countries have customs rules requiring marks of origin.

markup. v. To increase the value of assets to show an improvement in their market value. N. An increase, in dollars or percentage, between cost and selling price. See also *variable markup policy*.

mass appeal. N. Nondirect marketing method purporting to appeal to all possible users of an item or service; best to be used when the item or service crosses all demographic and psychographic boundaries.

mass communication. N. The delivery of quantities of identical messages at the same time by communication firms or media.

massed promotion. N. Communication concentrated in peak periods, like holidays.

mass magazine. N. A magazine, e.g., *Reader's Digest*, that is not designed for or targeted at a particular readership, but instead has an editorial structure of a general nature and appeals to a diversified readership.

mass marketing. N. The approach used to sell large volumes of items to everyone. This usually requires distribution in discount stores and supermarkets.

mass medium. N. An advertising medium used and accepted by a significant portion of the population.

mass merchandiser. N. To be an outlet with a discount image and following, it requires the handling of at least three merchandise lines within a floor space of ten thousand or greater square feet.

mass production. N. The utilization of mechanization to produce a large quantity of standardized items. Synonymous with *large-scale production*.

mass promotion. N. Sales promotion activities concentrated at a specific time, for example, the summer season.

master contract. N. See *blanket contract*.

master schedule. N. A schedule in production control that applies only to a completed product and its major elements.

matchbook cover. N. A protective covering on a book of paper matches where advertising is found; printed on the outside or inside cover and distributed locally or nationally.

matched sample. N. A sample group for test purposes that is the same as another group in terms of demographics, size, and psychographics. Matched samples are primarily employed to reinforce results, or test variations of an item or communications.

material budget. N. A forecast of how much material will be necessary to achieve a result.

material cost. N. The cost of an item that is a direct result of the cost of raw material and does not include indirect expenses such as wages and overhead.

materialism. N. The importance consumers attach to worldly possessions.

material management. N. The material-handling functions as they relate to the physical distribution chain.

materials controller. N. An individual responsible for the physical movement of materials and goods. Synonymous with *stock-room supervisor*, *tool-crib supervisor*.

materials handling. N. The physical movement of materials and products within a work facility.

materials requisition form. N. A document used to request raw materials from the storeroom.

matrix. N. (1) A device for problem-solving by placing data in rows and columns for statistical analysis; used by market researchers in interpreting information. (2) An enclosure that gives form to what lies in it.

mature economy. N. The condition of a nation's economy with a declining rate of population growth and a decrease in the proportion of national income utilized for new capital investment, accompanied by a relative increase of national income used in purchasing consumer goods.

mature households. N. Households headed by people over age 50.

maturity date. N. The date on which a financial obligation becomes due for payment or the date an obligation or contract expires.

maturity stage. N. The beginning of the demise of a product. The product's life cycle conclusion is measured by the leveling off of demand, a decline in profit, and increasing competition. Small and financially insecure institutions tend to drop out of the market in the maturity stage.

maximax criterion. N. A basis for decision making with an advertising agency whereby a manager determines the greatest payoff for each possible strategy and then chooses the one that is most favorable, thus maximizing the maximum gain. See also *maximin criterion*.

maximil rate. N. The cost of a line of newspaper space that reaches a circulation of one million, based on the highest possible rate chargeable to an advertiser by the publisher.

maximin criterion. N. A basis for decision making with an advertising agency whereby a manager determines the most negative payoff for each possible strategy and then chooses the one that

maximizing 398

is most favorable, thus maximizing the minimum gain. See also *maximax criterion*.

maximizing. N. Decision-making behavior in which an advertising agency manager selects the best alternative from all possible alternatives.

maximum depth requirement. N. The maximum height or depth a print advertisement must be to claim a fractional column rate, instead of being charged for a full-column rate.

maximum distribution. N. The number, usually given as a percentage, of outlets that have stocked the item at any time since an earlier retail audit.

MBO. ABBRV. Management by objectives.

McGuire Act. N. See *Miller-Tydings Resale Price Maintenance Act of 1937*.

mean. N. (1) Any statistical measure of central tendency. See also *median, mode*. (2) The sum of all the numbers in a set of scores divided by the number of scores. The mean is a sound representation of quantitative data, for example, the mean number of items bought per catalog order; used in statistical work by market and consumer researchers.

measure of value. N. A function of money that gives the standard for identifying the results of production, using the monetary unit as the common denominator.

measures of central tendency. N. See *average, mean, median, mode*.

mechanical recorder technique. N. A way of measuring broadcast audience size by program using equipment attached to the set with the owner's permission. It automatically records when the set is placed on, to which station, and for how long.

media. N. (1) The means used by transmitters of messages to deliver them to the intended receivers in a communication system. The single form of communication is called medium. (2) In advertising, newspapers, radio, television, magazines, billboards, direct mail, and other such institutions that are used to carry advertisements. The four categories of media are: print media, broadcast media, out-of-home media, and direct-mail media. See also *advertising media, alternative media*.

media analysis. N. The study and evaluation of various media approaches for promoting items and services to a wide or specific audience. See also *zero-based media planning, audience study*.

media buy. N. Buying of time and space in an advertising medium.

media buyer. N. The person working in an advertising agency who places an order for advertising space or advertising time. See also *space buyer, time buyer*.

media buying service. N. An organization that buys print space or broadcast time for a sponsor. See also *rating*.

media class. N. The largest subunit of advertising media, e.g., national magazines, radio, or television.

media coverage. N. See *reach*.

media director. N. An advertising agency executive who is responsible for choosing the media to be employed and scheduling the appearance of promotional material in such media.

media flighting. N. Used when funds are limited or if the service or item is seasonal; scheduling advertising for a stated time period, followed with a period free of advertising, then completed with another sequence of advertising.

media kit. N. Packet of information detailing costs of advertising in a given medium, and the targeted audience.

media mix. N. Combining various media to be used in any promotional or advertising program. See also *media support*.

median. N. A statistical average indicating central tendency, identified by a midpoint. Half the items being averaged must fall below the midpoint and half above. See also *mean, mode*.

media option. N. A single purchasable unit of advertising space or advertising time; determines the size, color, and place of a print advertisement or commercial. Usually given in a media plan. See also *media plan*.

media owners. N. Those firms having the right to sell advertising space or advertising time; usually, newspapers, magazines, radio, and television stations. Somewhat of a misnomer in that they do not actually own the advertising media, but only the selling rights.

media placement. N. Generating print and broadcast publicity.

media plan. N. The dimensions of the media selected in an advertising plan; giving goals, strategy, funds available, and time schedule. See also *media option, media planning*.

media planning. N. Inclusive of the advertising strategy; answers questions of who should be reached, where they are located, what the nature of the message is, and when the advertising should be scheduled. See also *across-the-board*.

media reach. N. The size of an audience that is reached by an advertisement or commercial with a specific medium. Can also be determined by interviewing people; for example, to determine the reach of a particular magazine, asking people what magazines they had read within the last month. See also *exposure*.

media representative. N. The salesperson retained by a publication or broadcast station who is responsible for selling advertising.

media schedule. N. The choosing of the media to be used and the timing of media options comprising an advertising campaign.

media selection strategy. N. An approach used in selecting the appropriate advertising media. Usually it is determined by which media will effectively reach the target audience and establish a schedule to fulfill the advertising objectives.

media support. N. Advertising media in its totality that is used to back up a promotion. See also *media mix*.

media weight. N. (1) The total audience delivery. (2) The volume of audience delivery by an advertising promotion based on the number of advertisements and commercials, inserts, time dimensions, and budget.

medium. N. Plural of *media*.

megaselling. N. Selling orders of large quantities, or for significant sums of money. Synonymous with *big ticket selling*.

"me" generation. N. A consumer lifestyle that stresses being good to oneself.

member-get-member promotion. N. A sales promotion method used in getting new customers by providing an incentive to current customers who then make referrals. As contrasted with friend-of-a-friend promotion, this form of promotion only provides incentives to people who are existing customers. See also *friend-of-a-friend promotion*.

membership group

membership group. N. A reference unit to which a person belongs and participates in, such as clubs, unions, and religious organizations.

membership warehouse club. N. A retailing format in which final consumers and businesses pay small yearly dues for the right to shop in a huge, austere warehouse. Consumers buy merchandise at deep discounts.

memorandum sale. N. The sale in a retail operation of consigned goods whose title rests with the vendor for a stated period. At the end of the period, unsold items are eligible for return to the vendor, and the sold or held goods are billed to the merchant. See also *on consignment*.

mercantile agency. N. An organization that supplies its subscribers with credit data on individuals and firms. In addition, some mercantile agencies gather statistical information and serve as collection depositories of past-due accounts.

mercantile credit. N. Deferring payment between a buyer and the seller, both of whom are merchant middlepeople.

mercantile customer. N. Any merchant middleperson.

merchandise. N. Purchased articles of business held for sale. See also *goods*. V. In sales, to plan or promote the sale of goods.

merchandise budget. N. In retailing, a plan in dollars of identified efforts involving merchandise for a given time period; includes sales projections, inventories, markdowns, discounts, expenses, returns, and controllable net profits. Used for assessing current practices as well as for projecting future activities.

merchandise charge. N. Extraneous costs (including shipping, insurance, demurrage, etc.) added to the cost of goods prior to mark-on.

merchandise control. N. The collection and analysis of data on purchases and sales items, either by unit or by dollars.

merchandise inventory. N. Products held by an entity for resale to customers.

merchandise manager. N. An executive who is responsible for supervising the purchasing, selling, and inventory control activities in a store.

merchandise mart. N. A building, usually large, that contains manufacturers' showrooms where retailers can examine the goods and place orders. See also *resident buyer, sales office*.

merchandiser. N. A display unit that holds items to be sold on the floor of the store.

merchandise resource. N. The source of supply from which salable and reliable goods are purchased on a recurring basis with few complications, if any, over an extended time period. See also *resource*.

merchandise transfer. N. The transfer of goods from one accounting unit of a store to another. Merchandise can be transferred from department to department, from one branch store to another branch, or from home office to branch store.

merchandising. N. (1) In retailing, all activities connected with the buying and selling of merchandise, including displays, promotions, pricing, and buying. See also *loss leader*. (2) In manufacturing, the activities required in the attempt to make a product interesting to buyers (packaging, promotion, pricing arrangements, etc.) See also *marketing*. (3) According to the American Marketing Association, "The planning involved in marketing the right merchandise or service at the right place, at the right time, in the right quantities, and at the right price."

merchandising allowance. N. The lowering of the wholesale price as an incentive to middlepeople and to wholesalers by compensating the retailer for expenditures made to promote the merchandise.

merchandising conglomerate. N. A corporation of a number of diversified retailing organizations under a single management. Their stores may be of various types. Synonymous with *conglomerchant*.

merchandising group. N. Several members of a cooperative chain that join forces under a common name to facilitate their advertising and promotion.

merchandising leader. N. A store that promotes several items at attractive prices for the purpose of inducing customers into the store. See also *loss leader*.

merchandising service. N. Merchandising assistance provided by one of the communications media for the placing of copy, advertising, commercials, layouts, etc. Traditionally, this type of service is provided without charge to advertisers.

merchandising the advertising. N. Selling the advertising and sales promotion program to channel intermediaries in order to generate their enthusiasm and gain their support.

merchant. N. An individual who takes title to goods by buying them, for the purpose of resale.

merchantism. N. The responsibility of the merchant to his or her customers; deals with appropriate customer service, emphasizing merchandise awareness, and knowledge of the goods.

merchant middleperson. N. An intermediary that takes title to the products it distributes.

merchant wholesaler. N. A middleperson who receives title to merchandise purchases for resale to firms that plan to resell the goods or process them in some fashion for resale. See also *wholesaler*.

merge-purge. N. Combining two or more mailing lists in order to identify duplications and eliminate unwanted names.

merger. N. The combining of two or more entities through the direct acquisition by one of the net assets of the other. A merger differs from a consolidation in that no new entity is created by a merger, whereas in consolidation a new organization comes into being and acquires the net assets of all the combining units.

merit goods. N. Items for which the government determines or heavily influences levels of consumption according to the argument that individuals are not qualified to make the choices (e.g., education, automobile safety equipment, etc.).

message. N. (1) An idea that is to be conveyed from a source to a receiver. (2) Any communication between persons. See also *advertising message, message development*.

message channel. N. A vehicle for delivering a message.

message development. N. Determining what is to be said in the advertisement. Objectives are first established. See also *source, unique selling proposition*.

message feedback. N. The response of a message receiver to the message.

message impact. N. The effect of the message contained within an advertisement upon the target audience's perception of it and their reaction to it, especially as it leads to further buying of the item advertised.

message permanence. N. The number of exposures one advertisement generates (repetition) and how long it remains available to the audience.

metamarketing. N. The study of marketing by focusing all social, ethical, scientific, technical, and business experience on marketing, thereby setting a full range of experience with the human being.

methods study. N. The analysis of the flow of work, particularly the utilization of materials to permit more efficient use of manpower.

me-too product. N. A strategy of a market follower who tries to avoid losing market share to a competitor by offering a product that is a duplicate of the competitor's item. See also *me-too response*.

me-too response. N. A strategy of a market follower who tries to avoid losing market share to a competitor by imitating the activities of a competitor. See also *me-too product*.

metroarea. N. See *metromarket*.

metromarket. N. The area, usually the inner city and its suburbs, from which a retail store draws most of its customers.

metro rating. N. Households with television within a metromarket that is tuned into a specific program or station.

microanalytic sales model. N. Identifying the sales process by having all sales be the item of the number of purchasers within the market, the percent who purchase from the company, and the average rate of buying. See also *macrosales model, microbehavioral sales model, microcomponent sales model*.

microbehavioral sales model. N. Identifying the sales process by having awareness of the individual customer's knowledge, attitudes, actions towards products, and environmental variables affecting him or her so that the probability of a purchase can be determined. See also *macrosales model, microanalytic sales model, microcomponent sales model*.

microcomponent sales model. N. Identifying the sale process by displaying sales as composed of additive components, each subject to separate analysis. These variables can be sales by item, by customer, or by salesperson, etc. See also *macrosales model, microanalytic sales model, microbehavioral sales model*.

microeconomics. N. The examination of the economic behavior of individual units in the economy, such as households or corporations. See also *macroeconomics*.

microenvironment. N. Internal factors within the organization that influence the firm's marketing efforts, such as adequacy of capital, talent, absenteeism, etc. See also *macroenvironment*.

microlevel approach. N. A method used to respond to changes of small magnitude, such as for individuals or groups.

micromarketing. N. (1) The study of the economic exchange process of individual firms. See also *macromarketing*. (2) Strategically managing human and organizational exchange relationships so as to provide social responsible want and need satisfaction throughout the world while achieving the marketer's objectives.

microsegmentation. N. (1) A process in which industrial market segments are subdivided on the basis of characteristics of the buying center and individual participants. (2) In industrial marketing, where the market potential for items or services is determined by collecting data about the characteristics of potential customers, usually through the personal experience of salespeople.

midbuy evaluation. N. Analysis of the effectiveness of commercial advertising at the midpoint of the media buy.

middleman. N. See *middleperson*.

middle management. N. (1) Management personnel who report directly to top management. (2) The level of management responsible for carrying out the directives of top (senior) management.

middle-of-month dating. N. The fifteenth and the last day of the month are used as cut-off dates, where all invoices dated before the fifteenth are considered dated the fifteenth; with invoices dated on and after the fifteenth, the credit period begins with the last day of the month. Discount and due dates are counted as from one of the two cut-off dates. ABBRV. *MOM*.

middle-of-month terms. N. See *middle-of-month dating*.

middleperson. N. Formerly middleman (rarely middlewoman); an individual who buys merchandise with the expectation of reselling it for profit. At times, a middleperson may arrange for such transactions without actually having possession of the goods. Synonymous with *intermediary*.

milestones of life. N. When an individual passes from one stage of the life cycle to another one.

milking. N. (1) *(slang)* Management's attempt to squeeze the last remaining profits from the firm without leaving sufficient reserves for improvements or for a downturn period. (2) *(slang)* In marketing, a short-range strategy to get the largest possible profit from a product in the shortest amount of time, irregardless of the product's long-range projections for sales. Used most often when budgets are minimal and funds are in demand, so that profits from one item can be used to evolve other company items that could have an even greater profitability. See also *abandonment stage*.

Miller-Tydings Resale Price Maintenance Act of 1937. N. Federal legislation enabling manufacturers to take advantage of state fair

trade laws without being prosecuted for violation of the federal antitrust laws. See also *fair trade acts*.

milling in transit. N. See *transit privileges*.

mill net return. N. The amount the plant receives for an item sold on a delivered price basis after the actual freight cost to the factory is subtracted from the price. See also *freight absorption*, *phantom freight*.

mill supply house. N. (1) A general-merchandise wholesaler that operates in an industrial setting. (2) The industrial equivalent of a general line, full-service merchant wholesaler, often focusing on supplying one industry.

minimarket test. N. A type of controlled-sale market testing whereby the outlets used are a small, nonrepresentative sampling of the market. Product is usually placed into the outlets (not sold), and promotion is much less than planned ultimately. Primarily tests just the willingness to spend some money for a product trial.

minimax regret criterion. N. The directive to choose that alternative offering the lowest chance of loss or failure.

minimum depth requirement. N. A newspaper tradition that advertisements be in proportion, usually an inch in depth for every column in width. Consequently the practice is; for example, should an advertisement be three columns wide, it must also be three inches high.

minimum markup laws. N. See *unfair practices acts*.

miniwarehouse mall. N. A type of shopping center in which a large warehouse offers space to a variety of sellers, including both retailers and wholesalers.

minor innovation. N. A product that was not previously sold by the company but has been marketed by some other company.

mirror principle. N. A marketing approach suggesting that customers will respond in the same fashion as they are treated. See also *mirror response technique*.

mirror response technique. N. When the salesperson responds to a customer's objections to a product or service by repeating what the prospect is understood to have said. It attempts to have the customer reconsider the statement. Synonymous with *repeating technique*.

MIS. ABBRV. (1) *Management information system*. (2) *Marketing information system*.

misdirected marketing effort. N. See *eighty-twenty principle*.

misfeasance. N. (1) Illegal or improper exercise of a legal responsibility. (2) Failure to properly perform a lawful act, or performance of an action without proper notice to those involved.

misleading silence. N. A deceptive advertising practice where the advertising is silent, or fails to mention or identify, a potentially negative aspect of an advertised service or product. The Federal Trade Commission can consider this to be incomplete disclosure that can confuse or misrepresent the item or service to the public, and may follow with a letter of concern to the maker or the product or creator of the service.

mismarketing. N. A failed or curtailed marketing program, usually resulting from poor decision making and inappropriate information.

misredemption. N. The incidence of error and fraud in offering for redemption to the manufacturer coupons given to or secured by retailers as the result of a couponing effort.

misrepresentation. N. Giving a positive statement or claiming an alleged fact about a product or service that is not true, thus leading to a false conclusion.

missionary sales. N. The activity of personnel from a manufacturer who works closely with various firms and middlepeople to increase the product sales. See also *detail person*.

missionary salesperson. N. See *detail person*.

mission statement. N. A part of corporate or division strategy, the essential character of the business that is a necessary input to new product strategy.

mix. N. (1) In retailing, combining merchandise in a retail package or the complete variety of inventory of a retailer, wholesaler, or distributor. (2) In merchandising, the combination of goods, including various sizes of the same item, for a specific brand in a particular store. (3) In broadcasting, the combining of programs in a contract, for a series. (4) See *audience composition*, *product mix*, *promotional mix*.

mixed approach. N. An international marketing strategy that combines standardized and nonstandardized efforts to enable companies to maximize production efficiencies, maintain a consistent image, exercise some home-office control, and yet to be sensitive and responsive to local needs.

mixed brand method. N. A strategy where a manufacturer produces a number of similar items under differing brand names, or where the retailer or middleperson sells items under differing brand names, or where a retailer or middleperson sells items under a dealer or generic name as well as under the manufacturer's name.

mixed costs. N. Costs that include both fixed and variable elements within a relevant range of activity. Synonymous with *semivariable costs*.

mobile franchise. N. A conventional franchise except that the franchisee dispenses his or her merchandise from a vehicle that is taken from place to place.

mode. N. Used by consumer and marketing researchers, a statistical measure of common tendency or average that identifies the value of the variable that gives the greatest height on a graph of the frequency distribution. See also *mean, median*.

model. N. A theory used to analyze various forms of behavior. The closer the model is to the real world, the more useful it is for analysis.

model bank. N. The component of a marketing information system that contains mathematical marketing models that show relationships among various marketing activities, environmental forces, and desired outcomes.

model stock. N. The ideal sales situation of having the right goods at the right time in the right quantities at the right price. See also *assortment plan, basic stock*.

mode of reaction. N. How product testees give their reaction to a product use test. Options include like/dislike, preference,, and descriptive, diagnostic information.

modification. N. (1) Any adjustment of an existing product's style, color, or model. (2) Any product improvement or a brand change.

modified break-even analysis. N. A form of demand-based pricing that combines traditional break-even analysis with an evaluation of demand at various levels of price. It reveals the price-quantity mix that maximizes profits.

modified rebuy. N. In industrial purchasing, where adjustments are made in the price or specification of the item to be ordered, thereby making the process more complicated than a straight rebuy. See also *new-task purchasing*.

modular service agency. N. See *a la carte agency*.

MOM. ABBRV. Middle of month dating.

mom and pop outlets. N. An affectionate term for small stores, generally operated by members of a family with limited capital. See also *bluefinger*.

monadic test. N. A product-use-testing format where only the new item is tested.

money, authority, desire, access. N. In marketing strategy, a method of predicting sales and in measuring market potential. Money, authority, desire, and access attributes are assigned to differing populations to quantify consumers whose have the money to buy a product, the power to make the buying decision, the interest in making a purchase, and the actual ability to obtain it. ABBRV. *MADA*.

money illusion. N. The perception that an increase in all prices and incomes by the same proportion produces an increase in consumption, although real incomes remain the same.

money income. N. The amount of money received for work performed.

money pinch. N. See *pinch*.

money supply. N. The total sum of currency circulating in a country.

monger. N. A trader or seller, often used in a derogatory fashion.

monitoring results. N. Involves comparing the actual performance of a firm, business unit, or product against planned performance for a specified period.

monitor role. N. An informational role in which a marketer continually scans the environment to collect information pertinent to his or her campaign or unit he or she manages.

monopolistic competition. N. A form of competition in which the product of each competitor in a particular field differs from other competitors' products in some way so that an exact duplicate cannot be obtained from another source. Most competition in the United States is monopolistic competition.

monopoly. N. (1) The ownership of the source of a commodity or domination of its distribution. (2) The exclusive dominance of the supply and price of a commodity or product that is acquired by a franchise or government patent. See also *oligopoly*, *perfect monopoly*.

monopsonist. N. A purchaser working in a market where there are no other buyers.

monopsony. N. A market situation in which there is only one buyer for an item. See also *duopsony*, *oligopsony*.

monostasy. N. The fundamental drive in people that creates the desire to be independent from others.

montage format. N. In print and television media, advertising where a number of pictures or images are juxtaposed in such a manner that the overall impression is created in the mind of the viewer.

Monte Carlo method. N. Used by market analysts, the use of statistical sampling techniques to obtain a probabilistic approximation to the solution of a mathematical or physical problem. See also *Markhov chain*.

mood advertising method. N. Advertising without any explicit claim about an item or service; the claim is suggested by the mood, such as fun, sex, youth, etc., set around the item or service.

morale. N. The extent to which an employee's or customer's needs are met and the extent to which the person perceives that satisfaction as stemming from his or her total job and life situation.

morning drive. N. The radio broadcast time period from 6:00 a.m. to 10:00 a.m. from Monday to Friday. The largest listening radio audience is this time period plus the afternoon drive period (3:00 p.m. to 7:00 p.m.). See also *day parts*.

morphological research. N. A form of marketing research that focuses on how decisions are made.

mortality curve. N. See *decay curve*.

motivation. N. An important component of consumer buying; a stimulus that differentially energizes certain responses within a person. See also *rational buying motives, self-concept theory, trio of needs*.

motivational needs. N. Psychological forces that affect thinking and behavior (e.g., needs for self-actualization, belonging, feelings of security). A theory developed by A. Maslow details an individual's motivational needs. See also *motivator-hygiene theory*.

motivational research. N. A technique developed by E. Dichter, purporting to correlate behavior, needs, emotions, and desires with consumer activity. The information collected is useful to advertisers and advertising agencies in planning new items, planning advertising campaigns, and, in general, preparing new strategies. See also *consumer behavior research, hidden persuader, impact*.

motivation research. N. See *motivational research*.

motivator-hygiene theory. N. F. Herzberg's theory that identifies conditions that operate primarily to dissatisfy people when they are not present (i.e., hygiene factors, salary, job security, etc.) and job conditions that lead to high levels of satisfaction when present

motive

(e.g., achievement, growth, etc.). Failure to meet the latter conditions is not highly dissatisfying. See also *motivational needs*.

motive. N. A need or want that is activated by a particular stimulus and initiates behavior toward some goal. See also *drive theory*.

moving average. N. A perpetual inventory cost-flow assumption whereby the cost of goods sold and the ending inventory are determined to be a weighted-average cost of all merchandise on hand after each purchase.

MPC. ABBRV. Marginal propensity to consume.

MPI. ABBRV. Marginal propensity to invest.

MPS. ABBRV. Marginal propensity to save.

MRO. ABBRV. Maintenance, repair, and operating supply items.

MS. ABBRV. Multidimensional scaling.

multiattribute segmentation. N. Market segmentation that is based on two or more demographic factors, e.g., a firm can segment the market based on people's age and sex.

multibrand strategy. N. A product strategy based on the expectation that a firm will market two brands in the same market, will, with all else constant, hold a greater brand share than one brand will obtain on its own, and with the right circumstances, three brands can also achieve greater share than two, etc.

multichannel marketing system. N. The supplier's technique of making use of two or more channels to reach consumers with his or her items. It can create friction between the supplier and a middleperson when interchannel competition to sell the same item intensifies. When the channels are used for different goods there are rarely problems.

multidimensional scaling. N. In marketing research, the perceptions and attitudes of respondents are geometrically shown. The data is then analyzed to assist decision makers in solving marketing concerns, e.g. determining how a group of people perceive a particular product. See also *perceptual mapping, positioning, product design model.* ABBRV. *MS.*

multidomestic marketing strategy. N. A firm's worldwide marketing strategy that offers as many different product variations, brand names, and advertising programs as countries in which it does business.

multimedia. N. (1) A partnership of technology (the telephone, the television, and the computer) and commerce, advanced in each driving the other forward. (2) In advertising, advertising promotion using two or more mediums, usually with one serving as the primary medium, reinforced with the secondary medium; for example, a television commercial supporting a newspaper insert. The majority of more costly advertising campaigns include several mediums.

multinational marketing. N. Setting resources and goals of an organization on a global market basis. Involves the crossing of national borders, not only physically but also in terms of financial transaction, capital investments overseas, licensing, royalty payments, etc.

multipack. N. A container holding two or more separately packaged items.

multiple brand entries. N. Several brand names used by a manufacturer on essentially the same product to open up new market segments. See also *adaptive product.*

multiple buying influence. N. Any purchase decision that is shared among several people, usually at differing levels of management.

multiple packaging. N. Including more than one item in a single container (e.g., the six-pack approach to beverage packaging).

multiple pricing. N. A price reduction offered if more than one unit is purchased. See also *multistage pricing*.

multiple purchasing influence. N. The situation in industrial marketing where a number of people are required to approve the purchase of an important item. See also *key buying influence*.

multiple regression analysis. N. Used by market researchers, a technique for studying the relationship between independent and dependent variables with the derivation of a regression equation that is used to predict the latter from the former.

multiple retailers. N. See *chain store*.

multiple sales. N. The result of selection by customers of multiple rather than single items to purchase.

multiple source purchasing. N. Purchasing from more than one supplier of goods considered to be of particular importance to the company.

multiple unit packaging. N. Combining a variety of units of an item into one wrapping or container with the expectation that the purchaser will take the number as a unit item; for example, beer six-packs.

multiple-unit pricing. N. Pricing goods by "so many for a price," i.e., five for $1.00. See also *unit pricing*.

multiple-zone pricing. N. Pricing products the same when delivered within one of several specified zones or geographical areas, but with different prices for each zone depending on demand, competition, and distance. Synonymous with *zone-delivered pricing*.

multiplier principle. N. The reciprocal of the marginal propensity to save. The multiplier is a figure that identifies the changes in investment and spending to alterations in aggregate income.

multiproduct branding. N. A branding strategy in which a company uses one name for all products.

multistage pricing. N. A planning method where a broad price policy is set by integrating a series of individual pricing decisions into a coherent price framework for the company. A number of steps are taken in sequence, commencing with the selection of a target market and finishing with the formulation of a specific price. See also *multiple pricing.*

multistep flow of communication. N. The communication theory that suggests that opinion leaders not only influence, but also are influenced by others.

multiunit advertising. N. The practice of including two or more company products in a single advertisement to reduce media costs.

multivariable segmentation. N. Market segmentation where more than one factor, e.g., age, sex, etc., is used to segment the population.

Murphy's law. N. The theory that if something can go wrong, eventually it will.

musical advertising approach. N. In broadcast advertising, using music to communicate the product message.

mystery technique. N. A method of salespeople in the first few minutes of customer contact. A dangling statement is used to attract the prospect's attention.

N. ABBRV. Used by market and consumer researchers, the number of instances, of whatever sort, in the total population being studied.

n. ABBRV. Used by market and consumer researchers, the total number of cases or observations in a small group.

NAD. ABBRV. National Advertising Division.

Naderism. N. At times, used as synonymous with *consumerism*. Named for consumer advocate Ralph Nader. See also *consumerist*.

NAFTA. ABBRV. North American Free Trade Agreement.

nailed down. N. Goods advertised at an extremely low price but which the store makes every effort not to sell. See also *bait advertising*.

NAM. ABBRV. National Association of Manufacturers.

name advertising. N. See *retentive stage*.

name recognition. N. Degree to which a brand, firm, or institution has meaning to a consumer; suggests greater product credibility.

name slug. N. An advertiser's signature or logo(type).

NARB. ABBRV. National Advertising Review Board.

narrow market. N. A condition that exists when the demand for a product or service is so limited that small alterations in supply or demand will create major fluctuations in its price. See also *broad market*.

national account marketing. N. A marketing approach where the company's biggest and most important customers are provided with special recognition for their volume and profitability of sales they provide. Synonymous with *key account marketing, major account marketing.*

national accounts. N. See *direct accounts.*

national advertising. N. (1) The advertising of a manufacturer or wholesaler, whose goods or services are sold nationally, as contrasted with that of a retailer or local advertiser. (2) Advertisements that appear in national media, print, or broadcast. See also *nationally advertised brand, promotional advertising.*

National Advertising Division. N. A unit of the Council of Better Business Bureaus, which is the investigative arm of the advertising industry's self-policing organization, the National Advertising Review Board. National Advertising Division decisions can be appealed to the National Advertising Review Board. ABBRV. *NAD.*

National Advertising Review Board. N. The advertising industry self-policing organization created by the Council of Better Business Bureaus and three trade groups in 1971. The National Advertising Review Board reviews national advertising for deceptive practices and hears appeals brought against the National Advertising Division. ABBRV. *NARB.*

National Association of Manufacturers. N. A major organization of employers, founded in 1895 and structured with departments of trade, law, industrial relations, and publicity. ABBRV. *NAM.*

national brand. N. See *manufacturer's brand.*

national competition. N. The ability of a nation's producers to compete successfully in the world markets and with imports in their own domestic markets.

national income. N. Of major use by market analysts; the total of the incomes received by all the people in a country over a stated period. It is equal to the gross national product minus depreciation minus sales taxes and other small items.

nationally advertised brand. N. The basis for legal lexicography; a New Jersey case before the state's Alcoholic Beverage Commission in which Seagrams attempted to disenfranchise liquor distributors based on the statute permitting this action if the liquor or wine sold was not appropriately a "nationally advertised brand." Applying definitions from English dictionaries going back to the seventeenth century to the present, J. M. Rosenberg helped to convince the commission that Seagrams had improperly disenfranchised the distributors, since their products were indeed nationally advertised brands. See also *national advertising, word-of-mouth advertising.*

national plan. N. A geographic plan for using media where the intent is to reach the largest number of different customers over the entire nation at the lowest cost per thousand.

national rate. N. See *one-time rate.*

national rating. N. For a television or radio network system or program broadcast over the United States, the percentage of radio or television households or individuals estimated to be in the audience as measured over a specific period of time.

national treatment. N. Important in international marketing of goods; a form of friendship where laws governing the marketing of domestic items in nations that have signed treaties are extended to items designated as "foreign" or "imported." The United States accords national treatment in virtually every sector and believes that it should be granted unconditionally.

national wealth. N. The combined monetary value of all the material economic products owned by all the people in a country.

national wholesaler. N. A wholesaler whose activities can reach most of or the entire nation. See also *sectional wholesaler*.

natural account. N. An accounting category that reflects how money is actually spent.

natural brands. N. See *producer-controlled brands*.

natural business year. N. A twelve-month period, usually selected to end when inventory or business activity is at a low point.

natural expenses. N. A firm's expense items categorized according to the quality of its cost rather than reasons for which it was first incurred; a form of cost analysis.

natural fold. N. Folding a direct advertisement so that the continuity of the message is emphasized as the piece is unfolded.

natural monopoly. N. (1) A monopoly that results from natural conditions (e.g., a crop that demands special climate is subject to monopolization by a grower in the area having that climate). (2) Among industries that experience economies of scale, the situation in which cost per unit is lowest when there is only one company in the industry.

natural products. N. See *natural resources*.

natural resources. N. All materials furnished by nature (minerals, timber, water, etc.).

natural trading area. N. The geographic boundaries containing customers that use a particular store or company. In most studies, customers become fewer as the distance increases from the store or company.

near-pack premium. N. Discounted merchandise or gifts that are too large to include inside or to affix to the item being promoted.

neck hanger

Such premiums are placed near the product display so as to visually and physically connect the item and the premium.

neck hanger. N. The tag placed around a bottle's neck that becomes a coupon; it is a means of communicating information or offers a special product.

need. N. Something that is lacking that is necessary for a person's physical or psychological well-being.

need awareness. N. The degree to which customers become aware of their needs and are prepared to talk about them with others.

need directed. N. A customer's purchase that is based on his or her need for sustenance and survival. See also *VALS*.

need hierarchy model. N. See *motivational needs*.

needle trades. N. Apparel-producing industries.

need-satisfaction approach. N. A higher-level selling method based on the principle that each customer has different characteristics and wants. The sales presentation is adapted to each individual customer.

negative appeal. N. Advertising copy concept providing the negative conditions of life without the advertised item or service; appeals to the consumer's anxiety about not using the item or service by emphasizing the loss they would experience by not buying the merchandise or service. See also *positive appeal*.

negative authorization. N. Credit approval where a list of delinquent payments is maintained. Should a customer's name not appear on the list, his or her request for credit is then approved. See also *floor limit*.

negative demand. N. Where a major segment of a market does not admire an item so much that it will take proper action to avoid the item.

negative elasticity. N. The concept that demand moves in the same direction as price. See also *elasticity*.

negative group. N. Any reference unit whose lifestyle or action patterns an individual attempts to avoid. Synonymous with *negative reference group*.

negative option selling. N. Where the consumer informs the salesperson by a given date not to forward the items that he or she does not want. Used extensively by book clubs and record clubs. See also *positive option selling*.

negative reference group. N. See *negative group*.

negligence. N. A source of product liability, more common decades ago. If negligence occurs in the design or manufacture of a product, the manufacturer is liable for the injuries that result.

negotiable. ADJ. Anything that can be sold or transferred to another for money or as payment of an obligation.

negotiable instrument. N. As stated in the Uniform Negotiable Instruments Act: "An instrument, to be negotiable, must conform to the following requirements: (a) it must be in writing and signed by the maker or drawer; (b) it must contain an unconditional promise or order to pay a certain sum in money; (c) it must be payable on demand, or at a fixed or determinable future time; (d) it must be payable to order or to bearer; and, (e) where the instrument is addressed to a drawee, he or she must be named or otherwise indicated therein with reasonable certainty."

negotiated contract. N. A contract to buy goods or service where the buyer and seller negotiate specific terms for agreement. Often

negotiated price

used when there is only one supplier and therefore no competition in the market.

negotiated price. N. The result obtained by a purchaser who desires something different from what is available or is powerful enough to force the seller to accept prices lower than those usually charged. See also *upset price*.

negotiation. N. The act by which a negotiable instrument is placed in circulation by being physically passed from the original holder to another person.

neighborhood cluster. N. The centralization of several stores surrounded by a residential community. Most are convenience stores with the majority of customers from the area.

neighborhood showing. N. A group of posters used in outdoor advertising, the purchase of which is confined to a particular shopping district in which the advertiser's product is available.

nested. ADJ. Packaged one within another.

net. ABBRV. (1) Broadcast network. (2) Net amount.

net advertising circulation. N. A measurement of the number of people exposed to outdoor advertising, based on two considerations: (a) the effective circulation, i.e., the least number of persons comprising the traffic passing by an outdoor advertising display who have a reasonable physical opportunity to see the display; and, (b) space position value, i.e., the efficiency with which a poster panel dominates the traffic to which it is exposed.

net amount. N. That which remains after certain designated deductions have been made from the gross amount. ABBRV. *net*.

net back. N. The sale of an item less out-of-pocket expenses to move it from the factory to its point of sale. Such costs include freight expenses, agents' commissions, etc.

net cash flow. N. The net cash consumed or produced in a period by an activity or product during a unit of time, including all revenue and expenses except noncash items such as depreciation.

net circulation. N. The number of people viewing a billboard, display, or other outdoor form of advertising during a stated time period.

net controlled circulation. N. The number of copies of a publication that have been printed and distributed, whether paid for or not, to members of a specific industry, business, trade, or professional, equivalent to the total edition printed minus office and complimentary copies, samples, exchanges, unclassified copies, and copies delivered to advertisers, agencies, and prospective advertisers. See also *net paid circulation*.

net cost. N. The true cost of an item; determined by subtracting all income or financial gain from the gross cost.

net credit period. N. According to its terms of sale, the maximum time that a company takes to pay its bill. For example, 1/20, n/60 provides a net credit period of sixty days; following the twentieth day no discount can be taken and the bill is payable net.

net effective distribution. N. The measure of the intensity of the distribution accomplished.

net export of goods and services. N. Of major importance to international marketers, the excess of exports of goods and services (domestic output sold abroad and production abroad credited to U.S.-owned resources) over imports (U.S. purchases of foreign output, domestic production credit to foreign-owned resources, and net private cash remittances to creditors abroad).

net income. N. The remains from earnings and profits after all costs, expenses, and allowances for depreciation and probable loss have been deducted.

net loss. N. See *net profit.*

net national product. N. (1) The gross national product minus capital consumption (depreciation). (2) The market value of net output of goods and services produced by the nation's economy.

net paid circulation. N. The number of copies of publication that have been paid for by the purchasers, not for resale, under the following conditions: (a) if the sale be a single copy sale, it shall be paid for at not less than 50% of the basic single-copy price; (b) on term order for a year, the subscription must be paid for at not less than 50% of the basic annual price; (c) a term subscription for one year or more paid in accordance with this rule may be included; (d) a term subscription for less than one year may not be included after its expiration unless the amount actually paid equals at least 50% of the full basic annual subscription price and not simply 50% of a pro rata of the basic annual subscription price. See also *net controlled circulation.*

net price. N. The price after deductions, allowances, and discounts have been made.

net profit. N. The excess of all revenues over all costs and expenses incurred to obtain the income in a given enterprise during a given period of time. If the total expenses exceed the income, such amount is known as net loss. Synonymous with *net revenue.*

net purchases. N. The invoice cost of merchandise purchased plus the transportation charges for the items, minus the sum of returns, allowances, and cash discounts taken.

net rate. N. An advertising medium's published rate, less the agency commission. See also *fifteen and two.*

net rating point. N. One percent of the cumulative audience for a given broadcast commercial or program. These points are totaled to arrive at a program's rating. ABBRV. *NRP.*

net realizable value. N. The selling price of an item less reasonable selling costs.

net revenue. N. See *net profit*.

net sales. N. Gross sales, minus returns and allowances, over a stated period. See also *sales*.

net terms. N. Conditions called for the billed amount of an invoice to be paid in full, with no cash discounts permitted.

network. N. (1) The diagram of the sequence of activities that must be performed to complete a project. (2) In broadcasting, a group of broadcasting stations affiliated by contract and interconnected for instant broadcast of the same program. There are national networks, regional networks, cable networks, and tailor-made networks.

network buy. N. The buying of commercial time made directly from the network, in order that all affiliated stations with the network are purchased at the same time. Most advertisers who choose to advertise nationally purchase commercial time this way. See also *market-by-market buy*.

networking. N. (1) See *network*. (2) In broadcasting, radio or television station and programs banded together for network broadcasting.

network marketing. N. A system of direct sales in which buyers at each level of the hierarchy or pyramid secure the participation of further buyers, especially at a lower level.

network option time. N. Those hours that a station affiliated with a network system has contractually agreed to permit the network to sell, along with time over other affiliates, to a national sponsor.

network rating. N. The percentage of television or radio households or individuals among those in a specified area estimated to be listening to a network's broadcast over a specified time.

net worth. N. (1) The owner's equity in a business, represented by the excess of the total assets over the total amounts owed to outside creditors at a given time. (2) Referring to an individual, the figure determined by deducting the amount of all personal liabilities for the total value of personal assets.

neutral approach. N. In sales, the strategy is to use a minimum of effort, although constant, to maintain a share of the market.

never-outs. N. Items that should never run out of stock during a season because of continuous demand.

new-business man. N. An advertising agency executive whose job it is to contact advertisers and prospective advertisers and to persuade them to employ the services of the agency he or she represents.

new-buyer holdover effect. N. Similar to customer holdover effect, with the difference that no further marketing expenditures are made.

new-collar workers. N. A segment of consumers, primarily 21 to 40 years old, who occupy a gray area between professional and blue collar jobs; these people tend to hold many traditional values but are also receptive to new values and lifestyles.

new product. N. (1) Any item perceived by prospective customers to be significantly different from other available items. (2) For manufacturers and retailers, an item never before produced, either by being completely unique or significantly different from earlier products.

new product development. N. The process of bringing an idea or concept forward from its earliest development stages to a final commercialization of a product or service. See also *new product planning process*. ABBRV. *NPD*.

new product failure. N. A new product that does not meet the objectives of its developers. Depending on what those objectives are, a profitable new product can be a failure, and an unprofitable new product can be a success.

new product planning process. N. Involves idea generation, screening, analysis and evaluation, product development and production, branding, test marketing and positioning, and full-scale marketing and production. See also *new product development, brainstorming*.

new products management. N. The overall management of a new product project or a total product innovation program.

new products manager. N. A product manager with a new products assignment. May direct a single project team, or several teams, or an entire product innovation program. Is nonfunctional, or general management in perspective, regardless of the department he or she housed in.

new product strategy. N. A strategy that guides the product innovation program. Is unique to new products and is a spin-off from overall corporate or division strategy.

newspaper stuffer. N. The advertising copy inserted loosely in a newspaper supplement section. May be only one sheet of paper, or a booklet of numerous pages. Synonymous with *free-standing stuffer, giant insert, Sheridan stuffer, stuffer*.

news technique. N. A sales approach used within the first few minutes of communication with a prospect. The salesperson pulls news items for discussion, e.g., a neighborhood fire is mentioned to promote the sale of fire extinguishers.

new task purchasing. N. In industrial purchasing, where the purchasing agent buys a new item or service. New task involves particular attention to detail and in most cases, decisions are made by more than one person. See also *straight rebuy*, *modified rebuy*.

new unsought items. N. Items offering new concepts and uses of which the consumer is unaware; requires promotion to inform the customer of its potential. See also *regularly unsought items*, *unsought goods*.

next in, first out. N. Purporting to reflect the replacement cost of inventories in terms of existing financial statements that have been practicable in the past. See also *LIFO*. ABBRV. *NIFO*.

NGT. ABBRV. Nominal group technique.

Nice Agreement. N. See *Nice Agreement Concerning the International Classification of Goods and Services for the Purposes of the Registration of Marks*.

Nice Agreement Concerning the International Classification of Goods and Services for the Purposes of the Registration of Marks. N. Of importance to international sales of intellectual properties, a 1977 multilateral treaty signed by countries providing protection of intellectual properties. The treaty is administered by the World Intellectual Property Organization. Synonymous with *Nice Agreement*.

niche marketing. N. A marketing approach, usually undertaken by small firms or by divisions of larger companies, where a manufacturer or supplier defines a narrow market segment that he or she feels best equipped to compete in. Often items or services are especially created or made for a niche market. See also *concentrated marketing, market niche.*

Nielsen Drug (Food) Index. N. Developed by A.C. Nielsen, statements on the market change of products, by type and brand, issued through panels of experts from drugstores and other stores.

Nielsen Market Sectional Reports. N. Reports distributed by the A.C. Nielsen Company offering market research or broadcast analysis, broken down by geographic area; by product's sales, market share, and competition. Most popularly called upon for advertising within a geographic area rather than national programs.

Nielsen rating. N. The percentage of households tuned to a stated radio or television program, as reported by the A.C. Nielsen Company. A device called an audimeter is installed out of sight in each sample household and is electronically connnected to each television set in the home. The audimeter produces a minute-by-minute photographic record identifying the times the sets are turned on and off and the stations tuned in.

Nielsen station index. N. An audience measurement service of A.C. Nielsen Company, providing information concerning the size of local television viewing audiences in approximately two hundred twenty-five markets; purchased by subscription. ABBRV. *NSI.*

Nielsen television index. N. A syndicated national network television audience measurement of the A.C. Nielsen Company, providing audience estimated for commercially sponsored network programs in the country; utilizes one thousand, two hundred audimeters, located in private homes and two thousand, four hundred viewing diaries of people in television households; purchased by subscription. ABBRV. *NTI.*

NIFO. ABBRV. Next in, first out.

nixie mail. N. Letters or packages not easily deliverable because of incorrect, ineligible, or insufficient address.

no demand. N. See *absence of demand*.

no frills product. N. See *generic product*.

noise. N. Interference in a communication channel that may distort a signal or interfere with openness, thus rendering the message difficult or impossible to interpret.

nominal. N. (1) Used as a modifier to indicate that values are expressed in current money prices. (2) The probable level of a market, but that level is not based on actual transactions.

nominal group technique. N. Used to set marketing and advertising goals; a forecasting strategy in which seven to ten experts gather to exchange their ideas and projections. ABBRV. *NGT*.

nonadopters. N. Consumers who may try an item but fail to become regular users. See also *audimeter, Hooperating, laggards*.

noncommercial advertising. N. Advertising placed by not-for-profit organizations, such as governmental agencies, charitable institutions, and religious groups, to create enthusiasm and support for causes they sponsor or support. See also *institutional advertising, promotional advertising*.

noncumulative quantity discount. N. (1) A price reduction that is given based on the size of the individual order placed. (2) A quantity discount that is offered on each sale made to a particular buyer.

nondegradable pollutants. N. Impurities (e.g., glass, plastics, and certain industrial wastes) that do not disintegrate or dissolve naturally.

nondisguised survey. N. In marketing research, a means for gathering data in which respondents are told the true purpose of the inquiry.

nondumping certificate. N. Often used by global marketers, a seller's certificate indicating that the items described are being sold at a price no lower than that applicable to like sales in the country of origin.

nondurable goods. N. See *soft goods*.

nongoods service. N. Where no tangible item is offered for sale or rental, e.g., medical services.

nonliquid assets. N. Valuable property, i.e., real estate or jewelry, that can be difficult to turn into immediate cash.

nonmanufacturing expenses. N. Expenditures that are not closely associated with the manufacture of products, including selling and administrative expenses.

nonmarket production. N. Production that occurs outside the market (e.g., production regulated by custom or law rather than by prices). This is a common phenomenon in less-developed nations.

nonmarking. N. See *group marking*.

nonpareil. N. See *surrogate positioning*.

nonperformance. N. The failure of a contracting party to provide goods or services according to an agreement.

nonpersonal retailing. N. Where the prospect does not enter a store and still makes a purchase. This is done using a catalog, mail-order house, or vending machine.

nonpreemptible time. N. Broadcast media time sold with the expectation that the program to be inserted in that time period will not be pulled or removed in favor of another program. Usually, an extra charge per time unit is called for. See also *preempt*.

nonprice competition. N. Markets in which a seller maneuvers for influence on the basis of special aspects of the items to be sold, promotion, or marketing strategy. Most larger organizations avoid price competition by emphasizing nonprice marketing forces. See also *pricing, price competition*.

nonprobability sampling. N. Choosing a sample for research where judgement of the researcher enters the selection process. The three types are the convenience sample, the judgment sample, and the quota sample. This approach has its shortcomings; it may be biased and can lead to false or misinterpretations of data. See also *convenience sampling, judgment sampling, quota sampling*.

nonproduct. N. An item or service prepared for a specific segment of the market only to discover that the segment did not really exist. Should the item or service be offered, it almost always fails.

nonprofit marketing. N. The application of marketing concepts and activities to nonprofit organizations.

nonsampling error. N. Any deviation from correct data arising in marketing research because of a variety of poor judgements or statistical treatments.

nonstandardized approach. N. An international marketing strategy that assumes each country or region is different and requires a distinct marketing plan.

nonstore retailing. N. Activities of vending, mail order, and house-to-house sellers.

nontariff barriers. N. Of importance to international marketers, any law, regulation, or requirement that prevents or impedes the importation of goods without good cause. The most direct of these barriers are import licensing requirements and quotas. Other examples are subsidies that distort trade and injure competing firms, and requirements that specify a certain level of domestic content in a product being manufactured or sold. Some legal and regulatory protections for consumers or the environment can operate as nontariff barriers. See also *nontariff measures*. ABBRV. *NTB*.

nontariff measures. N. Of importance to international marketers, differing from nontariff barriers only in that it is an action by a government that may eventually have restrictive implications on goods traded in the world market. Though it cannot always be proven as such, a nontarrif measure is perceived as having a restrictive effect. See also *nontariff barriers*. ABBRV. *NTM*.

nontraceable costs. N. (1) Costs that are not directly identified with the responsibility center to which they are assigned. (2) Common costs that are assigned to functional areas on an arbitrary basis.

nonvariable price policy. N. See *one-price policy*.

nonverbal communication. N. (1) The sharing of ideas without the use of words. (2) The act of imparting or interchanging thoughts, attitudes, or information without words. (3) In marketing research, used as a factor in determining consumer attitudes and beliefs pertaining to a product or service.

nonzero sum situation. N. A competitive situation in which not only the winning group benefits, but the other group also wins or its position remains unchanged.

no-op. N. Telemarketing call initiated by an automatic dialing unit and picked up by an operator immediately after the call is answered by a live party; becomes an abandoned call if called respondent hangs up before the operator gets on line.

norm. N. (1) A point of reference; a standard used for comparison. (2) A rule that tells the members of a particular cultural group what behavior is correct in certain situations.

normal good. N. An item whose consumption changes directly with money income when prices remain constant (e.g., consumer goods). Synonymous with *superior good*.

normal price. N. The price to which the market price tends to return following fluctuations up or down. When the purchase price does not reflect all consideration given by the buyer to the seller, the value of the goods will be adjusted for customs purposes.

normal sale. N. The transaction that pleases both the buyer and the seller of an item and in which no unforeseen or abnormal situations surface.

normative forecasting. N. A forecasting technique that begins with the identification of some future objectives and works back to the present, identifying problem areas that will have to be surmounted along the way.

norms. N. See *norm*.

North American Free Trade Agreement. N. Effective January 1, 1994, a trade accord that can create challenges and opportunities for overseas marketing of U.S. sales and promotion of goods and services. The North American Free Trade Agreement (NAFTA) is the name given to economic links formed by the United States, Canada, and Mexico. NAFTA's major provisions include: (a) tariffs—approximately 65% of U.S. industrial and agricultural exports to Mexico will be eligible for duty-free treatment either immediately or within five years; (b) financial services—Mexico's closed financial service markets will be opened, and U.S. banks and securities firms will be allowed to establish wholly owned subsidiaries; (c) insurance—U.S. insurance firms will gain major new opportunities in the Mexican market. By the year 2000, all equity and market share restrictions will be eliminated; (d) telecommunications—opens Mexico's $6 billion telecommunications services and equipment market. It gives U.S. providers of voicemail or packet-switched services nondiscriminatory access to the Mexican public telephone network and eliminates all investment restrictions by July 1995; (e) trucking—U.S. trucks will no longer be forced to "hand off" trailers to Mexican drivers and return home empty; will permit U.S. trucking companies to carry international cargo to the Mexican states contiguous to the United States by 1995 and gives them cross-border access to all of Mexico by the end of the 1990s; (f) motor vehicles and auto parts tariffs—U.S. autos and light trucks will enjoy greater access to Mexico, which has the fastest-growing auto market in the world. Within five years, duties on three-quarters of U.S. parts exports to Mexico will be eliminated and Mexican "trade balancing" and "local content requirements" will be phased out over ten years; (g) auto-rule of origin—only vehicles with substantial North American parts and labor content will benefit from tariff cuts under NAFTA's rule of origin; requires that autos contain 62.5% North American content; (h) textiles and apparel—barriers to trade on $250 million of U.S. exports of textiles and apparel to Mexico will be eliminated immediately and another $700 million freed from restriction within six years under NAFTA. All North American trade restrictions will be eliminated within ten years; (i) agriculture—Mexico imported $3 billion in U.S. agricultural goods in 1991, making it the U.S.'s third largest market; (j) energy—provides increased access for U.S. firms to Mexico's electricity, petrochemical, gas, and energy services and equipment markets; (k) intellectual property rights—provides a higher level of protection than that in any other agreement; and, (l) investment—Mexican "domestic content" rules will be eliminated, permitting additional sourcing of U.S. inputs and for the first time, U.S. firms operating in Mexico will receive the same treatment. ABBRV. *NAFTA*.

no sale final. N. An organizational policy that a sale is not final until the customer is totally pleased with the purchase made.

nose-to-nose selling. N. See *belly-to-belly selling*.

notation credit. N. A credit that specifies that any person purchasing or paying draft drawn or demands for payment made under it must note the amount of the draft or demand on the letter or advice of credit.

note. N. An instrument, such as a promissory note, which is the recognized legal evidence of a debt. A note is signed by the marker, called the borrower, promising to pay a certain sum of money on a specified date at a certain place of business, to a certain business, individual, or bank, called the lender.

not-for-profit. N. Describing the activities of an organization established with the sole goal of providing services for society rather than for the purpose of making a profit.

noting delay. N. A delay response effect resulting from a time lag between the completion of the execution delay and the reception of the specific stimulus by the market. In a sales message, the noting delay is zero.

novelty. N. See *advertising specialty*.

nozzle. N. A round-fitting fastener permanently placed at the opening of a container to facilitate filling or pouring and to permit closure.

NPD. ABBRV. New product development.

NPV. ABBRV. Net present value.

NRP. ABBRV. Net rating point.

NSI. ABBRV. Nielsen station index.

NTB. ABBRV. Nontariff barrier.

NTI. ABBRV. Nielsen television index.

NTM. ABBRV. Nontariff measures.

nuclear family. N. (1) A husband and wife and their children. (2) A unit composed traditionally of at least two adults, with or without children. Recently the demand that the adult be of the opposite sex has been dropped.

nudum pactum. N. (1) An empty promise. (2) A statement for which no consideration has been given.

null. ADJ. Applied by consumer and marketing researchers; referring to an absence of information, as contrasted with zero or blank for the presence of no information.

null hypothesis. N. The logical contradictory of the hypothesis that one seeks to test. If the null hypothesis is proved false, its contradictory is thereby proved true. Essentially, the null hypothesis is that there is no difference greater that could be expected by chance.

nullification of agreement. N. Setting aside the terms of an agreement.

number of stock turnover. N. Stock turnover as determined by dividing average inventory at retail to net sales for a year.

nut. N. (1) *(slang)* Uneliminatable operating costs. Synonymous with *variable costs*. (2) *(slang)* In broadcasting, the complete dollar amount reflecting the advertiser's entire sponsorship of either a television or radio broadcast; e.g., a $1 million advertising expenditure for a program sponsorship.

nutritional labeling. N. (1) A form of labeling in which consumers are informed of the amounts of protein, fat, carbohydrates, and calories in a processed food product. (2) Showing on packaged foods the nutritional value of an item, especially the U.S. recommended daily allowances supplied by a particular quantity of the item, and the specific ingredients contained.

objection. N. In sales, the reason provided by a prospect for rejecting a salesperson's offer for a product or service. See also *linking phase*.

objective-and-task technique. N. A promotional budget method in which a firm outlines its promotional goals, determines the activities needed to satisfy those goals, and then establishes the appropriate budget.

objectives. N. The goals or specific aims of a business.

objective value. N. The price an item can command in terms of other items in the market.

objectivity. N. Free of bias.

obligation. N. The legal responsibility and duty of a debtor (the obligor) to pay a debt when due, and the legal right of the creditor (the obligee) to enforce payment in the event of default.

obligee. N. A creditor or promisee.

obligor. N. A debtor or promisor.

observational technique. N. (1) A research method that entails observing consumer behavior. (2) A research method in which a researcher observes people's behavior and records what they see but avoids direct interaction.

obsolescence. N. The state of being out of date and therefore of little use to society. See also *functional obsolescence, planned obsolescence, postponed obsolescence, product obsolescence*.

obsolete material. N. Inventory items that have little or no possibility of being used in the near future. Often found with merchandise that has undergone structural design changes or of products that have been discarded for new ones.

occasion. N. In broadcasting, synonymous with *spot*.

occupant list. N. The list of addresses for the sending of direct-mail advertising. The word "occupant" is used instead of a person's name.

occupational mobility. N. The extent to which individuals in a particular occupation move into work other than that for which they were specially trained.

oddball pricing. N. In the selling of an assortment or a group of related products at the same price that does not relate to cost, desired markup or margin, or customary price of any of the separate products.

odd-ending pricing. N. See *odd pricing*.

odd-even pricing. N. A means of pricing purporting to make the cost of an item or service psychologically attractive to prospects without markedly lessening the desired profit margin.

odd-number pricing. N. See *odd pricing*.

odd pricing. N. (1) A form of psychological pricing in which the price is an odd number or a number just below a round number. (2) Pricing at odd amounts (e.g., at ninety-nine cents instead of at a dollar). Synonymous with *odd-ending pricing, odd-number pricing, off-even pricing, psychological pricing*. See also *persuasive pricing*.

OEMs. ABBRV. Original Equipment Manufacturers.

off-brand. N. A brand that is not considered acceptable to a consumer.

off-card. N. A special rate to the advertiser for advertising space or time; does not show on the medium's rate card.

offensive warfare

offensive warfare. N. The marketing warfare strategy for firms not in the lead in a product market; demands attacking the market leader, basing movements on the principles of: (a) after examining the strength of the leader, focusing an attack on lessening the leader's market share; (b) finding a weakness in the leader's dominance and attacking at that point; and, (c) launching the attack on as narrow a front as is possible, by going after one of the leader's items at a time.

offer. V. To present for acceptance or refusal. N. A contractual agreement made by a seller pending acceptance by a purchaser.

offering. N. The sum total of benefits or satisfaction provided to target markets by an organization. An offering consists of tangible products or services plus related services, warranties or guarantees, packaging, etc.

offer list. N. Of importance to global marketers, the list of items, usually prepared in conjunction with multilateral trade negotiations, on which a country is prepared to negotiate trade liberalization; may also identify merchandise that will be exempted from discussion.

offer test. N. A promotion test that assesses responses to differing prices or terms of quantities. For example, usually the price of $9.95 results in greater purchases than $10.00. See also *package test*.

off-even pricing. N. See *odd pricing*.

off factor. N. A chain discount brought to a single percent. This is the complement of the on-factor. See also *on-factor*.

official value. N. Used by global marketers, the value for duty purposes officially assigned by a country to certain imported items. It is usually compared with the invoice value, and ad valorem duties are levied upon the higher value.

off peak. N. See *prime time*.

off-price store. N. A discount store that buys manufacturer's overruns and end-of-season goods at below-wholesale prices and resells them at prices significantly lower than the regular department store price.

ogive. N. Used by market researchers, a distribution curve characterized by cumulative frequencies.

oligopoly. N. (1) A competitive situation in which a few firms account for a large percentage of the industry's sales and in which there are substantial barriers to entry. (2) An industry in which a small number of producers sell identical products. See also *monopoly, differential oligopoly, perfect monopoly*.

oligopoly price. N. A price that develops when there is a market of numerous buyers and few sellers, thus resulting in the sellers having the greatest power.

oligopsony. N. Control by a number of buyers who attempt to influence the demand for a specific item. See also *duopsony, monopsony*.

oligopsony price. N. A price that develops when there is a market of few buyers and numerous sellers, thus resulting in the buyers having the greatest power.

OMAs. ABBRV. Orderly marketing agreements.

omnibus cooperative advertisement. N. For wholesaler agreements, a full-page advertisement from a retailer over his or her own name. The retailer bills each manufacturer a pro rata share of the cost of the entire advertisement based on earlier cooperative advertisement agreement with the manufacturers.

on account. N. (1) A payment made toward the settlement of an account. (2) A purchase or sale made on open account.

on-air method. N. A technique applying audience feedback for evaluating the talent, format, and quality of a broadcast program or commercial that is being considered for a later broadcast. Real broadcast material is used for testing factors such as audience recall, attitude shifting, etc.

on-approval offer. N. A proposition made to a consumer whereby he or she is permitted to see, feel, taste, use, or otherwise experience the nature of a product without first paying for it and without being placed under the obligation to buy. Usually a time limit is given for such an offer, at the expiration of which the consumer is expected to return the product or to pay for it.

on consignment. N. Items turned over by an owner (the consignor) to someone else (the consignee) with the expectation that the items (the consignment) will be sold by the consignee. If all the items are not sold, the owner is entitled to the return of the items. See also *memorandum sale, purchase allowance, consignment.*

one-cent sale. N. A sale's offer where two products are sold with each other for the price of one of the items, plus one additional penny. Often used to introduce a new product. The general practice of manufacturers is to indicate in advertisements that the offer is restricted to a specific market area and good for a limited time.

one hundred percent location. N. The location within a given shopping area that is the best possible place for a specific type of store.

one hundred showing. N. A standard showing of outdoor posters. The number of panels in the poster in a one hundred showing varies with market size.

one-level channel. N. A marketing channel where there appears only one intermediary, usually the retailer, between the manufacturer and the consumer.

one-more-yes close. N. A salesperson's closing method based on the concept that people are creatures of habit and tend to say "yes." Consequently, the seller raises questions about the prospect's feelings toward the merchandise, with the final question suggestive of a positive reply from the prospect.

one-price policy. N. (1) A situation in which the price of goods is firm and cannot be negotiated. (2) A pricing policy in which the marketer assigns a price to the product and sells it at that price to all customers who purchase the same quantity of the product under the same conditions. Synonymous with *nonvariable price policy*. See also *single-price policy*.

one-sheet poster. N. A printed sheet of advertising matter pasted on a panel on display on subway platforms as a form of transit advertising.

one-shot promotion. N. A one-time promotion that involves items that cannot be reordered at a later time. At times, a supplier can be persuaded to provide items manufactured especially for a specific event.

one-side messages. N. Messages in which only the benefits of a good, service, or idea are mentioned by a firm.

one-time purchaser. N. A customer found on a list who has made only one purchase since an initial order.

one-time rate. N. The advertiser's rate paid when there is not enough space or time purchased to earn volume discounts. Synonymous with *general rate, national rate*. See also *rate differential*.

on-factor. N. The difference between 100% and the single discount representing a chain discount. For example, a chain discount of 40% and 10% equals a single discount of 46%. The on-factor is 100% less 46% or 54%. See also *local rate, off-factor, single-rate*.

on-line advertising. N. Advertising messages presented on a computer screen through a proprietary online service or the World Wide Web.

on order. N. Goods paid for but not yet received.

on pack. N. A package with a display card used by hanging on hooks, to which an item has been attached without using any cover. See also *in-pack, with-pack premium*.

on-spec. ABBRV. On-speculation.

on-speculation. N. Advertising, or another work effort, that is carried out for a client without a contract or order. The client pays for the service only should the work be used. Working on-spec is done by advertising agencies seeking to enhance their reputation. ABBRV. *On-spec*.

open account. N. (1) Credit extended that is not supported by a note, or other formal written evidence of indebtedness (e.g., shipments of merchandise for which a buyer is billed later). (2) An arrangement between the seller and purchaser where the purchaser receives no written confirmation of a purchase.

open ad. ABBRV. Open advertisement.

open advertisement. N. A want advertisement identifying both the position and the name of the potential employers and their address. See also *blind advertisement*.

open assortment. N. An assortment where the consumer does not have at hand all the items usually needed. See also *closed assortment*.

open bid. N. The offer to perform a service or provide merchandise to a buyer with an adequate public communication in order that all interested bidders are aware of the price submitted.

open charge account. N. See *charge account*.

open circuit system. N. A marketing system providing for feedback from all the influences that impact the firm. Data is often taken into account rapidly so that action can be taken quickly.

open code dating. N. See *open date labeling*.

open credit. N. Credit that is allowed without immediate proof of a customer's credit-worthiness.

open credit account. N. A credit arrangement in which a buyer receives a monthly bill for goods and services bought during the preceding month. The account must be paid in full each month.

open-date labeling. N. Clearly printed, the date marked on merchandise with limited shelf life, usually an item that can spoil, identifying the last date that the item can safely be sold to the public without danger of deterioration or spoilage. Synonymous with *open code dating*.

open dating. N. See *open date labeling*.

open display. N. Products placed where they can be handled and studied by prospects. See also *closed display*.

open distribution. N. The distribution of the same merchandise by a given area or region, by differing dealers. The dealers carry competitive lines and there are no barriers regarding the number of items a deal sells, offers, or delivers to a retailer. See also *exclusive distribution, intensive distribution, selective distribution*.

open-end commercial. N. (1) In broadcasting, a commercial designed to accommodate a dealer tag at its conclusion. (2) In advertising, the ending to a network program or commercial that is left blank for local advertising.

open-end contract. N. An agreement whereby a supplier contracts to meet the buyer's requirements for a specific item during a stated period, whatever those requirements may be. The agreement is open-end because all the terms are left indefinite.

open-ended. N. Pertaining to a process or system that can be cut back.

open-end pricing. N. Where a purchase order is released without a fixed price agreed to. Happens where the price is set by the free market and the supply is more critical to the company than is a fixed price.

open-end program. N. Any broadcast program that permits the inclusion of local commercials.

opening. N. The first showing of a new season's line of items by a manufacturer or an entire industry.

opening price point. N. The lowest price line of a particular item, such as the least costly of several brands of toothpaste.

open interest. N. The number of outstanding contracts in the market or in a particular class or series.

open market. N. A condition of trading that is not limited to any particular area or persons.

open order. N. (1) An order made without price or delivery stipulation. (2) An order shipped to a market representative without specifying the vendor.

open pricing. N. Marking merchandise with shelf life expiration dates clearly shown in acceptable symbols. See also *open-date labeling*.

open rate. N. (1) An advertising rate that is subject to discounts for volume or frequency. See also *base rate*. (2) A rate for space

open stock. N. Replacement items or additions of goods carried in quantity and retained in a warehouse for several years.

open the kimono. V. *(slang)* To reveal to prospective customers company plans regarding future products, to impress upon the buyer that the firm is ahead of its competitors in developing new or superior items.

open-to-buy. N. The quantity of goods that a store can receive in stock over a stated time without exceeding its planned inventory levels. ABBRV. *OTB*.

open trade. N. Any transaction that has not yet been closed.

operant conditioning. N. A motivation approach that focuses on the relationship between stimulus, response, and reward.

operating budget. N. A quantitative expression of a plan of action that shows how a firm, including an advertising agency, will acquire and use its resources over a specified period of time.

operating cycle. N. The general pattern of business activity whereby cash and other resources are converted to inventory and operational assets and eventually into a product or service that can be sold and for which cash and other resources are received.

operating expenses. N. (1) Any expense incurred in the normal operation of a business. See also *margin of profit*. (2) Expenses of furnishing transportation services, including the expense of maintenance and depreciation of the plant used in the service.

operating income. N. Income to a marketing and/or advertising business produced by its earning assets and by fees for services rendered.

operating leverage. N. The extent to which fixed costs and variable costs are used in the production and marketing of products and services.

operating losses. N. Losses incurred in the normal operation of a marketing or advertising business.

operating profit ratio. N. The ratio of a firm's operating profit to its net sales.

operating statement. N. A statement for a store's management, providing net sales, costs, expenses, and the net operating profit or loss for a fixed period.

operating supplies. N. Materials consumed during the manufacture process that do not appear in the final consumer or industrial product.

operational buying motives. N. Consumer motives based on how the item being considered for purchase works or performs.

operational diversification. N. Extending a company's offerings based on some degree of gain in the market, such as the lowering of cost through economies of scale, or the increasing of the customer family. See also *congruent production diversification*.

operations budgeting. N. The setting of immediate goals for sales, production, expenses, costs, and the availability of cash.

operations control. N. The practice of assessing how well an organization performs marketing activities as it seeks to achieve planned outcomes.

opinion. N. Used by consumer and marketing analysts, feelings that contribute to the formation of attitudes that are less subject to change or shift and are more likely to influence behavior. See also *activities, interests, opinions*.

opinion leader. N. A member of an organization who, because of ability, power, access to information, or prestige, can influence the attitudes, opinions, or behavior of those around him or her. See also *reference group*.

opinion research. N. Market research to determine a prospect's thoughts and beliefs toward a given object or situation.

opinion strategy. N. A method of salespeople who display the item under consideration to the prospect and invite opinions. The prospect is directly involved in the conversation.

OPM. ABBRV. (1) Operations per minute. (2) Other people's money.

opportunistic sampling. N. See *convenience sampling*.

opportunity. N. An unsatisfied want or need that arises from a change in the organization's environment.

opportunity cost. N. A maximum alternative profit that could have been obtained if the productive good, service, or capacity had been applied to some other use. See also *domestic-exchange ratio*.

opportunity cost of capital. N. The expected rate of return from employing funds effectively in the company.

optimum capacity. N. The quantity of output that permits the minimum cost per unit to be incurred.

optional consumption. N. The buying of items and services that are not required for daily fulfillment and well-being. See also *luxuries*.

optional product pricing. N. A pricing method for items offered to the public with several options, e.g., refrigerators with a host of options. Decisions have to be made as to which options are included and those not included in the base price, or those requiring additional costs to the consumer.

orange goods. N. In merchandising, consumer goods, such as clothing, that will eventually have to be replaced as they wear out, at a rate, or at the consumer's discretion. See also *brown goods*, *red goods*, *yellow goods*.

orbital structure. N. Any marketing operative or organization that is not fixed in space, e.g., a truck jobber or a traveling salesperson.

order. N. A request to deliver, sell, receive, or purchase goods or services.

order card. N. A self-addressed post card, postal card, business reply card, or similar form without self-addressing mailed to or otherwise delivered to prospects by an advertiser for their convenience in mailing an order for goods or services, an inquiry for information, or any other response to the sales message usually accompanying the card.

order cycle. N. Includes the activities of the vendor. Divided into four parts: (a) order transmittal—what happens and how long it will take to get the order to the vendor from the moment of initiation; (b) order processing—what the vendor does and how long it takes from the time of receipt of the order to notification of the proper warehouse to get the order prepared for shipping; (c) order picking—what occurs at the warehouse and how long it takes to prepare the order for pickup and to place the shipment into the hands of the chosen carrier; and, (d) order delivery—what occurs and how long it takes during the process of pickup and final delivery to the customer. Synonymous with *lead time*.

order delivery. N. See *order cycle*.

order entry. N. Approaches used in entering customer orders into an order-processing system, to provide an efficient and accurate means to ensure that customers receive their merchandise quickly and as ordered.

order-filling cost. N. A marketing cost incurred in storing, packing, shipping, billing, credit and collection, and other similar aspects of selling merchandise.

order form. N. A form for requesting goods or services from a wholesaler, manufacturer, or direct mail retailer; often included in such direct-marketing materials as catalogs.

order-generating costs. N. Costs that are revenue-producing, such as advertising and personal selling.

order getter. N. A salesperson, using highly developed approaches in dealing with prospects in a creative fashion.

order-getting cost. N. A marketing cost incurred in an effort to attain a desired sales volume and mix.

ordering cost. N. A major cost component that is considered in inventory controls decisions. Each time the firm orders items for inventory, it must formally contact the supplier, which usually involved some clerical and administrative work. Labor is also used in placing the order and putting the items in inventory. The clerical, administrative, and labor costs make up the ordering cost element in inventory control models.

orderly marketing agreements. N. Bilateral agreements limiting imports from one country to another; generally undertaken to avoid imposition of unilateral import restrictions. ABBRV. *OMAs.*

order margin. N. The total cost of items sold, including product, selling, and delivery expenses but not including promotional costs subtracted from the total sales revenue generated, and divided by the number of units sold. A promotion budget should not exceed the order margin, and this budget must be small enough to have a profit margin remain.

order picking. N. See *order cycle.*

order processing. N. See *order cycle*.

order processing costs. N. Expenses associated with recording and handling orders, such as order entry, computer-information handling, and merchandise handling.

orders. N. Requests made for the delivery of goods or services.

order size. N. The appropriate amount of merchandise, parts, and other items to purchase at one time. It depends on the availability of quantity discounts, the resources of the firm, the inventory turnover rate, the costs of processing each order, and the costs of maintaining goods in inventory.

order taker. N. A salesperson whose function is primarily to receive calls and who accepts orders for items and services.

order transmittal. N. See *order cycle*.

ordinal scale. N. Used by market researchers, a level of measurement that describes a variable in terms of a rank order.

ordinary course of trade. N. A principle that places the dutiable value of merchandise at the price at which it would normally sell if customary channels of distribution were observed.

ordinary interest. N. Interest that is calculated based on three hundred sixty days to the year.

ordinary terms. N. As found in invoices, where a cash discount is deducted should the bill be paid within the discount period. If not, the full payment is due at the end of the cycle shown. The cash discount and the net credit periods are both counted from the date of the invoice, which is traditionally the date of shipment.

organization. N. (1) All the activities involved in getting ready to carry out a strategic plan. (2) Any structured system of roles and functional relationships designed to carry out a firm's policies or, more precisely, the programs such policies inspire.

organizational buying objectives. N. Includes the availability of items, reliability of sellers, consistency of quality, delivery, price, and customer service.

organizational climate. N. A set of properties of the work environment perceived by consumers and assumed to be a major factor in influencing their behavior.

organizational consumer. N. Includes manufacturers, wholesalers, distributors, retailers and government units, and not-for- profit organizations. Usually these institutions use the items they receive to make other products, to maintain their operations, or to be offered for resale.

organizational consumer expectations. N. The perceived potential of alternative suppliers and brands to satisfy a number of explicit and implicit objectives.

organizational consumer's decision process. N. Consists of expectations, the buying process, conflict resolution, and situational factors.

organizational learning. N. The process whereby individuals within an organization learn as a group and apply that learning to their work. Traditionally, thought to vary with amount of experience (as measured, for example, by number of units produced), but is increasingly seen as an independent variable that can be managed as a source of competitive advantage.

organizational market. N. The market segment made up of people and firms that buy merchandise and services for reasons other than for individual consumption, such as goods to be used in the manufacturing of other goods. Its purchasers engage in large-volume, highly professional, and detail-oriented purchasing efforts. See also *consumer market*.

organizational mission. N. A firm's long-term commitment to a type of business and a place in the market. It can be expressed in terms of the customer group(s) served, the goods and services offered, the functions performed, and/or the technologies utilized.

organizational structure. N. A set of relationships among individuals with different responsibilities.

organization marketing. N. The methods used by not-for-profit institutions to sell their goals and/or receive contributions.

organizing function. N. The managerial activity involved with creating a formal structure of tasks and authority.

original equipment manufacturers. N. (1) An organization that purchases industrial goods to incorporate into other products. (2) Used in reference to the right to appeal. In 1990, the European Union's Court of Justice ruled that original equipment manufacturers may have the right to appeal from regulations of the commission and council imposing antidumping duties. Previously, this had been limited to complaining parties, producers/exporters, and related importers. ABBRV. *OEMs*.

original order. N. The first order received from a specific customer; important to maintain records of sources of original orders so that first-time purchasers can be concentrated on the best sources.

original retail. N. In the retail accounting method, the sales price of items that is a total of the cost plus the original markon.

original source. N. See *original order*.

OS&D. ABBRV. Over, short, and damaged.

OTB. ABBRV. Open-to-buy.

other directed. N. Individuals easily influenced by others.

others self-image. N. Our mental picture of ourselves as we believe others see us.

outbid. V. To offer a higher price for an item than that offered by other bidders.

outbound telemarketing. N. A direct-marketing approach of seeking out customers and prospects using the telephone; involves sales representatives calling individuals to both generate and qualify leads. See also *in-bound telemarketing, telemarketing.*

outdoor advertising. N. An advertising medium where the message is not delivered to an audience as it will be with media that enters the home, but the units are, instead, carefully situated locations where they are seen by an audience on the move. Communications from this medium are usually brief, read easily as the reader has only a few seconds to see the advertisement. Outdoor advertising is a splendid reminder medium and is frequently used in an advertising program to supplement other media. See also *approach phase, billboard.*

outdoor buyers. N. Media purchasers who specialize in outdoor advertising purchases.

outer-directed. N. A consumer purchase that is based on how the consumer perceives others see him or her and his or her actions. Such purchase behavior is affected by the person's wish to conform to peer group pressures.

outer envelope. N. The envelope, in direct-mail, that includes the package's promotional materials.

outgo. N. Any expense or other cost in the running of a business.

outgoing. N. A post or painted bulletin that displays the advertiser's message to traffic passing to a central part of a shopping or urban area.

outlay. N. Any expenditure.

outlays costs. N. The actual cash outflows directly associated with the production and transfer of goods or services.

outlet store. N. See *factory outlet*.

out-of-home. N. Advertising media viewed outside the household that is not available in the home, such as display on shopping carts and advertising in subways. See also *in-home*.

out-of-home media. N. Advertising viewed or listened to by people outside of their residence; includes billboards, transit advertising, outdoor displays, and skywriting. See also *alternative media*.

out of pocket expense. N. A cost incurred by an individual, often when on a business trip. The item or service is paid for in cash or by check or charge account, and the employee expects reimbursement from the company.

out of stock. N. Goods that are not in the store when requested by a customer. See also *periodic stock control*.

out of stock cost. N. Estimated profits that are never realized because of insufficient inventory available to fulfill the demands of customers. Customers and sales are lost through a stock-out.

out pack. N. Any premium attached to the outside of a package. See also *outsert*. Synonymous with *zip advertising*.

out post display. N. Items placed with signs at well-crossed points within a store away from the traditional selling department of the merchandise.

output. N. (1) The quantity yielded in any operation. (2) The average dollar gross domestic product produced in a stated period.

outsert. N. Separate printed material attached to the outside of a package.

outshopper. N. An individual who travels outside of his or her usual community or local area to obtain products or services. See also *outshopping*.

outshopping. N. (1) The number of shopping trips made outside a buyer's usual community or local area over a given time period. (2) The proportion of dollars spent made away from the buyer's usual community or local area. See also *outshopper*.

outside dimensions. N. The outer measurements of a container, a package, or any of its parts.

outside-in. N. Determining from consumers or industrial readers what media they follow so as to determine what form of media should be used as a preferred match.

outsizes. N. See *end sizes*.

outsourcing. N. Contracting work that formerly was done in-house by employees such as those in marketing research, advertising, and public relations departments too small, outside firms.

outstanding. N. Any unpaid or uncollected debt.

outward processing. N. See *production sharing*.

overall expenses technique. N. A method for determining the cost of goods sold by dividing the seller's total expense over time by the number of products sold during that time frame; prevents the seller from failing to include relevant expenses in the calculation and is a helpful measure of the change in expense realized relative to a change in the number of sold units.

overall market capability. N. The quantity of an item or service that is absorbed in the general market without allowing for price or market considerations. For example, the overall market capability for television sets includes everyone who owns a television and everyone who would like to own a television but hasn't purchased one to date. See also *potential demand, potential market saturation*.

overall objectives. N. The broad, measurable goals set by top management.

overbought. N. (1) Reflecting an opinion about price levels of an item that has had a sharp rise or of the market as a whole after a period of vigorous buying, which some argue has left prices too high. (2) When some element in the planning process has not evolved as anticipated, leading to a zero open-to-buy. (3) Where the store finds that it is overstocked with merchandise in excess of its demand.

overcapitalize. V. (1) To provide an excessive amount of capital to a business. (2) To place too high a value on the nominal capital of a company.

overcarriage. N. In international merchandising, the transportation of goods beyond the initially intended destination; usually resulting from the goods being refused at the destination.

overcoverage. N. In marketing research, a nonsampling error when some of the units in the sample are repeated on the lists given to separate interviewers, thus creating a bias.

overdue. N. A payment that has not been made at the time it was due.

overextension. N. Credit received or extended beyond the debtor's ability to pay.

overfull demand. N. Where demand for an item or service exceeds the capacity of suppliers to supply or manufacture it. In this situation, firms often engage in demarketing, which is marketing to less demand on a temporary or permanent basis, either by increasing the price of the item or service, or by decreasing service or promotional efforts. See also *demand states*.

overhead. N. Costs of materials and services not directly adding to or readily identifiable with the product or service of the entity. Synonymous with *burden*.

overheating. N. Excessive price or money activity that some economists believe will lead to inflation.

overkill. N. An expensive promotional effort that yields diminishing returns because it repels rather than attracts prospect interest.

overlay. N. (1) A unified theme that unites all the elements in an advertising campaign. (2) A transparent flap over art work to allow writing of instructions or corrections or to indicate color breaks.

overnights. N. The tentative report of household ratings and audience share of network program time slots in the top twenty-five markets in the nation; estimated audience figures that are gathered the day following the program's appearance.

over (or short). N. The difference between established sales statements and the actual audited figure. This discrepancy is often a result of errors in making change or missing sales checks.

overproduction. N. Producing more than can be sold at any price or at a profitable price. See also *Say's law*.

overproduction theory. N. The idea that an excessive expansion of productive capacity occurs whenever demand increases. See also *underconsumption theory*.

overrun. N. (1) Excess production. (2) The number of pieces of printed advertising in excess of the specified quantity. A 10% overrun is usually acceptable at pro rate cost. Overruns are produced to permit distribution of copies to prospective buyers or advertisers, as well as to readers who may request back issues. See also *underrun*.

overseas marketing research. N. The systematic gathering, recording, and analyzing of data to assist in minimizing uncertainty and aid in the decision-making process in overseas markets. It tends to be more costly than domestic marketing research, as it is broader in scope.

overseas sales branch. N. A branch or subsidiary of an exporting company that is in a foreign country, thereby permitting the exporter greater exposure and control in the foreign market. It also minimizes the dependence upon a domestic-based export department with other personnel. See also *direct exporting*.

over, short, and damaged. N. Used in international marketing, the discrepancy between the amount or condition of cargo on hand and that shown on the bill. See also *clean bill of lading, short merchandise*. ABBRV. *OS&D*.

oversold. ADJ. The situation of a manufacturer who has become obligated to deliver more than he or she is able to supply within the stated period.

overstock. N. See *remainder*.

overstored conditions. N. Where retail operations are opened longer than the need for extended hours suggests. It leads to an extra expense and overinvestment.

owe. V. To be obliged to pay something to someone for something received. An indebtedness results.

own brand. N. An item bearing the name or brand of the store selling the item rather than the name of the producer.

owned-goods service. N. A service that provides a customer with a service that had previously been used, e.g., plant maintenance.

owner-operator. N. A regular driver who owns equipment and is a subcontractor to a carrier on a long-term basis.

ownership. N. Possession of a legal title with the rights to enjoy the benefits derived from any assets accompanying or accruing from such title.

ownership utility. N. The value or satisfaction added to a product or service when it is in the possession of the correct person at the proper moment. Synonymous with *possession utility*.

P

P. ABBRV. Each of the Ps of the marketing mix: product, price, promotion, and place.

pack. V. (1) To add to the total cost of merchandise charges for items not included or inflated charges. (2) To give an undeserved discount without lowering the actual price.

package. N. (1) In merchandising, any container or wrapping in which goods are placed for shipping or carrying. (2) In broadcasting, the combination assortment of time units, sold as a single offering at a set price. (3) In broadcasting, a program, purchased as a unit for a lump sum, including all components ready for the addition of commercials.

package band. N. Advertisements, announcements, and other price offers printed on a paper strip that usually creates a band around the package.

package consolidating agency. N. See *freight forwarder*.

package design. N. The planning and deciding on the form and structure of a product's package.

packaged goods. N. Consumer items packaged by producers and sold through retail stores, e.g., food, tobacco, beauty aids, household cleaners, etc. Firms usually promote packaged items heavily with mass media advertising.

package enclosure. N. See *in-pack*.

package engineering. N. A discipline of scientific and engineering principles applied to solving problems of functional design, formation, filling, closing, or preparation for shipment of containers, regardless of the type of product enclosed.

package goods. N. Items found within a container designed for display and handled by the retailer, e.g., detergents, paper goods, cereals, etc.

package insert. N. (1) Printed material found with the item to explain its operation. (2) Advertising material placed in a package; usually identifies a firm's different product. (3) See *package stuffer*.

package plan. N. Spots devised by broadcast stations or networks that are offered to broadcast advertisers at a special price. Synonymous with *total audience plan*.

package stuffer. N. See *package insert*.

package test. N. In direct mailing, a small scale survey to set response rates and, thereby, determine which package elements are to be placed in the full mailing. Direct mailers, by applying an independent variable, alter only one factor in a test package because, should more than one factor be altered, it is difficult to conclude which change affected the higher response. See also *offer test*.

packaging. N. (1) The preparation of merchandise for shipping and marketing. (2) All activities that are related to designing and producing the container or wrapper for a product.

packaging functions. N. Consists of containment and protection, usage, communication, segmentation, channel cooperation, and new-product planning.

packaging wants. N. The variable address in the attempt to impart the subconscious feeling that an item will satisfy basic psychological wants other than the obvious needs for which it was produced.

packing house. N. See *freight forwarder*.

packing list. N. A list showing the number and kinds of items being shipped, as well as other information needed for transportation purposes.

packing slip. N. The form used for listing items to be shipped and to identify the recipient of the shipment. The slip goes with the shipment and, upon arrival at its destination, is used for confirming that the shipment is sound and complete.

packing wants. N. See *packaging wants*.

page traffic. N. The measure of the number of readers of a newspaper or periodical who look at a particular page or a particular advertisement.

paid circulation. N. The total number of copies of a magazine or other periodical sold through subscription or by single-copy sales in stores or newstands.

painted display. N. In outdoor advertising, where the advertising communication is hand-painted on the display.

painted wall. N. See *painted display*.

painting the bus. N. *(slang)* Altering the appearance of a presentation, proposal, or idea without changing any of the basics. See also *window dressing*.

paired-comparison. N. A mode of product-use testing where the new product is paired with (usually) the category leader, and direct comparisons are made.

pallet. N. A portable platform for retaining material while in storage or shipment.

panel. N. (1) In marketing, a group of people used for obtaining information on perceptions, attitudes, etc., toward a product, service, or organization. Synonymous with *test panel*. (2) In advertising, that portion of an outdoor sign that has a message or advertisement painted or pasted onto it. (3) In advertising, a printed unit that comprises the entire advertisement on an outdoor sign.

panel research. N. See *panel (1)*.

Pan-European marketing. N. Standardizing products or marketing communications to be used in European Community nations. This form of marketing requires changing merchandise and promotional strategies to deal with different languages and cultures. See also *Euro-Advertisement, Eurobrand, Harmonized System, standardization*.

pantry check. N. The physical examination of items possessed by respondents.

paperboard. N. A board made of matted or felted fibrous material that is more than 0.012 inches (twelve points) thick.

par. N. In marketing, the present value of a continuity customer over the active life of the customer; used to assess various sources of new customers.

parallel exporting. N. Impacting the profits of international marketers, a situation where, in addition to the official route by which the goods are exported by the exclusive distributor into a given territory, there is also a second parallel route, by which another trade in the territory exports the goods, which he or she has obtained from a third party outside the territory. The parallel exporter is a source of competition for the exclusive distributor. See also *parallel importing*.

parallel importing. N. Impacting the profits of international marketers, the importing of goods by an independent operator that is not part of the manufacturer's channel of distribution. The parallel importer may compete with the authorized importer or with a subsidiary of the foreign manufacturer that produces the item in the local market. See also *parallel exporting*.

parameter. N. (1) In marketing and consumer research, a quantity to which arbitrary values may be assigned. (2) A variable that is given a constant value for a specific purpose or process. (3) A definable characteristics of an item, device, or system.

parasalesperson. N. Usually a sales trainee who rarely completes the closing with a customer, but is assisted in this task by a more experienced salesperson.

parasite store. N. A store depending on traffic flow, originating from events external to those generated by the store itself, which is usually negligible compared to the total traffic flow.

parcel shipment. N. A small package restricted as to value, generally samples of goods, or advertising matter.

parentage. N. See *surrogate positioning*.

parent store. N. A controlling organization that owns or manages store properties. See also *flagship store*. Synonymous with *main store*.

Pareto's law. N. Of interest to marketing analysts, the theory of Vilfredo Pareto, an Italian sociologist and economist, that income tends to become distributed in the same proportion among consumers throughout the world, regardless of differing forms of taxation.

pari delicto. N. Fault or blame that is equally shared.

Parkinson's laws. N. As developed by C. Northcote Parkinson, concepts stating that: (a) work invariably expands to fill the time available for its completion, and (b) expenditures climb to reach income. Called "laws" but there is no legislative decisions involved.

partial equilibrium analysis. N. An inquiry that looks at only one market of an economy under the assumption that solutions in other markets will not be altered by a change in the market examined.

partial monopoly. N. A situation that exists where there are so few sellers or an item or service that each may alter the price and market. See also *perfect (pure) monopoly*.

partial payment. N. A payment that is not equal to the full amount owed and is not intended to constitute the full payment.

participating announcement. N. An advertising message broadcast as one of many such announcements for several sponsors during a participating program heard over a radio or television station. See also *particpating program*.

participating program. N. The broadcast program sponsored by more than one advertiser. See also *participating announcement*.

particular average. N. Damage or loss less than the total value; partial loss.

partnership. N. A contractual relationship between two or more people in a joint enterprise who agree to share, not necessarily equally, in the profits and losses of the organization. See also *joint venture*.

parts. N. Unit components of a product that are complete without additional processing but are useful only when incorporated into the product. See also *raw materials*.

party plan selling. N. See *party selling*.

party selling. N. Door-to-door selling where a hostess is convinced to invite friends to a mid-day event for a salesperson to demonstrate items. Usually, a free gift is given to the hostess for her participation. Synonymous with *group plan, party plan selling*.

pass. N. One cycle of processing a body of data.

pass-along circulation. N. The cycle of a periodical or magazine without having been purchased by the reader. For example, readers find the issue in a doctor's office, in a public library, etc. A magazine's total circulation includes both paid and nonpaid circulation, and pass-along circulation. Such readers are referred to as secondary readers. See also *primary circulation*.

pass-along deal. N. An arrangement to induce the retailer to lower the price of merchandise, thus increasing the volume and perhaps share of the market for the manufacturer.

passive philosophy. N. A philosophy of competitive behavior where the company participates in only minimal competitive tactics to remain in the market. See also *aggressive philosophy*.

patent. N. (1) A government grant to an inventor to protect the results of an invention. (2) The legal right of exclusive use and licensing granted by a government to the person who invents something. An invention is patentable if it is a useful, novel, and nonobvious process, machine, manufacture, or composition of matter. See also *patent applied for*.

patent applied for. N. A form showing the actual application by an inventor for a U.S. patent. If the inventor is dead, the administrator of his or her estate must apply for the patent. The application must contain a written description of the invention, a drawing, an oath of inventorship, and a government filing fee. See also *patent pending*.

patent pending. N. After filing for a patent, the patent office's statement that a search is being conducted in the United States and other countries to determine whether the invention is in fact new and patentable under the law. Should the patent be rejected, an appeal is permitted in the patent office and, if necessary, in the federal courts. See also *patent applied for*.

patronage discount. N. A discount permitted on the basis of the amount of business carried out with a company. Synonymous with *deferred discount, quantity discount, volume discount*.

patronage dividend and rebate. N. Wholesaler vouchers given to retailers to be used as incentive builders by wholesalers to generate increased retailer sales and goodwill. The patronage dividend occurs when the wholesaler offers the retailer a pro rata share of earnings from one or many of the wholesaler's goods. A patronage rebate occurs when the wholesaler refunds part of the retailer's original payment for merchandise. In both cases, payment is issued to retailers in the form of a merchandise credit voucher or a bank check.

patronage institutional advertising. N. Advertising intending to convince an audience to use the sponsors as the source of supply for reasons other than the obvious merits of the offering. See also *public relations institutional advertising*.

patronage motives. N. The reasons that customers shop in a particular retail outlet.

patronize. V. (1) To frequent a store. (2) To be a regular customer.

payback. N. (1) The return on investment equal to the original marketing expenditures; represents the minimum amount of dollar sales that must be generated to offset the cost of an advertising campaign. Synonymous with *payout*. See also *break-even point*. (2) In marketing, the time, usually in years, from the point of full-scale market introduction of a new product until it has recovered its costs of development and marketing. The market testing stage is usually considered a part of the evaluation process (and not in the payback period).

payback period. N. The period of time that passes before the incoming cash equals the outgoing cash on a specific project, order, or other effect.

payee. N. The person or organization to whom a check or draft or note is made payable. The payee's name follows the expression "pay to the order of."

payment guarantee. N. A guarantee to the supplier of merchandise that if he or she performs his or her obligations, payment will follow.

payola. N. *(slang)* A gift or other valuable item offered to people who have the potential for using their influence in the promotion or sale of a product or service.

payout. N. See *payback*.

pay-per-view. N. An increasing service, individualized programming provided by a cable television service.

peak. N. An exceptionally busy period in a business.

peak season. N. The period of days or months in which an item is in greatest customer demand (e.g., charcoal for barbecuing during the summer months).

pecuniary exchange. N. Any trade that uses money.

peddler. N. *(slang)* A person who travels and sells small quantities of merchandise.

pegged price. N. An artificial price kept at a given level below which it cannot drop even if market forces indicate the need for a change. Government intervention, often in the form of subsidies, control pegged prices.

peg point. N. The pay rate for a major task that becomes the base from which rates of pay for other related tasks are derived.

penetration. N. The degree of effectiveness of an advertisement as its impacts the general public, i.e., an ethnic food item such as kosher meat would have a high penetration in the large, urban cities in the United States, and a lower penetration in small towns or in rural communities. Firms try to increase their penetration by applying aggressive marketing strategies, such as increased advertising, preparing special promotions, and raising incentives for their sales people or channel intermediaries. See also *penetration strategies*.

penetration pricing. N. (1) An approach in which the price of an item is set low in order to enter the market quickly. (2) A pricing strategy in which the initial price is set at a low level in order to generate the greatest possible demand for the product.

penetration strategies. N. There are two forms of pricing and promotional strategies used when merchandise is first introduced: (a) rapid penetration—setting a low product price and placing aside a large amount of money for promotion to get the fastest market penetration and the largest market share. This method is used where there is a low level of product awareness and the market is large; and (b) slow penetration—setting a low product price and allocating little money for promotion, thereby suggesting a rapid market acceptance of the item, because of its low price, and keeping costs down; used when the market is large and when product awareness is quite high. See also *market penetration, penetration, skimming price*.

pen name. N. Pseudonym given by direct marketers to sign sales or service correspondence to customers; attempts to conceal true name of writer.

pennysaver. N. See *shopper*.

people meter. N. An instrument that is attached to a television set for measuring consumer broadcast preferences, viewer habits, and viewing frequencies.

people's capitalism. N. Of interest to marketing analysts, the full range of income levels in the population of a community being represented in the ownership of the business.

per annum. ADV. *(Latin)* By the year.

per capita income. N. Used by marketing/advertising researchers, total income divided by the number of individuals. Per capita income can be adjusted to reflect changes in prices or purchasing power over a stated time period to show real per capita income.

per capita output. N. The gross national product of a nation divided by its population. This is often used to identify a country's standard of living, which is of special interest to both marketers and advertisers.

perceived equitable rewards. N. The rewards people feel they should receive as the result of their performance.

perceived risk. N. The hazards a customer believes to be related to the buying of a specific term (e.g., difficulty of obtaining servicing, cost of servicing, lifetime of the item, or obsolescence of the item). Perceived risk can be socially based. Marketers try to understand reasons for perceived risk and therefore they provide product information to assist people in their buying decisions. See also *dissonance-reduction*.

perceived value. N. Benefit a customer expects to receive from a service or product; may be tangible or intangible.

percentage of sales method. N. A method of setting a marketing budget based on a forecast of sales. A budget allocation approach for advertisers that is both simple and can relate advertising costs directly to sales. Two shortcomings of this technique include a failure to recognize that as conditions are altered, advertising costs must change with them; also this approach can falsely lead to excessive spending for large established brands and an inadequate budgeting for items that would profit from further advertising, such as new brands.

percentile. N. Used by market researchers, one of the 99 point scores that divide a ranked distribution into groups or parts, each of which contains 1/100 of the scores or persons. The points are located to coincide with the obtained score below which, in each division, 1/100 of the cases fall. Scores are numbered from 1 to 99.

per centum. N. *(Latin)* By the hundred.

perception. N. A process by which individuals attend to incoming stimuli and translate such stimuli into a message indicating the appropriate response; a major force in consumer behavior. See also *product image, selective perception, symbol.*

perceptual defense. N. The subconscious screening out of stimuli that the individual chooses to reject because of a belief, value, etc.

perceptual gap. N. A gap that appears on a mapping of products where the positions of the products are determined by user opinions, not necessarily fact.

perceptual mapping. N. Creating a graph of brand attributes, one product at a time, as noted by consumers on a scale of low to high. Helps to identify the positioning of all brands in a product category where consumer preferences are not being well provided for. See also *multidimensional scaling, product positioning.*

per contra item. N. A balance in one account that is offset by a balance from another account.

perfect competition. N. A description for an industry or market unit consisting of a large number of purchasers and sellers, all involved in the buying and selling of a homogenous good, with awareness of prices and volume, no discrimination in buying and selling, and a mobility of resources. See also *imperfect competition, pure competition.*

perfect hedge. N. A hedge where the loss or gain on the commodity transaction equals the loss or gain on the finished items transactions.

perfect (pure) monopoly. N. A situation in which one person or organization has total control over the manufacture and marketing of an item. See also *monopoly, oligopoly.*

performance analysis. N. A means to compare the actual performance of a marketing strategy with the expectations for the plan. It is used to upgrade the operations of the program, spot trouble areas, and correct shortcomings.

performance based compensation. N. In advertising, the payment by firms to their agencies based on the agencies' performance, usually based on the sale of the item being advertised, instead of on a retainer or project basis.

performance budgeting. N. Grouping of budget accounts into categories related to a specific product or service that is produced, and the evolution of product-cost measurements of these activities.

performance label. N. A label affixed to a product describing the operating characteristics and features of performance for that item. See also *label.*

performance monitoring research. N. Research designed to provide information about the outcomes of marketing activities.

performance standard. N. The measure of performance against which the actual performance is to be compared.

perimeter advertising. N. The collective term for posters, billboards, and signs placed in public structures to attract spectators. Often used at sporting events.

per-inquiry payment. N. Payment based on the percentage of all funds received from an advertiser's inquiries or actual sales, instead of on published time or space rates. Per-inquiry arrangements are often carried out in order to introduce advertisers to new media.

period cost. N. See *fixed cost*.

period expense. N. An expenditure that cannot be associated with or assigned to a product, and so is reported as an expense in the period in which it is incurred. See also *product costing*.

periodical. N. See *magazine*.

periodic stock control. N. A unit control system in which stock is identified and recorded periodically and sales for intervening time slots are calculated. See also *inventory control, out of stock*.

peripheral service. N. An added service offered without charge to a basic item or service. These services, which add to operating costs, enhance an advertising agencies' image and hopefully competitive advantage.

perishability of services. N. Where some services cannot be stored for future sale. The service supplier attempts to manage consumer usage so there is consistent demand throughout various periods of the week, month, and/or year.

perishable distinctiveness. N. A product having serious competition over the coming years, usually five. At first the item may have an exclusive distinctiveness, but with the passing of time, as others capture a larger share of the market, the product passes into a stage of declining distinctiveness.

perishable goods. N. Items that are subject to rapid decay unless given proper storage (e.g., meat and dairy products).

PERK. ABBRV. Perquisites.

permanent income hypothesis. N. Where expenditures are based on average income expectations over a period of time, where consumers average out their expenditures.

perpetual inventory. N. A book inventory identifying the stock on hand by means of a detailed record, enabling the firm to know the composition of its inventory at any point in time. See also *inventory, perpetual inventory control*.

perpetual inventory control. N. A unit control system whereby orders, receipts, and sales are identified as they occur and inventory is computed. See also *inventory, perpetual inventory*.

perpetual inventory system. N. Keeping a record of the firm's inventory by constantly noting the movement of merchandise into and out of the company. Usually involves the recording of orders and receipt quantities, and requisitions of sale quantities. See also *perpetual merchandise control*.

perpetual merchandise control. N. Similar to perpetual inventory system, but limited to retailing.

perquisites. N. Additional compensation furnished by management, usually in goods or services, over and above the general payment of wages. ABBRV. *PERK*.

personal care items. N. Hair dryers, electric shavers, toothbrushes, facial cosmetics, and the like.

personal consumption expenditures. N. The funds spent by households for consumer items. Disposable personal income minus savings equals personal consumption expenditures.

personal demographics. N. The basic identifiable characteristics of individual final consumers and organizational consumers and groups of final consumers and organizational consumers.

personal disposable income. N. See *disposable income*.

personal distribution of income. N. The distribution of natural income among individuals or households; used by advertisers in setting strategies.

personal income. N. Used by marketers, national income less various kinds of income not actually received by individuals, not-for-profit institutions, and so on, plus certain receipts that do not arise from production. See also *disposable income*.

personal influence. N. The power of people to sway or influence the purchasing decisions of others. For this reason, marketers attempt to identify those people who exert influence over others. See also *bluefinger*.

personal interview. N. A survey technique in which respondents are questioned in a face-to-face setting, homes, shopping malls, offices, etc. It is considered the preferred method, although costly, in the early stages of research when there is a lack of certainty as to the best questions to ask.

personality. N. In broadcasting, synonymous with *format (2)*.

personalized advertisement. N. A specially bound periodical insertion that features the individual subscriber's name.

personalizing shoppers. N. One of a four-way sociological classification of consumers who seek out retail outlets that they are most secure in, in particular those with salespeople they feel they can relate best with. For other categories, see also *apathetic shoppers, economic shoppers, and ethical shoppers*.

personal saving. N. Of special importance to advertisers and marketers, the difference between disposable personal income and personal consumption expenditures, including the changes in cash and deposits, security holdings, indebtedness, reserves of life insurance companies and mutual savings institutions, the net

personal selling

investment of unincorporated enterprises, and the acquisition of real property net of depreciation.

personal selling. N. (1) A promotion method involving interpersonal communication between individuals. (2) In salesmanship, verbal presentation to a prospective customer for the purpose of making a sale. As contrasted with advertising, personal selling is usually more effective.

persuasion. N. A primary objective of advertising, the act of influencing an individual or group to work for a desired objective.

persuasion vehicles. N. See *advertising media*.

persuasive impact. N. The impact of a message upon a prospect.

persuasive label. N. The label, whose primary objective is to attract the consumer to buy the item, not to inform him or her with information.

persuasive pricing. N. Psychological pricing that tends to convey a sense of extra-good value to the consumer. See also *odd pricing*.

PERT. ABBRV. Program evaluation and review technique.

PERT/COST. N. A modified PERT system that, in addition to time, deadlines, and schedules, includes all cost considerations.

phantom market. N. A market that when examined carefully does not exist at all or is too small to demand attention.

phantom shoppers. N. Sellers' representatives who pose as customers to assess methods used by dealers in selling some items. They may receive prizes if preferred methods are being used.

phase zero. N. The preliminary evaluation or study preceding the decision to go ahead with a project or strategy.

phony list price. N. The list price presented to a prospect to indicate that the price has been discounted from list. At times, customers wind up paying more for the item or service than the actual market price. This practice is outlawed by the Wheeler-Lea Amendment. See also *list price*.

physical distribution. N. (1) The movement of merchandise from manufacturer to consumer. (2) The movement of materials from sources of supply to producers. See also *distribution*. (3) All the activities that provide for the efficient flow of raw materials, in-process inventory, and finished goods from the point of procurement to the ultimate consumer.

physical distribution concept. N. A theory requiring all physical handling and the trade channel system be looked upon as one total system.

physical distribution manager. N. The corporate person responsible for the flow of materials that are used in manufacturing and in distributing finished merchandise to the market; coordinates the work of corporate departments responsible for the procurement of raw materials and, eventually, delivering finished items to channel intermediaries or end-users. Synonymous with *logistics manager*.

physical distribution strategy. N. The transportation form(s) to be used, inventory levels, and warehouse form(s), and the number and locations of plants, warehouses, and shopping facilities employed in moving goods from one place to another.

physical inventory. N. Inventory calculation obtained by making an actual listing of stock on hand.

physical obsolescence. N. (1) Any worn out, broken item resulting from normal wear and tear. (2) Obsolescence that results when products are built to last only a limited time.

physical product. N. The actual physical entity or service that is offered to consumers.

physiological motives. N. Motives whose satisfaction is needed for survival. See also *psychological satisfaction*.

physiological needs. N. See *primary needs*.

pick-and-pack. N. Goods shipment method where merchandise is chosen from a warehouse based on what has been ordered by each customer, and then packed for shipment.

pickup. N. See *pickup materials*.

pickup materials. N. Advertising materials that can be used over again, in part or total, in a different advertisement. Synonymous with *pickup*.

piece goods. N. Fabrics that are purchased in required lengths for home sewing.

piece rate (wage). N. The amount of money received for each unit of output. When wages are so determined, an incentive wage system is in operation.

piggyback. N. (1) Trailer trucks transported by railroad cars. (2) In broadcasting, two commercials by an identical advertiser that appear one following the other; may be for the same or for different items. See also *bookends*.

piggyback commercial. N. In broadcasting, two or more commercials aired one to follow another, with different merchandise of the same sponsor. Advertisers like piggyback commercials to get two or more unrelated advertising messages into the time allocated for one, without the increase of commercial time. See also *bookends*.

Pigou effect concept. N. The concept that a lowering of the overall price level creates higher consumption of time and services.

pilferage. N. The taking of another's property while such goods are in transit or being stored. See also *inventory shortage, shoplifting.*

pilot film. N. A filmed television program produced in order to demonstrate to prospective sponsors and advertising agencies the format, talent, and quality of the entire series that is project for future filming.

pilot marketing. N. A marketing method to test the feasibility of the proposed course of action; provides the firm with valuable marketing experience while forging ahead with manufacturing plans and demands of the market.

pilot plant scale production. N. Production of a modest number of units in small facilities designed to prove methods that may be used in full-scale plants.

PIMS. ABBRV. Profit impact of marketing strategy.

pinch. N. (1) A bind or tight situation. (2) A sudden, unanticipated rise in prices. When money rates go up suddenly, it is called a money pinch.

pinochle season. N. *(slang)* In the garment industry, the off-season.

pioneering advertisements. N. Advertisements that tell what product is, what it can do, and where it can be found.

pioneering innovativeness. N. A strategy of trying to be the first to market new types of products. The highest order of innovativeness (others are adapting and imitating), it is often based on technical breakthroughs.

pioneering stage. N. The first stage in the product life cycle. Emphasis is placed on achieving a demand for sale of the item. Synonymous with *primary stage.* See also *spiral stage.*

pipeline. N. A manufacturer's inventory purchased by wholesalers and retailers, but not as yet purchased by consumers.

pirate parts. N. Replacement units made and sold by producers specializing in only making replacement parts. Traditionally the makers are firms other than the makers of the machines that the pirate parts match.

pirating. N. Where a nonsubscriber to rating reports tries to persuade a subscriber to permit the non-subscriber to use them.

pitch. N. (1) A presentation to a prospect by the salesperson in order to obtain an order or new business, as in a sales pitch. (2) The presentation by one or more people from an advertising agency to a prospective account.

place. N. One of the four Ps of marketing, dealing with strategies and distribution channels for making a product physically available to consumers; concerned with physical handling and distribution of items, such as warehousing, packaging for transportation, modes of transport, and the number of wholesale and/or retail outlets through which the item is made available. See also *P*.

place-based media. N. Advertising media alternative that places messages in locations that attract a specific target audience, such as airports, doctors' offices, and health clubs.

place utility. N. (1) The additional value in having a product where it is utilized or consumed. (2) The satisfaction that buyers receive from having a product available at the appropriate place. See also *utility*.

plan. N. A written document that specifies resource requirements, costs, expected benefits, and activities necessary to achieve a goal.

planned economy. N. A system whereby the government has a major influence in directing economic resources for deciding what to manufacture, in what quantity, and often for whom.

planned gap. N. (1) The difference between a forecast and a plan. (2) The difference between what will occur assuming that no changes are made (forecast) and a projection of what the organization wants to accomplish (plan).

planned impulse buying. N. A form of impulse buying where the customer plans to use the store's stock as a shopping list. See also *impulse buying, pure impulse buying, reminder impulse buying*.

planned obsolescence. N. An approach of consciously making an item out of fashion in the eyes of the consumer by repeatedly bringing out new models or products featuring improvements that are promoted as being superior or beneficial. There is a question of the value to the consumer of these systematic changes. The weakest-link theory claims that the least durable component in a product will determine its useful life. See also *product obsolescence, weakest-link theory*. Synonymous with *managed obsolescence*.

planned presentation. N. See *canned presentation*.

planned purchases. N. (1) In retailing, the means to determine the dollar value of merchandise to be drawn into stock during a given season or cycle; helps ensure having adequate stock on hand to fulfill increased demand. (2) In marketing, in consumer purchasing process, carried out prior to the prospect's entry into the outlet and prior to the prospect having direct contact with the item.

planned shopping center. N. A retail location that consists of centrally owned or managed facilities. It is planned and operated as an entity, ringed by parking, and based on balanced tenancy. The three types of planned centers are regional, community, and neighborhood.

planning. N. An organizational activity that requires establishment of a predetermined course of action, beginning with a statement of goals. See also *market planning, strategic planning, tactical planning.*

planogram. N. A computerized diagram used in merchandising to design the ideal display of merchandise on retail store shelves.

plans board. N. A group of advertising agency executives who meet regularly to discuss and plan the advertising and marketing strategies for the agency's clients.

plant. N. (1) An establishment that manufactures or distributes items and services. (2) In advertising, a group of outdoor structures and display areas used for the presentation of advertising messages and consisting of poster panels, metal and wood bulletins, walls of buildings, and electric spectaculars and semispectaculars, located in a city or an area characterized by a great volume of traffic and is owned and operated by an individual or firm.

plant operator. N. An individual or organization servicing advertisers by offering outdoor display facilities for the presentation of sales messages.

plant turnover ratio. N. The relationship between an organization's sales income and cost of operating its physical plant. It gives the sales volume generated for each dollar invested in physical facilities.

plasticity of demand. N. When consumer choices are in part influenced around a given point on the demand curve. See also *price elasticity, promotional elasticity of demand.*

plateauing. N. When salespeople cease expanding their sales efforts because of a variety of variables, including the lack of motivation.

PLC. ABBRV. Product life cycle.

pledging. N. The offering by a borrower of his or her assets as security for the repayment of a debt.

plow back. V. To put earnings from sales back into the business operation. N. Appropriating funds representing net profit received during an earlier period to the advertising budget; used by advertisers who wish to invest maximum dollars in their promotions.

plug. V. To work hard and steadily. N. (1) In packaging, a type of closure made to be inserted into the opening of a container. (2) In advertising, a testimonial that is received without charge.

plunge method. N. See *task method*.

p.m. deal. N. A monetary payment made to retail salesclerks by a manufacturer for every item sold by the clerks under a special incentive plan. In order to induce clerks to push the product and to encourage them to favor his or her item over those of competitors, a manufacturer may offer a special payment or bonus for each unit sold during the life of the offer.

point of equilibrium. N. The point at which supply equals demand.

point of ideal proportion. N. In a production process, the point at which the most profitable relative amounts of the forces of production (land, labor, capital, and management) are used.

point of indifference. N. In production, the point at which the cost of an added increment of land, labor, capital, or management merely equals the money return of the additional item made because of that increase. See also *diminishing returns*, *diseconomies of scale*.

point of origin. N. The location at which goods are received for transportation.

point-of-purchase. N. See *point-of-sale*. ABBRV. *POP*.

point-of-purchase advertising. N. See *POP advertising*.

point-of-sale. N. In retailing, the location within the store where a sale is completed, i.e., the cash register, where merchandise is picked up. Synonymous with *point-of-purchase*. ABBRV. *POS*.

point-of-sale terminal. N. A communication and data-capture terminal located where payment is made for goods or services. ABBRV. *POST*.

Poison Prevention Packaging Act of 1970. N. Federal legislation requiring manufacturers to use safety packaging on items containing substances considered dangerous or harmful to children.

policy. N. A plan of action.

policy rights. N. In purchasing, the authority given managers to set procurement goals.

political advertising. N. Advertising ideas, attitudes, and interests related to public policy issues, including political candidates and their arguments on various social issues. See also *political marketing*.

political marketing. N. Marketing of ideas and opinions that relates to public or political issues or to specific candidates for office. See also *political advertising*.

polybag. N. A bag employed by direct marketers for shipping multiple pieces of items of goods or sheets of promotional material. See also *shrink wrapping*.

polycentricity. N. One of a three-way classification of the policies of a company involved with international marketing that concentrates on the legal, cultural, and demographic differences and similarities among markets, where each is looked upon as different so that only local managers can understand and react to local conditions. See also *ethnocentricity, geocentricity*.

pony spread. N. Print advertising composed of two junior page advertisements appearing on opposite pages in a magazine or periodical. The spread consists of two advertisements that use equal portions of the adjoining pages but are united to visually form one advertisement. Synonymous with *junior spread*.

pool. N. (1) An agreement between two or more companies to curtail output, divide sales areas, or to avoid competition in any other way. (2) A combination of resources of funds, for some common purpose or benefit.

pooled interdependence. N. The relationship between units of an organization such that their separate products can be added together to form the total final product.

pooled marketing. N. Where two of more manufacturers offer each other's products as a premium when purchasing a certain number of units of the first's product. See also *symbiotic marketing*.

pooled purchasing. N. A number of independent middlepeople who combine their orders to keep costs lower. Synonymous with *informal buying group*.

pooling. N. Uniting several manufacturer's items without trying to keep separated the contribution from any one producer.

POP. ABBRV. Point-of-purchase.

POP advertising. N. Promotional material placed at the point of purchase, such as interior displays, printed material at store counters, or window displays. See also *point-of-sale, position media*.

pop-in. N. A short paid announcement by a broadcast advertiser that is usually of special interest to the viewer or listener, e.g., during the Christmas holiday where the company wishes the public a happy holiday without mentioning any of its products available on the market. Synonymous with *image liner*.

population. N. In marketing research, the full group under study and for which the researcher will attempt predictions, forecasts, and draw conclusions. See also *sampling*.

pop-up. N. Print advertising and magazine inserts created to rise when the reader opens it.

Porter-Lawler model. N. An extension of the expectancy theory that draws together individual, job, and organizational characteristics to describe the motivational process.

portfolio. N. A set of things. Most often applied to that group of projects currently active in a research laboratory but may apply to all new projects under way.

portfolio analysis. N. A technique by which an organization individually assesses and positions every business unit or product. Company efforts and resources are allocated and separate marketing mixes are aimed at their chosen target markets on the basis of these assessments.

POS. ABBRV. Point-of-sale.

POSDCORB. ABBRV. The seven functions of administration: planning, organizing, staffing, directing, coordinating, reporting, and budgeting.

position. N. (1) The location of an advertisement or commercial in a given vehicle. Advertisers often pay a premium for a preferred position. See also *island position, positioning*. (2) The space occupied by an advertisement in a publication in relation to its

positioning. N. (1) In marketing, the projection of an item as possessing a desired image, to make it attractive to a part of the market for that type of merchandise (e.g., a low-priced sports car that looks like an expensive model). See also *market target*, *multidimensional scaling*. (2) In marketing, a process in which a marketer communicates with consumers to establish a distinct place for its product or brand in their minds. Synonymous with *market positioning*. See also *repositioning*. (3) In advertising, the place on the page when an advertisement appears in relation to its placement on the page. (4) In broadcasting, programs or time spots felt by advertisers to be particularly attractive.

positioning advertising. N. Advertising where a segment of the market is targeted and the item or service is then presented to appeal directly to that segment.

position media. N. Inclusive of both outdoor and transit advertising media but does include nonstandardized signs and point-of-purchase advertising. See also *point-of-sale*, *POP advertising*.

positive appeal. N. Advertising copy method purporting to alleviate a person's anxiety about purchasing and using an item. Emphasis is given to the positive components of an item and the ensuing gains from purchasing the product. See also *negative appeal*.

positive concept of valuation. N. Used in international marketing, an application of ad valorem duties holding that duties should be applied on the actual value of the transaction, as defined by the buyer and seller.

positive conversion. N. See *boomerang (2)*.

positive file. N. An authorization system file that contains information about every account holder and is capable of providing a

positive option selling. N. A direct-mail method where a consumer indicates whether or not he or she wishes to receive a regularly scheduled product shipment. With a positive option, there is less revenue per customer than a negative option, but the positive option usually attracts more purchasers. See also *negative option selling*.

positive reinforcement. N. The administration of positive rewards, contingent on good performance, that strengthens desired behavior in the future.

possession utility. N. See *ownership utility*.

POST. ABBRV. Point-of-sale terminal.

postage stamp pricing. N. See *freight allowed*.

postbuy analysis. N. Measure of advertising impact at the end of the media buy; usually based on consumer recall and recognition tests.

poster. N. See *billboard*.

posterior analysis. N. In marketing research, data that leads to a change in marketing decisions and strategy because of new insights or new information. See also *preposterior analysis, prior analysis*.

posting. N. The physical placing of an advertisement on an outdoor advertisement. See also *posting date, posting period*.

posting date. N. The date on which a display of an outdoor advertisement commences; usually every fifth day, starting with the first of the month.

posting period. N. The amount of time remaining on a display, e.g., a billboard's posting period is anywhere from three to twelve months.

postmark. N. An impression on letters and packages, showing the time, date, and post office or sectional center of origin.

postmark advertising. N. Advertising printed by a postage-meter machine on an envelope as part of its postmark. Postmark advertising is required to fulfill certain U.S. Postal Service requirements; must also be nonpolitical and noncontroversial and cannot confuse the public by having a design that appears as a regular postal marking.

postmortem. N. The analysis of an operation after its completion.

postponed obsolescence. N. Obsolescence that occurs when technological improvements are available but are not introduced until the demand for existing products declines. See also *obsolescence*.

postponement. N. Reducing risks in marketing by having the inventory location take place at the last possible moment. It may allow the greatest possible sorting while the item is relatively undifferentiated as its presently exists.

postpurchase anxiety. N. A customer's feeling of doubt following his or her purchase commitment. See also *postpurchase behavior*.

postpurchase behavior. N. The final stage in the consumer adoption process, includes the continued evaluation of the item or service, maintenance, and if the item or service should be repurchased. See also *postpurchase anxiety*.

postscript. N. A sentence or block of copy added to a direct-mail letter immediately beneath the advertiser's signature as a means of calling attention to an important point that should be impressed upon the reader.

post test. N. A procedure to the assessment of an advertisement or advertising campaign. Post testing by advertisers is used to obtain insight into consumer responses to certain advertising methods and to minimize costly mistakes in the future; measures both the impact of an advertising message as well as its ultimate impact on product sales. See also *pretest*.

potential competition. N. The possible entry into the market of new companies, substitute products, or materials of similar or superior quality or benefit, all perhaps introduced at equal or lower prices.

potential demand. N. Demand that can be expected to become effective at a future date (e.g., when purchasing power is increased). See also *overall market capability*.

potential market saturation. N. The maximum number of potential users (or buyers) during a specified period.

potential need satisfier. N. Any item, service, or consideration perceived by a prospect as a possible means of satisfying their need. See also *risk reduction*.

poverty. N. (1) The absence of most of the comforts of life and undersupply of the necessities. (2) The point at which deprivation makes the level necessary for physical efficiency impossible.

poverty of time. N. A consumer lifestyle where the quest for financial security means less free time because the alternatives competing for time expand.

power. N. In marketing, the ability of one member of a marketing channel to influence the trading behavior of another.

power of attorney. N. A written instrument, usually acknowledged before a public officer or witness, in which one person grants to another the rights of utilization, tenancy, transfer, or disposal of assets owned by the first person as though he or she were exercising these rights. A power of attorney has the force of law; it may be limited with respect to the assets listed in the power of attorney, or it may give full power over all assets owned.

practical capacity. N. The maximum level at which a plant or department can economically operate most efficiently.

praise method. N. Using compliments by the salesperson to convince a prospect to purchase an item or service.

preapproach. N. The step in the sales process of finding critical data about a potential customer prior to contact. See also *canvass*.

preaudit. N. The examination of a creditor's invoices, payrolls, claims, and expected reimbursements before actual payment, or the verification of sales transactions before delivery.

precautionary motive. N. A rationale used by firms and consumers for retaining a portion of their assets in cash, to ensure their ability to satisfy unexpected demands easily.

precedence. N. In product innovation, the order of market entry. A product is first to market, second, etc.

preclusive purchasing. N. Buying materials with the expectation of denying their use to a competitor.

preclusive specification. N. A specification that only one or few suppliers qualify to bid on, placing the buyer at a disadvantage by having so few potential suppliers.

predatory pricing. N. Cutting prices with the objective of harming one's competitors. The opposite of umbrella pricing. See also *extinction price, rate war*.

predictive research. N. The category on the level-of-outcome dimension when the outcome of a research effort is to predict

predictor variable

the future. Predictive research is the third level, preceded by the first level of descriptive research, which states that something does exist or has occurred in the past. Evaluative research is the second level and adds value judgments to data in order to form comparisons. See also *forecasting*.

predictor variable. N. See *independent variable*.

preempt. N. In broadcasting, removing a program from the air and replacing it with another. See also *preemption, nonpreemptible time*.

preemptible rate. N. In broadcasting, a discount rate to advertisers for the time that may have to be surrendered if another advertiser is willing to pay even more.

preemption. N. The prerogative of customs authorities to seize and sell items that an importer has deliberately undervalued to avoid the payment of duties. See also *preempt*.

preemptive marketing. N. Advertising a service or product prior to its availability in the marketplace so as to put off the purchasing of a competitor's product or service, already available.

preemptive price. N. A price that is so low that the market is unattractive to possible entrants who might eventually become strong competitors. Synonymous with *keep-out price, stay-out price*.

prefabricate. V. To manufacture standardized components of a larger unit in a factory, thus making possible the assembling of the item elsewhere (e.g., the buyer's home) without production facilities.

preference gap. N. An opportunity first discovered on determinant gap maps or perceptual gap maps and then evaluated using maps based on customer preferences; often coincides with areas of no preference.

preference item. N. A consumer's choice of a particular item even when similar items are less costly (e.g., insisting on Coca Cola, although a chain grocery store's cola-type soft drink is less expensive).

preferences. N. In international sales, special trade advantages given by governments to trading partners in order to promote export growth and development. Licensing practices, quotas, or preferential application of other measures, including taxes, can also be granted in the nontariff areas.

preferential tariff. N. Of importance to international marketers, a tariff that grants lower rates of duty on goods imported from certain "preferred" countries than on the same goods from other nations.

preferred position. N. (1) Any advertisement position for which the advertiser pays a premium when specifically requested. It could be a right-hand page, top of a column, or space surrounded by editorial materials, a sport's manufacturer requesting a sports page, etc. Publications often have a special higher rate for preferred position advertisements. (2) The advertisement's placement in the section of the medium that is appropriate to the advertised merchandise or service. See also *split run, fixed location/position, premium, prime time, upfront selling period.*

preferred resource. N. A seller chosen by the consumer as his or her first choice source of supply for a particular time of goods or services.

prejudice. N. A human characteristic of special importance to advertisers; a mental bias tending toward some preconceived judgment or opinion, thus affecting one's attitude toward work or employees. See also *bias, proactive inhibition.*

pre-launch. N. The first stage of the launch cycle. Involves getting ready to launch the product, including getting distribution and building necessary field service capability.

preliminary expenses. N. Expense incurred in the establishment of an advertising agency (e.g., costs for developing and circulating a prospectus).

preliminary market analysis. N. A type of market research that follows ideation and entry evaluation. Often used to gain greater knowledge of a particular market prior to setting up a concept test plan.

premarketing. N. See *prepricing*.

premarking. N. When some manufacturers provide a service where items have the purchaser's selling price placed directly at the factory.

premium. N. (1) In merchandising, a product that is offered free or at less than the regular price in order to induce the consumer to buy another product. (2) In retailing, an offer of merchandise, at a minimal cost or at no charge, as an inducement to the customer to purchase a given item. See also *coupon, direct premium, referral premium*. (3) In advertising, the higher charge paid for special advertising, as with a preferred position. Synonymous with *premium pricing*. See also *trade premium*.

premium jobber. N. A wholesaler of incentive items who usually deals with a full range of merchandise. See also *jobber*.

premium money. N. See *push money*.

premium offers. N. They are (a) a free gift; (b) the free, send-away premium (a free gift in exchange for proof of purchase); and, (c) a self-liquidating premium where the consumer sends both money and proof of purchase to obtain the offer.

premium pricing. N. See *premium (3)*.

premium representative. N. (1) A manufacturer's representative working with premium users; offers factory price, support, experience, and personal attention. (2) A commission salesperson serving a host of manufacturers on a direct-factory-price basis.

prepackaging. N. (1) Packaging of fresh foods (meat, vegetables, cheeses, etc.) in consumer units for self-service sales. (2) In merchandising, avoiding repackaging by the retailer by having the manufacturer package merchandise such as chinaware and furniture so that it may be sold directly to the consumer without opening. Synonymous with *prepak*.

prepaid. ADJ. Indicating that shipping charges have already been paid or are to be paid at the point of delivery.

prepaid expenses. N. (1) Payment for items not yet received. (2) A charge deferred for a period of time until the benefit for which payment has been made occurs.

prepak. N. See *prepackaging*.

prepay. V. To pay before or in advance of receipt of goods or services.

prepayment. N. Payment of a debt before it actually becomes due.

prepayment clause. N. The privilege of repaying part or all of a loan in advance of date or dates stated in a contract.

preposterior analysis. N. In marketing research, the attempt to determine if further information is worth the cost of generating it. See also *posterior analysis*.

prepricing. N. The manufacturer at times prints the retail or suggested price of an item directly on the packaging of the item. Although it saves the dealer the cost and time of pricing merchandise, it locks him or her into a situation where the items cannot be sold to a customer at a higher price. Synonymous with *premarketing, preticketing*.

preprint. N. (1) Making a copy of an advertisement before it is run in a print medium. Such advertisements are usually larger thatnthey will actually appear when printed and are also mounted on a board for display purposes. (2) Materials printed ahead of the publication's regular printing time schedule, e.g., freestanding inserts and advertisements printed on special paper stock.

prepurchase activity. N. The stage following the buyer becoming aware of the assets in purchasing a product; involves seeking information, sources of supply, and the lowering of uncertainty, with assessments each step of the way.

preretailing. N. Assignment by the retailer of retail prices to goods at the time an order is made, thus allowing the determination of retail values of items on order. This practice also speeds up the checking and marking procedures when merchandise arrives.

prerogatives. N. The rights, powers, and privileges of an individual that others do not possess.

prescreening. N. Those evaluation steps that follow ideation and precede the full screen. Involves entry evaluation, preliminary market analysis, and concept testing and development.

present value. N. The discounted value of a certain sum that is due and payable at a specified future date.

presold market. N. Buyers waiting for the arrival of a new product or service.

press. N. (1) The print news media. (2) A casual expression for publicity received for a service, item, accomplishment, or other effect from a company/marketing activity. Synonymous with *press coverage*.

press coverage. N. See *press*.

prestige advertising. N. Advertising to enhance the prestige of a firm or a firm's services or products. See also *corporate advertising*.

prestige pricing. N. Increasing the price of an item to establish a quality image of the product or the seller.

pressure-sensitive labels. N. Labels with an adhesive back that can be readily removed from their original sheets and attached to the mailing envelopes. Is assumed to be one of the incentives for recipients to respond to a mailing.

presumption. N. An assumed fact, which can serve as evidence until facts are obtained.

pretest. N. (1) A test given to determine an individual's performance in some area in advance of training, education, or some other condition that is expected to improve performance. See also *post test*. (2) In marketing, the measure of the acceptance of a concept, item, or service presented to prospects; usually accomplished with interviews and impacts on selling strategy.

preticketing. N. See *prepricing*.

prewrap. V. To wrap or package merchandise before it is placed on the floor for sale.

price. N. (1) That which the buyer gives up in exchange for something that provides satisfaction. (2) The amount of money a seller receives for goods or services at the factory or place of business. Price is not what the seller asks for the product or service, but what is actually received; one of the four Ps of marketing, and the only part of the marketing mix that produces revenues. See also *pricing*.

price agreement plan. N. A central purchasing accord where the purchaser for the stores arranges prices, colors, sizes, etc., in addition to the shipping terms. Synonymous with *catalog plan*.

price analysis. N. A purchaser's study of a supplier's costs to manufacture an item with the purpose of assisting the purchaser in negotiating a price similar to the supplier's cost to make.

price appeal. N. The practical instead of emotional approach to advertising, where the promotion of an item or service is based on the price of the service or item.

price-based shopping products. N. Products for which consumers believe the attributes of alternatives are relatively similar and look around for the least expensive items or stores.

price ceiling. N. A government-established maximum price.

price competition. N. Competition among firms that purport to differentiate their merchandise based on price alone. Items are marked as being preferred based on how much less they will cost. See also *nonprice competition*.

price control. N. (1) Regulation of the prices of goods and services with the intent to reduce increases in the cost of living. A government-imposed strategy that is rarely used. (2) In merchandising, the result of the demand by a manufacturer that the buyer for resale not be able to determine a resale price for the goods. See also *fair trade price*.

price cutting. N. Used usually when firms have excess capacity and wish to generate additional business without increasing selling efforts, adding the cost of advertising, or improving the item. Price cutting offers goods or services for sale at a price below that recognized as typical or appropriate by buyers and sellers. Coupons, rebates, larger packages at the same price, and lowering

price discretion. N. Reflected in the decision of a sales representative to alter the price of an item for purposes of making a sale.

price discrimination. N. The practice of charging different prices for the same quality and quantity of merchandise to different buyers. Should this practice result in reducing competition, it is illegal under the antitrust laws. See also *Robinson-Patman Act of 1936, functional discount.*

priced out of the market. N. See *price out of the market.*

price elasticity. N. Reflected in a reduction in sales when the price of an item is raised. See also *price inelasticity, elastic demand, income elasticity of demand, plasticity of demand.*

price equalization. N. A competitive pricing policy leading to a company's delivered price to a customer; composed of the price of the item at the factory plus the freight cost to the customer as if the shipment began at the shipping point of the company's competitor nearest to the company's customer.

price escalation. N. Advanced in the final price of an item or service because of unanticipated or miscalculated costs of distribution, transportation, tariffs, etc.

price fixing. N. An agreement by competing organizations to avoid competitive pricing by charging identical prices or by changing prices at the same time. Price fixing is in violation of the Sherman Antitrust Act. See also *conscious parallel action, price stabilization, price negotiation.*

price floor. N. The lowest price at which a company can sell an item or service and still realize a profit.

price-floor pricing

price-floor pricing. N. A form of cost-based pricing whereby a firm determines the lowest price at which it is worthwhile to increase the amount of goods or services it makes available for sale.

price guaranty. N. A seller's agreement to make a proportionate refund to a customer on all items in the buyer's inventory at the time of a price reduction. Usually has a time limit following purchase. Synonymous with *guaranty against price decline, price protection*.

price index. N. A measure to illustrate the changes in the average level of prices. See also *purchasing power of the dollar, wholesale price index*.

price inelasticity. N. A change in price that yields a disproportionately small change in demand. See also *price elasticity*.

price inflaters. N. Charges placed on top of the list price of an item or service which thereby increases its true selling price. Would include credit charges, service contracts, handling fees, etc.

price leader. N. See *price leadership*.

price leadership. N. (1) A situation in which prices can be determined by one major manufacturer in an industry, thus influencing others to accept the prices as determined. See also *administered price*. (2) Merchandise whose price has been significantly dropped to enhance store traffic. See also *loss leader*.

price level. N. The value of money in comparison with a specified base period.

price lining. N. (1) In retailing, placing several items of varying costs together and selling them all at the same price. This practice is used frequently in retailing. See also *loss leader*. (2) In marketing, a pricing strategy in which prices are used to sort products into

price planning

"lines" based on an attribute such as quality, prestige, or style. See also *price lining*.

price loco. N. The price at the place where a purchase occurs.

price-minus pricing. N. A method for determining the price of an item or service by initially estimating the price that the item or service would find a share of the market, and then developing the item or service to be profitable at that found price.

price mix. N. A firm's strategy of raising and lowering prices in order to meet competition head on.

price negotiation. N. Price fixing based on the belief that the purchaser is a price-maker rather than a price-taker. See also *price fixing*.

price-off. N. A price reduction that is used to induce trial or increase usage of a product. The percentage reduction is traditionally noted on the product package. See also *price leadership*.

price out of the market. N. Items that have been made so expensive that they are no longer purchased in their usual market (e.g., vendors of $12 ice cream cones would find themselves priced out of the juvenile market). See also *inelastic demand*.

price pack. N. Items available at a lower price to consumers. Two forms of price packs are: (a) reduced-price packs—two single packages sold together at a lowered rate, such as three for the price of two; and, (b) banded price packs—two related items, bound together and sold at a price lower than what it would cost if they were bought separately, such as shaving cream and a razor. See also *economy pack*.

price planning. N. Systematic decision making by an organization regarding all aspects of pricing.

price point. N. The standard retail price used by marketers for some items that vary slightly in wholesale cost but share a similar level of perceived value to the consumer, e.g., instead of selling five shirts on an absolute profit margin, resulting in prices such as $19.95, $18.75, $18.00, $17.50, and $17.00, the marketer could price all of them at $18.25. Small differences in price tend to have a disproportionate impact on sales.

price protection. N. See *price guaranty*.

price quality association. N. The belief that consumers equate high prices with higher quality and low price with lower quality. See also *prestige pricing*.

price reducers. N. Methods for lowering the selling price, i.e., providing free services, rebates, discounts, etc.

price repression. N. The deliberate reduction of domestic prices when imported items that are competitors are sold at significantly lower prices than the domestically produced items. Synonymous with *price suppression*.

price rigidity. N. A long-term lack of concern for prices of raw or produced items in relation to the inflationary aspects of a depression or recession.

price sensitive. N. The tendency of the demand for an item or service to vary based on the variations in price. Some items or services are more price sensitive than others, impacted by demand, availability etc. Marketers of price-sensitive items often test new prices before implementing them to assess the impact on demand. See also *elasticity, price elasticity*.

price shading. N. Where discounts are available to wholesalers, retailers, and consumers with the expectation that an increased demand will evolve.

price space. N. The distance between price points in the product line, i.e., the distance from one price to another.

price-specie flow theory. N. A theory stating that imports of precious metals increase the supply of funds and therefore advance the price level of items that use these metals.

price stabilization. N. Keeping prices at a state level. This is primarily a government strategy, especially during wartime or periods of rapid inflation, but it is illegal when practiced by private companies. See also *Sherman Antitrust Act of 1890*, *price fixing*.

price suppression. N. See *price repression*.

price system. N. The market system of resource allocation.

price takers. N. Firms that have no market power over price. Therefore, the market dictates price for them.

price war. N. A combative competition between firms by the lowering of prices in the attempt to undersell each other for sales. Often the result of a price war is the failure of one or more competitors.

price zone. N. Price lines that appeal to a group of a store's customers. See also *price lining*.

pricing. N. Setting or changing the cost to the consumer for a service or item. See also *price*, *pricing above the market*.

pricing above the market. N. Establishing prices lower than those of the competitor so as to maximize the use of price as a competitive factor.

pricing constraints. N. Factors that limit a firm's latitude in the price it may set.

prima facie. ADV. *(Latin)* At first view. That which appears to be true, until contrary evidence is given. ADJ. *prima facie.*

primary advertising. N. Used most by trade associations, advertising where the marketer tries to increase demand for a product category. Synonymous with *generic advertising.*

primary audience. N. In advertising, the target group for a particular advertising campaign. When a strategy is under discussion, the features and purchasing habits of a primary audience are to be evaluated carefully.

primary boycott. N. See *boycott.*

primary circulation. N. The number of households that purchase a particular publication. See also *pass-along circulation.* Synonymous with *primary readership.*

primary data. N. (1) Data that are collected specifically for use in a particular research project. (2) Information collected by a researcher from the original source. See also *secondary data.*

primary demand. N. (1) Demand for a product type. (2) Market demand for a product class rather than a particular brand.

primary demand advertising. N. (1) Advertising purporting to create primary buying motives with consumers. See also *selective demand advertising.* (2) Advertising in which the marketer attempts to create awareness of and provide information about a type of product.

primary groups. N. (1) Reference units to which a person belongs that provide a major influence on attitudes and behavior. (2) Groups that are small and intimate enough so that all of their members can communicate with one another face to face.

primary market. N. See *local market.*

primary market area. N. The major area of sale and distribution for an advertiser's goods or services, e.g., the primary market for bathing suits would be southern states or other warm climate areas. Synonymous with *heartland*.

primary needs. N. Based on Maslow's hierarchy of needs theory, the basic physiological needs are: hunger, thirst, shelter, and sex. Synonymous with *biogenic needs, innate needs, physiological needs*.

primary processed items. N. They are lumber, stone, clay, and glass; blast furnace and steel work products; nonferrous and other primary metals; fabricated metals; textiles; paper; chemicals; petroleum; and, rubber. See also *primary product*.

primary product. N. Any product of a farm, forest, or fishery, or any mineral, in its natural form or that has undergone such processing as is customarily needed to prepare it for marketing in substantial volume in international trade. See also *primary processed items*.

primary readership. N. See *primary circulation*.

primary research. N. Gathering market data in the field by a firm or individual to examine a specific marketing problem or situation.

primary service area. N. The geographical area surrounding a radio or television station in which the ground waves are not subject to objectionable interference or fading.

primary stage. N. See *pioneering stage*.

primary source list. N. Name and address records originally created by an owner rather than purchased or rented from other sources.

primary trading area. N. The geographic boundary in which a marketing organization has dominance, and often control.

prime time. N. In broadcasting, the few hours during the day that attract the largest audience, usually in the early evening. May differ for radio and television stations, and may be affected by the product described within the commercial, such as toys are best advertised on Sunday morning while children are watching television. See also *day parts, preferred position, drive time.*

principal. N. The face value of an instrument, which becomes the obligation of the maker or drawee to pay to a holder in due course. Interest is charged on the principal amount.

principal markets. N. The chief places in the nation of exportation where the items are freely sold or offered for sale, not necessarily the place where they are manufactured or delivered.

Principal Register. N. A classification of trademarks established by the Trade-Mark Act of 1946 in which certain qualified trademarks may be included.

principle of diminishing utility. N. As ownership usage decreases, the number of its units increases.

principle of marketing relativism. N. See *marketing relativism.*

principle of massed reserves. N. A concept of reducing the size of many inventories at the retail level while at the same time increasing the size of inventories carried by wholesalers, with the impact of lowering the total stock carried in the store.

principle of minimum total transactions. N. The inclusion of an intermediary between buyers and sellers that should reduce the number of transactions.

principle of postponement. N. See *postponement.*

principle of relative loss. N. A producer's failure to sell his or her goods to a retailer and thus retain unused capacity and unrealized profit opportunities.

prior analysis. N. Analysis that offers the reasons for selecting among alternative courses of action, all based on existing information. See also *posterior analysis, preposterior analysis.*

prior donor file. N. Computer listing of people who have already bought gifts from a marketer in a completed sale transaction. Prior donors are usually fine prospects for additional gift promotions.

prioritize. V. To set in order of preference or priority the attributes or needs of an organization. Assignments are made from this list of priorities.

priority practices. N. Unfair trading acts that are or will become trade barriers to an exporting nation.

prior source. N. A source from a previous order from a client who has ordered again. It is important to know who these people are, as they tend to become repeat buyers.

Privacy Act of 1974. N. Federal legislation designed to protect citizens from invasion of privacy by the federal government and permitting individuals, for the first time, to inspect information about themselves contained in federal agency files and to challenge, correct, or amend the material. The act prohibits an agency from selling or renting an individual's name or address for mailing list use.

private brand. N. (1) A middleperson-owned brand name or trade mark (e.g., Sears Roebuck owns the Kenmore brand). Synonymous with *private label*. (2) A brand sponsored by a wholesaler, retailer, dealer, or merchant, e.g., a supermarket item bearing a store label with an item's name, as contrasted with a brand having the name of a manufacturer or producer; usually priced lower than manufactured brands and appeals primarily to bargain conscious customers.

private cost. N. The cost of a specific item to an individual.

private label. N. See *private brand*.

private rate of return. N. The financial rate of return anticipated by businesspeople prior to investing their monies.

private sector. N. The segment of the total economy composed of businesses and households but excluding government. See also *public sector*.

private warehouse. N. See *warehouse, private*.

prize broker. N. The person who arranges the exchange of an advertiser's goods for free broadcast time or radio or television "plugs." Synonymous with *barter broker*.

prizm. N. Information used in segmenting a market based on a combination of geographic and demographic variables. The data defines areas by zip code, census tract, and block group. Such data is used in developing marketing mix variations and media planning to attempt to reach prospects most likely to purchase the sellers' merchandise.

proactive inhibition. N. An existing barrier resulting from a consumer's previous experience; an attitude that interferes with his or her learning of new relationship, concepts, etc. See also *prejudice*.

probability. N. Used by market and advertising researchers, the likelihood of the occurrence of an event, estimated as a ratio between the number of ways in which the event may occur and the number of ways in which alternative events may occur. See also *probability sampling*.

probability chain. N. An informal communication chain in which information is passed on a random basis.

probability sampling. N. Used by advertising analysts, a sampling technique in which each unit of the population has an equal chance of appearing in the sample. See also *random sample*. Synonymous with *random sampling*.

probability theory. N. See *probability*.

probable error. N. Used in market research, a measure of dispersion, variation, or scatter on both sides of the arithmetic mean, yielding a space that includes one-half the total number of cases. It is computed by multiplying the standard deviation by 0.6745.

problem. N. A situation where a decision maker must resolve questions involving uncertainty.

problem analysis. N. A part of the problem find/solve method of concept generation. Relates to finding the problems and involves the study of users to learn their dissatisfactions and unmet needs.

problem awareness. N. The stage in the final consumer's decision process during which the consumer recognizes that the good, service, organization, person, place, or idea under consideration may solve a problem of shortage or unfulfilled desire.

problem child. N. *(slang)* A high growth item that can only attract a low market share. If prolonged, the company either must abandon the item or invest more money into it to alter its appearance or for promotional activities.

problem definition. N. The first stage in marketing research, where a clear and detailed statement of the problem emerges.

problem detection analysis. N. A study focusing on the complaints or problems that consumers have with the item or service.

problem find/solve. N. A general method of concept generation, usually thought to be the best. Requires finding problems faced by customers and other users and solving them. In the solutions are found new product concepts.

problem identification. N. The first stage of the problem analysis method of ideation. Involves finding, describing, and analyzing the problem(s) of target market participants.

problem-solution advertisement. N. An advertisement that concentrates on a consumer issue and provides a solution to the problem, e.g., a cigarette smoking kit for ceasing the habit will remind viewers and listeners of the health risks in smoking.

problem solving. N. An activity resulting in suggestions or recommendations that express in concise, quantified terms the advantages and disadvantages to a firm of pursuing a possible future course of action or the advantages of various alternative operations.

proceeds. N. (1) The actual amount of funds given to a borrower, following deductions for interest charges, fees, and so on. (2) The funds received by a seller after deductions for the payment of commissions (e.g, proceeds from a sale).

process analysis. N. The study of the approaches used for producing a part or a product for purposes of yielding the lowest cost and most efficient process that will produce items of adequate quality.

process average. N. In purchasing, noting the average percent of defective parts found in a supplier's shipment. It helps in deciding the degree of inspection where it is to be determined by sample.

process control. N. A monitoring method to assure that the production system is functioning properly.

process costing. N. A method of product costing whereby costs are accumulated by process or work centers and averaged over all products manufactured in those centers for a specified period.

process departmentation. N. Grouping jobs into subunits based on the sequential processes involved in an organization's operations. This is common in one-product plants, such as oil refineries.

processing in transit. N. See *transit privileges*.

process inspection. N. Inspection at intervals during or between production operations. See also *quality control*.

process machinery. N. See *installations*.

process-related ethical issues. N. Involves the unethical use of marketing strategies or tactics.

procurement. N. The purchase of goods for resale to a store's customers. Synonymous with *purchasing*. See also *purchasing agent*.

produce. V. To make or manufacture. N. In food retailing, fresh fruits and vegetables and the store's department where they can be purchased.

produce exchange. N. A market for perishable agricultural products.

producer. N. (1) An individual who manufactures goods or offers services. (2) In advertising, a person working on the staff of an advertising agency or an advertiser, or even on a freelance basis, who is responsible for the production of advertisements or commercials. (3) In marketing, creators of goods and services that are made for consumers of for a particular target market.

producer commodity cartel. N. An organization of producers of a key raw material commodity in world trade (e.g., the Organization of Petroleum Exporting Countries).

producer-controlled brands. N. Brands owned or controlled by firms that are primarily in the manufacturing business. Synonymous with *natural brand*.

producer cooperative. N. A member-owned wholesale operation that assembles farm products to sell in local markets.

producer goods. N. Items intended to be used and worn out in the course of producing other items in the future (e.g., ink in newspaper printing).

producer market. N. A set of buyers that purchase goods and services and use them to make other products.

producer price index. N. See *wholesale price index*.

product. N. (1) Goods and services made available to consumers; the total of benefits offered. See also *goods*. (2) In marketing, one of the four Ps of marketing; an offering that may satisfy a need or a want, which is offered to a target market for use. The item will project its benefits, styling, quality, brand name, and packaging to give it its own unique image or distinguishing characteristics.

product adaptation. N. Altering items to fulfill local or regional requirements, e.g., changing the current fixtures for items sold overseas.

product adoption process. N. The sequence of stages that individuals and firms go through in the process of accepting new products. The stages vary greatly in usage but tend to include (a) becoming aware of the new product; (b) seeking information about it; (c) developing favorable attitudes toward it; (d) trying it out in some direct or indirect way; (e) finding satisfaction in the trial; and, (f) adopting the product into a standing usage or repurchase pattern.

product advertising. N. Advertising whose goal is the attempt to create adequate demand for a product or service. Synonymous with *brand advertising*.

product assortment. N. The brands and types of items in a product class available to consumers.

product attributes. N. The characteristics by which products are identified and differentiated. Usually comprises features and benefits.

product augmentation. N. A technique for maintaining sales of items marketed in their mature life cycle stage. The life may be extended by repackaging, reducing its selling price, etc.

product buy-back agreement. N. See *buy-back agreement*.

product champion. N. A person who takes an inordinate interest in seeing that a particular process or product is fully developed and marketed. The role varies from situations calling for little more than stimulating awareness of the item to extreme cases where the champion tries to force the item past the strongly entrenched internal resistance of company policy or that of objecting parties.

product characteristics. N. Attributes that buyers and sellers use when deciding if a product or service meets a particular need.

product class. N. A group of items that are treated as natural substitutes or complements by most consumers.

product concept. N. The general belief that consumers are interested in purchasing quality items at fair and reasonable prices, thus the manufacturer concentrates on means to fulfill these characteristics, such as improving the item's performance at minimal cost.

product costing

product costing. N. The assignment of manufacturing costs to products in order to determine the cost of finished goods. See also *absorption costing, variable cost, period expense.*

product deletion. N. See *simplification.*

product depth. N. The number of items in each product line that is available for purchase.

product design model. N. In the new product development process, a concept to determine the most desirable characteristics for a net item by creating the ideal relationship between product features and attributes to advance its marketability. See also *conjoint analysis, multidimensional scaling.*

product development. N. The generation of new ideas for new or improved goods to be added to or to replace existing items.

product differentiation. N. See *differentiation.*

product disfeature. N. A characteristic of a product that the consumer does not like; frequently, its price.

product driven. N. The manufacturer's strategy of concentrating on the production of items with minimal concern for the needs of the prospect. The assumption is made that if the item is a quality one or can create a need, people will purchase it.

product elimination. N. Removing a product from a company's list of offered items, usually after the product has passed the decline stage of the life cycle.

product feature approach. N. Determining channels of distribution by assuming that size, unit value, perishability, etc., is used for fitting the item into a channel set to handle them.

product fit. N. The degree to which a product fulfills the needs of the marketplace.

product form. N. The physical shape or nature of a good or the sequential steps in a service. Form is provided by one or more technologies and yields benefits to the user; for example, many technologies go to make a front-wheel drive form of an automobile. Products of the same form make up a group within a product class (for example, all front-wheel drive automobiles). Differences in form of service separate discount and full-service stock brokers.

product hierarchy. N. An organizational chart-type array of the products offered in a given market, breaking first into class, then form, the variations on form, then brand. There are various options within these product hierarchy dimensions, so the array can be designed to fit the needs of the analyst. The hierarchy concept fits services as well as goods.

product image. N. How a prospect or user perceives one or more characteristics of an item. This image may be as important, or more important, to the specific real usage of the item. See also *brand awareness*, *perception*, *product positioning*.

product improvement. N. Activities for increasing sales by upgrading an item's attributes to attract either new customers or to encourage existing customers to buy the product more often. Product improvement is carried out by: (a) quality improvement—increasing the function of the product, such as making it stronger to last longer; (b) feature improvement—where new features are added to introduce versatility or convenience for people, such as the adding of accessories; and, (c) style improvement—altering the item to enhance its physical or aesthetic appeal, such as a new design for a television set. Synonymous with *product modification*.

product innovation gap. N. The difference between a firm's projected sales/profit goals and what its current product line is expected to produce. The gap must be filled by some form of product innovation.

product innovation strategy. N. The decision by management to compete with another firm in the introduction of a new product, and not on the basis of price, promotion, etc.

product introduction. N. The first stage of the product life cycle, during which the new item is announced to the market and offered for sale. See also *divest-and-exit strategy*.

production. N. (1) Any form of activity that adds value to goods and services, including creation, transportation, and warehousing until used. (2) A criterion of effectiveness that refers to an organization's ability to provide the outputs demanded of it by the environment. (3) Usually, but not always, the same as manufacturing.

production costs. N. Funds used in manufacturing an item for market consumption, either as fixed or variable.

production effect (of a tariff). N. The increase in domestic production of an item as a result of its increase in price resulting from a protective tariff.

production era. N. Devotion to the physical distribution of products due to high demand and low competition. Consumer research, product modifications, and adapting to consumer needs are unnecessary.

production fit. N. The compatibility of a new product with established manufacturing equipment and processes.

production inventory. N. The stock of items that is consumed in manufacturing, such as raw materials, parts, supplies, etc.

production oriented diversification. N. See *congruent production diversification*.

production sharing. N. A situation in which a product is manufactured in one country, assembled in another, and marketed in a third. See also *re-export*. Synonymous with *outward processing*.

product item. N. A specific model, brand, or size of a product that a company sells.

productive efficiency. N. A situation that exists when there is no possibility of increasing the yield of one item without decreasing the yield of another item.

productivity. N. A measurement of the efficiency of production; a ratio of output to input (e.g., ten units per manhour).

product liability. N. Liability imposed for damages caused by accident and arising out of goods or products manufactured, sold, handled, or distributed by the insured or by other trading under his or her name. The accident must have occurred after possession of goods had been relinquished to others and away from premises owned, rented, or controlled by the insured. In the case of food products, however, the accident does not have to occur away from the premises (e.g., in a restaurant). See also *warranty, consumer protection legislation*.

product life cycle. N. (1) A sequence of stages in the marketing of a product that begins with commercialization and ends with removal from the market. (2) The six stages of market acceptance of any goods: pioneering, growth, maturity, saturation, decline, and abandonment. See also *growth stage*. ABBRV. *PLC*.

product line. N. The assortment of items presented by a firm, or a group of items that are closely related because they either satisfy a need, are used with each other, are sold to the same consumer, are marketed within the same outlets, or are within similar price ranges. See also *line, product mix, service line*.

product management. N. The business activities dealing with the evolution of new items or brands, their introduction to the market, and their management through the product life cycle.

product manager. N. An executive responsible for marketing approaches, such as promotion, pricing, distribution, and establishing product characteristics. The product manager deals more with the planning aspects than with the actual selling to the consumer. Synonymous with *brand manager, program manager, project manager.* See also *marketing management, sales manager.*

product manager system. N. A product management organizational format under which a middle manager focuses on the performance of a single product (brand) or a small group of products (brands). This manager handles both new and existing products and is involved with everything from marketing research to package design to advertising.

product market. N. See *consumer market.*

product market grid. N. Used primarily in developing market coverage strategies, a chart that identifies market segments that are to be or have been targeted.

product/market opportunity matrix. N. Identifies four alternative marketing strategies that may be used to maintain or increase sales of business units and products: market penetration, market development, product development, and diversification.

product markets. N. Markets in which firms sell the outputs that they produce.

product/market segment. N. That portion of a product marketed defined in terms of geographic area, end-use application, customer demographic characteristics, type of customer institution, or buyer behavior.

product mix. N. The composite of items offered for sale by one company. Some firms have a wide product mix geared toward a diverse consumer group, while others maintain a narrow product mix geared toward a particular market segment. See also *mix*, *product line*.

product modification. N. See *product improvement*.

product motives. N. Why people purchase a particular product.

product obsolescence. N. The effect on items that become less attractive to the consumer because of the introduction of newly improved items that do the job less expensively or better, or perhaps both. See also *planned obsolescence*.

product pattern. N. An organizational pattern whereby jobs and activities are grouped on the basis of types of products or services.

product planning. N. The process leading to the identification of goals and procedures as well as the precise nature of the merchandise to be marketed. See also *marketing research*.

product-planning committee. N. A product management organizational format staffed by high-level executives from various functional areas including marketing, production, engineering, finance, and research and development. It handles product approval, evaluation, and development on a part-time basis.

product portfolio. N. (1) A group of products marketed by the same company. (2) A company's product mix viewed from a strategic perspective; a set of products or brands that are at different stages in the product life cycle.

product positioning. N. The way in which a product is characterized to attract consumer interest and purchase. A product may be positioned in a variety of ways, such as economical, durable, stylish, safe, convenient, and so forth. See also *perceptual mapping, positioning, product image, product space*.

product proliferation. N. An excess of products performing the same or similar function. Usually results from too many firms entering into the manufacture of competing products.

product protection. N. In advertising, separating advertisements of competing items so that either time or pages keep readers from seeing one item after the other. Synonymous with *commercial protection, separation*.

product quality. N. (1) An objective measure of a product's conformance to requirements, to perform as intended and advertised. See also *ISO, ISO 9000*. (2) A subjective measure of a product's performance as determined by user's reaction to the items' price, packaging, promotion, service, and channel of distribution.

product recall. N. Calling back of an item because of imperfection, defect, or other problem. At times a governmental agency demands that a product be recalled when violations of a law is determined. See also *recall*.

product-related ethical issues. N. Involves the ethical appropriateness of marketing certain products.

product relaunch. N. A product management strategy that focuses on finding new markets and untapped market segments, new product uses, and ways to stimulate increased use of a product by existing customers.

product reliability. N. The probability that a product will perform a stated function under specific conditions for a specified period without failure. See also *guarantee*.

product reputation advertising. N. See *commercial advertising, promotional advertising*.

product research. N. See *qualitative market analysis*.

product screening. N. The process of eliminating proposed products from future consideration.

product segmentation. N. In industrial marketing, the subdivision of a market on the basis of product specifications that fulfill the needs of the purchaser.

product/service life cycle. N. The market phases for most products and services.

product shifting. N. The switch from the manufacture and export of one item to the manufacture and export of still another.

products market equilibrium. N. A situation in which aggregate demand equals aggregate supply.

product space. N. The dimensions of a product, including those impacted by human senses, such as touch and smell, but also including price and size. See also *product positioning*.

product-specific buying factors. N. Product-based variables that lead to either autonomous (independent) or joint decision making. These variables include perceived risk, purchase frequency, and time pressure.

product-specific investments. N. Capital investments made for facilities, equipment, and personnel resources for use in stocking, selling, and servicing a specific product line.

product spotter. N. Any eye- or ear-catching device, such as a colored spotlight, for attracting consumer's attention to a product or package. Used most frequently in promoting a new item.

product-structured sales force. N. A sales force organization where sellers are assigned particular items or item lines. Used most often by sellers of sophisticated or technical products enabling the sales force to be experts in the workings of a specific product. See also

product testing

market-structured sales force, territory-structured sales force, sales force.

product testing. N. A system for testing and certifying products, calling for the mutual recognition of testing and certification so that a product approved by authorities in one country would be marketed anywhere else. See also *market testing.*

product usage segmentation. N. Ane of a four-way classification of the strategies of segmentation that relates observed factors of use to the way in which consumers with specific characteristics respond to certain marketing mixes. See also *benefit segmentation, state-of-being segmentation, state-of- mind segmentation.*

product use test. N. One of several key evaluation steps in the product development process. Involves giving some of the new product to persons or firms in the intended target market and asking them to use it for a time and report their reactions to it. The purposes of a product-use test are (a) to see if the item developed by the organization has the attributes prescribed for it; (b) to learn whether it satisfies the market needs identified during the ideation process; and, (c) to disclose information about how and by whom the item is used.

product width. N. (1) The number of product lines that a company offers to the public. (2) When a large variety of different items is available within a classification.

professional advertising. N. (1) Advertising by professional people, i.e., doctors, lawyers, etc. (2) Advertising by manufacturers or distributors whose message is pointed to a professional group seeking their support, approval, or at times their endorsement.

profile analysis. N. Used by consumer and marketing analysts, a method for appraising individual uniqueness and characteristics

profile sheet. N. A form that displays the characteristics of a proposed product at the time of screening. Scores are plotted on a diagram for easier analysis.

profit. N. (1) The reward to the entrepreneur for the risks assumed by him or her in the establishment, operation, and management of a given enterprise or undertaking. See also *uncertainty theory*. (2) The monies remaining after a business has paid all its bills. (3) In marketing, the excess of the selling price over all costs and expenses incurred in making a sale. See also *profit impact of marketing strategy*.

profitability. N. A firm's ability to earn a profit and its potential for future earnings.

profitability measures. N. The ratios of net profit to capital, to total assets, and to sales.

profit and loss statement. N. The summary listing of a firm's total revenues and expenses within a specified time period. Synonymous with *income and expense statement*.

profit-based pricing objectives. N. Those that orient a firm's pricing strategy toward some type of profit goals; profit maximization, satisfactory profit, return on investment, or early recovery of cash.

profit center. N. A segment of a business that is responsible for both revenues and expenses.

profit impact of marketing strategy. N. A program that provides individual companies with a database summarizing the financial and market performance of a few thousand business units representing several hundred firms. It focuses on the links between various factors and profitability/cash flow. ABBRV. *PIMS*.

profit margin. N. Sales less all operating expenses divided by the number of sales.

profit maximization. N. Corporate strategy to fulfill maximum long-term profits from a marketing effort, as opposed to emphasis on capturing or marketing or fulfilling a social need of consumers, which may or may not be as profitable. Synonymous with *profit optimization*.

profit optimization. N. See *profit maximization*.

profit oriented audit. N. Assessing a marketing plan in relation to expenses and revenues generated by that plan.

profit taking strategy. N. See *milking*.

profit target analysis. N. Determining the volume of sales required to pay for all the costs of operation and still command a predetermined profit for the firm.

pro forma invoice. N. A preliminary invoice indicating the value of the items listed and informing the recipient that all have been sent. It is not a demand for money.

program evaluation and review technique. N. A method to facilitate planning and to give management tools for the control of specific programs. Original PERT programs were developed by the U.S. Navy. See also *critical path method, PERT/COST*. ABBRV. *PERT*.

program manager. N. See *product manager*.

program merchandising. N. Combined efforts of a retailer and a key source to make merchandising and promotion plans for a store.

pseudo sale. N. A category of market testing methods wherein the customer does various things to indicate reaction to the product and to its marketing strategy but does not actually spend money.

psychic income. N. Nonmonetary income regarded by an individual as desirable to fulfill his or her needs, wants, and psychological demands. Power, control, independence, and actualization are examples of psychic income. Synonymous with *intangible rewards*.

psychographic market segmentation. N. In segmentation, choosing people who react in the identical fashion to a particular emotional appeal, or who share common behavioral patterns. See also *demographic segmentation*.

psychographic segmentation. N. See *psychographic market segmentation*.

psychographics. N. Psychological profiles of prospects within a given market.

psychological discounting. N. Offering an illusionary lowering of prices by providing artificial comparisons of present price with an earlier price, where the earlier price never even existed. Illegal today. Synonymous with *was-is-pricing*.

psychological moment. N. That point when the salesperson feels he or she is ready to attempt the trial close.

psychological pricing. N. See *odd pricing*.

psychological product. N. The physical product along with its warranties, services, and psychological overtones.

psychological satisfaction. N. The satisfaction received from the intangible benefits of a product, such as a feeling of self-worth. See also *physiological motives*.

psychometric. N. A technique used by market researchers; any quantitative measurement of an individual's psychological traits or assets.

publication. N. Any material published in any format, e.g., magazines and newspapers.

publication-set. N. An advertisement that is set in type by the publication where it is to appear, ready for final publication. ABBRV. *pub-set*.

public consumption monopoly. N. A governmental monopoly created to regulate the consumption of specific items that are considered harmful. See also *sumptuary laws*.

public domain. N. Federally owned land.

publicity. N. (1) Any message about an organization that is communicated through the mass media but is not paid for by the organization. (2) Any event or communication, through established media or otherwise, free or paid, solicited or not, that attracts attention to a product or service. See also *advertising, public relations*.

publicity agent. N. A person or organization whose responsibility it is to disseminate news and information about clients through such channels of communication as newspapers, magazines, radio stations, and other media, the use of which is not paid for by the clients.

public policy. N. Any conduct that affects the public good.

public relations. N. (1) Any communication or activity created or performed primarily to enhance prestige or goodwill for an individual or organization. See also *publicity*. (2) In marketing, a promotional activity that aims to communicate a favorable image of a product or its marketer and to promote goodwill. Differs from

public relations institutional advertising. N. Advertising directed toward enhancing the image and reputation of a company. See also *patronage institutional advertising, public service advertising.*

public responsibility. N. The responsibilities of individuals or groups that are presumed to reflect the broader and more pervasive needs of the entire community, state, or nation.

publics. N. Groups, such as customers, shareholders, government agencies, etc., to which a firm markets its merchandise and services or that affect the firm's ability to succeed in achieving its goals.

publics' demand. N. The characteristics and needs of employees, unions, stockholders, consumer groups, the general public, government agencies, and other internal and external forces that affect company operations.

public sector. N. The segment of the total economy that includes all levels of government and excludes businesses and households. See also *private sector.*

public service advertising. N. (1) Advertising with a central focus on the public welfare, usually sponsored by a not-for-profit organization, religious institutions, political group, or trade association. (2) Advertising related not to the marketing of products, but to social betterment goals, (e.g., preventing forest fires, promoting traffic safety, securing blood donations, etc.). See also *Advertising Council, patronage institutional advertising, public relations institutional advertising, advocacy advertising, social advertising.*

public warehouse. N. An organization offering storage space for a fee to any person who seeks out the service. See also *warehouse.*

publisher letter. N. See *lift letter*.

publisher's representative. N. An independent organization or person that sells advertising space for a publication.

pub-set. ABBRV. Publication-set.

puff. N. *(slang)* A free promotion of a product or service.

puffery. N. (1) A story or news release lacking news value or perceived to be overly self-serving. (2) In advertising, an exaggerated advertising campaign or promotion, often with words such as "the best," "the greatest," "the longest lasting," etc. Deception can be the next step.

pull. N. The ability of an advertisement to enhance sales, as the "advertisement pulled well."

pull communication strategy. N. The practice of creating initial interest for an offering among potential buyers, who in turn demand the offering from intermediaries, ultimately "pulling" the offering through the channel. The principal emphasis is on consumer advertising and consumer promotions. See also *push communication strategy*.

pull date. N. The date stamped on perishable products (e.g., bakery and dairy goods), after which the items should not be sold.

pulling power. N. (1) The ability to draw an audience. (2) In advertisement, the power of an advertisement or of an advertising medium in which a sales message is placed to draw response from the advertiser's prospects and customers, usually measured by the number of orders or inquiries received after publication of the advertisement.

pull strategy. N. A promotional strategy in which each channel member attempts to persuade the next member in the system to handle and promote the product. See also *push-pull strategy*.

pulsation. N. Using advertisements on a sporadic basis, with spacing so as not to saturate the market. Money is also saved. Synonymous with *wave scheduling, waving*. See also *pulsing strategy*.

pulsing strategy. N. A media scheduling strategy in which a continuous campaign is combined with short bursts of heavier advertising. See also *pulsation*.

purchase allowance. N. A lowering of the price of an item when the merchandise as requested does not meet the expectations as identified on the invoice. See also *on consignment, returns to vendor*.

purchase contract. N. An agreement between a buyer and seller that itemizes items and services to be bought and sold, respectively.

purchase decision. N. The final stage in the buying process culminating in the choice to buy the item or service from a particular supplier.

purchase discount. N. A reduction in the price of an order that has been paid promptly.

purchase distribution. N. The percentage of all retail outlets that received a shipment of the product since a previous audit, whether or not they were in stock then or at the current audit.

purchase frequency. N. The frequency of purchase of a specific product.

purchase history. N. A customer record of purchases over a time period.

purchase order. N. A statement permitting a vendor to deliver merchandise or materials at an agreed-upon price.

purchase price. N. The amount for which an item or service is bought.

purchase privilege offer. N. See *semi-liquidator, trade cards*.

purchaser. N. (1) A buyer. (2) A person who obtains title to or an interest in property by the act of purchase.

purchase requisition. N. See *requisition*.

purchase research. N. See *value analysis*.

purchase returns and allowances. N. A contra-purchases account in which the returns or allowances for previously purchased merchandise are recorded.

purchasing. N. See *procurement*.

purchasing agent. N. An individual who buys products for store maintenance and daily operation, not for resale to customers. Some purchasing agents are employed as company staff, others are independent middlepeople who work for a company on a contractual basis and are paid on commission. See also *procurement*.

purchasing leverage. N. The impact of effective purchasing on profitability.

purchasing power. N. (1) The value of money measured by the items it can buy. See also *real value of money*. Synonymous with *buying power*. (2) In marketing, the capacity to purchase possessed by an individual buyer, a group of buyers, or the aggregate of the buyers in an area or market.

purchasing power of the dollar. N. A measurement of the quantity of goods and services that a dollar will buy in a specified market, compared with the amount it could buy in some base period. It is obtained by taking the reciprocal of an appropriate price index.

pure competition. N. A situation in which there are many sellers and buyers of a standardized product or service with free entrance to the market and no collusion. The primary characteristics of pure competition are: (a) a large degree of homogeneity between items; (b) the number of sellers is so large that the marketing mix variations by one seller does not impact market prices; and, (c) where sellers have no need for a price policy since the market will determine price, thus reflecting what consumers are actually willing to pay. See also *imperfect competition*, *perfect competition*.

Pure Food and Drug Act of 1906. N. Federal legislation prohibiting manufacturers' mislabeling of the contents of food, liquor, and medicine containers.

pure impulse buying. N. Impulse purchasing where the customer purchases because he or she becomes consumed with the uniqueness or worthiness of the offering. See also *planned impulse buying*, *reminder impulse buying*.

pure market economy. N. A competitive economic system of numerous buyers and sellers, in which prices are determined by the free interaction of supply and demand.

pure monopoly. N. See *perfect (pure) monopoly*.

pure premium. N. A premium, arrived at by dividing losses by exposure, to which no loading has been added for commissions, taxes, or expenses.

pure profit. N. See *economic profit*.

pure public item. N. An item consumed in equal amount by all people, even though the item may have different value to these people. No one can be excluded from being a customer of a pure public item (e.g., air, water, a sidewalk).

push incentive. N. Some form of compensation, traditionally money, offered to retail salespersons to push the sale of a particular item; offered by a manufacturer, the head of a chain store, or the executive of a larger department store. Synonymous with *spiffs*.

pushing strategy. N. See *push-pull strategy*.

push money. N. See *spiffs*.

push communication strategy. N. The practice of "pushing" an offering through a marketing channel in a sequential fashion, with each channel representing a distinct target market. The principal emphasis is on personal selling and trade promotions directed toward wholesalers and retailers. See also *pull communication strategy*.

push or pull distribution strategy. N. See *push-pull strategy*.

push-pull strategy. N. (1) A promotional strategy in which the producer uses mass promotion to stimulate demand in the consumer market, thereby causing intermediaries to want to carry the product. (2) The balance between a firm's attempts to stimulate the demand for its products by pushing them forward through the channels through efforts aimed at the middleperson and pulling the goods through the channels to the consumer through promotional efforts aimed directly at the market. Synonymous with *push strategy*. See also *pull strategy*.

push strategy. N. See *push-pull strategy*.

putting-out system. N. The second stage in the evolution of a materially productive civilization, initially characterized by an entrepreneur's agreement to take all the output an individual (or family) can produce at a fixed price. This stage eventually progressed to the stage at which the entrepreneur provided the workers with the raw materials and paid them on a piece-rate basis for finished goods.

pyramiding. N. See *pyramid selling*.

pyramid ratio. N. A tool used in the analysis of management and income to determine the relationship of profits and capital.

pyramid schemes. N. See *pyramid selling*.

pyramid selling. N. Business opportunity frauds, usually promoted through advertisements for job opportunities guaranteed to yield enormous or quick profits, requiring little education or demanding a minimal personal investment. There are government regulations against certain pyramid schemes. The pyramider induces many people to buy his or her products, which they are to resell at a higher price. For example, if ten people buy fifty units each but can sell only fifteen each, the pyramider is still ahead, because he or she has sold five hundred units. See also *fraud, roll-out*.

Q&A format. N. See *question-and-answer format.*

QERs ABBRV. *Quantitative restrictions.*

Q-rating. N. In research conducted on audience behavior, the level of awareness people have about a broadcast program or personality; measures how many television viewers or radio listeners are familiar with a particular program and if they regard it as their favorite. Synonymous with *Q-score.*

QR inventory system. N. See *quick response inventory system.*

QRs. ABBRV. *Quantitative restrictions.*

Q-score. N. See *Q-rating.*

Q-sort. N. A personality inventory in which the individual sorts a considerable number of statements into piles that represent the degrees to which the statements apply to him or her.

Q-system. N. An inventory control system that holds the reorder quantity constant and shifts the reorder period. Synonymous with *reorder system.*

quadrangle. N. See *advertising quadrangle.*

qualified lead. N. (1) In retailing, a person who shows interest, usually by making an inquiry from a retailer, in purchasing an item or service. (2) In merchandising, an individual possessing the financial ability to purchase an item or service; a valid potential customer. See also *qualifying.*

qualified prospect. N. A potential customer who is able to buy a product and has the authority to make a decision to purchase. This conclusion is often arrived at following a check on the individual's credit.

qualifying. N. Determining whether or not a sales prospect is a serious and potential customer, and, therefore, worth following. Attempts are made to minimize lost time and to avoid involvement with people who are not interested in or able to make a purchase. Criteria used are: (a) the seller determining if the prospect has the funds to purchase the item or service; (b) whether the prospect has the authority for making the decision to buy; and, (c) whether the prospect has a need to secure the product or service. See also *prospecting*.

qualifying decisions. N. See *qualifying dimensions*.

qualifying dimensions. N. Characteristics of people in a target market making them eligible to purchase a product or service. Synonymous with *qualifying decisions*.

qualifying (descriptive) variables. N. A set of variables that allow or qualify an individual to be a member of a particular market segment.

qualitative factor. N. A factor that is significant but cannot be measured precisely and easily.

qualitative market analysis. N. The examination of the market with the goal of gathering data that can affect the product or service. Synonymous with *product research*.

qualitative research. N. To gain awareness that is useful in defining a group or situation, market research that is not statistical in nature; describes the nature, type, or components of a consumer group or market situation. Qualitative research generated cannot be extrapolated to larger populations. See also *quantitative research*.

quality. N. A product's or service's characteristic making it appropriate for its intended goal; a product or service that is valid.

quality control. N. (1) The attempt to ensure the presence of qualitative factors in a product or standards of performance in a service. See also *process inspection*. (2) The traditional approach to quality in which problems are detected after manufacturing and an effort is made to remove substandard products before shipping them to customers.

quality creep. N. A new product that is better than it needs to be to fulfill needs of its target customers.

quality description. N. A message to the supplier of the type and features of the item required.

quality discount. N. A lowering of price offered by the seller as a way to get the purchaser to buy large quantities of the item.

quality market. N. A market in which quality is more important than price.

quantitative export restrictions. N. See *voluntary restraint agreements, quantitative restrictions*. ABBRV. *QERs*.

quantitative factor. N. A factor that affects decision making and can be measured numerically.

quantitative research. N. Involves representative sampling of respondents; a market research technique of a statistical nature that involves the measurement of quantifiable amounts; entails collecting data, the result being statistics that are assigned specific characteristics or values as variables. See also *qualitative research*.

quantitative restrictions. N. Of concern to global marketers; specific limits on the quantity or value of goods that can be imported or exported during a specific time period. Synonymous with *export quotas, quantity restrictions*. ABBRV. *QRs*.

quantity demanded. N. The amount that would be purchased at a particular price, at a moment of time. See also *marginal propensity to invest*.

quantity discount. N. See *patronage discount*.

quantity restrictions. N. See *quantitative restrictions*.

quantum meruit. N. *(Latin)* As much as is merited; a principle of business law providing that when a service is given without a written estimate of price, there is an implied promise by the purchaser of the service to pay for the work as much as it is worth.

quais. N. As if; that which resembles.

quarter showing. N. The display of car-card advertising in one fourth of the subway cars, buses, or other means of transportation included in the transit advertising service offered to advertisers.

quasi-chain. N. Independently owned retail outlets that are affiliated with a form of central organization. See also *voluntary chain*.

query. N. A customer or prospective customer's request for information on his or her account or about the item or service involved. See also *customer service, inquiry*.

question-and-answer format. N. In advertising, a method for writing copy where the advertiser or a spokesperson for the advertiser responds to questions posed by the customer or prospective customer. Primarily used in print media. ABBRV. *Q&A format*.

question mark. N. A strategic-business unit that has a low relative market share and is in a high-growth market.

questionnaire. N. Used by marketing and advertising researchers, a set of questions seeking objective data or subjective opinion on a given subject. The questions are intended not to test an individual's ability to answer the questions (e.g., to arrive at a score), but rather to elicit responses with respect to the subject at hand.

quick response inventory system. N. A cooperative effort between retailers and their suppliers aimed at reducing retail inventory while providing a merchandise supply that more closely addresses the actual buying patterns of consumers.

quid pro quo. N. *(Latin)* Something for something; a mutual consideration; an advantage or a concession received in return for a similar favor.

quota. N. (1) The amount of production expected from the average employee in order to receive the specified base pay. See also *sales quota, trade quota*. (2) In merchandising, a specific limit on the number of items of a particular kind that my be imported.

quota cartel. N. An agreement among firms to a specific industry by which each participant is assigned a portion of market demand.

quota control sampling. N. See *quota sampling*.

quota sample. N. See *quota sampling*.

quota sampling. N. A sampling technique in which interviewers look for specific numbers of candidates with special characteristics. All units in the population do not have known or equal chances of being chosen. Synonymous with *quota control sampling*. See also *area sample, nonprobability sampling, sampling*.

quotation. N. An offer to sell goods at a stated price and under specified conditions.

quoted price. N. The stated price for an item or service.

R

rack

rack. N. The floor stand for holding goods on shelves, hooks, or in pockets. See also *rack jobber*.

rack jobber. N. (1) A limited-service wholesaler that supplies nonfood products to supermarkets, grocery stores, and drug retailers. (2) A wholesaler who maintains stocks of convenience-type merchandise, primarily in supermarkets, drugstores, and other related retail operations. He or she delivers merchandise by vehicle, sets up the displays and makes frequent visits to stores and refills the inventory of display items. See also *jobber*, *rack*.

Radiation Control for Health and Safety Act of 1968. N. Federal legislation establishing performance standards and limits of radiation that may be emitted from consumer items (television sets, microwave over, etc.)

radiation selling. N. Using a specific sale as a starting point for future related sales, based on the first sale as the example of need (e.g., selling the camera that will lead to sales of film and film processing services).

radio. N. A form of broadcast advertising medium. Its advantages include: being able to control when an advertisement appears, creating advertisements best adopted to sound, and being less expensive than television.

radio network. N. A group of radio stations linked to each other by telephone wire and simultaneously broadcasting programs originating from one of the stations.

rag business (trade). N. *(slang)* The sentimental name given to the fashion apparel industry. See also *rags*.

rags. N. *(slang)* Garments made by the apparel industry. See also *rag business*.

rain-lap posting. N. A method of posting outdoor advertising messages on panels in which one sheet or section is laid beginning at the bottom of the poster panel, the succeeding upper sections overlapping each other until the top of the panel is reached.

random demand. N. A change in market demand that has no pattern and cannot be forecasted.

random-digit dialing. N. A method for choosing household telephone numbers to be called during a research study; a sample method where numbers are randomly generated. In practice, the first three digits are retained, thus ensuring that all calls come from the same geographic area. Only the final four digits are chosen at random. Securing unlisted telephone numbers is the key to an accurate survey.

randomization. N. The process of choosing a sample on the basis of chance. See also *random sample*.

random sample. N. A limited number of observations chosen by chance from an entire aggregate of a phenomenon. In this form of sampling, every item in the population has the same chance of being chosen as any other items. See also *area sample, randomization, probability sampling, quota sampling*.

random sampling. N. See *probability sampling*.

range. N. A measure showing the approximate extent of total variability or dispersion, found by determining the difference between the lower limit of the lowest class interval and the upper limit of the highest class interval.

rate. N. (1) The movement and handling of goods or persons, the determining factor used in arriving at the charge or fare for services rendered. (2) The determining factor used to assess tariff duties. (3) In advertising, the cost of advertising space or

rate base 556

commercial broadcasting time in a medium, as set by owners of the medium; based on the circulation of the publication or the size of the listening or viewing audience, the quality of the medium's recipients, etc. The rate can vary once the advertiser exceeds a certain minimum dollar volume, or when payment of advertising expenses are made within a given time period.

rate base. N. The circulation of a periodical guaranteed as the base for its rate structure. The advertiser usually receives a refund should circulation fall below the agreed-upon rate base. See also *rate protection*.

rate book. N. Manufacturer's record listing products for sale and their prices.

rate card. N. A brief printing of media owners providing charges, a price list, for units of advertising space or advertising times. The card provides the advertiser with all necessary relevant information for advertising with a particular medium.

rate differential. N. The separation between the higher rate charged by the advertising media to national as contrasted with local advertisers. Should the difference be extreme, management must decide in the wisdom and expense for national advertising. See also *one-time rate*.

rate holder. N. (1) In advertising, an advertisement, usually the smallest space a publication will permit, that has been placed by an advertiser to "hold" a contracted discount rate offered by the publisher for a minimum number or insertions and/or lines. (2) In broadcasting, as above, where advertisers can purchase a ten-second spot for the same purpose.

rate protection. N. How long a time period the advertiser is guaranteed a specific rate base; usually from three months to a year from the time of contract signing. See also *rate base*.

rate war. N. A negative form of competition in which sellers drop their prices below their costs for purposes of putting the competition out of business. See also *predatory pricing, underselling*.

rating. N. (1) A traditional method of performance appraisal in which a judge evaluates performance in terms of a value or index that is used in some standard way. It traditionally involves global rating scales. (2) In outdoor advertising, an estimate of the number of people exposed to an outdoor advertisement. Each sign is rated in terms of the number of people who pass by it on a daily basis as compared to the total population in the community where the structure is found. The rating is used in determining the cost per thousand for outdoor advertising. (3) In broadcasting, the size of an actual listening or viewing audience for a specific program or commercial as contrasted with the size of the potential audience. Programs with high ratings deliver a large audience to advertisers for their commercials. See also *audience measurement*.

ratio analysis. N. Analysis of financial statements through a comparison of one figure, such as net profit, to another, such as sales or total investment.

rational appeals. N. Messages for the industrial prospect purporting to stimulate sales by promoting the item's economic and technical superiority instead of attempting to emphasize emotional or behavioral factors.

rational buying motives. N. All costs of money, use, labor, and profit that affect a purchaser. See also *motivation*.

rationality. N. The process of making decisions that serve to maximize the firm's goals.

rationalization. N. Any approach that has the potential to increase efficiency or output.

rationing. N. A technique for limiting purchases or usages of an item when the demanded quantity of the item exceeds the quantity available at a specific price. This occurs most often during wartime and under extremes of natural conditions (e.g., drought).

ratio of finished goods inventory to the cost of goods sold. N. A ratio determined by dividing the cost of goods sold by the average finished-goods inventory. The resulting figure is the number of times the investment in the finished-goods inventory has turned over during the period under consideration. The present ratio is compared with a similar ratio for several previous periods, since it portrays the stability and trend of sales or a possibly overstated or expanded inventory.

ratio of notes payable to accounts payable. N. A ratio whose desirability is determined by consideration of three quantitative factors: (a) notes issued in payment of merchandise; (b) notes issued to banks and brokers; and, (c) notes issued to others. If a relatively large number of the outstanding notes were issued to merchandise creditors, this might indicate that the firm is unable to take advantage of the cash discounts offered in the trade and that other lending agencies might consider the firm's credit unfavorably.

ratio of notes receivable to accounts receivable. N. A ratio that, if large as compared with other firms in a similar line of business, indicates that the firm with the high ratio may have a lax credit policy or may be extending credit to customers whose ability to pay promptly is dubious.

ratio of raw-materials inventory to cost of manufacture. N. A ratio determined by dividing the cost of goods manufactured by the average raw-materials inventory. The resulting figure is the number of times the investment in raw-materials inventory has turned over during the period under consideration. When the present ratio is compared with a similar ratio for a previous period, it portrays

reactive management

the trend and steadiness of production or indicates a possibly overstated or overexpanded inventory. See also *raw-materials inventory*.

raw data. N. Data that has not been processed or reduced.

raw material. N. Nonprocessed resources utilized in producing an item. The act of production results in an alteration in the form of the original material. See also *fabricated parts*.

raw-materials inventory. N. The items purchased by a manufacturing firm to be used in production. See also *ratio of raw-materials inventory to cost of manufacture*.

reach. N. (1) The percentage of total prospects that are exposed to a specific advertisement in a specified period. (2) The total audience a medium reaches, without duplication. See also *audience, coverage, exposure, frequency, cumulative audience*. Synonymous with *media coverage*.

reach and frequency. N. Components for determining the gross rating points obtained by a broadcast media schedule. Indicates how many household can be exposed to the schedule, and how often each households will be exposed. Multiplied together they show, by percentage, the total potential audience exposure in a particular market.

reactance. N. A boomerang effect that sometimes occurs when consumers are threatened with a loss of freedom of choice; they respond by doing the opposite of the behavior advocated in a persuasive message.

reactive management. N. A management style in which decision makers respond to problems rather than anticipating problems before they occur.

reactive selling. N. When customers seek out a particular vendor.

reader interest. N. Readers' expression of interest in an advertisement found in a particular publication.

reader response. N. The measurement of advertising and editorial readership based on orders and requests resulting from the appearance of an advertisement or editorial copy.

readership. N. (1) The total audience of a publication, including those who purchase the periodical or newspaper and those who secure it by other means. See also *pass-along circulation, circulation*. (2) In audience measurement, the percentage of an audience who can recall reading a print advertisement.

readership profile. N. A description of the people who read a particular magazine or newspaper. Describes their lifestyle, income, social relationships, etc.

readers per copy. N. The number of people who read a particular issue of a magazine; determined by dividing the total audience of the publication by its circulation of a typical issue of the magazine or periodical.

reading-and-noting. N. A survey of actual readers of newspapers and magazines, indicating which pages or advertisement they read or studied.

reading notice. N. A printed advertisement appearing as editorial material. However, it should always be marked as an advertisement so as not to confuse the reader. See also *advertorial*.

read-most. N. People or a grouping of people who read more than 50% of a particular advertisement.

real income. N. (1) The sum total of the purchasing power of a nation or individual. (2) Income that has been adjusted for the effected of inflation.

reallocation. N. See *reapportionment*.

real other. N. How a consumer perceives other people's views of his or her skills, personality, etc.

real people. N. Individuals found in advertisements to represent actual consumers instead of actors.

real price. N. The price of goods and services measured by the quantity of manpower needed to earn sufficient money to purchase the goods or services.

real self-image. N. Our mental picture of ourselves as we think we really are.

real value of money. N. The price of money measured in terms of goods. See also *purchasing power*.

reapportionment. N. Allocation of the costs of operating the service departments to the various production departments in proportion to the relative benefits or services received by each production unit. Synonymous with *reallocation*.

reason-why approach. N. See *factual approach*.

rebate. N. (1) Any refund of a payment. (2) In sales, any deduction made from a payment or charge. In contrast to a discount, a rebate is not deducted in advance, but is returned to the consumer following payment of the full amount (e.g., a GE appliance costs $24, with a rebate of $5 after the consumer has mailed in a coupon from the appliance package). See also *discount*. (3) In sales, any refund given to a consumer for sending in proof-of-purchase following a sale. See also *refund offer*.

rebate offer. N. See *refund offer*.

rebuild strategy. N. Investment and marketing efforts designed to increase or exceed sales, profits, or market share levels that were held at an earlier time.

recall. N. In manufacturing, the return of a distributed production for purposes of adjustment, repair, or other necessary work. If found unsatisfactory, may result in returning the cost of the item to the customer. See also *product recall*.

recall testing. N. A means for determining advertising effectiveness; measures the degree that a person remembers aspects of an advertisement. In studies of recall people describe the advertisement by responding to questions on its message, points made in the copy, its campaign theme, etc. The two form of recall tests are: (a) aided recall, when the researcher presents the advertisement to the respondent to be followed with questions, and (b) unaided recall, when, without showing the advertisement, the researcher merely asks the respondent questions about the advertisement. See also *recognition*.

receipt. N. Written acknowledgment of value received.

receipt of goods dating. N. Under this condition of sales, the date for payment and the discount period are determined from the date the buyer obtains shipment, rather than from the invoice date. This procedure is primarily employed when great shipping distances are involved. See also *regular dating*. ABBRV. *ROG dating*.

receiver. N. The audience that is the target of a message.

receiving apron. N. A statement used in the receiving department of a store that contains all pertinent data concerning an incoming shipment. The form is used to identify the shipment for purposes of accounting and control. See also *pro forma invoice*.

recency/frequency. N. The measure of the value of a customer or group of customers based on the number of purchases made and the length of time in between purchases as well as the time passed since the last purchase. The most valued customer has a high degree of recency and frequency. See also *recency/frequency/ monetary value*.

recency/frequency/monetary value. N. The measures for determining the value of a customer or group of customers based on time since the last purchase, the number of actual purchases, and the dollar value of the bought merchandise. See also *recency/frequency*.

receptivity to innovation. N. The extent to which a person or firm is willing to consider and hopefully purchase a new item or process.

recession. N. A phase of the business cycle that shows a downswing or contraction of the economy.

reciprocal demand. N. The situation created when one person offers what another person desires, and vice-versa.

reciprocal trade agreement. N. An international agreement between two or more countries to establish mutual trade concessions that are expected to be of equal value.

reciprocity. N. (1) In merchandising, the purchasing of goods by one firm from another on a preferential basis, with the expectation that the second firm will preferentially buy the goods of the first. (2) In international marketing, a provision of a guarantee of similar or at least nondiscriminatory opportunities for enterprises to operate in foreign markets on the same basis as local firms.

reclamation. N. The act of obtaining useful materials from waste products. See also *recycling*.

recognition. N. (1) In advertising, acceptance of an agency by a medium. A recognized agency receives standard agency discounts. (2) Consumer awareness of having seen or heard an advertisement or commercial. Should there be found a high degree of recognition of the advertising message, then the advertiser believes that the advertisement is accomplishing its goals. See also *aided recall*, *recall testing*.

recognized agency. N. The advertising agency that is acknowledged by the media as acceptable to receive a commission or fee for the time or space it purchases for advertisers. It bills its clients at full rate.

recommendations. N. The transmittal to media members by a media association of the latter's evaluation of the financial and related conditions of an applicant advertising agency and of the association's assessment of the agency's qualifications to receive credit and agency commission from the association's members.

reconsignment. N. Any alteration, including a route change, made in a consignment before the items have arrived at their billed destination.

recording delay. N. The delayed response effect indicating a time lag between the actual buying of merchandise and the manufacturer's knowledge of the purchase in his or her accounting records. Important, as it impacts on reorders, promotional needs, etc.

recovery. N. (1) The period of the business cycle that follows a depression. (2) In sales, the difference between the purchasing price and the selling price of goods or services.

recycling. N. The conversion of waste products (i.e., empty beer cans) to usable material for the purpose of reducing pollution, saving money, and/or conserving resources. See also *reclamation*.

recruiting. N. (1) Personnel department activity involving the search for employees to meet the specific needs of an organization. In addition, the company may utilize the services of outside recruiting firms. (2) In sales, the activity of locating skilled salespeople and inducing them to apply for employment.

Red Book. N. See *Standard Advertising Register*.

red clause. N. A clause, printed in red, on a letter of credit, authorizing a negotiating banker to make advances to a beneficiary so that he or she can buy the items, and deliver them for shipment.

redemption. N. Returning, usually to a retailer, coupons or proofs-of-purchase in order to receive a discount or premium. Firms follow these numbers to measure the effectiveness of a promotion. See also *redemption center*.

redemption center. N. A store or outlet established by a trading-stamp firm where holders can redeem filled stamp booklets for goods. See also *redemption*. Synonymous with *redemption store*.

redemption store. N. See *redemption center*.

red goods. N. Food items and other consumer goods that are consumed and replaced at a rapid rate and have a low profit margin. See also *brown goods*, *orange goods*, *yellow goods*.

rediscount. V. To discount for the second time.

red label. N. A shipping label indicating flammable contents.

reduced-price pack. N. A package clearly marked with a price that is less than regular retail.

reduced rate. N. (1) See *allowance*. (2) See *discount*.

reexport. V. To export already imported items, without duty charges, in basically similar form to a third country. See also *production sharing*.

reference group. N. (1) A sociological unit from which an individual takes his or her behavior cues. (2) Any set of people that influences an individual's attitudes or behavior. Includes membership groups, where people actually belong, and aspirational groups, groups that people would like to be belong to. See also *opinion leader*.

reference media. N. Sources of statistical, commercial, or demographic information periodically printed for advertisers and other businesses.

referral. N. See *referral leads*.

referral leads. N. Names of potential customers given to a sales representative, usually by satisfied customers. Referrals respond to promotions at a much higher rate than other prospects. See also *friend-of-a-friend promotion, lead*.

referral premium. N. A reward offered to a satisfied customer when a prospect recommended by the customer purchases a product or service. See also *premium*.

reflation. N. Upon recovering from a depression or a recession, the period during which prices are turned to the level they had attained during a period of prosperity by lowering the purchasing power of money.

refund. N. Dollar returned by a seller of goods or services in exchange for the return of some part of an item or service, e.g., returning empty soda bottles.

refund check. N. A statement for a customer's purchase that is returned.

refund offer. N. Sales-promotion technique guaranteeing the purchaser a refund if not completely satisfied. See also *trial offer*.

refusal to sell. N. The right of a seller to choose the dealers that will handle his or her merchandise. Invoking this right, which is recognized by law, a seller may refuse to deal with firms that do not meet certain standards or qualifications. See also *franchise*.

regiocentrism. N. A marketing strategy where the marketing effort targets regions instead of individual nations, or the entire global marketplace. Such regions can be composed of nations that possess any or all of the following: (a) are contiguous to each other; (b) share a common language; (c) are at similar levels of economic and technical development; and, (d) belong to the same economic community or trading zone. See also *geocentricity*.

regional edition. N. A national publication with a particular advertising section aimed at a specific geographic location, enabling local advertisers to participate without having to pay the rate for national advertising. Their distribution is limited to the specific geographic area involved in the advertising. Synonymous with *sectional edition*.

regional marketing. N. A form of geographical segmentation that develops marketing plans to reflect specific area differences in taste preferences, perceived needs, or interests.

regional rollouts. N. Introducing a new product sequentially into geographical areas to allow production levels and marketing activities to build up gradually.

regional store. N. A branch store, usually located far from the central store, that functions under the name of the parent store. In most cases a regional store operates as an autonomous unit. See also *branch store*.

regional wholesaler. N. See *sectional wholesaler*.

register. V. To record a trademark, patent, copyright, etc., with a governmental unit so as to claim exclusivity. N. (1) Machine for temporarily storing information while or until it is used, i.e., a store's cash register. (2) In transportation, a written document prepared by a customs official that allows a ship to engage in foreign trade.

registry. N. A listing by a country of ships that fly its flag and are under the regulation of maritime law.

regression. N. A means of coping with anxiety by reverting to a typically immature act; a form of returning to an earlier behavior stage.

regression analysis. N. A method for predicting the values of a quantitative variable from scores of a correlated variable.

regular dating. N. Terms of a sale under which the period for discount and the date on which payment is required are determined from the date of the invoice. See also *ROG dating*.

regularly unsought items. N. Products that are regularly required by consumers, but which they will not go out of their way to purchase; for example, reference books for their children or insurance coverage. These items are often heavily promoted to increase consumer awareness and sales. See also *new unsought goods*, *unsought goods*.

regular wholesaler. N. See *service wholesaler*.

reinforcement. N. The extent to which satisfaction is derived from a response to an aroused need.

reinforcement advertising. N. Advertising that guarantees the buyer of a product or service that he or she has made a wise decision and suggests forms of satisfaction that are to be realized following purchase.

reinforcement schedule. N. The timing or scheduling of rewards.

reinforcement theory. N. A motivation approach that examines factors that energize, direct, and sustain behavior.

reinforcer. N. A stimulus that follows an act and (a) reduces the need motivating the act, and, (b) strengthens the habit that led to the act in the first place.

reinstatement. N. (1) Restoration of a worker to a former position without the loss of seniority or benefits. (2) In marketing, placement of a customer's record back into active status after being suspended, canceled, or becoming inactive.

reinvoicing. N. In international marketing, a strategy employed by global firms where one of its national companies imports commodities through an offshore firm and following, dumps the profits made on the transaction in the offshore tax haven, thus lifting its apparent costs to lower taxes on the mainland firm.

related-item display. N. See *cross merchandising*.

relationship analysis. N. A category of fortuitous scan methods of ideation in which the essential element is bringing together things not normally so considered.

relationship marketing. N. Exists when firms seek to develop and maintain continuous long-term ties with their suppliers, distribution intermediaries, and customers.

relative advantage. N. The potential market's perception of the amount of utility a replacement item has over the item it replaces or with which it will compete.

relative income concept. N. The hypothesis that spending is a function of a family's relative place in the income distribution of similar family units (i.e., people who earn the same amount tend to spend the same amount of money).

relative market share. N. (1) The market share held by a company or service or item as compared to the market shares of competitors. (2) An organization or strategic business unit's market share divided by that of its largest competitor.

relative product failure. N. Occurs if a firm makes a profit on an item but the product does not reach profit objectives or adversely affects the firm's image.

relaunch. N. The reintroduction of a product, service, or promotional program after a period of inactivity. Usually, follows a discontinuance of the item or service. Relaunching will proceed by creating a change in the item or service, or a new promotional approach prior to its beginning.

release. N. (1) The cancellation or resolution of a claim against another person. (2) In advertising, a legal instrument authorizing an advertiser to utilize the name of a person or his or her photograph.

relevant costs. N. Expenditures that (a) are expected to occur in the future as a result of some marketing action, and, (2) differ among marketing alternatives being considered.

release date. N. A given day, and often time, when a product or promotion is announced to the public or the media.

relevant range. N. The band of activity in which budgeted sales and expense relationships will be valid.

reliability. N. (1) Accuracy and dependability. (2) In market research, the quality data have when repetition of the same research produces essentially the same results. (3) In retailing, the consistency of performance of goods, i.e., a hair dryer is guaranteed to continue to work the same way over and over again until the warranty date passes. See also *product reliability, validity*.

remainder. N. (1) In merchandising, goods that remain unsold at their original price because of a lack of demand; then sold at a lower price. (2) In publishing, an unsold book that has never been retailed. Remainders are often offered by the publisher to special stores for sale at reduced prices. (3) See *overstock*.

remarketing. N. A technique for reviving the demand for an item or service that has been experiencing a period of decline.

reminder advertisements. N. Advertisements used to reinforce previous knowledge of a product.

reminder impulse buying. N. Impulse buying where the customer is reminded within the store of the value in replenishing his or her stock. See also *planned impulse buying, pure impulse buying*.

remit rate. ABBRV. Remittance rate.

remittance. N. Funds forwarded from one person to another as payment for purchased items or services.

remittance rate. N. That part of a subscription sales price remitted to the publisher by a subscription agent following the deduction of the agent's commission. ABBRV. *Remit rate.*

remote delivery. N. Sending goods from a central warehouse to customers via area delivery stations located in the suburbs or by truck.

renege. V. To go back on a promise; to pull out of an agreement.

renewal promotion. N. Sending by mail a reminder of the expiration of a periodical to subscribers, hoping that it will encourage a renewal of the subscription. The mailing is often carried out three to six months prior to the expiration date.

rented-goods service. N. Involves the leasing of a good for a specified period of time.

reorder system. N. See *Q-system*.

rep. ABBRV. Representative.

repeat demand. N. The demand created for items that are frequently requested and bought.

repeating technique. N. See *mirror response technique*.

repeat purchasing. N. Purchasing the same item or service from the same source of supply over a given time period.

repeat rate. N. The number of times an item or service is bought by a consumer within a time frame. When the repeat rate is low, it can indicate that the item or service could use more advertising, or if that fails, the item or service might be redesigned or even dropped from the market.

repeat sales. N. Sales perpetuated by going back to the same store or retailer to make a purchase.

repetition. N. The repeated frequency of an advertising message, slogan, or concept so as to reinforce it with consumers.

replacement demand. N. Capital goods or consumer items that are in demand because of depreciation or obsolescence.

replacement potential. N. As measured in units or dollars, the sales potential of merchandise to present consumers who will require replacing the item within a fixed time period.

replacement rate. N. The frequency with which merchandise is bought by consumers.

reply envelope. N. Used primarily in direct-mail packages, a self-addressed envelope from a direct marketer for the return on orders and other types of responses. As an incentive to the consumer, most reply envelopes are postage-paid. Studies show that postage-paid reply envelopes lead to a higher response return rate.

repositioning. N. By changing a product's target market, a strategy for increasing sales of an already existing item. It requires altering the original positioning strategy, especially when a competing product starts to dominate and a new or revised strategy is required, or when the decline stage of the product life cycle begins. See also *positioning*.

repossession. N. The reclaiming or taking back of items that were bought on an installment sales contract on which the buyer has fallen behind in payments.

representative. N. In advertising, the person who sells space or time for an advertising medium. ABBRV. *Rep*. Synonymous with *sales representative*.

reprint. N. In advertising, the reproduction of an advertisement after it has been shown in a publication.

repurchase agreement. N. An agreement between a seller and a buyer that the seller will buy back the property at the expiration of a stated period or upon completion of certain conditions, or both.

required rate of return. N. A financial hurdle that is a firm's cost of capital adjusted for the risk of the project. Most new product projects have more risk than ongoing operations, so most required rates are well above costs of capital. See also *risk premium*.

requisition. N. A written demand from a department to its purchasing department to release on a specific date materials to be used in a production process or other activity of consumption within an organization. See also *stores requisition*.

resale. N. The selling of goods or services that have been bought by the seller from another person in essentially the same form.

resale price maintenance. N. (1) The practice by a supplier of prescribing, and taking action to enforce, retail or wholesale prices for the resale of items. (2) A supplier's control over the selling price of his or her goods at various stages of distribution by means of contractual arrangement under fair trade laws or other means. See also *fair trade price*.

rescale. N. See *resizing*.

rescind. N. See *right of rescission*.

rescission. N. Making void or annulling. See also *right of rescission*.

research and development. N. Applying the findings of science and technology in creating a firm's products or services. ABBRV. *R&D*.

research design. N. An overall plan for conducting a research project, including the choice of the method that will be used to achieve the goals of the research.

research study. N. An activity to gather market research information on a particular market problem or situation.

reseller. N. See *jobber*.

reseller markets. N. Firms and individuals who buy products in order to resell them to others. Most products are sold through such selling intermediaries.

reserve stock. N. See *backup merchandise, buffer stock*.

reserve stock control. N. A technique for earmarking appropriate stock for the maintenance of business until new merchandise is purchased.

reshipper. N. A shipping container in which empty containers (e.g., soda bottles) intended to be used again are received.

resident buyer. N. Any person or firm located in a market area who aids retailers in making market contracts and assists in their purchasing. See also *merchandise mart*.

resident salesperson. N. A supplier's salesperson located within the structure of one of the supplier's primary accounts. He or she provides full attention to the customer's needs.

residual. N. A fee paid to an individual for repeated transmission (e.g., on radio or television) of a performance in which he or she originally participated. The residual can be paid for by the television or radio station or advertiser. Synonymous with *re-use fee*.

resistor. N. A person who has a history of not replying to direct-mail promotions.

resize. N. See *resizing*.

resizing. N. The production of the means of running an advertisement in several sizes in order to fit different units of space. Synonymous with *rescale*.

resonance. N. A literary device, frequently used in advertising, that uses a play on words (a double meaning) to communicate a product benefit.

resource. N. (1) Anything a country uses to produce goods and services (manpower, minerals, oil, etc.). (2) In merchandising, a producer or wholesaler from whom a merchant buys goods for resale. See also *merchandise resource*.

respondent. N. (1) The person who provides information in an inquiry or on a questionnaire. (2) A person who participates as a subject and provides information in a poll, study, or other research-gathering service.

response. N. (1) Whatever occurs as a reaction to an aroused need. (2) Replies and reactions to a stimuli. See also *response analysis*, *response rate*.

response analysis. N. A statistical treatment of the reply to a direct-mail promotion indicating how the varying elements of the promotion performance.

response function. N. In marketing, the impact of any shift in the four Ps and the result it produces on sales and profits. It is usually plotted as a curve on a graph showing the effects of changes in the component marketing mix elements.

response projection. N. Forecasting of a response to a promotion based on the number of responses received to date or based upon earlier experience with the promotion, product, or service.

response rate. N. Usually less than 5%, the gross or net responses received as a percentage of total promotions mailed.

response variable. N. See *dependent variable*.

restrained exporters. N. Nations that use voluntary export restraints to slow down the export of particular items to identified markets. See also *protected markets*.

restraint of trade. N. Of critical importance to marketers, the effect of any contract, combination, or agreement (e.g., a monopoly) that impedes free competition. See also *Robinson-Patman Act of 1936*, *Sherman Antitrust Act of 1890*.

restricted articles. N. Articles that are handled only under certain conditions.

restrictive business practices. N. Acts of enterprises, public or private, that limit access to markets or indirectly restrain competition.

restrictive license. N. An agreement under whose terms an owner of a patented item allows a licensee to sell the patented good under certain limited conditions.

retailing

retail advertising. N. The dissemination of sales messages by retail store operators through local media such as newspapers and non-network radio and television radio directed toward those consumers living within the trading area of the advertiser. See also *local advertising*.

retail chain. N. Involves the common ownership of multiple units. See also *factory outlet*.

retail cooperative. N. A voluntary association of independent retailers who jointly own and operate their own wholesale facilities and often serve together as a buying club to achieve the economies of large-scale purchasing.

retail display allowance. N. A decrease in the funds paid by the retailer to the manufacturer in exchange for a more favorable display of the item in the store or on the shelf.

retailer. N. (1) A merchant whose primary activity is to sell directly to consumers. (2) An intermediary that sells products primarily to ultimate consumers. There are store retailers (operators of department stores, outlets, supermarkets, boutiques, etc.), and nonstore retailers (firms that sell through mail-order catalogs, have direct-selling procedures, or operate vending machines).

retail franchising. N. A contractual agreement between a franchisor (a manufacturer, wholesaler, or service sponsor) and a retail franchise, which allows the franchisee to conduct a certain form of business under an establishment name and according to a specific set of rules.

retailing. N. (1) The activity of purchasing for resale to a customer. (2) All activities undertaken by intermediaries whose primary function is to sell goods and services to ultimate consumers. The four functions of retailing are: (a) buying and storing merchandise;

(b) transferring title of those items; (c) providing information on the nature and uses of those goods; and, (d) in some situations, extending credit to buyers. See also *wholesaling*.

retailing mix. N. The retail store's combination of controllable variables giving it its unique image and position in the market. Variables include product, price, promotions, place, operating policy, purchasing, personnel, service, etc.

retail installment credit account. N. See *all-purpose revolving account*.

retail marketing. N. Where sales objectives are set based on market potential with heightened attention to the consumer's behavior; concerned with who is purchasing what and the underlying reasons for this action.

retail method of inventory. N. An accounting technique for recording all inventory inputs, including sales, purchases, markdowns, and so on, at their retail values. Purchased items are recorded at cost. See also *markdown, markdown cancellation, markup, markup cancellation*.

retail outlet. N. A store that sells directly to the customer.

retail price. N. The price at which goods are identified for sale or are sold.

retail price maintenance. N. Allowing a manufacturer, under protection of state law, to set retail prices for his or her products. This is in accord with the terms of the fair trade acts. See also *fair trade acts*.

retail rate. N. See *local rate*.

retail salesperson. N. An individual who works inside a store, where customers come to him or her.

retail store cooperative. N. A store that is owned and operated by a number of people as a source of supply for at least a certain kind of product.

retail store strategy mix. N. Consists of an integrated combination of hours, location, assortment, service, advertising, prices, and other factors retailers employ.

retainer. N. A method of compensating an advertising agency or other organization for services rendered. Usually it involves providing a standard monthly fee to be paid by the company to the client. Out-of-pocket expenses, e.g., travel, are billed to the client separately from a retainer's fee.

retention cycle. N. The time an inactive customer's record is retained.

retentive stage. N. A product's stage when its acceptance of a particular brand is so broad that the advertiser need only keep reminders before his or her customers, accomplished with little effort and expense. Throughout loyalty is preserved. See also *spiral stage*.

return. N. See *returns*.

return card. N. See *return postcard*.

return on investment. N. The amount earned in direct proportion to the capital invested. ABBRV. *ROI*.

return percentage. N. See *response rate*.

return postcard. N. A self-addressed card used in direct-mail packages to offer recipients an easy way to request information or order goods or services. The postcard is traditionally paid for by the advertiser.

returns. N. (1) Any response to a direct-mail campaign. (2) Goods returned to a supplier for credit, and sometimes, refunds. See also *returns and allowances*.

returns and allowances. N. In retailing, the total dollar amounts of items that were returned to the seller by dissatisfied customers (returns) and the total price reductions/discounts that were granted to consumers by the seller (allowances). The monetary amount of returns and allowances deducted from the outlet's gross sales to arrive at total net sales. See also *returns*.

returns to vendor. N. Goods sent back to the vendor by a store for various reasons (e.g., damaged merchandise, lateness of delivery). See also *vendor chargebacks, purchase allowance*.

reusable packaging. N. Containers that have another use subsequent to their service as merchandise containers.

re-use fee. N. See *residual*.

revenue. N. The granted total of all resources received from the sale of a firm's product or service during a stated period; not to be confused with general revenue.

reverse distribution. N. See *backward channel*.

reverse elasticity. N. Where a brief increase for a product or service triggers an increase in purchasing and a decrease in price along with a decrease in buying. This is caused by buyer anticipation that the initial act will be followed by other price cuts.

reverse marketing. N. The effort by organizational buyers to build relationships that shape suppliers' products, services, and capabilities to fit a buyer's needs and those of its customers.

reverse-order perception. N. The rate occurrence when consumers prefer to purchase the more expensive item because of the

revolving account. N. See *revolving charge account*.

revolving charge account. N. A credit system permitting the customer to have repeated purchases on account as long as the charge balance does not exceed a set amount and the customer make his or her agreed-upon payments on time. See Truth-in-Lending Act of 1968. Synonymous with *all-purpose revolving account, revolving account*.

revolving credit. N. A regular thirty-day charge account that is paid in full or in monthly installments. Paid in full within thirty days of the statement date will not commence any finance charge.

rhochrematics. N. A way of managing the material flow process, which has an integrated system for making and marketing an item.

rifle technique. N. (1) The sales practice of concentrating on selling only a few items, using a carefully prepared style of presentation that will lead to a rapid decision. See also *shotgun approach*. (2) Distributing of publicity materials to select news media instead of mass mailing them to numerous different media.

rigged market. N. The situation that exists when purchases and sales are manipulated to distort a normal supply and demand price.

right of rescission. N. The privilege, guaranteed by the Truth in Lending Act, of canceling a contract under certain circumstances within three business days, without penalty and with full refund of all deposits that have been submitted. See also *Truth in Lending Act of 1968, voidable contract*.

rights of consumers. N. A doctrine enunciated by President John F. Kennedy, stating that consumers have the right to be safe, to be informed, to choose, and to be heard.

risk. N. Any chance of loss. Marketers try to comprehend the forces that create risk in consumers' minds and take appropriate actions to lower it. See also *marketing risks*.

risk analysis. N. A strategic planning activity where the external threats of the marketplace are identified and evaluated in terms of their potential impact on the organization and the chances of occurrence.

risk matrix. N. A matrix of the risks at any particular point in a new product's evaluation process. It shows the risk of rejecting a product idea that would ultimately succeed and the risk of going ahead with a project that would ultimately fail.

risk premium. N. The amount by which cost of capital is raised to reflect added risks of any particular new product proposal. Such addition yields the required rate of return. See also *required rate of return*.

risk reduction. N. The effort by a customer to solve a problem and make a purchase while at the same time cutting down on the uncertainties linked with a product or service. The customer is provided with a host of materials, information brochures, etc., to reduce this risk. See also *potential need satisfier*.

risk taker. N. One who is willing to take chances and may aggressively seek out risky situations that offer the possibility of significant payoffs or profits. See also *risk taking*.

risk taking. N. A marketing function that accepts the possibility of failure or loss in the selling of a product or service. See also *risk taker*.

risky shift phenomenon. N. The concept that the action of people as individuals is often radically different from their group behavior and thus that the shift away from conformity can be risky.

roadblocking. N. Where the advertiser, early in a program, will engage the same time period on all of the major networks to provide for maximum exported with the public.

Robinson-Patman Act of 1936. N. Federal legislation, amending the Clayton Antitrust Act of 1914, in which price discrimination practices are more clearly identified. Quantity discounts in excess of the cost savings realized by selling in such quantities are declared illegal, as are false brokerage deals. Promotional allowances must be made to all buyers on a proportionately equal basis, and price discrimination is acceptable if it is done to meet a proper low price of a competitor and if the price does not restrict competition. Synonymous with *chain store law*. See also *price discrimination, restraint of trade, unique user, volume bonus*.

rock bottom. N. *(slang)* The lowest level that will be entertained in a business transaction (e.g., the rock bottom price is the lowest price at which a seller will agree to sell his or her goods).

ROG dating. ABBRV. Receipt-of-goods dating.

ROI. ABBRV. Return on investment.

role. N. Behavior patterns expected from people in various economic, social, or other status positions.

role expectations. N. The rights, privileges, duties, and responsibilities that are associated with a particular role.

role of marketing. N. Determined by top management, which notes its importance, outlines its activities, and integrates it into the firm's overall operation.

role theory. N. An approach to the study of group influence that recognizes that people conduct their lives by playing many roles, each of which is accompanied by a certain range of acceptable behaviors.

roll-out. N. (1) The expansion of a new item into previously unknown markets from a local introduction. (2) In merchandising, an approach to new-product introduction in which the product is launched in a series of geographic areas over an extended period. (3) In direct mail, the largest mailing in a campaign. See also *pyramid selling*.

ROP. ABBRV. Run-of-paper.

Rorabaugh reports. N. Quarterly statements on spot advertising expenditures in television that are released by a private advertising consultant every three months.

ROS. ABBRV. Run-of-schedule.

rotated merchandise control. N. Counting a retailer's inventory on a rotated or staggered basis by scheduling counts on specific days.

rotation. N. Advertisements repeated in sequences after the entire series has been run.

rough. N. A preliminary, sketchily drawn layout of an advertisement designed to indicate the relative size and placement of the various units comprising the advertisement, usually as a prelude to a more carefully drawn layout.

round turn. N. The execution at different time periods for the same principal of a purchase transaction and a sale transaction that offset each other. Synonymous with *turn*.

routine. N. In broadcasting, the opening of a broadcast program. See also *billboard*.

routine consumer decision making. N. In consumer behavior, a decision requiring minimal discussion and planning because of the routine nature of the purchase. Such items are usually inexpensive, carrying little consumer risk.

routing. N. The selection of a path and steps in the operation performed on materials during the manufacturing process. Salespeople use routing in the hope of ensuring that a territory is adequately covered at the lowest possible cost to the selling organization. See also *territory management, traffic*.

ROW. ABBRV. Run-of-week.

rubricated account. N. See *flagging an account*.

rule line. N. The straight line used as a border or dividing line in an advertisement; used for decoration or to clearly define a panel by creating a boundary, or other aspect of the advertisement.

rule of reason. N. The Supreme Court decision in 1911 that only unreasonable restraint of trade was illegal, thereby permitting companies to become as large as they wished, under the argument that the law did not outlaw mere size. This interpretation has largely been reversed since World War II.

rules of content. N. See *rules of origin*.

rules of origin. N. Critical in international marketing and sales, products that are treated differently in international commerce according to their country of origin. Shifting percentages of content rules inevitably stirs criticism. Most accords set 50%–60% as a minimum of parts that must come from one of the nations involved. Rules of origin remain a set of criteria by which to determine what country a given product is made in; that a product's country of origin is to be the last country where assembly or processing operations "substantially transformed" the inputs or components into a new product. Strong rules of origin provisions assist customs inspectors to make determinations of what passes free of tariffs or duty while not unduly inhibiting and impeding trade. See also *dumping, rule of content*.

running. N. In merchandising, a best-selling item, especially one that is continually kept in stock because of its heavy sales volume. See also *sleeper, fill-ins*.

running costs. N. Direct or indirect costs that result from keeping an operation and/or machinery functioning. These costs include wages, rent, and taxes.

run-of-paper. N. A media buyer's ordering instruction thereby controlling the use and placement of an advertisement. The advertiser presents an advertisement to the publisher and the publisher will decide where it shall appear. Should the advertiser prefer a preferred position, the advertiser will negotiate the cost to have the advertisement run in a specific location. Synonymous with *run-of-press*. See also *run-of-schedule, run-of-week*. ABBRV. *ROP*.

run-of-press. N. See *run-of-paper*.

run-of-schedule. N. In broadcasting, the equivalent of run-of-paper; the situation where the advertiser provides a television commercial and its air time is set by the station management, with possible negotiation occurring for a preferred position with an agreed-upon revised rate. See also *run- of-paper*. ABBRV. *ROS*.

run-of-week. N. A media buyer's ordering instruction, where the advertisement appears in whatever newspaper, magazine, etc., the media owner selects. See also *run-of-schedule*. ABBRV. *ROW*.

run sizes. N. The number of items manufactured at one time in a given lot.

S

sacrifice. v. To make a sale at a loss for purposes of raising cash, with the awareness that the profit will be lowered.

safety. N. In magazine advertising, the space between the perimeter of the advertisement and the edge of the page, thus allowing binding of pages without losing the boundaries of the advertisement.

safety stock. N. A minimum inventory that provides a cushion against reasonably expected maximum demand and against variations in lead time. See also *cushion*.

sag sale. N. See *residual*.

sale. N. (1) The transfer of title to an item or items. (2) The agreement to perform a service in return for cash or the expectation of cash payment.

sale-below-cost laws. N. See *unfair practices acts*.

sales. N. (1) Revenue received for the sale of goods. (2) Final sales plus producer item sales. See also *net sales, selling*.

sales agent. N. A middleperson who undertakes to sell the entire output of items of a business that he or she represents. As controlled by the manufacturer's contract, sales agents can or cannot exercise control over setting prices and other terms of the exchange between purchaser and seller. See also *selling agent*.

sales allowance. N. A lowering of the price of an item when merchandise delivered is not exactly what was ordered by a buyer.

sales analysis. N. An aspect of market research involving the systematic study and comparison of sales information; carried out for specific territories, products, or salespeople, quarterly, monthly, or annually. See also *systems selling, cost analysis*.

sales anchors. N. Concepts and statements used by sales representatives when attempting to overcome customer resistance.

sales aptitude. N. The capability to achieve success in the sales field, as acknowledged by a sales department and measured by means of interviews and recommendations.

sales audit. N. An audit that is a comprehensive assessment of sales strategy of fulfilling sales objectives with the aim to improve the overall effectiveness of the salespeople. This audit purports to determine whether or not the objectives set are realistic, appropriate, and reachable. It can also determine the firm's sales plans and policies. Usually, a sales audit is carried out by an independent consulting organization.

sales-based pricing objectives. N. Goals that orient a company's pricing strategy toward high sales volume and/or expanding its share of sales relative to competitors.

sales branch. N. A producer's outlet that maintains inventory and delivers to buyers from that stock.

sales broker. N. An agent who, though not physically handling merchandise that he or she deals with and has little control over the terms of a contract between principal and third party, serves a critical phase in the relationship between parties in the production and distribution process.

sales budget. N. A budget based on forecasted sales for a coming period; usually includes all marketing expenditures of which selling is only a part. Will have an impact on the funds provided to the sales department over a set time period.

sales call pattern. N. A pattern of effort where salespeople in the field call on prospective customers. The pattern evolves by: (a) the universe of target customers and their geographical distribution;

(b) the frequency of calls required by each customer; (c) the cost-effectiveness of calling; and, (d) the selling culture of, and competitive sales pattern in, the particular universe of customers.

sales clerk. N. An individual in a retail store who records the customers' purchases, who usually is responsible for maintaining stock, and who at times helps the customer in making a selection from the available stock. A minimum of salesmanship need be employed by a sales clerk.

sales closing. N. See *close (1)*.

sales company. N. A corporate entity established in a foreign country by the parent firm to sell goods or services imported from the parent firm and other foreign affiliates.

sales compensation. N. Money paid to salespeople in the form of straight compensation, salary, or a combination of both. The three primary forms of sales compensation are: (a) straight salary—paying a salesperson a fixed annual amount; (b) commission basis—compensation based on the salesperson's performance, e.g., as a percentage of sales that he or she generates; and, (c) combination compensation—mixing a straight salary arrangement with a commission.

sales component analysis. N. A tool for controlling marketing programs that traces sales revenue to their sources such as specific products, sales territories, or customers.

sales contest. N. A sponsored competition, usually by a dealer or manufacturer of an item, where outstanding sales efforts and results are rewarded.

sales control. N. A system of supervision involving the use of such devices as records, statistical analyses, correspondence, and personal contact for the purpose of carrying out or adjusting marketing policies and plans.

sales conversion rate. N. The number of sales made relative to the number of actual contacts made; used primarily in telemarketing.

sales decline stage. N. In the cycle of a product, the period when sales fall and will continue in that direction unless remedies are taken.

sales demonstration. N. Illustrating how an item functions and its potential. Synonymous with *demonstration*.

sales discount. N. See *cash discount*.

sales effectiveness test. N. A means for determining the ability of an advertising program or communications medium to sell a product or service.

sales efficiency. N. The correlation between sales volume or value and individual and total selling expenses.

sales engineer. N. A person who sells products that require technical knowledge and training. Synonymous with *technical salesperson*.

sales era. N. Involves hiring a sales force and sometimes advertising to sell inventory after production is maximized. The role of the sales force and advertising is to make the desires of consumers fit the attributes of the products being manufactured.

sales exception reporting. N. Where products are documented as either slow- or fast-selling.

sales expense budget. N. A budget allocating expenditures relating to personal selling efforts. Impacts budget setting.

sales fertility. N. The amount of marketing effort needed to achieve a stated sales volume.

sales finance company. N. A financial organization that purchases installment contracts from dealers and finances dealers' inventories.

sales force. N. Canvassers and sales representatives who contact potential purchasers of goods and attempt to persuade them that they should buy items being sold. These people are organized by geographic territory, type of merchandise, the market, or any combination of these factors. See also *market- structured sales force, product-structured sales force, territory-structured sales force.*

sales forecast. N. A dollar or unit sales estimate made for a specified period in a marketing campaign. See also *forecasting, sales forecast opportunity variance.*

sales forecast opportunity variance. N. A measure of the differential between scheduled capacity and the master budget sales forecast capacity, usually expressed in dollars. See also *forecasting.*

sales incentive. N. Offered by the manufacturer, traditionally money provided for a salesperson for exceeding some preset sales goal. Other perks include free trips and special prizes.

sales invoice. N. The main written, typed, or computer-generated source of sales analysis data.

sales journal. N. A book in which records of sales are entered.

sales lead. N. Providing the salesperson with information or a contact to assist in his or her selling efforts.

sales letter. N. A correspondence from a selling firm that is sent to prospective or existing customers, providing information on

sales management. N. Management activities in the development of a skilled sales force. Involves recruiting, selecting, and training, plus follow up activities of supervision and motivation. See also *sales analysis, sales audit, sales manager.*

sales manager. N. An executive responsible for planning, directing, and controlling the activities of sales personnel. The manager plans the firm's sales objectives and strategies for achieving these objectives. Also organizes and directs efforts of the sales force, develops sales programs, and monitors overall sales performance in relation to stated sales goals. See also *role set, sales management, product manager.*

salesmanship. N. The art of selling goods or services by creating a demand or need for a particular item or service and realizing an actual order. See also *creative selling, hard sell, low-pressure selling, service selling, conmanship.*

sales manual. N. A book describing the product, merchandise, or service to be sold and suggesting approaches for selling to a customer.

sales mix. N. A combination of the various company products leading to a firm's total sales.

sales objective. N. See *sales quota.*

sales office. N. A facility for taking orders and handling adjustments that serves as a contact point for suppliers and customers. No inventory is maintained at the office. See also *merchandise mart.*

sales penetration. N. The degree to which a firm is achieving its sales potential as measured by: sales penetration = actual sales ÷ sales potential.

salesperson. N. A person who practices salesmanship. Synonymous with *sales representative*.

sales pitch. N. A strong statement aimed at persuading a potential customer to buy the salesperson's product or service.

sales plan. N. A merchandise budget that contains a detailed projection of sales for a given period, specifying the purchases, inventory, and so on, needed to achieve this goal.

sales potential. N. Fulfilling the identified market share or market objective with consumers. See also *market potential*.

sales potential forecast. N. A forecast of total potential sales for the firm for a specific time period.

sales presentation. N. The total selling process of describing to a potential customer the product or service, including the attempt to plan an order. See also *trial close*.

sales promotion. N. The array of techniques that marketers use to stimulate immediate purchase, including using: coupons, rebates, continuity programs, price packs, premiums, samples, contests, sweepstakes, incentives, point-of-purchase advertising, and events marketing. See also *promotion*. Synonymous with *demand creation, demand stimulation*.

sales promotion agency. N. The firm specializing in supplying broad sales promotion services to clients. See also *advertising agency*.

sales promotion conditions. N. Requirements that channel members or consumers must meet to be eligible for a specific sales promotion.

sales promotion orientation. N. The focus of sales promotion—channel members or consumers—and its theme.

sales quota. N. A projected goal for sales of a product. Usually the quota is established as part of a marketing campaign. Assessing a salesperson's performance is frequently based on the actual sales generated contrasted with a sales quota. See also *activity quota, quota, trade quota*. Synonymous with *sales objective*.

sales reports. N. Written reports summarizing back to management results of sales performance and salesperson's activities. These reports can detail customers' reactions to items, services, or company procedures, in addition to competitors' efforts.

sales representative. N. See *manufacturers' representative, resentative, salesperson*.

sales response function. N. The relationship between the expense of marketing results obtained. Measures of marketing results include sales revenue, profit, units sold, and level of awareness.

sales results test. N. An effort to measure the impact on sales of a specific advertisement or campaign.

sales returns and allowances. N. A contra-sales account in which the returns or allowances for previously sold merchandise are recorded.

sales revenue. N. Total income derived from sales for a stated time period.

sales tax. N. A tax levied by a state on items at the time of their purchase. It may be a tax on the sale of an item every time it changes hands or only upon its transfer of ownership at one specific time. The sales of manufacturers are taxed when the items are considered to be completed goods; the sales of wholesalers are taxed when their goods are sold to retailers; and, retail sales are taxed when the goods are purchased by consumers.

sales terms. N. See *terms of sale*.

sales territory. N. The segment of a firm's total market; defined by prospect, customer, or by geographic boundaries. In sales, synonymous with *territory*.

sales to thirds. N. See *trade sales*.

sales trainee. N. A recently hired sales representative who is engaged in learning the basic concepts of selling. Usually the trainee receives a small salary during this period.

sales training. N. A firm's program for training sales personnel; may be carried out externally, with the hiring of consultants or sending candidates to specialized programs or classes, or within the organization itself.

sales variance analysis. N. A method of data analysis in which data on actual sales are compared with quantitative sales objectives.

sales volume analysis. N. A method for assessing performance in the marketplace by measuring the target market's reaction to the firm's offering of items.

sales wave method. N. A measure in market testing where an item is placed in the prospect's home on a trial basis and made available for purchasing.

salon. N. A shop within a store for the selling of high-price apparel and accessories. See also *boutique*.

salting. N. In direct-mail, inserting fictional names and addresses into a mailing list to hopefully uncover any unauthorized usage of the list.

salutory items. N. Where a consumer holds an item or service in low esteem because the high-priced item or service has yet to provide the satisfaction or benefit to the consumer.

salvage. N. (1) Equipment or property that is no longer used for its initial purpose. (2) In merchandising, goods that are soiled beyond reclamation for purposes of sale and thus usually disposed of by other means. See also *salvage value*.

salvage value. N. The expected worth of a depreciable item at the end of its service life.

sample. N. (1) Items selected so that they represent the entire unit. (2) In merchandising, an item of a product that is a proper representative of all the units of that product. (3) In retailing, a portion of an item given away free to a prospective consumer. (4) In market research, a subset of a population drawn for testing activities under the assumption that the results will forecast the results or behavior of the entire population. See also *sampling*.

sample buyer. N. A person who buys at a special introductory rate or obtains at no cost a product sample. See also *trial size*.

sample package. N. See *trial size*.

sampling. N. (1) Choosing a representative portion of a population to characterize a larger population. See also *Monte Carlo method*. (2) In salesmanship, the method where a market is exposed to new items, packages, or package sizes by providing prospects with a miniature or actual unit of the item, hoping successful usage will lead to future purchases. (3) In marketing research methods, used to provide information about a large population from data gathered about few units from that population. There is probability sampling where every member of the total universe of respondents has an equal and known chance of being chosen; nonprobability sampling is based on criteria to ensure that some members of the population have a greater probability of being chosen than others. See also *cluster sample, convenience sampling, judgement sampling, population, quota sampling, sample, simple random sampling, stratified random sampling*.

sampling accuracy. N. The degree to which the parameter of the population characteristic is properly estimated by the chosen sample. See also *sampling error*.

sampling buying. N. In industrial buying, purchasing an item after studying a portion of the potential shipment for quality.

sampling error. N. An error occurs when the sample used is not representative of the population it was designed to represent. Sampling error points to the difference among figures generated in repeated measurements of the population and will decrease as the size of the sample increases. See also *standard error*.

sampling frame. N. The sampling units from which the sample will be taken, such as a listing of people, geographic location, firms, etc. See also *universe*.

sampling unit. N. The segment of the total population to be sampled in marketing research.

sanction. N. A penalty for the breach of a rule of law.

sandwich board. N. An old-fashioned, but still-used, form of advertising, with two boards, one hung from in front of the person, the other behind. Announcements or advertisements are usually placed on both sides.

satisfaction. N. (1) A criterion of effectiveness that refers to an organization's ability to gratify the needs of its employees. Synonymous with *morale, voluntarism*. (2) An enjoyed purchase.

satisfaction of demand. N. Involves product availability, actual performance after purchase, perceptions of safety, after-sale service, and other factors.

satisficing. N. Decision-making behavior in which the manager selects an alternative that is good enough (i.e., one that will yield a satisfactory return to the organization).

saturated market. N. A situation occurring when there is a greater supply of a particular item than there is demand for it. A company's item can gain market share at this point, only at the expense of another item.

saturation. N. The phase of the product life cycle in which an item is no longer able to be sold because most consumers who are likely to be interested in it have already purchased it. See also *burst advertising, life cycle of product, product life cycle, saturation campaign.* Synonymous with *horizontal saturation.*

saturation campaign. N. Intensive use of radio or television advertising to promote or sell a product in a market. There are usually special low rates for saturation-level advertising. See also *flight saturation, saturation.*

saving. N. The amount of existing income that is not spent on consumption.

Say's law. N. Used by market analysts, a concept developed by Jean Baptiste Say in the late eighteenth century that the supply of all economic items must always equal the full demand for them. Therefore, any increase in output is an increase in demand, and overproduction is an impossibility. See also *overproduction, underconsumption theory.*

SBUs. ABBRV. Strategic business units.

scaling method. N. In marketing research, purports to measure the nature and strength of an individual's attitudes or opinions toward a specific object, concept, or idea.

scanner. N. In merchandizing and retailing, an electronic instrument that reads bar codes and other graphic information found on product packages, coupons, and mailing envelopes. See also *scanner market, universal product code.*

scanner market. N. A type of controlled market testing where products are offered for sale in stores where scanners have been installed, and special arrangements are made to gather all relevant information about them and their buyers. See also *scanner*.

scarcity value. N. An increase in value caused by a demand for an item whose supply cannot be increased (e.g., works of art from the nineteenth century).

scare purchasing. N. (1) Purchasing to hoard. (2) Unusually heavy buying of items in short supply.

scatter plan. N. (1) Purchasing a number of specially selected spots on television. (2) A broadcast media plan that schedules advertising announcements to run during a program, giving the advertiser a wider audience for his or her money than would be achieved by being a single program sponsor.

scenario. N. The sequence of events that may occur in the future. Useful to the firm in planning product strategies of the future. See also *scenario analysis*.

scenario analysis. N. A forecasting technique in which market researchers develop a subjective picture of several possible futures by identifying cause-and-effect relationships and following them to their logical conclusions. See also *scenario*.

schedule. N. (1) A systematic plan for future operation over a given period. (2) In advertising, a list of advertisements, by stated media, giving dates of appearance, space, time, and so on.

scheduled production. N. The rate of activity assigned for the production of a given item in a specified period.

schedule of variance. N. The difference between actual production and scheduled production.

scheduling. N. The organization and control of the time needed to carry out a sales effort.

schlock (shlock). N. *(slang)* Cheap, inferior items or services.

scientific method. N. A philosophy for marketing research based on objectivity, accuracy, and thoroughness.

scientific tariff. N. A duty to cover foreign and domestic manufacturing costs.

scintilla of evidence. N. A small amount of evidence that assists in the proof of an allegation.

scoop. V. To beat out a rival. N. A considerable profit following a transaction that is likely to involve advance notice over or exclusion of competitors.

scoring model. N. A weighted-factor checklist used to screen new product proposals. Factors are scored, and the scorings are weighted and then totaled to yield a judgment on the concept.

scrambled merchandise. N. (1) The practice of carrying any product line, however dissimilar from other lines carried; must yield a profit. (2) An approach by retail outlets of maintaining types of goods not normally found in those stores (e.g., clothing and large appliances sold in a drugstore).

scrap. N. Equipment or material that has not be used and therefore has been discarded. Synonymous with *excess*. See also *waste*.

scrap value. N. See *salvage value*.

scratch and sniff. N. A device for advertising an area impregnated with a fragrance that is released by scratching its surface. See also *action device*.

scratch off. N. Found in sales promotions materials, a card where the consumer scratches away a portion to reveal a message, usually indicating whether the person is an instant winner of a contest and what the prize is.

screening stage. N. In new product development, when new concepts are assessed to determine which of them have the potential for development.

screwdriver duties. N. A means of reducing costs to global marketers, where imported components of foreign products made within a national country or member of an international trade agreement might be vulnerable to antidumping duties unless an adequate proportion of the final unit is made outside the foreign nation.

scruff. V. *(slang)* To earn sufficient monies for the basic necessities of life.

s-curve effect. N. Occurs if sales of a product rise sharply after it is introduced because of heavy initial promotion effort (advertisements, coupons, samples, etc.), drop slightly as promotional support is reduced, and then rise again a positive word-of-mouth communication takes place.

SEA. ABBRV. Single European Act.

sealed bid pricing. N. A pricing technique in a competitive bid situation; the firm bases its price on what it anticipates its competitors will charge, i.e., what the competitors will bid as contrasted to the company's own costs or demands. Sealed-bid pricing requires the submission of confidential bids, all within a stated time of a particular day, with a contract usually going to the lowest bidder.

sealing. N. (l) In advertising, reducing or enlarging an illustration or advertisement. (2) In packaging, holding a closed box or package adequately by cord, tape, glue, or other means.

seal of approval. N. An award in the form of insignia made by a consumer magazine or an association to a manufacturer whose product specifications have met the standards set up by the magazine's testing bureau or by the association's committee. Such seals are valued by advertisers.

search. N. Where buyers gather and interpret information enabling them to decide whether or not to purchase an item or service, including consideration for alternative items or services.

search goods. N. Items whose qualities are easily determined prior to purchase. See also *experience items*.

seasonal dating. N. See *advance dating*.

seasonal demand. N. See *seasonality*.

seasonal discount. N. (1) A discount that is offered to customers who purchase a product or service during a season when the demand for that product or service is low. (2) A price reduction given for purchases made out of season (e.g., ski equipment can usually be bought at a discount in the spring). See also *static inventory problem*.

seasonal employee. N. A worker who is employed for limited periods of activity (e.g. for working in a department store over the Christmas buying season).

seasonal fluctuations. N. Regular and predictable shifts in business activity created by changes in the season (e.g., housing construction increases during spring).

seasonal forecast. N. Changes in market demand that depend primarily on the time of year.

seasonal industry. N. An industry that has high peaks of employment at specified times of the year and down periods during other seasons.

seasonality. N. A time, the changing of the seasons, that is characteristic of a market, product, or promotional campaign that indicates some variation in sales, e.g., trying to sell ski equipment in the summer may fail unless other incentives, such as bargain prices, are introduced. See also *demand states*, *erratic demand*. Synonymous with *seasonal demand*.

season dating. N. See *advance dating*.

secondary data. N. Information not received by a user from its original source, but that came instead from references gathered earlier. See also *primary data*.

secondary group. N. A large group whose members have a shared goal but do not engage in face-to-face communication.

secondary research. N. In marketing research, using data from already available published sources, such as those previously conducted, the census bureau as contrasted with primary research information gleamed from original field research. Secondary research differs from primary research in that the latter is for a particular firm and the information gathered is often proprietary, not for free circulation.

secondary shopping district. N. A series of stores outside the urban center, but within the city limits, that services a larger population. Convenience items are particularly important in these stores.

secondary source. N. Data that have been collected for a purpose other than the research project in question.

secondhand. ADJ. (1) Not new. (2) Merchandise offered for sale that has already been used.

seconds. N. Goods bearing defects that have possible effects on wearability and appearance. See also *bargain store*, *thirds*.

second sale. N. (1) A sale achieved by building on a customer's receptive mood following an initial purchase. (2) An additional sale to the same person.

sectional edition. N. See *regional issue*.

sectional wholesaler. N. A wholesaler who limits his or her activities to a fixed and small number of geographic areas, or states. Synonymous with *regional wholesaler*. See also *local wholesaler, national wholesaler*.

secular inflation. N. The most serious economic problem of the 1970s. In contrast to cyclical inflation, which moves in and out of the economic system roughly every two years, secular inflation is primarily a long-term social phenomenon; impacts sales and advertising investments.

secular stagnation. N. A low level of economic movement measured over an extended time period; impacts sales and advertising investments.

secured distribution. N. A field warehousing technique where carload lots are shipped to a distributor's premises for release based on the bonded warehouse's arrangement as the distributor requires the items.

security agreement. N. The agreement between a seller and a buyer that the seller shall have an interest in the goods. The security agreement must be signed by the buyer and must describe the goods.

seed trends. N. Current trends used to spot possible scenarios. See also *scenario*.

segment. N. (1) A portion of a message. (2) In marketing, a subgroup of people found within a market. See also *market* *segmentation.* (3) In broadcasting, television or radio advertising time within which there is no variation in the unit charge.

segmentation. N. Dividing a market into subunits with similar motivations and needs. Used to increase product or service acceptance by recognizing item appeals. Demographics, geographics, personality, attitudes, values, and preferences are the most popular base for segmenting a market. See also *demographic segmentation, market segmentation, fragmentation.* Synonymous with *market cleavage.*

segmentation pricing. N. When prices are fixed at different levels for different segments of the population, e.g., the airline industry, which provides different classes of service.

segmentation research. N. A form of marketing research that uncovers new bases for market segmentation. See also *market segmentation.*

segmentation strategy. N. See *differentiation.*

segmenter. N. A marketing organization that uses the single target market approach or the multiple target market approach in the evolution of a strategy. See also *imaginative segmenter, innovative segmenter.*

selection criteria. N. The basis for choosing a subset from a group.

selective demand. N. The demand for a particular brand. See also *primary demand, selective demand advertising.*

selective demand advertising. N. Advertising purporting to determine selective buying motives within a particular audience. See also *primary demand advertising.*

selective distribution. N. (1) An approach to distribution that involves the use of a limited set of outlets in a given territory. (2) Choosing retail outlets that will be permitted to receive one's merchandise for sale; traditionally used with hard goods, such as appliances, VCRs, refrigerators, furniture, etc. Permits manufacturers to maintain greater control over the way their merchandise is sold and reduces price competition among sellers of the items. See also *exclusive distribution, intensive distribution, open distribution.* Synonymous with *limited distribution, selective selling.*

selective headline. N. A headline directed to the interest of a specific market segment.

selective perception. N. People's cognitive abilty to shield themselves from the onslaught of external stimuli to which they have been exposed so as to create order and reduce psychological disruption. The three aspects of selective perception used by consumers and that one of importance to marketers are: (a) selective exposure—suggests that consumers choose only some communications from the mass of external stimuli that have been presented to them; (b) selective distortion—when confronted with general, limited, or dissonant data, people will unconsciously supplement the information with their own perception, the goal and result of which is a message that is comprehendable and consistent with their feelings and beliefs; and, (c) selective retention—people's tendency to recall external stimuli that are similar to their preconceived notions and beliefs, and to forget other stimuli that are not. See also *consumer behavior, perception.*

selective selling. N. See *selective distribution.*

selective stage. N. See *competitive stage.*

selective stocking. N. Balancing the cost of service with the expense of maintaining inventory to determine what merchandise should be stocked at every distribution center.

selectivity index. N. In media planning, a measurement method that compares print advertising media in a stated geographic area; determined by dividing a medium's audience size by the percentage of the target market potential population. See also *cost per thousand*.

self-concept. N. See *self-image*.

self-concept theory. N. The notion that two factors influencing an individual's purchasing behavior are how the person perceives himself or herself and how he or she wishes to be perceived by others. See also *motivation*.

self-fulfilling forecast. N. A forecast that encourages behavior that causes itself to be realized.

self-fulfilling prophecy. N. A situation in which a firm predicts sales will decline and ensures this by reducing or removing marketing support.

self-image. N. Peoples' concepts of themselves and their roles in relation to others. Synonymous with *self-concept*. See also *ideal self image, self-concept theory*.

self-liquidating. N. An asset that can be converted into cash or is subject to total recovery of invested money over a period of time.

self-liquidating offer. N. See *self-liquidating premium*.

self-liquidating premium. N. A premium for which the buyer pays all or part of the cost, where the advertiser offers something of value that enhances the item's image without incurring any cost. See also *trade cards*.

self-liquidator. N. See *self-liquidating premium*.

self-mailer. N. In direct-mail advertising, a piece structured so that it can be addressed directly on the piece, and then it is folded or mailed without being enclosed in an envelope.

self-reference criterion. N. Where the firm concludes that if a product prospers in the domestic market it should do equally as well or better in an overseas market. Therefore, they conclude that no new market research effort is required.

self-selection selling. N. A merchandising approach that allows customers to make their choices without the initial assistance of sales help.

self-service. N. A sales outlet or store in which the customer chooses the items to be purchased, removes them from the shelves, carries them to a checkout counter for completion of the transaction, and carries or sends them to the place of use.

seller concentration. N. The number of sellers found in a single industry. As the number of sellers increases, the less the chance that it is that one firm can influence prices.

seller's lien. N. The seller's privilege of holding onto certain items until the buyer has delivered payment. See also *general lien, vendor's lien*.

seller's market. N. A market in which demand is greater than supply, resulting in sellers setting the prices and terms of sale. It is a market characterized by rising or high prices. See also *buyer's market*. Synonymous with *tight market*.

seller's surplus. N. The difference between the price a seller actually receives and the lowest price that he or she would accept.

sell-in. N. The manufacturers' attempts to convince retailers to distribute and stock his or her merchandise. See also *sell through*.

selling. N. The process of assisting and/or persuading a potential customer to buy merchandise or services, or to act favorably on an idea. See also *sales*.

selling against the brand. N. When artificially inflated prices are kept on some items to increase sales on other items.

selling agent. N. An agent that handles the entire marketing function for a manufacturer. These agents usually work on an extended contractual basis with the manufacturer and traditionally have full authority for setting prices. They differ from sales agents, in that sales agents do not have control or influence over prices and terms of sales and rarely get involved in advertising and promotional activities.

selling calendar. N. A schedule for promotions identifying specific dates for each intended special selling event.

selling costs. N. Marketing costs (e.g., advertising and sales promotion) necessary to attract a potential buyer to an item or service.

selling error. N. When inappropriate, error-filled selling methods are employed; often leads to markdowns of merchandise. See also *buying error*.

selling formula approach. N. A selling method that assumes that all consumers are alike or at least will respond in a predictable way to a set sales presentation.

selling price. N. The cash price that a customer must pay for purchased items or services.

selling process. N. Involves prospecting for customer leads, approaching customers, determining customer wants, giving a sales presentation, answering questions, closing the sale, and following up.

selling short. N. See *short selling*.

sell off. N. Reselling advertising space and time that has already been contracted for to another advertiser.

sell out. V. (1) To betray a person, organization, or cause, usually for profit or special treatment. (2) In merchandising, to dispose of an entire stock or set of products.

sell through. N. The manufacturer's attempt to increase sales of merchandise at the retail level. See also *sell-in*.

semantic differential scale. N. A method to determine consumer attitudes. It is a scale of opposite pairs of words separated by a line divided into seven parts. By connecting the checks, the market researcher is left with a picture of consumers' attitudes.

semi-direct channel. N. A channel of distribution with a limited number of middlepeople—often only one—between the producer and consumer. See also *indirect channel*.

semi-finished items. N. See *fabricated parts*.

semi-jobbing. N. When the retailer makes wholesale sales or when the wholesaler makes retail sales. See also *split function wholesaler*.

semi-liquidator. N. A premium offer paid in part by the consumer. Synonymous with *purchase-privilege offer*, *semi-self-liquidator*, *self-liquidator*.

semi-manufactured items. N. Raw materials that have passed several stages of production but still have other processes to pass into before items can be used. Synonymous with *fabricated parts*.

semi-self liquidator. N. See *semi-liquidator*.

semi-spectacular. N. An outdoor advertising message hand-painted on a panel of wood or metal placed adjacent to a highway or railroad line or in a metropolitan district containing heavy traffic and making use of an electrical, mechanical, or three-dimensional device or animated copy or figures.

semivariable costs. N. See *mixed costs*.

sensitive market. N. A market characterized by fluctuations determined by the announcement of favorable or unfavorable news.

sensitive products. N. Products in sectors that are deemed highly vulnerable to injurious import competition.

sensory thresholds. N. The upper and lower limits on the ability of human sensory processes to perceive increases or decreases in the intensity of a stimulus.

separation. N. See *product protection*.

sequential interdependence. N. The relationship between units of an organization such that the product of one is passed along to the next in order, after which the final product results.

serendipity. N. The ability to gain knowledge from accidental events. Many famous new products have been discovered accidentally, but many potential discoveries were overlooked because the observer was not serendipitous (having a prepared mind).

serpents in the garden. N. Inducements and displays placed near the doors of a store to attract customers' immediate attention.

serrated edge. N. A saw tooth edge, as around the mouth of a paper bag.

service. N. A deed, act, or performance.

service area. N. See *accommodation area*.

service blueprint. N. A visual portrayal of the service plan by a firm. It is essentially a detailed map or flowchart.

service costs. N. The operating costs of service departments that are usually allocated to production departments.

service department. N. An organizational unit that does not directly produce goods but serves other departments.

service charge. N. A payment by a financial institution against an individual or organization for services rendered.

service fee. N. Funds paid to the advertising agency by the advertiser. Usually, the agency is paid a retainer for a wide variety of services. Other extraordinary services are compensated at special rates.

service line. N. The offering of a sales organization that may be called upon by a client when marketing its products or services. See also *product line*.

service mark. N. (1) A trademark for a service. (2) A mark used in the sale or advertising of services to identify the services of one person and distinguish them from the services of others, such as the names, symbols, titles, designations, slogans, character names, and distinctive features of radio or other advertising used in commerce.

service marketing. N. (1) Efforts to raise the sale or delivery of a service. (2) Encompasses the rental of goods, the alteration or maintenance or repair of goods owned by consumers, and personal services.

services. N. (1) Work offered by people or organizations for others without transferring goods or commodities, e.g., insurance companies or banks. (2) Privileges for customers of a firm beyond the items themselves, such as credit, assortment, home delivery, and gift wrapping.

service salesperson. N. Usually interacts with customers after sales are completed. Delivery, installation, or other follow-up tasks are undertaken.

service selling. N. Efforts by a salesperson who satisfies a consumer's needs and thus retains goodwill.

services marketing. N. See *service marketing*.

service wholesaler. N. The merchant selling to retailers, industrial users, and wholesalers. Complete services are provided including credit, delivery, variety of items, etc. Synonymous with *regular wholesaler*.

setback. N. A reversal or partial loss in an activity.

setup. N. The time or costs needed before production of an item can commence.

shading. N. *(slang)* Giving a small reduction in a price or terms of sale.

shadow boxes. N. Boxes that can display small items in retail stores; usually a framed box with tiny shelves.

share. N. (1) Stock that names the holder and indicates ownership in a corporation. (2) In broadcasting, the percentage of households in a specific geographic location with television sets tuned to a particular program as compared to the percentage of households tuned in. See also *audience share, brand share*.

shared services. N. Common carriers, a combined captive sales force, or public warehousing shared by several marketers at any one time.

share of advertising method. N. A method of setting the advertising budget based on a share of the total advertising expenditures in a specific field.

share of audience. N. The percentage of radio or television sets in use or households watching a particular program. See also *audience flow, Hooperating, Nielsen rating*.

share of the market. N. See *market share*.

share of voice. N. The level of advertising by a brand in a particular product category in contrast to others within the same category. The greater the brand's share of voice, the greater the number of advertising messages being offered to consumers. Companies that advertise most frequently usually gain a greater level of market share in the product category.

share points. N. Percentage points of market share; used as the common basis of comparison to allocate marketing resources effectively.

sharpening. N. A cognitive process in which the information retained becomes more vivid and important than the event itself.

shelf life. N. The time identified on the package or label that a certain item can remain in stock or on the shelf before deterioration of a significant nature occurs. When that date arrives, the product should not be sold to the consumer. See also *stock rotation*.

shelf miser. N. See *space miser*.

shelf stock. N. Items available to store customers who remove what they desire from the shelves on which the merchandise are placed. See also *floor stock, forward stock*.

shelf talker. N. Printed advertisement hung from the shelf in a retail store, supermarket, or a variety store.

shell firm. N. An organization that is incorporated but does not function or produce any goods or services.

Sheridan stuffer. N. See *newspaper stuffer*.

Sherman Antitrust Act of 1890. N. Federal legislation aimed at preventing business monopoly. Some courts, however, applied the sanctions of the law against strikes, and unions were fined triple damages for acts that were considered to be in restraint of trade. See *price stabilization, restraint of trade*.

shipment. N. (1) Delivery and transport of items by a carrier. (2) In distribution, a collection of items that are transported as a unit. (3) In merchandising, merchandise sent to a manufacturer to be processed, or items sent from the manufacturer to a wholesaler or retailer. See also *drop shipper, middleperson*.

shipper's agent. N. An international service facilitating intermediary who buys cargo capacity on transport modes and then resells it to shippers.

shipper's cooperative. N. (1) A group of shippers that pool shipments of similar items in order to benefit from lower freight rates. (2) An incorporated firm, owned by shippers of goods and run on a not-for-profit basis, that performs the functions of a foreign freight forwarder.

shipping order. N. Instructions of shippers to carriers for forwarding all goods; usually the duplicate copy of the bill of lading.

shipping permit. N. Authority issued by a transportation line permitting the acceptance and forwarding of goods against the movement of which an embargo has been placed.

shirt-board advertising. N. An advertising medium in which a sales message is printed in full color on a specially processed shirt board inserted in each shirt sent out to customers by laundries.

shoehorn. N. *(slang)* Adding copy or visuals to an already exisiting advertisement, such as last-minute changes.

shoplifting. N. Thievery of a store's items by a customer or employee. See also *inventory shortage, pilferage, shrinkage*.

shop merchandising. N. Establishing certain locations in a store for serving buyers with special interests (e.g., tennis shop, teenage corner).

shopper. N. The individual engaged in a search for goods or services. Synonymous with *pennysaver*.

shopping center. N. (1) A cluster of stores and other related facilities (restaurants, rest rooms, etc.) planned and built to service a trading area. (2) A group of retail stores at a single location that is planned, developed, and controlled by one organization. See also *superstore*.

shopping goods. N. Consumer goods that are purchased only after the buyer compares the offerings of more than one store. See also *convenience goods, specialty merchandise*.

shopping mall. N. See *mall*.

shopping mall intercept. N. A form of personal interview in which respondents are approached or intercepted as they pass a particular spot in a shopping mall.

shopping plaza. N. See *mall*.

shopping products. N. Goods and services about which consumers will seek information before making a purchase.

shopping radius. N. The area around the store from which customers are usually attracted.

shopping store. N. A retail outlet that is favored by consumers who are shopping for a certain type of product.

shortage. N. (1) An excess of quantity demanded over quantity supplied, indicating that the price is below equilibrium. See also *short merchandise.* (2) A deficiency in quantity shipped.

shortage advertising. N. The advertising run when an item or service is in short supply resulting from production problems. Rather than attempt to influence the customer to purchase more of the item or service, the advertisement turns to education or other forms of influence while stock is replenished.

short hour. N. Part-time workers who work during peak store hours.

short merchandise. N. (1) Goods bought in small quantities, usually in extreme sizes, to complete an assortment. (2) In merchandising, purchased goods that were not included in a shipment.

short of destination. N. Prior to reaching the final port, warehouse, or destination.

short rate. N. The higher rate an advertiser pays when he or she fails to use the space or time contracted for.

short run. N. (1) A one-time job. (2) The time during which a firm can alter the price or output of its goods but not change the size of its plant or close down operations.

short selling. N. Selling items and purchasing them at a lower price to receive a profit. Synonymous with *selling short.*

short term. N. See *short run.*

shotgun approach. N. (1) A disorganized approach to selling or advertising, aimed at reaching a large number of potential customers without expecting to make sales to all. See also *rifle technique.* (2) In publicity, the mailing of news releases to different media outlets.

showing. N. The number of outdoor advertising displays bought for the placing of advertisements. For example, a one hundred showing indicates that the entire combination of units bought will be exposed to the entire population of a market at least once during any given day. A fifty showing indicates that half the population will pass by the advertising at least once during any given day, etc.

shrinkage. N. The gradual loss of inventory over time due to damage, misplacement, or theft. Shoplifting is a major cause of shrinkage. See also *inventory shortage (shrinkage), shoplifting*.

shrink wrapping. N. A plastic coating applied over a package. When subjected to heat, the coating conforms to the shape of the package; used in mailing multicomponent promotion packages, such as catalogs and fliers.

SIC. ABBRV. Standard Industrial Classification System.

sideline stores. N. Stores whose primary interest is other than retailing (e.g., a wholesaler who also sells to the consumer as an accommodation).

signature. N. (1) In advertising, the advertiser's name as mentioned in the advertisement. (2) In broadcasting, the sound effect or music that is used to identify a commercial or program.

significance. N. Statistical importance; the degree of probability that, in an infinite series of measurements of the type in question, the value actually obtained will not occur with meaningful frequency by chance alone and hence can be attributed to something other than chance.

silent salesperson. N. A point-of-purchase display, direct-mail item, or money used in a vending machine.

similitude. N. The practice of customs authorities when an imported article does not conveniently fit into any existing classification within the customs tariff. Articles are then compared with similar articles listed in the tariff for justification.

simple random sampling. N. Used by market researchers, probability sampling in which respondents are chosen at random from a complete list of the members of the population. See also *sampling*.

simple regression analysis. N. See *regression analysis*.

simple trend analysis. N. Used by market researchers, a forecasting technique in which managers review historical data and use the rates of change to project future trends.

simplification. N. Cutting down on the different products in a company's lines. See also *diversification*. Synonymous with *product deletion*.

simulcast. N. A program that is broadcast simultaneously over radio and television.

simulated test market. N. A type of market testing where consumers are presented with a simulated purchase situation to determine their reactions and feelings toward the merchandise, advertising campaign, or marketing mix combinations.

simulation. N. (1) The representation of certain features of the behavior of a physical or abstract system by means of the behavior of another system. (2) A method of reviewing an operation or problem that overcomes the difficulty of not being able to study it in real-life form. A model of the system or process is subjected to a series of assumptions and manipulations in an effort to find one or more acceptable solutions.

singing commercial. N. A radio or television advertising message delivered in the form of a song, usually accompanied by one or more musical instruments.

single customs document. N. For international marketers, the one document that replaces some seventy different forms once used in trade across the European Community's internal borders. Effective 1988, this document attempts to harmonize and simplify trade procedures and alleviate the long delays at Europe's border crossings.

Single European Act. N. Of importance to international marketers, this amendment to the original treaty set new objectives for the European Union with the completion of the internal market, "an area without internal frontiers in which the free movement of goods, persons, services and capital is ensured in accordance with provisions of this Treaty." It took effect on January 1, 1993, with fiscal and trade barriers eliminated among the twelve nations. ABBRV. *SEA*.

single-item pricing. N. See *unit pricing*.

single-line store. N. A store that carries a wide variety of one type of goods.

single-line wholesaler. N. A full-service wholesaler that carries only one or two product lines but offers considerable depth in each.

single market. N. See *Single European Act*.

single-price policy. N. Selling the entire assortment of a given category of items at one fixed price in order that the purchaser can concentrate only on the item offered, e.g., all gloves are $10.00. See also *one-price policy*.

single product strategy. N. Manufacturing only one item or a single item with a limited number of options.

single-rate. N. A radio or television station's charge that does not differentiate between local and national advertisers. See also *local rate, one-time rate*.

single-source data collection. N. A technique that allows research firms to tract the activities of individual consumer households from the programs they watch on television to the products they purchase at a store.

single-sourcing. N. Purchasing all the firm's requirements for a specific product or service from one source of supply.

single-stage sampling. N. See *cluster sampling*.

single target market method. N. A marketing segmentation approach where one homogeneous group is chosen as the target market and one marketing mix is employed to market the item.

single variable segmentation. N. The simplest form of market segmentation where only a single factor, e.g., a person's age, is used to segment the population.

singularity. N. The number of other products against which a new item will be tested. If one, singularity is monadic. If two, the singularity is paired comparison.

sister-store concept. N. See *equal-store concept*.

situational analysis. N. An assessment of the marketing environment; key part of the marketing plan. The firm's strengths and weaknesses are assessed as well as its products; may also include data on market characteristics, consumer needs, buying patterns, and other factors that influence the outcome of the marketing effort. Synonymous with *market review*.

situational factors. N. Those factors that can interrupt the organizational consumer's decision process and the actual selection of a supplier or brand. They include strikes, machine breakdowns, organizational changes, and so on.

six Cs. N. In marketing, in preparation for making decisions, the following are to be examined carefully: commodity, company, competitors, channel members, consumers, and community.

six-sheet poster. N. A printed sheet of outdoor advertising matter measuring four feet, four inches high, and nine feet, ten inches wide, adopted as a standard of outdoor advertising service.

skewness. N. Used by consumer and marketing researchers, the property of a distribution curve that is not symmetrical. See also *kurtosis*.

skimming. N. See *skimming price*.

skimming price. N. Use of a high introductory price followed by a series of price reductions, designed to get all the trade the market will bear at one price level before lowering the price and also to appeal to the more price-conscious consumer. Synonymous with *skim-the cream price*. See also *penetration strategies*.

skim-the-cream price. N. See *skimming price*.

skip. N. A customer who moves from a known address without paying the bill of a business or utility.

skip loss. N. See *skip*.

skywriting. N. Out-of-the-home advertising medium where a short message is written in the sky by an airplane. Small puffs of smoke, from a chemical mixture, forms letters leaving a message for a few seconds, and then disappear.

slack. N. (1) The time in which a minor operation can be completed in advance of the next major operation that depends on it. (2) A dull or inactive business period (i.e., a slack season).

slack filling. N. Employing deceptively oversized boxes or other packages. An unlawful practice as regulated by the Federal Trade Commission.

sleeper. N. A fast-selling item that has the potential to become a runner. See also *running*.

slice of life. N. (1) In broadcasting, a commercial indicating how a person overcomes a barrier by utilizing the advertised item or service. These commercials are often a mini-drama where a common problem is solved by using the advertised item. (2) In advertising, advertising that portrays consumers in realistic situations that are consistent with consumers' perceptions of their own lifestyles.

sliding scale. N. A reason for increasing or decreasing charges to a customer in relation to the volume of activity or usage over a stated time (e.g., a gas company may charge for gas on a sliding scale, with lower rates for greater consumption).

sliding scale tariff. N. A customs tariff in which rates of duty vary according to the price of a given import. Usually, as the price of the merchandise falls, the duty is lowered.

slippage. N. (1) Lost time. (2) In merchandising, people who purchase an item intending to redeem a coupon, request a rebate, or send in for a premium, and then fail to do so.

slogan. N. Verbal material found in an advertisement that is repeated and recalled precisely as presented. Highly memorable slogans ultimately define the features of the product or service that is advertised. Can be printed or verbal.

slug. N. In advertising, the signature of the advertiser on the print advertisement. Either a logo, trademark, or just the name of the advertiser that is given for purposes of identification.

slump. N. A short-lived decline in the activity of a business or economy.

small order. N. Small orders for merchandise. See also *small order problem*.

small order problem. N. Orders to purchase items that are so small that the transaction may not produce a profit.

smorgasbord plan. N. A sales compensation method allowing the person to choose among salary, commissions, bonuses, and other fringe benefits that he or she prefers as a means to fulfilling individual needs.

smuggling. N. Removing from or putting in goods or persons without permission. Smuggling can be done across the borders of countries or other political entities (e.g., cigarette smuggling across state lines).

snapper. N. An added incentive used to encourage prospects to buy a heavily promoted item or service.

sniffer. N. A display that provides an aroma or odor to attract prospects or to enhance the appeal of an item.

snob impact. N. The degree to which demand for an item is discounted because too many other people use it.

snowballing method. N. A means for evolving media advertising schedules where the climax of a campaign is looked upon as important and therefore receives the greatest proportion of the budget. Synonymous with *crescendo method*.

social benefit. N. The value to society resulting from a specific act or action (e.g., the discovery of penicillin and the invention of the automobile).

social channel. N. Others familiar with the prospect who share information and attitudes about products and services. See also *social classes*.

social classes. N. Employed in marketing research and market segmentation, categories of status and position that are often overlapping and impossible to adequately define. These social stratifications are: upper-upper (social register), lower-upper (nouveau riche), upper-middle, lower-middle, upper-lower, lower-lower. See also *social mobility, social channel*.

social contract. N. A model conceptualizing the relationship between a firm and society as a whole, whereby the organization is granted freedom to exist and is obligated to function in the public interest.

social cost. N. The price paid by people for the side effects of economic performance (e.g., pollution or the destruction of forests). See also *comparative advantage*.

socialization. N. A formal and informal process of training, guidance, indoctrination, influence, or even coercion, whereby a new or potential organization member is made to internalize the norms, values, attitudes, or behavior patterns of the organization.

social marketing. N. The use of marketing philosophy and techniques in the dissemination of societally useful ideas. The concept was propounded by Phillip Kotler and Gerald Zaltman in the 1970s. Synonymous with *societal marketing*. See also *advocacy advertising, public service advertising*.

social mobility. N. Moving from one social class or stratification into another. See also *social classes*.

social performance. N. How a person carries out his or her roles as worker, family member, citizen, and friend.

social responsibility. N. The expectation that companies should act in the public interest and contribute to the solution of social and ecological problems.

social styles model. N. A classification system for segmenting organizational consumers in terms of a broad range of demographic and lifestyle factors. The model divides the personnel representing those consumers into various lifestyle categories.

societal marketing. N. See *social marketing*.

socioecological view of marketing. N. Examines all the stages in a product's life span from raw materials to the junkpile. It incorporates the interests of all consumers influenced by the use of a good or service. See also *eco-audit*.

socioeconomic segmentation. N. Market segmentation based on age, income, occupation, education, etc. Usually, a variety of these variables are used together to help identify potential purchasers of specific items or services.

sociogram. N. A means of describing the preferences people have in being with others. The sociogram is used in choosing teams, work partners, and so on.

sociographics. N. A means to describe group influences on consumer behavior.

soft goods. N. Ready-to-wear clothing, piece goods, linens, towels, and small fashion accessories. See also *capital goods*. Synonymous with *nondurable goods*.

soft market. N. See *buyers' market*.

soft sell. N. A selling technique that is convincing, subtle, and indirect. See also *hard sell, consultative selling*.

soft technologies. N. A way to industrialize services by substituting preplanned systems, such as prepackaged vacation tours, for individual services.

SOH. ABBRV. Stock on hand.

solo mail. N. A direct-mail promotion used for one item or service.

sort. V. To segregate items into groups according to some definite rules, such as grade and quality. See also *assorting*.

sort and count. N. Gathering of results from people who respond to an advertiser's request to respond to the advertisement. Responses are usually coded for future usage by an advertiser in breaking down the information into useful information.

sorting. N. A process in which products are brought together at one location and then divided up and moved in smaller quantities to locations closer to the ultimate buyers.

sorting out. N. See *sort*.

source. N. (1) The originator of a message. (2) In marketing, the channel of sale generating an order or customer. See also *source evaluation*. (3) In advertising, the individual who communicates an advertising message. See also *message development*.

source effect. N. The public's reaction to an advertisement as dictated by their perception of the source of the message.

source evaluation. N. A critical part of direct marketing enabling marketers to concentrate their promotion resources on the best sources. See also *source (2)*.

source marking. N. Where vendors price merchandise before shipment.

source migration. N. An order pattern made by a customer over a time period where orders in response to varying promotions are made.

space. N. The area of medium in which an advertisement is placed.

space allocation. N. The quantity of shelf space in a retail store set aside for the display of merchandise.

space buyer. N. An advertising agency executive who assists in the planning of printed media campaigns and chooses and purchases space in the media. See also *time buyer*.

space contract. N. An agreement between a publisher and an advertiser on the rate structure for the publication.

space miser. N. A point-of-purchase display created to hold items that can be readily removed, as well as carry a promotional message. Frequently placed on a shelf where the item is available. Synonymous with *shelf miser*.

space position value. N. The effectiveness of outdoor advertising, based on four factors: the distance from where the advertisement is seen, the speed of traffic approaching, the angle seen, and the number of competing outdoor advertisements in the area; expressed as a percentage from zero to one hundred, with zero indicating zero visibility.

space spots. N. Newspaper advertisements of small size that are volume bought by national advertisers.

span of control. N. The extent of a supervisor's responsibility, usually identified in the organizational chart by lines of authority. Synonymous with *span of supervision*. See also *evoked set*.

span of recall. N. The number of brands a person can name when asked to do so. See also *evoked set*.

span of supervision. N. See *span of control*.

special event pricing. N. Promotional pricing where a sale is advertised, frequently linked with an event or holiday. The goal is to bring inventories into line with consumer demand or to raise cash.

special events. N. See *events marketing*.

special features. N. Regularly run broadcasts of continuing interest to the public, i.e., weather reports or sports. Traditionally sold to advertisers at a higher rate than other programs.

specialization. N. Reducing an operation or task into separate simplified, individual activities.

special order. N. An order that may be priced below the normal price in order to utilize excess capacity and thereby contribute to company profits.

special-line retailer. N. See *specialty store*.

special position. N. The particular location of an advertisement in a newspaper, magazine, or other periodical.

specialties. N. See *advertising specialty*.

specialty. N. See *advertising specialty*.

specialty advertising counselor. N. See *specialty distributor*.

specialty advertising field. N. Utilizing advertising novelties as the advertising medium. See also *Specialty Advertising Information Bureau*.

Specialty Advertising Information Bureau. N. An organization within the specialty advertising field purporting to maintain an interest in the subject by sharing information and educating users about the advantages of the medium. See also *specialty advertising field*.

specialty discount store. N. An outlet that carries a single item category and sells it at below regular retail prices.

specialty distributor. N. A wholesaler in the specialty advertising field; handles a variety of advertising novelties and assists in advertising campaigns of these items. Synonymous with *advertising specialty distributor, specialty advertising counselor*. See also *direct selling house*.

specialty goods. N. See *specialty merchandise*.

specialty-line market research firm. N. A research organization that provides data gathering or analysis to other researchers or company marketing research units. See also *syndicated service*.

specialty line supplier. N. A research firm that specializes in one aspect of the marketing research process.

specialty line retailer. N. A limited-line retailer that carries only one or two product lines, but offers substantial depth and expertise in those lines.

specialty merchandise. N. Consumer goods that have special features for which buyers are willing to make a major purchasing effort (e.g., imported foods, hi-fi equipment, cameras, etc.). Synonymous with *specialty goods*.

specialty-merchandise wholesalers. N. Full-service merchant wholesalers that concentrate their efforts on a relatively narrow range of products and have an extensive assortment within that range. Synonymous with *limited-line wholesalers*.

specialty products. N. Goods and services for which there are no acceptable substitutes in the consumer's mind, e.g., some luxury cars, consumer electronics equipment, designer fashions, etc.

specialty salesperson. N. A salesperson, other than retail, who specializes in the sale of one product or a few products of a line of one or more manufacturers or producers.

specialty selling. N. Usually the sale of products or services at a person's home or place of work, i.e., the selling of insurance, encyclopedias, vacuum cleaners.

specialty shops. N. See *specialty stores*.

specialty stores. N. Retail outlets that maintain a large selection in a limited line of merchandise (e.g., men's apparel stores). Synonymous with *special-line retailers*, *specialty shops*.

specialty supplier. N. A company that processes advertising novelties for sale through a host of outlets. See also *direct selling house*, *specialty advertising counselor*, *specialty distributor*.

specialty wholesaler. N. See *specialty distributor*.

specification. N. A written identification of the work to be done and materials to be used in the completion of a task or product. See also *job specification*. ABBRV. *specs*.

specific identification. N. A method of valuing inventory and determining cost of goods sold whereby the actual cost of specific inventory items are assigned to those items of inventory on hand and to those that have been sold.

specific tariff. N. A tariff based on a fixed amount charged per unit of the goods imported.

specs. ABBRV. Specification.

spectacular. N. An outdoor advertising display characterized by the use of electric or neon lights and lavish color, and sometimes by such special effects as flashing lights, laser beams, billowing smoke, and animation.

speculation. N. The employment of funds by a speculator. Safety of principal is a factor secondary to increasing capital. See also *speculator*.

speculative pitch. N. See *speculative presentation*.

speculative presentation. N. An expensive demonstration by an advertising agency to a prospects, indicating what the agency can do should it be awarded the contract; involving considerable and expensive time for the agency and therefore usually done for large accounts. Synonymous with *speculative pitch*.

speculative purchasing. N. Buying items when prices appear lowest, with the expectation that there will be a future price increase that will make a profit possible.

speculator. N. One who is willing to assume a relatively large risk in the hope of gain. The speculator's principal concern is to increase capital rather than dividend income. Speculators may buy and sell the same day or may invest in enterprises that they do not expect to be profitable for years. See also *speculation*.

spendable earnings. N. Considered by market analysts; net earnings after deductions for taxes, or the amount available for spending. Synonymous with *take-home pay*.

spiffs. N. See *push incentive, push money*.

spillovers. N. See *externalities*.

spin-out. N. A form of new product team organization in which the team is broken out from the ongoing organization. It is the ultimate

spiral stage

in projectization and used only in cases where the project will have major barriers to overcome.

spiral stage. N. In advertising, the manner in which a product or service develops in terms of its acceptance by prospective consumers. Contains continuous stages and ceases as a given point, while others continue. See also *competitive stage, pioneering stage, retentive stage*.

split function wholesaler. N. A merchant wholesaler who is vertically integrated to operate on two or more levels of the channel of distribution. See also *semi-jobbing*.

split item. N. Merchandise that a firm both produces and purchases simultaneously.

split-off point. N. See *joint production costs*.

split order. N. A large order that is separated into smaller units that are sold over a period of time. When purchasing or selling goods, a very large transaction could cause substantial price fluctuation, and the splitting is supposed to prevent this.

split run. N. Two or more advertisements of equal size with the identical position in different copies of the same publication issue. This affords a means of determining the impact of differing versions of an advertisement, and it allows an advertiser to feature different products in regional printings of a national publication. See also *copy testing, preferred position*.

spoilage. N. Merchandise found to be defective.

spokesperson. N. (1) A manager's role in speaking for the unit and representing it to others. A key concept of the spokesperson's role is that of representation; the manager must act as an advocate for subordinates. (2) In advertising, the person who delivers the message in a testimonial. See also *celebrity testimonial, media training.*

sponsor. N. A radio or television advertiser who runs one or more advertisements during a program. Usually, sponsoring a program requires the advertiser to buy the majority of commercial announcements made on the program. See also *sponsorship, sustaining program.*

sponsor identification. N. The association of a radio or television program with the name of the sponsor or the brand name of his or her product, as elicited from listeners or viewers during or after the broadcast.

sponsorship. N. Financial backing of an advertisement. See also *alternate sponsorship, sponsor.*

sports marketing. N. Sponsorship in sporting programs or events. See also *events marketing.*

spot. N. In broadcasting, a place or position in a listing or schedule (e.g., a spot on television). Synonymous with *occasion, time slot.*

spot advertising. N. A campaign wherein advertisers choose specific stations to be used. This contrasts with network or local advertising. See also *flight saturation.*

spot announcement. N. A brief commercial, usually one minute long or less, inserted between portions of a radio or television program. See also *spot broadcasting.*

spot broadcasting. N. The use of a local radio or television station in a specified market by a national advertiser; permits an advertiser to select individual markets closely matching his or her areas of distribution, and those trading zones in which special sales or distributive problems must be solved. See also *spot announcement.*

spot campaign. N. An advertising campaign using spots.

spot delivery. N. Immediate delivery.

spot display. N. Items clearly set down along store aisles with an attention-getting device attached.

spot market. N. (1) A market in which commodities are sold for cash and delivered quickly. (2) A market in which transactions between buyers and sellers take place at spot prices, which fluctuate daily, and, sometimes, hourly to reflect supply and demand conditions.

spread. N. (1) The differences between the bid and asked prices of an item. (2) In retailing, the difference between two prices. (3) In broadcasting, stretching a live broadcast to fill the entire time slot allotted it. (4) In advertising, an advertisement appearing on two facing pages in a periodical or magazine. Should they appear in the center of the magazine, the piece is called a center spread.

SRDS. ABBRV. Standard Rate and Data Service, Inc.

SRO method. N. In sales, a closing approach where the prospect is told that, should the sale not be concluded immediately, the chances are small that the item will be available to the person at a later time. Considered by most as an unethical practice.

stability. N. The objective of creating a sense of predictability, control, and certainty in an organization.

stable environment. N. An environment that is characterized by relatively small changes in technology and customers who have a minimal impact on the internal operation of the organization.

stable market. N. A market with few short-term price fluctuations, where purchasers are able to do little to influence prices. See also *unstable market*.

stacker. N. A freight handler who loads a vehicle.

staff. N. Employees who advise and assist line managers and employees but are not directly engaged in the production of the final good or service.

staff department. N. A department that provides assistance and support to line departments in attaining basic objectives of the organization. In a manufacturing firm, purchasing and accounting would be staff departments.

stagflation. N. Impacts marketing and advertising revenues; inflation coexisting with economic stagnation. Prices for goods and services continue to increase during a period of minimal capital investment in equipment, research and development, and so on.

staging. N. Planning the location and actions to be executed for a commercial.

stagnation. N. Impacts marketing and advertising revenues; conditions of minimal growth rate, or growth that is increasing at a lower rate than expected.

stake. N. The degree of dependency one channel member has over another for its success or failure.

Standard Advertising Register. N. The Standard Directory of Advertising Agencies and the Standard Directory of Advertisers are the two companion directories in the field; referred to as the Red Books, because of their red cover. The former provides information on advertising agencies, and the latter lists the seventeen thosuand firms that advertise throughout the country, with their agencies and annual advertising budgets.

standard advertising units. N. The standard sizes of advertising space set by newspapers for all national advertisers; units sizes of differing columns and inches so as to simplify the buying of advertising space by these advertisers. See also *column inch.*

Standard Container Acts of 1916 and 1928. N. Federal legislation that fixed the standard sizes for baskets and containers for fruits and vegetables.

standard costs. N. An estimate of what actual costs should be under projected conditions.

standard deviation. N. Used by market researchers, the square root of the arithmetic mean of the squares of the deviations from the mean of the series.

Standard Directory of Advertisers. N. See *Standard Advertising Register.*

Standard Directory of Advertising Agencies. N. See *Standard Advertising Register.*

standard error. N. (1) Used by consumer and market researchers, a measure or an estimate of the sampling errors affecting a statistic. (2) A measure of the amount a statistic may be expected to differ by chance from the true value of the statistic. See also *sampling error.*

Standard Industrial Classification System. N. A numerical system developed by the U.S. Bureau of the Budget to classify establishments by type of activity for purposes of facilitating the collection, tabulation, presentation, and analysis of data relating to such establishments and for promoting uniformity within U.S. agencies. ABBRV. *SIC.*

standardization. N. (1) The determination of basic limits or grade ranges in the form of specifications to which produced items should conform. Greater standards compatibility removes structural barriers to markets and increases the competitiveness of firms. Standards define certain technical specifications that products must meet in order to establish an acceptable level of safety. Usually referred to as harmonization in the European Union. See also *grade labeling, Pan-European marketing, standards* (2) In manufacturing, establishing specific criteria levels (size, quality, weight, etc.). Industrial standardization is achieved by an elaboration of standards throughout nations that trade with each other. See also *ISO, ISO 9000*.

standardized approach. N. An international marketing strategy in which a firm uses a common marketing plan for all nations in which it operates. Synonymous with *global approach*.

standardized marketing data sources. N. External sources of marketing data collected by outside organizations for several information users who have common information needs.

standard markets. N. Sites where companies test market a product through normal distribution channels and monitor the results.

standard of living. N. A consideration for marketers when planning strategies, the level of material affluence of a nation as measured by per capita output.

standard package. N. The quantity of an item usually shipped in just one carton.

Standard Rate and Data Service, Inc. N. An organization that releases up-to-date data on advertising rates, standards, and so on, of various media. SRDS is considered the prime source of advertising media information. ABBRV. *SRDS*.

standards. N. The mutual recognition, which removes technical barriers to trade, irrespective of whether these involve technical rules, standards, tests, or certificates. See also *standardization*.

standard volume. N. The expected sales over a given business cycle reduced to an annual basis.

standing details. N. In advertising, elements that appear in each advertisement, e.g., logo, trademark, photograph of item, etc.

standing order. N. An authority to a vendor to ship specific products as available, or on a fixed-quantity basis per time interval.

standstill. N. In international marketing of goods, where participants agree not to take any restrictive or distorting measures inconsistent with global trade agreements, such as the General Agreement on Tariffs and Trade.

staples. N. See *staple stock*.

staple items. N. See *staple stock*.

staple stock. N. Goods on hand that are in continuous demand, such as milk, bread, sugar, etc. Staple stock items are marketed primarily on the basis of price. Synonymous with *commodity products*.

star. N. (1) When a product line has a high growth rate and a significant share of the market. (2) A strategic business unit that has a high growth rate and a high relative market share.

Starch test. N. A posttest that assesses the extent of consumers' recognition of an advertisement appearing in a magazine that they have read.

state. N. One of the fifty geographic and governmental units of the United States, as well as the nation's capital, Washington, D.C., and all U.S. territories.

state bonded warehouse. N. See *warehouse, state bonded.*

statement. N. A summary of transactions between a creditor and his or her debts or a presentation of names and amounts of accounts to show a financial condition (e.g., an IRS statement).

state-of-being segmentation. N. One of a four-way classification of the strategies of segmentation. Refers to the physical, demographic, or geographic features of a population. See also *benefit segmentation, product usage segmentation, state-of- mind segmentation.*

state-of-mind segmentation. N. One of a four-way classification of the strategies of segmentation. Refers to the psychological features of the population, especially as it deals with the relationship between attitudes and behavior. See also *benefit segmentation, product usage segmentation, state- of-being segmentation.*

static analysis. N. The determination of an equilibrium at a single point in time without considering the impact of the passage of time.

static inventory problem. N. The tendency of items bought for a specific selling season to lose value, either partly or completely, because of changes in the market at the season's end. See also *seasonal discount.*

station break. N. Giving the call letters or identification of a radio or television station; an advertising message or announcement is delivered during that interval.

station option time. N. Time over which a network affiliate station has priority on first sales.

station poster. N. Advertising billboards displayed in bus, train, airline, and subway stations.

statistical demand analysis. N. Uncovering the direct relationship between sales and real demand factors. This analysis, based on multiple regression analysis, assists in overcoming forecasting problems.

statistical process control. N. The use of statistical analysis (usually by line employees) to measure and manage specific work processes. Commonly used in total quality programs designed by marketers.

statistics. N. The mathematics of gathering data and the approaches used in describing and analyzing numerical information.

status. N. (1) An individual's relative social or power position in a group. See also *social classes*. (2) The position of an organization in a broad social context.

status consensus. N. The agreement of group members about the relative status of members of the group. Synonymous with *status consequence*.

status consequence. N. See *status consensus*.

status float occurrence. N. An attempt to explain the influence of fashion on different levels of social class. Numerous contradictions appear as to dress and code of dressing. See also *trickle-down theory*.

status quo. N. The existing state of affairs.

status-quo based pricing objectives. N. Those that orient a firm's pricing strategy toward continuing a favorable business climate for its operations or stability.

status quo pricing. N. To minimize chances of a price war with competitors, prices are kept at the level charged in the mature stage of the product life cycle.

status symbol. N. An item or service purchased in the hope that it will communicate one's desired or real status to others.

stay out price. N. See *preemptive price*.

steady schedule. N. A scheduling approach in which advertising is run at a steady schedule throughout the year.

stepped costs. N. Costs that climb by increments with increased volumes of activity.

step-up. N. See *upgrade*.

stereotypes. N. Preconceived notions, often based on superficial characteristics, that often distort communication between people. See also *bias*.

stickers. N. Items that have not been purchased after a reasonable time and occupy space considered important for better-selling items. See also *dead stock*.

stimulation marketing. N. Efforts purporting to bring the affected market segment from a lack of interest in buying to the recognition of the value in the product and a reasonable level of positive demand.

stimulus. N. Any change that interacts with a sense—vision, hearing, taste, smell, and touch.

stimulus-response. N. The basic unit of learning (habit) in both the classical and instrumental conditioning models.

stock. N. (1) Merchandise held for sale (e.g., inventory). (2) Material in inventory.

stock ahead. V. To maintain sufficient quantities of goods in inventory to cover an anticipated surge in future demand for the items.

stock control. N. Regulating inventory levels so that stock on hand is balanced between demand and production ability.

stock cover. N. The ratio of current average weekly sales to current stock, providing information on the quantity remaining in stock before new items need to be ordered.

stock depth. N. Merchandise determined to be needed to maintain assortments without too many lost sales because of an out-of-stock situation. See also *stockout*.

stocking allowance. N. A special allowance by a manufacturer to encourage distributor organizations to carry a particular product.

stocking representative. N. A manufacturer's representative carrying an inventory for his or her principal and then shipped for the principal from that inventory.

stock in trade. N. The business activity that is usually carried on by a firm.

stockless purchasing. N. Purchasing where financial responsibility for stock lies with the vendor. See also *systems contracting*.

stock levels. N. The inventory carried by a business firm.

stockout. N. A condition that occurs when all inventory has been used or sold. Stockouts are very costly, as other inputs must then be utilized. See also *stock depth*.

stock-room supervisor. N. See *materials controller, tool-crib supervisor*.

stock rotation. N. Putting new incoming products behind those of the same kind already on the shelf, so that inventory remains fresh. See also *shelf life*.

stock-sales ratio. N. The inventory retail value at the beginning of a given month, divided by sales for that month. This relationship is used to control the sales and inventory balance.

stock shortage. N. A condition that occurs when the dollar value of the real inventory in stock is less than that which is shown on the inventory books.

stock spotting. N. In warehousing, where items are warehoused close to the customer instead of near the factory of production so as to shorten delivery time and lower transportation expenses.

stock-to-sale method. N. Planning inventory levels from planned sales for a given month. The ratio of stock to sales of the same month in the prior year is used as a guide for the plan in the following year.

stock-turn. N. In retailing, synonymous with *turnover*.

stop and hold. N. The record status of an inactive customer; used when merchandise is undeliverable or when a cessation of service to the customer is needed.

storage. N. The holding of goods for future use.

store. N. Any place where merchandise, goods, or services can be purchased, or a place for storage. See also *department store*, *specialty stores*.

store audit. N. A count of the merchandise carried and sold in a retail outlet.

store brand. N. A brand whose copyright is owned by the retailer, though the item may have been prepared for the store by a supplier. Usually the latter applies and a store label is affixed to the item.

storecast. N. A radio broadcast appearing in a store. Retailers using storecast place loudspeakers around their store to receive musical programs as well as merchandise-related messages.

store check. N. A study of items in a store by nonsales personnel whose primary responsibilities and duties include running in-field examinations, such as determining how effectively merchandise is displayed; how the sales force sells items; and, how well the merchandise is indeed selling.

store count distribution. N. A measure of distribution based on the number of stores. A product sold in 90% of all grocery stores would have 90% store count distribution.

store image. N. The image of a store as perceived by customers or prospects.

store redeemable coupon. N. A merchandise discount certificate that is redeemed in any retail outlet where the item is sold, as contrasted with a certificate that can only been redeemed through the mail.

stores. N. Plural of *store*.

stores requisition. N. The form for securing materials that are held in normal stock. It goes directly to the stores department from which materials are then supplied for use. See also *requisition*.

store traffic. N. The number of customers coming and going in a store.

storyboard. N. See *storyline format*.

storyline format. N. A form of advertising where a story begins and presents the product or in some fashion relates its history to some present-day useful activity.

straight commission. N. Where salespersons receive a fixed percentage of their total sales as their only compensation. See also *straight salary*.

straight extension. N. An international product-planning strategy in which a company makes and markets the same products for domestic and foreign sales.

straight rebuy. N. (1) A purchasing situation in which the organization has bought the item or service before and is likely to reorder from the same vendor. (2) An undramatic repurchase of an item previously bought. See also *modified rebuy, new-task purchasing*.

straight-rebuy purchase process. N. See *straight rebuy*.

straight salary. N. Compensation for a salesperson based on a fixed rate and at regular intervals, independent of performance considerations. See also *straight commission*.

strategic alliance. N. See *joint venture*.

strategic business units. N. (1) Divisions composed of key businesses within multiproduct companies, with specific managers, resources, objectives, and competitors. Strategic business units may encompass a division, a product line, or a single product. (2) One or more products, brands, divisions, or market segments that have something in common, such as the same distribution system. Each strategic business unit has its own mission, it own set of competitors, and its own strategic plan. ABBRV. *SBUs*.

strategic clusters. N. A means of identifying competitors by the grouping of international firms of overlapping activities within geographic proximity to their primary customers and to their supply networks.

strategic information scanning system. N. A formal structure of people, equipment, and procedures to obtain and manage information to support strategic decision making.

strategic marketing. N. To make a store or company more customer oriented, the correlation between marketing activities and strategic planning activities are measured and provided with a greater percentage of the firm's budget.

strategic plan. N. A long-term plan covering a period of three, five, or sometimes ten years. See also *strategic planning*.

strategic planning. N. (1) A basic type of planning by which a firm formulates its long-range goals and selects activities for achieving those goals. Decisions include whether to enter a new untapped market, to grow an existing market, to dominate an existing market, or to dominate a small segment of an existing market by replacing competitors or by satisfying an unmet desire. (2) The process of developing a long-range plan that is designed to match the organization's strengths and weaknesses with the threats and opportunities in its environment. See also *planning*.

strategic planning gap. N. The difference between the present position of a company and its desired future position.

strategic resource monopoly. N. An organization that has a monopoly by virtue of controlling a vital input to a production process, e.g., DeBeers of South Africa owns most of the world's diamond mines.

strategic window. N. The time period, as when the window is open, when a firm's abilities to produce items in demand by the public are matched with sales. When the window closes, such as when the firm waits too long to act appropriately, the firm may have lost its marketing opportunity.

strategy. N. Guidelines for making directional decisions that influence an organization's long-run performance. See also *market strategy*.

stratified random sampling. N. Probability sampling in which the total population is divided into subgroups, or strata, and a random sample is chosen from each subgroup. See also *sampling*.

stratified sample. N. See *stratified random sampling*.

stratifying the market. N. Determining the number of consumers who may purchase the item or service at various price levels.

strict liability. N. An extreme variant of product liability (in common practice today) in which the producer is held responsible for not putting a defective product on the market. Under strict liability, there need be no negligence, sale no longer has to be direct from producer to user (privity of contract), and no disclaimer statement relieves the producer of this responsibility.

strip center. N. An uncovered shopping center as contrasted with an enclosed mall.

stripped down price. N. An item offered for sale at a lower price, and then upon visiting the store, the customer finds that the item contains fewer features than originally thought. For example, a stripped down car has no air-conditioning or stereo.

strip programming. N. See *across-the-board*.

strong market. N. A market that has a greater demand for purchasing than for selling.

structural inflation. N. Increasing prices caused by an uneven upward demand or cost pressures in a key industry, even when total demand remains in balance with total supply for the economy as a whole.

structured question. N. A question that limits respondents to a specific set of replies.

stuff. V. *(slang)* To sell goods that are not genuine or have been stolen.

stuffer. N. See *newspaper stuffer*.

stuffing. N. Loading cargo or goods into a container or envelope.

style. N. (1) A characteristic or distinctive method of expression, presentation, or conception in the field of some art. (2) A particular design.

style modification. N. Altering a product in order to present a new image or to differentiate it from other brands that perform a similar activity or service.

style obsolescence. N. Obsolescence that occurs when the physical appearance of a product is changed to make existing versions seem out of date.

style-out. N. Identifying which characteristics of specific items attract customers' purchasing attention by separating the fast-moving products from the slow-moving products and then studying the fast-moving products to uncover the common features that may be the explanation for the greater sales.

subcaption. N. See *subheadline*.

subculture. N. A smaller cultural group within a society that reflects geographic, religious, or ethnic differences; important in analyzing consumer behavior since subculture members tend to display similar preferences for a variety of items and services, such as food, art, recreation, politics, etc. Subcultures represent a distinct market segment. However, stereotyping creates a bias as dissimilar features also exist. See also *market segmentation, target marketing.*

subhead. N. See *subheadline.*

subheadline. N. A restatement of the idea of interest to a newspaper reader in a different and more direct fashion than appears within the headline. Usually a subheadline is set in a smaller type than the headline but is larger in type than the type used in the text of the body. Synonymous with *subcaption.*

subject bid. N. A bid that is negotiable, rather than firm.

subjective method. N. Used by consumer and marketing analysts, a forecasting method based on the subjective opinions of people who are knowledgeable about the field for which the forecast is being made.

subjective price. N. A consumer's perception of the price of a good or service as being high, fair, or low.

subliminal advertising. N. The delivery of a message below a receiver's awareness level, to be registered subconsciously. The receivers do not realize that they have seen or heard these messages, by which advertisers attempt to promote sales of a product or service. Since the 1960s subliminal advertising has not been used on television as it has been declared illegal. See also *hidden persuaders, supraliminal awareness.*

subliminal awareness. N. See *subliminal advertising.*

submarginal. N. Yielding less than enough to cover the cost of production.

submarket. N. A portion of the market separated on the basis of common motivations. See also *segmentation.*

suboptimization. N. Operating at a less-than-optimal level in one segment of a firm in order to optimize the functioning of the organization as a whole.

subordinate product advertising. N. Advertising carried out in order to encourage consumer demand for the producer of a product that has utility, in part or whole, as a component of another item, e.g., shoelaces for shoes. Synonymous with *end-product advertising*.

subscriber. N. One who agrees in writing to purchase a certain offering.

subscription. N. A contractual agreement between a buyer and a seller to provide the buyers with a service or item to be delivered as stated in a contract or agreement at the total price based on the length of the service to be rendered. Discounts are often employed with new or long-term subscribers, but not for renewed customers.

subset. N. Used by market analysts, a group of items that is contained in a larger grouping of items.

subsidiary. N. An organization whose voting stock is more than 50% owned by another firm.

susidies. N. See *subsidy*.

subsidy. N. (1) In the United States, impacts cost to marketers; federal payments to an individual or organization for which the government receives no products or services. The primary objective of a subsidy is to allow for production of the goods at prices that will attract buyers. (2) In international usage, financial encouragements provided, usually by a government, to support businesses. Such subsidies can take the form of lower taxes, tax rebates, or direct payments. There are two general types: (a) export subsidy—a benefit conferred on a firm by the government that is contingent on exports, and (b) domestic subsidy—a benefit not linked to exports, conferred by the government on a specific industry or enterprise or group of industries or enterprises; impacts profits of marketers.

substandard. N. Conditions that make a risk less desirable than normal for its class.

substantiation. N. A consumer-protection legal concept that requires a firm to be able to prove all the claims it makes in promotion messages. This means thorough testing and evidence of performance are needed prior to making claims.

substitute goods. N. Items that can easily replace one another either in production or in consumption (e.g., natural and synthetic fibers, strawberries and raspberries, etc.). An increase in the price of one substitute good encourages purchase of the other(s).

substitution law. N. The economic statement that if one product or service can be a replacement of another, the prices of the two must be very close to each other.

suggested retail price. N. Though not mandatory, the list price of merchandise as stated by the manufacturer as a fair price to be charged by the retailer. Manufacturers hope and expect that stores maintain a price close to their suggested retail price. See also *discount*.

suggestion selling. N. See *suggestive selling*.

suggestive selling. N. The strategy of suggesting to a potential purchaser that he or she might have an additional need related to what has already been purchased (e.g., it might be suggested that a women who has bought a dress also select appropriate shoes or a sweater). See also *complementary products*, *derived demand*.

sumptuary laws. N. Laws that attempt to minimize the consumption of items that are believed to be harmful to individuals or to society in general. See also *public consumption monopoly*.

sunk cost. N. (1) A cost that has already been incurred and is now irrelevant to the decision-making process. (2) In marketing, a cost that represents expenses already incurred in the development of a new product; have been written off, involve no capital asset, and no anticipated salvage value. For purposes of net present value, sunk costs are ignored. After the project is over, an overall recap will include all costs, whenever spent.

superior goods. N. Products and services that are demanded in larger quantities as incomes rise (e.g., expensive cars, caviar, fur coats).

superdeductive. N. (1) A U.S. Customs procedure in determining the deductive value of merchandise for assessment of ad valorem duties. (2) Affecting marketers costs, an alternative valuation method that allows a deduction from the value of the items for duty purposes of further processing within the United States prior to sale to the ultimate buyer. Synonymous with *further processing method*.

superette. N. See *bantam store*.

superior good. N. See *normal good*.

supermarket. N. A retail operation, having at least eight employees, occupying approximately twenty-five thousand square feet, that sells food and nonfood items. See also *bantam store, superstore*.

superstore. N. A combination of a general-merchandise discount operation and a supermarket; usually ranges in size from fifty thousand square feet to two hundred thousand square feet. Established to fulfill all consumer needs for every type of food and

supplement. N. An added newspaper section that enhances the content and prestige of a newspaper and allows advertisers in the supplement the ability of reaching a mass audience, especially if the newspaper is national.

Supplemental Register. N. A classification of trademarks established by the Trade-Mark Act of 1946 in which certain qualified marks may be included.

supplier. N. The firm that provides goods that are used in the manufacturing process but that are not included in the item itself.

supplier-active. N. A new product development process where the manufacturer studies customers to obtain information for new items, which is then analyzed and eventually developed into a new product.

supplier/distribution intermediary contracts. N. Focuses on price policies, conditions of sale, territorial rights, the services/responsibility mix, and contract length and conditions of termination.

supply. N. The quantity of items available for sale. See also *Say's law*.

supply and demand. N. Theory relating to the amount of product to be placed on the market over a time period (supply) and the number of the product units to be sold within that same time frame (demand). Used by marketers in setting a marketing strategy, since supply and demand patterns impact product pricing. For example, when supply of an item is low and demand for it is high, prices can be set at higher levels, and vice versa. See also *demand states*.

supply curve. N. A graphic representation of the quantity of output supplied as a function of price. See also *excess supply curve*.

supply price. N. The lowest price needed to product a specified output. It is the lowest price a seller will accept for the act of supplying a given quantity of a commodity.

supply schedule. N. A table of prices and corresponding quantities offered for sale in a given period.

supporting the market. N. Placing purchasing orders at or somewhat below the prevailing market level in order to maintain and balance existing prices and to encourage a price rise.

supportive service. N. In marketing, a benefit or service, e.g., extending credit, which contributes to an items attractiveness to a consumer.

support level. N. The point at which demand for a product or service is reached. It is the moment when the resistance level is overcome.

supraliminal awareness. N. The detection of stimuli by a person on the conscious level. See also *subliminal advertising*.

supramarginal. N. Yielding more than the cost of production.

surcharge. N. A charge above the usual or customary charge.

surface changes. N. Shifts in consumer preferences and interests that direct spending patterns from one activity to another without signaling a basic change in fundamental cultural values.

surplus. N. Anything remaining or left over.

surrogate positioning. N. Product positioning that eschews product features and benefits, turning instead to one of perhaps eight or ten substitutes, or surrogates. The two most popular surrogates are nonpareil (our product is simply the best available, no features or benefits cited) and parentage (our product is good because it was designed by the designers or producers of product X). See also *surrogate question*.

surrogate question. N. Any question to which the answer can yield an answer to another question that cannot be answered at this time, if ever. For example, if the key question is "What retaliation will our chief competitor offer to our new product?" a surrogate question that can be answered would be "What retaliation did that competitor offer to its most recent serious competitive threat?" See also *surrogate positioning*.

survey. N. A unique inquiry using a sample as a database for each new study.

survey approach. N. A research method in which researchers use personal interviews, telephone interviews, or mailed questionnaires to question a group of people directly.

survey area. N. The geographic area represented by a sample group or that is found in a radio/television market.

survey-feedback activities. N. Activities that focus on collecting survey data and designing a plan of action based on the interpretation of the data.

survey of buying power. N. A detailed demographic, geographic statistical study of consumer power to purchase goods of various types.

survey research. N. Research to provide descriptive data about a marketing problem or situation, often by purporting to gain insight into buying behavior of prospects and existing customers.

suspend. V. See *stop and hold*.

sustainable competitive advantage. N. A strength, relative to competitors, in the markets served and the products offered.

sustainer. N. See *sustaining program*.

sustaining program. N. An unsponsored broadcast program on radio or television, where the cost of preparing and broadcasting the program is sustained by the station or network. See also *sponsor*.

swap. V. To exchange or barter. See also *exchange (3)*.

sweeps. N. The month-long time period when the audience size of network television time slots is determined. Its results set advertising rates for local stations. Consequently, networks air popular shows and films to attract the widest possible audience because the large the viewing audience, the higher the rates to be charged.

sweepstake. N. A sales promotion method where participants compete for awards by merely entering the contest. No skill or strategy on the part of the participant is required. A contestant merely submits an entry form with his or her name and address. See also *contest*.

swell allowance. N. A reduction from invoice cost to provide for the loss of item value due to damage in shipping.

switching customers. N. Bringing in a sales specialist when the salesperson who originally served a customer is unable to close a sale.

switch selling. N. An unethical practice of using high-pressure tactics to sell an item that is more expensive than one advertised at a lower price. See also *bait and switch advertising*.

SWOT analysis. N. Strengths, weakness, opportunities, and threats, which are part of strategic marketing planning. Used for forecasting by comparing present and future information.

symbiotic marketing. N. Where one company sells and promotes a product made or controlled by another firm. See also *pooled marketing*.

symbol. N. (1) A representation of characteristics or transformations of ideas or things. See also *perception*. (2) The single capital letter or combination of letters acquired by a corporation when it is to be listed on an exchange, e.g., International Business Machines is IBM.

symbolic pricing. N. Using price to create an impression about a product or a brand in the minds of consumers.

symmetrical balance. N. See *formal balance*.

syncromarketing. N. Marketing aimed at attempting to bring inconsistent or seasonal demand levels in synch with supply levels in synch with supply levels, for example, the restaurant's early-bird special.

syndicate. N. (1) The association of two or more individuals, established to carry out a business activity. Members share in all profits or losses in proportion to their contribution to the resources of the syndicate. (2) In advertising, a group of newspapers forming a chain, owned or managed by the same person or organization. (4) In newspapers, a group of newspapers owned by the same company. See also *syndication*. V. (1) In broadcasting, to sell or distribute a program to one or more local stations.

syndicated research. N. Research based on samples or from panels of people, where all or part of the same results are supplied to different users.

syndicated service. N. A research firm that periodically compiles specific types of data for sale to marketers. See also *specialty-line market research firm*.

syndication. N. The sale or distribution of radio and television programming to local stations by the owner of that programming. Broadcast syndication falls into two categories: (a) first-run syndication—the distribution of original programs that were produced specifically for the syndication market, such as films and specials, and (b) off-network syndication: the distribution to local stations of shows that previously aired in prime time on network television, e.g., *I Love Lucy* reruns. See also *syndicate*.

syndicator. N. (1) A company that supplies products and associated brochures, envelopes, and other materials. (2) People who sell merchandise via the mail. See also *bangtail*.

synectics. N. Like brainstorming, an idea-generating method where discussion evolves from an idea related to a problem, rather than the problem by itself. Used by advertisers and advertising agencies when preparing a campaign. Four concepts are used: (a) the identification of a particular leader; (b) knowledge of a common understanding of the situation, issue, or problem; (c) a common acceptance that all ideas contain some merit; and, (d) the importance of equality from participants in the sharing of ideas and suggestions. See also *brainstorming, idea generation*.

synergy. N. The feature of a system whereby, when the parts are properly interrelated and functioning, an output is achieved that is greater than or superior to the effects obtained when the parts function independently.

system. N. (1) Any purposeful organization of resources. (2) An assembly of methods, procedures, or techniques that are united by regulated interaction to form an organized whole.

systematic error. N. The tendency toward error when making a judgment.

systems analysis. N. The analysis of business activity to determine precisely what must be accomplished and how to accomplish it. See also *operations research*.

systems buying/selling. N. (1) Purchasing or selling of a multifaceted product or service. Firms that participate in systems buying do not choose to make different buying decisions when purchasing a complex item, such as a telecommunications network. They prefer, instead of coordinating their efforts with multiple groups or vendors, to deal with one contractor who is fully responsible for the bidding and assembling of subcontractors to provide the complete package. (2) Firms that provide systems selling market the capability to assemble all the items and services required by the purchaser.

systems completing product. N. A product that makes available to a large population an already accepted and used technology.

systems contracting. N. Buying that permits for little or no stock to be handled by the purchaser. The purchase agreement is based on a catalog furnished by the supplier for the item agreed upon. Can benefit both the supplier and the purchaser. See also *blanket order, stockless purchasing, systems selling*.

systems design. N. The formulation and graphic outlining of the nature and content of input, files, procedures, and output in order to display the necessary connection processes and procedures.

systems selling. N. The merchandising of a group of items that has some functional relationship to one another as a package, rather than as single items, e.g., matching tie and handkerchief sets. See also *systems contracting, sales analysis, systems buying/selling*.

T

table 664

table. N. In marketing research, a statement of factual information, usually assembled for reference purposes.

tabloid. N. Appearing as a magazine, but truly a newspaper with a page size smaller than that of the standard newspaper.

tabloid inserts. N. Separate, preprinted supplements of advertisements found inside newspapers, usually in weekend editions.

tactic. N. An approach used to attain certain goals that relate directly to the overall objectives of an organization.

tactical planning. N. A short-term plan that specifies the activities necessary to carry out a strategic plan. See also *planning*.

tactical product-line adjustment. N. The determination of the number of variations of any given item that is offered. See also *strategic product-line adjustment*.

tactics. N. Effort for executing the strategies outlined within a marketing plan; steps for manipulating the context in which an item is sold.

tag. N. (1) In merchandising, see *Kimball tags*. (2) In broadcasting, an addition to a commercial broadcast (e.g., a voiceover message following a transcribed statement, or an announcement or insertion of music serving as a conclusion).

tag line. N. See *tag (2)*.

tailor-made. ADJ. (1) Just right. (2) Made according to individual specifications.

take. N. *(slang)* In retailing, the funds in the cash register of a retail store at the close of a business day.

take-and-pay contract. N. A guarantee to purchase an agreed amount of a product or service, provided that it is delivered. See also *tale-or-pay contract*.

take-home pay. N. See *spendable earnings*.

take-one. N. The print advertisement featuring coupons, refund blanks, or contest entry forms in a pad or pocket that is affixed to the advertisement. It carries an extra charge to the advertiser, which covers maintenance services provided.

takeover time. N. The time required in marketing for a superior new product to go from 10% to 90% displacement of an inferior older product.

take stock. V. To make an inventory of items on hand.

take-withs. N. See *carryouts*.

taking inventory. N. The procedure of counting all inventory on hand at a time set aside for this purpose. See also *unit control*.

tale-or-pay contracts. N. An unconditional guarantee to purchase an agreed amount of the product or service, whether or not it is delivered. See also *take-and-pay contract*.

talon. N. A special coupon (e.g., a voucher stub).

tame cat distributor. N. A wholesaler owned and controlled by a manufacturer.

tamperproof container. N. A container designed so that it cannot be opened and resealed without leaving evidence of tampering.

tangible assets. N. Physical and material (perceptible to touch) assets, as distinguished from intangible assets, which are imperceptible to touch (e.g., cash, land, buildings, etc.).

tangible product. N. A basic physical entity, service, or idea with precise specifications and offered under a given description or model number.

tape plan. N. A promotional strategy, usually run by supermarkets, offering premiums in return for cash register tapes totaling a specified amount. Synonymous with *cash-register-tape redemption plan*.

tare. N. An unproductive weight; an amount that is part of the gross weight of an article (e.g., the weight of a truck, a package, or any other container or vehicle). Net weight is gross weight less the tare.

target. N. (1) The one to whom a selling message is addressed. (2) A market where a selling effort is made. See also *target audience*. (3) The marketing goal toward which organizational resources are directed.

target audience. N. That portion of the population to which marketing efforts and advertising are directed; defined in terms of geographic, demographic, or psychographic factors. Used by marketers to develop promotional activities. Synonymous with *audience (2), target market*. See also *market segmentation, target marketing, market target*.

target customers. N. The people who are the objects of a store's total efforts to attract business. See also *market target*.

target market. N. See *target audience*.

target marketing. N. A process in which the marketer evaluates a number of market segments, decides which one or ones to serve, and develops and implements a unique marketing mix for the targeted segment(s). The three target marketing steps are: (a) market segmentation—where the firm defines its market segments based on factors of geography, demographics, etc.; (b) market targeting—the firm decides which of the market segments to follow by assessing the potential profit for each segment, then setting a market coverage tactic; and, (c) positioning—where the firm makes decisions on how to present the merchandise offerings so as to make them more attractive to consumers than those of competitors. See also *subculture, target audience*.

target marketing strategy. N. See *target marketing*.

target population. N. The population from which a sample is taken.

target pricing. N. A technique of establishing prices to reach a profit objective.

target return on investment. N. An amount of income equivalent to a certain percentage of the firm's investment; this amount is set as a goal to be achieved through pricing. See also *target return pricing*.

target return pricing. N. Setting a product's price to yield a specific return on investment using a formula.

target return price. N. An equation where target return price = desired return X invested capital unit cost + unit sales. See also *target return on investment*.

tariff. N. (1) Any list of prices, charges, duties, and so on. (2) A schedule of taxes on items imported or exported. In the United States, tariffs are imposed on imported goods only. See also *General Agreement on Tariffs and Trade, specific duty*.

tariff bindings. N. Of importance to global marketers, the agreement by contracting parties to maintain the duty rates on specified goods at negotiated levels or below.

tariff escalation. N. The common situation whereby raw materials and less processed goods are generally duties at lower rates than more processed versions of the same or derivative goods. For instance, the import duty in most countries is generally higher for petrochemicals than for the petroleum and other raw materials necessary for their production. It is argued by primary commodity exporting nations that this situation confers a higher degree of protection for the processing industries of importing countries than nominal tariff rates would suggest.

tariffication. N. Of importance to global marketers, to convert quotas and other restrictions to tariffs that would be reduced over time. For example, nations with strict import controls would start with prohibitive tariffs of several hundred percent. Tariffication includes provisions to guarantee a minimum level of imports at reduced tariff rates. Its intent is to permit high tariffs to shrink over a period of time and thus have a minimum tariff quota expanded. Synonymous with *tariffy*.

tariff rate. N. The charge rate or schedule established by the rating organization that has jurisdiction over a given class and territory (e.g., a schedule of freight rates for transporting different items to various cities).

tariff war. N. A form of competition between nations as evidenced by tariff discrimination of various forms.

tariffy. N. See *tariffication*.

task force. N. A team of individuals, often representing various departments or interests, that has responsibility for coordinating a study or other efforts that involve a number of organizational units.

task interdependency. N. The extent to which two or more groups or individuals rely on each other for services, information, and goods to accomplish their own goals.

task method. N. A means of arriving at an advertising budget by setting a sales objective and then deciding the cost of reaching that objective through advertising. Synonymous with *plunge method*.

tastemakers. N. Those who are the first to adopt product innovations, recognizing their influence on followers.

tax-and-board. N. Charges included in premiums (almost always percentages of the paid premium) for state or local taxes and for the support of various rating offices, bureaus, and boards.

taxpayer. N. (1) A small building or store. (2) A person who pays taxes. (3) An owner of property who pays taxes.

TCPA. ABBRV. Telephone Consumer Protection Act.

team. N. That group of persons who serve as on-site managers for a new products program. Each team member represents a function, department, or specialty, and together they form the management for that product. Team members may be full-time or part-time, and persons may move on and off a team depending on the continuing need for their specialty.

team selling. N. A selling technique using several salespeople, especially with highly technical or complex products since no one person could be expert in all the features of the offering. See also *systems buying/selling*.

tear sheet. N. A page bearing advertisement to appear in a publication that is sent to the advertiser for purposes of proofing. Usually the tear sheet accompanies an invoice for the advertisement, as many advertisers will not pay their bill without evidence that the advertisement ran as ordered. See also *checking copy*.

teaser advertisement. N. An advertisement that purports to increase curiosity by holding back the name of the advertiser or the product but pledging additional data in future statements. These advertisements are the front running of an advertising program.

teaser ad. N. See *teaser advertisement*.

technical approval. N. A favorable technical assessment of a product's fitness for use for a particular purpose, based on its meeting the specific requirements.

technical barrier to trade. N. A specification that sets forth characteristics a product must meet (such as levels of quality, performance, safety, or dimensions) to be imported.

technical level. N. A low organizational level that is concerned primarily with the production and distribution of goods and services.

technical managers. N. Low-level managers who are concerned with turning out goods and services as economically as possible. These managers tend to have an engineering point of view.

technical regulation. N. A document that lays down goods' characteristics or their related processes and production methods, or services characteristics or their related operating methods, including the applicable administrative provisions, with which compliance is mandatory. It may also include or deal exclusively with terminology, symbols, packaging, marking, or labeling requirements as they apply to a good, process, production, or operating method. See also *technical specification*.

technical salesperson. N. See *sales engineer*.

technical specification. N. Lays down goods' characteristics or their related processes and production methods, or services characteristics or their related operating methods, including the applicable administrative provisions. It may also include or deal exclusively with terminology, symbols, packaging, marking, or labeling requirements as they apply to a good, process, or production or operating method. See also *technical regulation*.

technological obsolescence. N. Obsolescence that results when technological improvements are made in a product.

technology. N. (1) Industrial science, especially when applied to the replacement of skilled labor by advanced equipment. (2) Applied scientific knowledge utilized in the resolution of practical issues and problems, in the evolution of new products and new processes of manufacture, and in the introduction of major changes in techniques of physical distribution.

technology driven. N. A new products strategy or operation based on the strength of a technology; yields new products, which are then offered to the market. Market driven is the alternative form of thrust. Dual drive uses both at the same time and is the preferred form today.

telecollections. N. Utilizing outbound telemarketing to reach debtors and to collect debts. See also *telemarketing*.

telemarketing. N. (1) Product and services sales using the telephone; carried out at both consumer and industrial levels of the marketplace. Such calls interrupt the consumer by requesting immediate attention and are not identifiable as a promotion before the consumer has been interrupted, thereby at times leading to an antagonized prospect. See also *teleshopping*. (2) Sales of items and services via an interactive system or two-way television. Prospects are often preselected such as current or prior customers or likely prospects selected from a rented list. (3) See *teleselling*.

telephone agency. N. A firm that makes and/or receives telemarketing calls for another organization or person.

telephone coincidental method. N. Once a preselected sample of people are identified, they are called during the running of a television program and asked questions about their reaction to the program, how many people are watching it, etc.; the most popular form of audience research.

Telephone Consumer Protection Act of 1991. N. U.S. legislation of the Federal Communications Commission dealing with automatic dialers, prerecorded telemarketing messages, unsolicited facsimile transmission advertising, and other telephone marketing methods. ABBRV. *TCPA*.

telephone interview. N. Survey technique in which respondents are questioned by telephone.

telephone retailing. N. Selling by telephone at the retail level, usually to the consumer. See also *telemarketing, teleshopping*.

teleselling. N. See *telemarketing*.

teleshopping. N. When customers use telephones to secure products or services that have been seen in advertisements, or on radio and television. For toll-free encouragement, 800 telephone numbers are frequently employed. See also *telemarketing*.

television. N. An electronic communications medium with a capability to yield impactive advertising messages by using the combination of sound and picture.

television home. N. A home with one or more television sets; becomes the basic unit of measurement used in determining the size of a program's audience. Synonymous with *television household*.

television household. N. See *television home*.

television ratings. N. See *rating (3)*.

television support. N. An advertisement seen on television to serve as a secondary part of a multimedia promotion, such as informing the viewer that a supplement will appear in tomorrow's newspaper.

temporary employees. N. Nonpermanent members of an organization's work force, often hired to do clerical or sales work. Popularly used during busy retail store season.

tender. V. To offer money in satisfaction of a debt by producing the money and stating to the creditor a desire to pay.

tension concept. N. A theory of consumer behavior that when a need has not been satisfied adequately, a condition of stress developed leading the person to seek equilibrium via the searching and finding of an appropriate satisfaction.

tent card. N. A card used for the display of an advertisement, imprinted and folded to be read on either side of the fold that stands freely.

term. N. (1) The prescribed time a person has to make installment or other payments as identified in a loan or credit contract. (2) The duration of an agreement, subscription, etc.

terms of sale. N. Identification of a vendor's given time to pay an invoice, any discounts offered, and other conditions of the sale. Synonymous with *sales terms*.

terms of trade. N. The number of units of items that must be surrendered for one unit of goods obtained by a group or nation that is a party to a transaction.

territorial departmentalization. N. Organization of a department according to geographic location (e.g., a company with four major divisions: eastern, midwestern, western, and foreign.)

territorial franchise. N. See *territorial rights*.

territorial potential. N. The full potential demand for a particular item within a defined area of territory.

territorial rights. N. An agreement where the supplier grants the exclusive right to develop the potential demand in a geographic area for an item to one distributor.

territory. N. See *sales territory*.

territory screening. N. See *canvass (2)*.

territory-structured sales force. N. A sales force organization where each person is assigned an exclusive geographic area. It provides the salesperson with a clear knowledge of his or her responsibility; it increases the salesperson's chances for evolving closer relationships with prospects, customers, and local businesspeople; and, it saves on travel costs. See also *market-structured sales force, product-structured sales force, sales force*.

test. N. (1) Any instrument to identify a person's behavior or skills in a host of areas. (2) In advertising, the introduction of a new product or campaign on a small scale to determine consumer response; includes decisions regarding where to test, how long to test, and what to do in response to test results.

testimonial. N. (1) A statement by a satisfied customer praising a product or service that is used in advertising or sales promotion to influence others. See also *blurb*. (2) In advertising, an advertising message that is presented by someone who is viewed as an expert on the subject.

testimonial advertising. N. See *celebrity testimonial, testimonial (2)*.

testing. N. (1) The determination at relatively low cost, before insertion of an advertisement or the running of a campaign, of the probable performance of a product, copy, appeal, price, proposition, illustration, medium, or other element. (2) The determination of the success or effectiveness of an advertisement or campaign after it has been run.

test instrument. N. Any approach used for eliciting data for hypothesis testing in marketing research, e.g., a questionnaire, or psychological test.

test market. N. See *test marketing*.

test marketing. N. (1) Trial distribution of a new product in a small market to determine its likely acceptance in the total market. See also *market fit*. (2) The controlled introduction of a new product to carefully selected markets for the purpose of testing market acceptance and predicting future sales of the product in that region. See also *market fit, market testing, product testing*.

test panel. N. See *panel (1)*.

text. N. In advertising, see *body copy*.

Textile Products Identification Act. N. Federal legislation requiring that sellers of yarns and fabrics and household items made of these, which are made from natural or synthetic fibers other than wool, to attached labels indicating the percent by weight of each fiber they contain and to list the fibers by generic name set by the Federal Trade Commission.

TF. ABBRV. Till forbid.

theme. N. The major idea of an advertising campaign.

thin market. N. A market in which there are comparatively few bids to buy or offers to sell, or both. The term may apply to a single item or to multiple items.

third cover. N. See *inside back cover*.

third-party sale. N. A sale by an agency serving as the intermediary between a buyer and a seller.

thirds. N. Goods of extremely poor quality, lower in grades than seconds. See also *seconds*.

thirty. N. A symbol used in the newsfield to indicate the end of a broadcast or article; written as -30-.

thirty-three. N. *(slang)* A potential customer who refuses to make a purchase from one salesperson and is then turned over to another.

three Bs. ABBRV. Better Business Bureau.

three Cs of credit. N. Used to determine whether a person's credit is acceptable; character, as an indication of determination to pay; capacity, the measure of the ability to pay; and, capital, a person's financial resources or net worth.

three level channel. N. A marketing channel where there are three distinct levels of distribution between the manufacturer and the consumer. For example, an agent, a distributor, and a retailer.

three-sheet. N. An advertising circular, brochure, or handbill.

threshold companies. N. Firms that are on the threshold of corporate maturity in that they are not yet managed by professionals but are run intuitively by a handful of entrepreneurs.

threshold level of expenditures. N. The lowest amount a company must spend in order to participate in a market and receive sales from that market.

throughput. N. The distribution of merchandise via dealers and on to the consumer.

throughput agreement. N. An agreement to put a stated amount of merchandise through a production facility in an agreed time period, or if not, to pay for the availability of the facility.

throwaways. N. See *handbill*.

thumbnail. N. See *esquisse*.

tickler file. N. A follow-up diary or folder containing memos, letters, and so on, ordered by future dates and pulled periodically for review and action.

tie-in advertisement. N. Paid for by the retailers who sponsor it, a print advertisement relating to other forms of advertising, such as one carried by a retail store in conjunction with the manufacturer's advertisement for an item carried in that store. Can also be for several different items, from different manufacturers, that tie-in with a local sales promotion. See also *cross promote, tie-in sales*.

tie-in promotion. N. Marketing displays and approaches that connect with an active advertising campaign to create immediate sales, assist in introducing merchandise, or to enhance the advertising program. Synonymous with *cross-promotion*.

tie-in sales. N. Sales that are limited so that a buyer cannot purchase one product or service without purchasing something else from the same manufacturer. The Clayton Antitrust Act of 1914 made this practice illegal in interstate commerce. See also *tie-in advertisement, tying agreement*.

tight market. N. See *seller's market*.

till forbid. N. (1) Instructions to continue using an advertisement until told otherwise. (2) A standing order for goods or services, such as a request to run an advertisement in a time period, until told to stop running it. ABBRV. *TF*.

time budgeting of purchases. N. In order to even out changes in prices of merchandise, small units of items are purchased over short periods. This will assure that the firm's average price for each product will approximate the true average for the period. However, it tends to increase the total cost of purchasing.

time buyer. N. An executive in an advertising agency who assists in the planning of media campaigns and chooses and buys radio and television time. See also *media buyer, space buyer*.

time clearance. N. In broadcasting, setting aside a specific time period.

time discount. N. A reduction in an advertising rate determined by the frequency of appearance of an advertisement. See also *transient rate*.

time expenditures. N. Involves the types of activities in which a person participates and the amount of time allocated to them.

time order. N. An order that becomes a market or limited price order at a specified time.

time rate of demand. N. The quantity of an item that the market can absorb at a given price over a specified time.

time-series forecast. N. A method of forecasting in which historical trends are projected into the future.

time slot. N. In broadcasting, see *spot*.

time utility. N. (1) The satisfaction that buyers receive from having a product or service available at the appropriate time. (2) A feature of an item making it feasible to satisfy a desire or want based on time preference. Storage creates time utility. See also *utility*.

tinge. N. *(slang)* A salesperson who specializes in the sale of undesirable merchandise that earn him or her bonus payments.

tip in. N. An insert placed within a publication, such as an extra page of advertising. A tip in as contrasted with a tip on becomes an integral part of the bound product, requiring more complex application devices. See also *tip on*.

tip on. N. An item attached with glue or a glue stripping to a promotional piece or advertisement in a printed publication. A tip on is not considered an integral part of the bound material. See also *tip in*.

tipping. N. The process of attaching a tip on or tip in to printed material.

tire kickers. N. *(slang)* Inspectors or troubleshooters who are assigned to closely examine a project, item, or service for defects, flaws, or inadequacies.

title. N. Proper and rightful ownership.

title flows. N. The path of the title to or ownership of products as they flow through channels of distribution.

token order. N. (1) A small order placed to assess the desirability of an item. (2) A small order placed as a means of getting rid of a bothersome salesperson.

tombstone advertisement. N. (1) A solemn appearing advertisement, often only listing the item with the names of sources of supply. Such an advertisement is used in financial announcements, including major securities offerings. (2) A casual reference to an advertisement for a professional or organization that meets legal requirements and regulations imposed on the industry represented in the advertising.

tool-crib supervisor. N. See *materials controller*.

top credit. N. Ready credit.

top-down method. N. In retailing, a budget method where the budgeter commences with a gross amount and follows with specific amounts to designated classifications of merchandise. See also *bottom-up technique*.

top management. N. The top level of an administrative hierarchy. Managers at this level coordinate the work of other managers but do not report to a manager.

top of mind. N. A description of the brand or product name or advertising promotion that a respondent recalls in response to a research question.

top out. N. The peak period of demand for a product or service, after which demand decreases.

total audience. N. People 12 years of age or older who are targeted for most broadcast advertising. See also *audience share*.

total audience plan. N. See *package plan*.

total cost. N. The sum of a firm's total fixed costs and total variable costs.

total-cost approach. N. Determines the distribution service level with the lowest total costs, including freight (shipping), warehousing, and the cost of lost business. An idea system seeks

total variable costs

a balance between low expenditures on distribution and high opportunities for sales.

total fixed costs. N. The costs that do not change with an organization's output (e.g., payments on rent, property taxes).

total loss. N. Items that have been so badly damaged that they are not considered to be worth repairing (e.g., a car that has suffered a head-on collision with a truck, or merchandise that is party destroyed by fire).

total market approach. N. See *undifferentiated marketing*.

total net paid. N. See *total paid circulation*.

total paid circulation. N. The number of people who actually pay for a magazine or other periodical, as opposed to those who see it by other means, such as in a doctor's office, from a friend. Synonymous with *total net paid*. See also *controlled circulation*.

total product. N. The marketing mix of a firm.

total quality program. N. The most common rubric for Japanese-inspired efforts to build quality into a product or service as it is produced or performed. Total quality programs require the active involvement of the line workers themselves, which is generally best achieved via a radical change in corporate culture led by the chief executive.

total revenue. N. Total receipts of a company. It is equal to the price per unit times the number of units sold.

total variable costs. N. Costs that change directly with the firm's output, increasing as output rises over the total range of production, e.g., labor or fuel.

Toxic Substances Control Act of 1976. N. Federal legislation requiring chemical manufacturers to give the Environmental Protection Agency (EPA) at least three months' notice before beginning commercial production of a new chemical or before marketing an existing chemical for new use. If the EPA sees no risks, the firm may proceed.

traceable costs. N. Common costs that can be assigned to two or more specific functional areas.

tracer. N. A request to trace a shipment in order to determine its location, alter instructions, or affects its status.

tracking. N. (1) In marketing, the follow-up to a promotional campaign, either via direct marketing or resulting from an advertisement. Involves the analysis of various elements of the promotion by examining the four stages in the life cycle of a promotion: the early response, halfway point response, final response, and long-term results. (2) In merchandising, monitoring inventory received, ordered, and bought, to maintain optimum levels for future purchases.

tracking variable. N. A specific variable used to track a specific phenomenon. Distribution can be tracked, for example, by measuring the "percent of outlets that have stocked at least one package."

trade. N. Transactions involving goods or services from profit between legal entities.

trade advertising. N. (1) Advertising directed at wholesalers or retailers. (2) Consumer-product advertising used for stimulating wholesalers and retailers to buy merchandise for resale to their customers. See also *business-to-business advertising, consumer advertising*.

trade allowances. N. Incentives provided by the manufacturer to retailers and other channel intermediaries to stock, display, or promote the manufacturer's goods. See also *trade promotion*.

trade association. N. A nonprofit organization that purports to serve the common interest of its membership. Usually, members of trade associations work in closely related industries.

trade barrier. N. An artificial restraint on the free exchange of goods and services between countries, usually in the form of tariffs, subsidies, quotas, or exchange controls. See also *barriers to competition, barriers to entry*.

trade cards. N. Where retailers punch into a card the amount spent by a consumer until a total is reached qualifying the buyer to purchase a premium at a self-liquidating price. Synonymous with *purchase-privilege offer*.

trade channel. N. See *channel of distribution*.

trade character. N. People, objects, animals or characteristics of animals, etc. used in advertising a brand. Trade characters come to be identified with that brand.

trade creation. N. The formation of commercial transactions because of the displacement of domestic production by lower cost imports.

trade credit. N. Credit from producers and wholesalers to their customers on a short-term basis.

trade deal. N. See *deal (2)*.

trade deficit. N. A negative trade balance, where a nation's imports are greater in value than the nation's exports. See *trade surplus*.

trade deflection. N. The entrance of imports into nations that offer the lowest tariffs to avoid the higher tariffs of other member nations in international trade agreements.

trade discount. N. A deduction from the agreed price, usually expressed as a percentage or a series of percentages, that is used in commerce to encourage prompt payment of bills. Trade discount should not be entered in the books of account, nor should it be considered to be a type of earnings. Synonymous with *functional discount*.

trade down. N. See *trading down*.

Trade Expansion Act of 1962. N. Federal legislation permitting the president to negotiate additional tariff reductions, eliminate or reduce tariffs on items of the European Community, reduce tariffs on the basis of reciprocal trade agreements, and grant technical and financial assistance to employers whose business is adversely affected by tariff reductions.

trade in. V. To surrender an old product for a new one, accompanied by additional payment to make up for depreciation of the item traded in.

trade industry. N. In industrial marketing, wholesalers and retailers who purchase for resale to others or for use in conducting their own business.

trade magazine. N. A magazine with editorial content of interest to people engaged in a specific industry, profession, or occupation; provides advertisers with an opportunity to reach highly defined business audiences in both print and by way of the acquisition of mailing lists for direct marketing. Synonymous with *business publication*.

trade margin. N. The difference between unit sales price and unit cost at each level of a marketing channel; usually expressed in percentage terms.

trademark. N. (1) A brand that is given legal protection because it has been appropriated exclusively by one marketer. (2) A distinctive identification of a manufactured product or a service in the form of a name, logo, motto, and so on. A trademarked brand has legal protection, and only the owner can use the mark. Organizations that file an application at the U.S. Patent Office and use the brand for five years may be granted a trademark. A firm may lose a trademark that has become generic. Generic names are those that consumers use to identify the product, rather than to specify a particular brand (e.g., escalator, aspirin, or nylon). See also *Lanham Act of 1947*.

Trade-Mark Act of 1946. N. Federal legislation, known as the Lanham Act; governing the registration of trademarks used in commerce.

trade marketing mix. N. See *retailing mix*.

trade name. N. The name under which an organization conducts business or by which the business or its goods and services are identified. It may or may not be registered as a trademark.

tradeoffs. N. Activities that provide benefits also incur certain disadvantages and vice versa.

trade-oriented sales promtions. N. Sales tools used to support a company's advertising and personal selling efforts directed to wholesalers, distributors, or retailers. Three common approaches are allowances, cooperative advertising, and salesforce training.

trade paper advertising. N. The dissemination of sales messages by a manufacturer to retail store owners, distributors, and others engaged in the resale of an advertised product directly to ultimate consumers.

trade preferences. N. Trade concessions, usually preferential tariff treatment, granted by a country to a certain nation but not to others.

trade premium. N. An incentive, such as vacations, prizes, free merchandise, etc., from a manufacturer to a retailer or wholesaler who achieves a specific level of sales of the manufacturer's merchandise. See also *premium*.

trade price. N. The manufacturer's price to a middleperson.

trade promotion. N. Sales promotion efforts directed toward retailers and wholesalers offering incentives, such as gifts, price-off discounts, trips, merchandise, etc., to middlepeople who will carry the manufacturer's items or will increase their inventory of the manufacturer. See also *advertising allowance, promotion*.

trade quota. N. A form of trade restriction that sets limits on the amount of goods that can be imported into a country. See also *quota*.

trader. N. Anyone who is engaged in trade or commerce.

trade rate. N. A special price given by wholesalers, distributors, or manufacturers to retailers.

trade reference. N. A person or firm to which a seller is referred for credit data on a potential customer.

trade sales. N. See *sales to thirds*.

trade salesperson. N. A salesperson whose primary duties are promotional, by assisting customers to promote a firm's items or services. They write orders but spend most of their time dealing with established customers.

trade secret. N. In contrast to getting a patent on an invention, the inventory or firm can simply attempt to keep secret the new aspect of the product. The Coca-Cola formula, for example, is a famous trade secret.

trade show. N. Where manufacturers, wholesalers, or both from a specific industry meet for the purpose of showing their merchandise; serves as a vehicle to generate new sales leads and to maintain existing customer relations.

trade specialty house. N. An industrial distributor who serves a specific type of customer, with a full line of items requested by him or her, e.g., barber shop supplies or shoe repair supplies.

trade style. N. The unique manner in which a firm displays its name in print in advertising and on letterheads.

trade surplus. N. Where the value of a country's exports exceeds the value of its imports. See also *trade deficit*.

trade up. N. See *trading up*.

trading across. N. When a store alters its marketing strategy to try to appeal to a different market segment. Shifting can be very difficult and expensive.

trading area. N. The region or shopping district whose limits are determined by the costs of delivering merchandise to the area.

trading companies. N. Firms that develop international trade and serve as intermediaries between foreign buyers and domestic sellers, and vice versa.

trading down. N. Attempting to increase the market of a store or item with an established reputation by lowering price or quality or by changing promotional strategy to appeal to a larger potential market, which is frequently in a lower socioeconomic level. By trading down, the image of the item is often sacrificed for gains in profit. See also *social classes, wheel of retailing, trading up.*

trading house. N. A business that specializes in the import and export of items from overseas nations or regions.

trading stamp. N. A promotional device; a stamp given to customers that is worth a small percentage of the total amount paid for purchases. When a large number of stamps have been accumulated, they can be redeemed at the store or at a warehouse for merchandise. See also *box-top offer.*

trading up. N. Attempting to improve the image of a store or item by increasing prices or quality or by altering advertisement approaches, usually to appeal to a market in a higher socioeconomic level. See also *social classes, wheel of retailing, trading down.*

traditional break-even analysis. N. Determines the sales quantity in units or dollars that is needed for total revenues to equal total costs at a given price: breakeven point = total fixed costs

(units) price–variables costs (per unit)

break-even point = total fixed costs

(sales dollars) 1–variables costs (per unit)

_____price

traditional department store. N. A department store that has a great assortment of goods and services, provides many customer services, is a fashion leader, and often serves as an anchor store in a shopping district or shopping center. See also *department store.*

traffic. N. (1) Business done by a transportation or communications company. (2) In merchandising, the flow of people who are exposed to a store's goods. Measurement of traffic (i.e., counting the people) is usually done as customers enter and leave the store's premises. See also *routing*.

traffic appliances. N. Portable appliances, including toasters, blenders, irons, etc.

traffic builder. N. (1) A low-cost premium offered as an inducement to enter a store for a demonstration of a product. (2) A popular item whose price has been lowered to attract customers to the store or outlet.

traffic count. N. Estimating poster advertising where the poster is monitored as people walk by it.

traffic department. N. The department that schedules the work responsibilities of other units in an advertising agency and has primary responsibility for ensuring that deadlines are met.

traffic items. N. Consumer products that have a limited life and will in time attract consumers back into a store to purchase new replacement items.

traffic management. N. The planning, selection, and direction of all means of transportation involved in the movement of goods in the marketing process.

traffic system. N. A method of advertising agency office management designed to route work from department to department according to a predetermined schedule and to permit the agency to maintain control of the progress of the work at any time.

trailer tests. N. Advertising pretesting procedures that recruit respondents from shopping malls for forced exposure to ads in a trailer near the mall or in a room in the mall itself.

transaction. N. Any agreement between two or more parties that establishes a legal obligation. See also *exchange (3)*.

transactions motive. N. The holding, by consumers and businesspeople, of some of their assets in liquid form to make possible participation in day-to-day spending activities.

transfer costs. N. The costs that a department accepts for items supplied by other departments.

transfer impact. N. A feature of an offering making it possible for that item or service to force a transfer of a consumer's allegiance to the offering source.

transfer price. N. (1) Raising the price of a product shipped to a foreign affiliate in order to increase the amount of profit transferred from the affiliate to the parent firm. (2) The price charged by one segment of an organization for a product or service it supplies to another part of the same firm. See also *transfer costs*.

transfer pricing. N. See *transfer price*.

transient rate. N. (1) The fee paid for a single nonrepeated advertisement. (2) The one-time rate for an advertisement, without quantity or frequency reductions. See also *time discount*.

transit advertising. N. Advertising for an audience en route from one point to another using public transportation, usually a bus or train. It serves a large number of people, within a well-defined geography, and has a high rate of repetition. See *one-sheet poster*. Synonymous with *transportation advertising*.

transition time. N. See *fringe time*.

transit privileges. N. The privilege offered a shipper by a shipping company of unloading merchandise in transit for a future processing, then reloaded and delivered to their destination without additional costs. Synonymous with *milling in transit*, *processing in transit*.

transportation advertising. N. See *transit advertising*.

transportation service companies. N. Marketing specialists that predominantly handle the shipments of small and moderate-sized packages. The three major kinds of service companies are government parcel post, private parcel, and express.

transhipping. N. (1) The transfer of items from one carrier to another. (2) In salesmanship, the shipment of merchandise by a dealer or distributor to another dealer or distributor beyond the usual selling area.

traveling sales representative. N. A salesperson who travels considerably to obtain orders.

tray pack. N. A point-of-purchase display where the top of the case of goods can be opened and folded back so that the case actually becomes a display tray that is readily placed on a shelf or counter in the store.

trend extension. N. Used by market researchers, forecasting sales for existing items based on previous data information and projecting that information to the future.

Trendex. N. A research firm that issues statements on the relative popularity of network television programs. Most of the Trendex data are gathered by using the coincidental-telephone approach.

trend forecast. N. The long-term changes in market demand.

trial. N. Within the adoption process of a consumer, the period when a product is first used. This is a critical point in determining the continued acceptance of the item by consumers.

trial and error pricing. N. Selling an item at varying prices in different locations and then assessing the response to each of the prices.

trial buyer. N. See *trial offer*.

trial close. N. An attempt, based on perpetual clues, to zero in on the close of a sale before the natural termination of the sales presentation. See also *check question, sales presentation*.

trial offer. N. A soft-sell method permitting a first-time purchaser to examine, use, or test an item for a short period of time before deciding to buy or decline the opportunity to purchase the item; may also include a special reduced rate. Synonymous with *free examination offer, free trial offer, soft offer, trial offer, trial subscriber*.

trial sampling. N. In sales promotion, encouraging a consumer to try an item, usually after being given a free sample. See also *trial size*.

trial size. N. A package that is smaller than the usual manufactured package; often used as a giveaway or sample. Can be free or sold at a lower price to attract buyers. Trial-size packages are traditionally delivered by mail or are available in retail outlets.

trial subscriber. N. A first-time buyer of a subscription at a reduced rate and/or for a short time period. See also *trial offer*.

trickle-down theory. N. The process by which federal funds flowing into the national economy stimulate growth by being distributed into organizations, as opposed to stimulating growth by direct payments. See also *status float occurrence*.

trigger price. N. The world price for a commodity or product, set by an international organization.

trio of needs. N. Basic motivations that make consumers purchase an item or service. They are needs for: power, affiliation, and achievement. See also *motivation*.

triple spotting. N. In broadcasting, running three commercials in succession without intervening news or programming. See also *back-to-back commercials*.

troubleshoot. N. The activity of an individual who is engaged in locating and eliminating the source of trouble in a task or operation.

trough. N. The lowest point of economic activity.

truck distributor. N. See *truck jobber*.

truck jobber. N. A middleperson who delivers at the time of sale (e.g., vendors of ice cream, lunch specialties, and other items that must be sold fresh). Synonymous with *truck distributor, truck wholesaler, wagon wholesaler*. See also *cash and carry wholesaler*.

truck/wagon wholesalers. N. Limited-service merchant wholesalers that generally have a regular sales route, offer items from the truck or wagon, and deliver goods at the same time they are sold.

truck wholesaler. N. See *truck jobber*.

true panel. N. A panel where respondents are measured repeatedly with respect to the same group of variables.

true prospect. N. A lead that can benefit from the use of the product, can afford to buy it, and has the authority to do so.

trunk show. N. The display of a vendor's total line of merchandise before an audience that is gathered for the purpose of inspecting the wares.

truth in advertising. N. The requirement of a firm to truthfully explain the attributes and benefits of products within their advertising. Firms that do not engage in truthful advertising can be cited for disciplinary action by the Federal Trade Commission. See also *Truth in Lending Act of 1968*.

Truth in Lending Act of 1968. N. Officially, the Consumer Credit Protection Act of 1968; requires that most categories of lenders disclose the true annual interest rate on virtually all types of loans and credit sales as well as the total dollar cost and other terms of a loan. See also *Fair Credit Billing Act, right of rescission, truth in advertising*.

Truth in Packaging Act. N. See *Fair Packaging and Labeling Act of 1966*.

turbulence. N. A stage in a product's evolution representing the critical survival period for marginal producers.

turn. N. In merchandising, turnover of items within an inventory. Synonymous with *round turn*.

turn and earn concept. N. Profit levels are determined in terms of inventory turnover as the major favorable.

turnaround. N. The movement by a freight carrier in which the driver returns to the point of origin following the unloading and reloading of cargo.

turnkey. N. A contractual agreement between a customer and an organization to provide full services or a complete product.

turnover. N. In retailing, the frequency with which an inventory is sold and replaced over a stated period, usually determined by dividing the net sales for the period by the average retail value of the inventory during that period. See also *demand sensitivity*. Synonymous with *stock-turn*.

twenty/eighty (20/80) rule. N. A rule of thumb that says that about 20% of consumers in a product category, the heavy users, account for about 80% of sales.

twenty-four-sheet poster. N. A printed sheet of outdoor advertising matter measuring eight feet, eight inches high, and nineteen feet, six inches long, posted on an outdoor, steel-faced panel in an area of great traffic volume.

twin pack. N. Traditionally sold at a lower cost, a retail product package of two containers of the same product bound under the same wrapping or in the same holder. See also *bonus pack*.

twin streams of innovation activity. N. The innovation process is building a product and also a marketing plan. The two processes go on simultaneously, and, in fact, the marketing plan may originate first if the firm's strategy is to develop new products for specific target markets.

two-dimensional matrix. N. A simple form of relationship analysis using only two dimensions. Contrasts with the morphological matrix of several dimensions.

two-for-one sale. N. An offer to consumers of two units of merchandise for the regular price of one, made by a seller for the purpose of encouraging sampling of the product and to unload dealers' shelves.

two-level channel. N. A marketing channel where two levels of distribution between the manufacturer/producer and consumer exist.

two-sheet poster. N. A printed sheet of advertising matter pasted on a panel on display on subway and elevated platforms as a form of transportation advertising.

two-sides messages. N. Communication in which a firm discusses both the benefits and limitations of a good, service, or idea.

two-step flow of communication. N. A theory stating that a message goes from the company to opinion leaders and then to the target market.

tying agreement. N. (1) A method of control over distribution in which the producer forces the dealer to buy additional products in order to secure one highly desired product. (2) An agreement where the manufacturer requires a dealer or middleperson to buy certain items in order to purchase certain other items, or in which the manufacturer requires that the dealer not sell competing items. In turn, the dealer is often granted exclusive rights to sales of the manufacturer's items in a specified territory. See also *tie-in sales*.

UBD. ABBRV. Undeliverable billing document.

ultimate consumer. N. The individual who actually uses the bought merchandise. See also *consumer, industrial user*. Synonymous with *final consumer*.

ultimo. N. The month prior to the present one.

umbrella brands. N. See *family brands*.

umbrella pricing. N. A large firm's strategy of maintaining the prices of its products at a level higher than needed so as to protect smaller competitors from overwhelming competition. The opposite of predatory pricing.

unaided recall. N. A means of determining a consumer's ability to remember an advertisement as a way of determining the effectiveness of the advertisement. Respondents are asked questions such as "What program did you watch this morning?" or "What commercials do you remember seeing yesterday?" In this method, respondents are not prompted in their replies as they are in aided recall. See also *aided recall*.

unbilled revenue. N. Fees earned in a given period for which bills have not yet been sent to the customers.

unbundled prices. N. A pricing method where customers are allowed to select specific services on an optimal basis. Unbundling of prices is based on the concept that one price is no longer quoted for a product or service package.

uncertainty theory. N. The theory that profit arises from uncertainties due to innovations, changes in taste, price fluctuations, and the vagaries of competition. See also *profit*.

unchanging list price. N. List prices that do not change over a determined time period, even when discounts from other competitors are offered. See also *list price*.

uncontrollable factors. N. Factors beyond the direct control of the manager (e.g., competitors' activities, international developments, and economic conditions).

undeliverable billing document. N. An invoice that is undeliverable as addressed and will be returned to the sender by the post office. ABBRV. *UBD*.

underapplied overhead. N. The excess of factory overhead incurred over factory overhead applied. In practice, this means that the actual cost of overhead incurred was more than the amount charged to the manufacturing process during the year.

undercharge. V. To charge less than the proper amount.

underconsumption theory. N. A concept presented by the English economist J. A. Hobson that prosperity must always be brought to an end because consumption lags behind expanding output. See also *overproduction theory, Say's law*.

underground economy. N. Of use to marketers in setting strategies, the part of a nation's income that, underreported or unreported, is not measured by official statistics.

underpackaging. N. The use of packaging methods that are inadequate for the level of protection needed.

underpayment. N. An invoice payment that is less than the billed amount, resulting in the seller billing again for the remaining funds, accepting the amount received as if full payment, or proportionately lowering the service or items to be delivered.

underrun. N. Printing fewer pieces of a publication or advertisement than was originally planned. See also *overrun*.

underselling. N. Selling at a price lower than that listed by a competitor. See also *price cutting, rate war*.

undifferentiated marketing. N. A marketing technique where one or more items are offered for sale to the total market, i.e., no effort is made to be concerned with individual market segments. It is an easier and less expensive strategy to execute than differentiated marketing. Synonymous with *market aggregation, total market approach.* See also *differentiated marketing.*

undiscounted. ADJ. Goods or services sold at the full price without discounts or any allowances. Such items or services are usually stable in demand and have little price elasticity.

undisplay advertising. N. See *classified advertising.*

undistributed profits. N. The profits of a partnership, syndicate, or joint venture prior to division among the individuals concerned.

undo. V. To reverse a transaction.

unduplicated audience. N. See *cumulative audience.*

unearned discount. N. Interest that is received but not yet earned.

unearned revenues. N. Amounts that are received before they have been earned.

unfair competition. N. Practices employed by a seller to increase profit by means of misleading advertising, selling below cost or dumping, obtaining rebates from suppliers, or utilizing other devices that unfairly take advantage of a competing firm.

unfair goods. N. Products or items that are not produced by members of a union.

unfair practices. N. The discriminatory commercial exchange activities of goods that are either unfairly subsidized or dumped, or are otherwise illegitimate, as with counterfeit items.

unfair practices acts. N. State regulations establishing minimum resale prices. Such laws stipulate that goods must be sold for cost plus some nominal percentage. In practice, there is little enforcement of these rulings. Synonymous with *minimum markup laws, sales-below-cost laws, unfair sales acts, unfair trade practices acts.* See also *tie-in sales, fair trade acts.*

unfair sales acts. N. See *minimum markup laws, unfair practices acts.*

unfair trade practices acts. N. See *minimum markup laws, unfair practices acts.*

uniform delivered price. N. A pricing method whereby all the products are sold at the same delivery price in a stated area, without regard for delivery costs.

unique selling proposition. N. Differentiating the quality of an item on which an advertising strategy has been based. The three characteristics of an effective unique selling proposition are: (a) it should make a proposition to the consumer, suggesting that purchasing the merchandise will offer a particular benefit; (b) the proposition should be unique and one that a competitor cannot make, therefore the brand or the advertising claim made must be unique; and, (c) the proposition must be sufficiently strong so as to attract a large number of new customers. See also *competitive advantage, message development.* ABBRV. *USP.*

unique user. N. In altering the specifications of materials or other products, a company may be the only one to use it that way, thereby avoiding the issues posed by the Robinson-Patman Act concerning "like kind." See also *Robinson-Patman Act of 1936.*

unit. N. (1) A basic element; a standard of measurements; a single person or group. (2) In marketing, a standard package size or quantity where an item is sold, such as a case of beer or one page in a print advertising medium.

unitary demand. N. A situation in which a percentage change in price brings about an equal percentage change in quantity sold.

unitary elasticity. N. The concept that a change in price will be compensated by a corresponding change in demand, so that total income will remain the same.

unitary falloff. N. A percentage drop in response or sales volume equal to the percentage increase in the price of a good or service.

unit billing. N. A list of all purchases by a customer, prepared on a single statement.

unit contribution margin. N. The excess of the sales price of one unit over its variable costs.

unit control. N. An approach for listing the quantity of goods bought, sold, in stock, and on order, with additional breakdowns as needed. See also *taking inventory*.

unit cost. N. The cost of producing or distributing one unit of a processed item.

united load. N. A load in which all the containers are bound together in one or more units.

unitize. V. To combine a number of freight pieces into one large piece by banding, placing in a container, stacking, or any other means of assembling into a unit.

unit pricing. N. (1) The quotation of prices given in terms of a standard of measurement (by weight, length, count, etc.). See also *ton-mile*. (2) The practice of pricing each product so that the price tag displays the price per unit of weight or volume in the package. See also *multiple-unit pricing*. Synonymous with *single-item pricing*.

unit-small batch technology. N. Custom manufacturing of individual items.

unit store. N. (1) An establishment of a company having but one place of business. (2) A single store of a chain.

unit train. N. A train that ships only one cargo, nonstop between two locations.

unity. N. In advertising, where all the factors used in an advertisement form in combination a single impression that supports the one principle idea suggested by the advertisement.

unity of command. N. The concept in classical management that a subordinate must be responsible to only one superior.

universal product code. N. Adopted by the food industry in 1973;,a categorization where each item is given a ten-digit number, premarked on the package by the producer in the form of a bar code over ten corresponding numbers. The bar code is easily read by an optical scanner at the checkout counter, all controlled by a computer. The first six digits are the same for all the manufacturer's items and represent the name of the maker. The following five refer to the item itself and are identified by the maker to the product of his or her choice. Retailers use this portion of the code to set prices on computers. The correct price is automatically pulled from the table and recorded on the register. The last digit of the universal product code is a check digit. See also *bar code*, *scanner*. ABBRV. *UPC*.

universe. N. The total population or market. Units of study to be examined in a marketing research effort are drawn from the universe via sampling. Therefore, the sample is a subset of the universe. See also *sampling frame*.

unloading. N. (1) Selling merchandise at a relatively low price. Slang for "dumping." (2) The practice of stimulating the movement of consumer goods across retail counters by offering consumers inducements to purchase merchandise through such techniques as premium offers, contests, and two-for-one sales.

unpaid balance. N. On a credit purchase, the difference between the purchase price and the down payment or the value of a trade-in; on a cash loan, the difference between the total loan and the amount that is still owed.

unplanned business district. N. A retail location that exists where two or more stores are located close to one another without the use of prior planning as to the number and composition of stores. There are four kinds of unplanned districts: central business district, secondary business district, neighborhood business district, and string.

unprotected consumers. N. People, usually children, the elderly, the sick, and the poor, who are unable to argue for their legal rights in the market. State and federal legislation has been written to assist these consumers.

unselfish display. N. A form of altruistic display that also carries items not sold by the store.

unsought goods. N. Products of which the market has not as yet recognized their values, or perhaps not even knowledge of their existence. See also *new unsought goods, regularly unsought items*.

unstable market. N. A market in which forces of disequilibrium are reinforced so that movements away from equilibrium are not reversible. See also *stable market*.

unstructured question. N. Used by consumer behavior researchers, a question that allows respondents to answer as they wish and does not limit the length of responses.

unstuffing. N. Unloading cargo from a container.

unsystematic freight equalization. N. Meeting competitors' locational discount and delivered prices so as to retain market share. This is an unfair pricing practice if used with predatory intent. A company with high fixed costs and significant capacity can have no other price-setting choices.

unwholesome demand state. N. A demand situation where a harmful item yields marketing activities that attempt to discourage consumers from buying it, such as products of alcohol and cigarettes. See also *demand states*.

UPC. ABBRV. Universal product code.

upfront selling period. N. The season, usually in May and June, when television networks negotiate with advertisers on the cost of commercial time for forthcoming fall shows. See also *preferred position*.

upgrade. N. See *upgrading*.

upgrading. N. (1) In retailing, offering superior goods and a greater assortment to customers. (2) In merchandising, an increase in the value of an order either at the time of the order or purchase, when a credit order is paid, or when a second order is requested.

upper turning point. N. A short period during which an upswing ends and a downswing begins.

upscale. N. People and households of well-above-average income and education. For advertisers and manufacturers, such people are the best prospects for purchasing expensive items, such as luxury cars, jewelry, cruise tickets, etc. See also *downscale*.

upset price. N. The minimal price at which a seller is willing to sell; the beginning price asked at an auction prior to public bidding. See also *marginal seller, negotiated price*.

upstream pricing. N. Forming a market value for commodities from which other items are derived or other by-products are produced.

upturn. N. See *business cycle*.

upwardly mobile. N. People within a market who are striving for and, to some extent, achieve a higher socioeconomic position. Numerous products are geared for these people.

urge line. N. In advertising, see *close*.

urgent consignments. N. Merchandise that, because of its character, requires expeditious release by customs officials, e.g., perishable goods.

usage rate segmentation. N. A method of market segmentation based on the rate at which consumers purchase and utilize these items; separates the market into heavy, light, and nonusers.

U.S. Customs bonded warehouse. N. See *warehouse, U.S. Customs bonded*.

U.S. Internal Revenue warehouse. N. See *warehouse, U.S. Internal Revenue*.

useless quality. N. Goods created with quality, dependability, or performance that is superior to that demanded by the public.

user. N. Anyone who requires the services of a system or product or who employs a service.

user-active. N. In new industrial product development, where the customer (a) develops the concept for the new item; (b) chooses a supplier able to make the item; and, (c) takes the initiative to purchase the item from the supplier, thereby assisting the diffusion of that new item.

user calls. N. Callbacks made by a sales representative to a customer who has already made a purchase from him or her or from the organization. See also *callback*.

user expectation. N. A sales forecast that is construed after a consumer survey or some other form of consumer research has been conducted.

use tax. N. A tax levied on the initial use of an item rather than on the merchandise when it is sold. See also *value-added tax*.

USP. ABBRV. Unique selling proposition.

utility. N. The capability or power of an item to satisfy a need, as determined by the satisfaction one receives from consuming something. See also *form utility, place utility, time utility*.

vacuumize

vacuumize. v. To remove air from a filled container before closing it.

vacuum packaging. n. Packaging in containers from which almost all air has been removed before the container is sealed.

valance. n. An identification strip or advertisement placed along the upper edge of a window, wall, counter, or shelf.

valence. n. A person's preference for a first-level outcome.

valid. adj. (1) A fact. (2) That which is sufficient to satisfy the requirement of the law; a fact.

validated export license. n. A required document for global marketers; issued by the U.S. government authorizing the export of specific commodities. This license is for a specific transaction or time period in which the exporting is to take place. See also *export license*.

validation. n. Undertaken to assure the quality of research data; the quality of being truthful or factual. It presupposes that the antecedent reasoning process is formal and correct. This quality is also a reflection on the quality of those researchers carrying out the research.

validity. n. (1) Used in the setting of marketing hypotheses, the degree to which a statistical technique accurately measures or predicts some value. (2) The quality of being truthful or factual. It presupposes that the antecendent reasoning process is formal and correct. See also *reliability*.

valorization. n. Government action leading to the establishment of a price or value for an item or service.

VALS. ABBRV. Market information based on consumer's values and lifestyles. VALS data can be used to understand a persons' buying decision making. VALS data group consumers into segments of three categories: (a) need directed—consumers who buy strictly on need; (b) outer directed—consumers whose buying practices are influenced by how they believe other people will perceive them; and, (c) inner directed—consumers whose buying practices are based primarily on satisfying their own psychological needs.

valuation. N. Setting a value for anything.

value. N. (1) Purchasing power. (2) The worth of property, goods, services, and so on.

value added. N. The part of the value of produced goods that is developed in a company. It is determined by subtracting from sales the costs of materials and supplies, energy, contract work, and so on, and it includes labor expenses, administrative and sales costs, and all other operating profits.

value-added reseller. N. A reseller that purchases goods from a primary producer and adds value through product assembly, modification, and/or customization. ABBRV. *VAR.*

value-added tax. N. (1) A government tax on the value added; a tax on the selling price of manufactured items less the cost of the materials and expenses used in their production. (2) A tax that is levied every time a product is sold to another member of the distribution channel. See also *domestic value-added, use tax.* ABBRV. *VAT.*

value analysis. N. A purchasing strategy of asking the buyer's engineers to project the costs of goods in an attempt to keep the vendor's prices low. Synonymous with *purchase research, value control.* See also *value engineering.*

value consciousness. N. Consumer concern for obtaining the best quality, features, and performance of a product or service for a given price.

value control. N. See *value analysis*.

value engineering. N. See *value analysis*, but applied at the items design stage.

value in use. N. The value of goods to the individual who uses them.

value judgement. N. In merchandising, the result of a consumer's comparison of the attractiveness of two or more alternative items or services.

value marketing. N. A concept integrating marketing, design, and communications into a mix created for a specific situation.

value of a customer. N. The total revenue coming from a buyer and over time placed together, minus all expenditures associated with obtaining that total revenue except the cost of advertising, which is associated with securing the customer.

values and lifestyles. N. See *VALS*.

vampire video. N. Attention-getting devices in a television commercial that are more powerful in securing customers than the sponsor's comments about the product.

van container. N. A standard trailer used to carry general cargo.

vanity sizing. N. The girth-accommodating practice of labeling clothes as the same size while actually making them larger.

VAR. ABBRV. Value-added reseller.

variability in service quality. N. Differing service performance from one purchase experience to another. Variations may be due to the service firm's difficulty in diagnosing a problem (for repairs), the inability of a customer to verbalize service needs, and the lack of standardization and mass production for many services.

variable. N. (1) A quantity that may assume any of a given set of values. (2) A value that shifts as a result of direct intervention (independent variable) or a shift in another variable (dependent variable). See also *dependent variable, independent variable*.

variable budget. N. A budget that divides expenses into fixed costs and variable costs. The latter are allowed to vary on a predetermined basis with differing levels of output.

variable cost. N. A cost that is uniform per unit but changes in total in direct proportion to changes in the related total activity or volume. See also *fixed cost, product costing*.

variable expenses. N. Expenses that vary with the level of factory output or plant capacity (e.g., the expenses of power, oils, and lubricants vary with the number of machines in operation). Generally, variable expenses are considered controllable.

variable inspection. N. A method of quality control in which measurements are used to determine the deviation from standards.

variable leader pricing. N. A strategy where specific products are offered to consumers at prices so low that they produce little or no profit; these prices are frequently changed each week.

variable markup policy. N. A form of cost-based markup pricing whereby separate categories of goods and services receive different percentage markups; recognizes that some items require greater personal selling efforts, customer service, alterations, and end-of-season markdown than others. See also *markup*.

variable presentation. N. In retailing, an approach to setting prices by examining customers' services, salesperson's knowledge of the product, store image, assortment and variety, competition factors, and the prospect's satisfaction in order to determine that perfect combination to give the price the customer anticipates and is prepared to pay. Synonymous with *variable sales presentation*.

variable pricing. N. A marketing method permitting a different price to be charged to differing prospects or at differing times; used especially at outdoor flea markets, antique stalls, street vendors, and the like. Its shortcoming is that at various times customers may learn that others have paid less for the same item. In addition, federal and state regulations protect competing retailers from discriminatory pricing that gives competitors an unfair advantage. See also *flat rate, market-minus prices*. Synonymous with *flexible price policy*.

variable sales presentation. N. See *variable presentation*.

variable slot location system. N. Utilizing computers to keep track of where merchandise is kept, placing items in a warehouse by assigning newly brought merchandise to whatever place appears to be empty at that time.

variance. N. (1) A disagreement between two sets of figures or facts. (2) The measure of dispersion within a distribution of events. (3) The difference between expected and actual production costs. See also *management by exception*.

variance analysis. N. The difference between the actual and standards costs.

variety. N. Different types of merchandise sold to consumers. See also *assortment*.

variety store. N. A retail operation that carries limited quantities of apparel and accessories for the family as well as other goods, with prices set somewhat lower than in retail stores.

VAT. ABBRV. Value-added tax.

Veblen effect. N. An economic theory of Thorstein Veblen (1857–1929) where the higher price will increase the demand for products, which, because of conspicuous consumption, have status attached to the higher price. See also *law of demand*.

vehicle. N. An advertising medium within a media category; for example, *Time* magazine is one vehicle in the media category of magazines. Advertisers create a media mix tactic for advertising campaigns that detail general media categories and the target vehicles within them.

vend. V. To offer to sell something.

vendee. N. The party who purchases or agrees to purchase something owned by another.

vending machine. N. Selling merchandise with coin-operated equipment.

vendor. N. A manufacturer, wholesaler, or importer from whom goods or services are purchased.

vendor analysis. N. The assessment of the strengths and weaknesses of current or new suppliers in terms of such factors as merchandise quality, customer service, reliability, and price.

vendor chargebacks. N. The return of goods or services to a vendor, accompanied by an adjusted invoice. Proof of delivery to the vendor is usually provided. See also *returns to vendor*.

vendor reliability. N. The capability of the seller to meet the conditions of the contract.

vendor's lien. N. An unpaid seller's right to take possession of property until the purchasing price has been recovered. See also *seller's lien*.

vent for surplus. N. The hypothesis that economic progress spreads from developing industrial locations to less-developed geographic locations by means of the increasing demand for items in former areas.

venture. N. A business activity or undertaking that involves some or considerable risk.

venture capital. N. Funds invested in enterprises that do not usually have access to conventional sources of capital (banks, stock market, etc.).

venture team concept. N. The new product development process, commencing with the creation of an idea or concept, through commercialization and sale to consumers.

VERs. ABBRV. Voluntary export restraints. See *voluntary restraint agreements*.

vertical audit. N. An in-depth analysis of one aspect of a firm's marketing strategy.

vertical channel system. N. A channel of distribution having centralization in management to coordinate efforts at all levels according to a set goal. See also *voluntary chain*.

vertical conflict. N. Conflict that occurs between channel members at different levels of the distribution system.

vertical cooperative advertising. N. See *cooperative advertising*.

vertical discount. N. A special lower rate for the buying of several broadcast time periods to be broadcast at intervals with a set time frame such as a day. The time slots are listed with hours vertically, and days horizontally.

vertical half page. N. A magazine advertising space dividing the page in equal halves vertically instead of horizontally. Space is then sold at the half-page rate. See also *vertical third page*.

vertical industrial market. N. A thin market for industrial products where nearly every industrial consumer is a possible customer.

vertically combined. N. A business firm that performs all the various stages of production of a single finished item. Synonymous with *vertically integrated*.

vertically integrated. N. See *vertically combined*.

vertical market. N. A market condition where the manufacturer's product is sold to buyers in only a single or a few industries. See also *horizontal market*.

vertical marketing system. N. Establishments that deal with the manufacture and distribution of a particular item or related group of items. Often leads to vertical integration. Vertical marketing systems were created to help firms control channel behavior, by, for example, reducing conflicts between channel intermediaries following their own financial goals. ABBRV. *VMS*.

vertical merger. N. The joining of firms that are responsible for different production stages of a particular product so that more of the entire process, from raw material to retail sales, is under the control of a single management.

vertical price fixing. N. A form of price fixing in which marketers at different levels of the distribution system get together to set retail prices.

vertical publication. N. In industrial advertising, the publication that reaches only people in one industry. See also *horizontal publication*.

vertical saturation. N. In broadcasting, numerous commercials from one sponsor who attempt to reach many people to build traffic for a sale to be held on the following day. See also *saturation*.

vertical third page. N. Print advertising space equal to one-third of the page, separated vertically into three units. See also *vertical half page*.

very profitable item. N. Merchandise that a retailer believes are quite easy to convince consumers to purchase from it as the preferred source of supply. ABBRV. *VPI*.

vest pocket supermarket. N. See *bantam store*.

video commercial. N. A commercial that appears at the beginning of a videotape film that has either been rented or bought.

Videodex. N. A research firm that supplies indices of television program popularity, employing the diary technique to obtain information. See also *diary method*.

video-shopping services. N. Allows retailers to efficiently, conveniently, and promptly present information, receive orders, and process customer transactions. Its two basic categories are merchandise catalogs on videodiscs and videocassettes, and in-store and in-home ordering systems.

VIEs. ABBRV. Voluntary import expansions.

viewer. N. A person who watches a television broadcast.

viewer impression. N. The reaction held by a person to a commercial or program on a television.

visualizing

viewers per viewing household. N. The estimated number of people who make up the viewing audience within any household where the television is tuned to a specific program or station, or during a stated time period. ABBRV. *VPVH*.

vignette. N. A display that stimulates a product in actual use.

vintage capital. N. A measure of capital stock that assumes that newly produced capital goods are more productive than older ones.

virtual reality. N. Realistic three-dimensional environment created by computer software and hardware; allows marketers to uniquely create presentations.

virtual storefront. N. Interactive media/electronic marketing permitting customers to view and order goods or services on their computer screens.

visible items of trade. N. See *visible trade*.

visible supply. N. Stock in distribution centers that has been brought there from production areas. See also *invisible supply*.

visible trade. N. The portion of commerce between nations that is shown by records of transactions involving the exchange of tangible items.

visual. N. In advertising, one of the first rough layouts prepared for an advertisement; a sketch showing the relative place of the elements to be placed within the advertisement.

visualizing. N. In advertising, interpreting and presenting a concept in a pictorial format. It is usually followed with a headline. When presented in a layout it can induce the reader to pause and examine, leading to the advertisement's great impact.

visual merchandise. N. In retailing, displaying items to be pronounced and placed in their greatest advantage.

vital statistics. N. Data on individuals having to do with dates of birth and death, ownership of a house, marriages, divorces, and so on. See also *demographics*.

VMS. ABBRV. Vertical marketing system.

VO. ABBRV. Voice over.

vocational advertising. N. Advertising used in such diverse areas as farming, trade, industrial, and the professions.

voice over. N. In broadcasting, the narration with the speaker removed off sight of the television audience. Synonymous with *announcer voice over*. ABBRV. *VO*.

void. ADJ. That which has no legal effect.

voidable contract. N. An agreement that can be rescinded by either of the parties in the event of fraud, incompetence, or other sufficient cause. See also *fraud, right of rescission*.

volume. N. A quantity, bulk, or amount.

volume bonus. N. A purchase incentive for customers who may be offered a discount on large purchases. See also *Robinson-Patman Act of 1936*.

volume discount. N. See *bulk discount, patronage discount*.

volume merchandise allowance. N. A manufacturer's discount offered to a wholesaler or retailer for purchasing large volumes of goods.

volume of trade transacted. N. The sum of all sales of all business activities in a nation's economy.

voluntary chain. N. A wholesaling organization established by independent retailers or wholesalers to gather increased purchasing power. See also *affiliated wholesaler, voluntary wholesaler*. Synonymous with *wholesale-sponsored voluntary chain*.

voluntary export quota. N. A quantitative restriction that a country places on the export of certain marketed items to another nation. Usually evolves from complaints from an importing nation that its domestic industry is being injured by continuing exports of the item from its trading partner.

voluntary export restraints. N. See *voluntary restraint agreements*. ABBRV. *VERs*.

voluntary import expansions. N. Under which a nation replies to another's threats of trade sanctions by agreeing to buy more of certain marketed items from that country. ABBRV. *VIEs*.

voluntary restraint agreements. N. A bilateral arrangement whereby an exporting country agrees to reduce or restrict exports without the importing country having to make use of quotas, tariffs, or other import controls. These agreements are generally undertaken to avoid action by the importing country against imports that may injure or in some way threaten the positions of domestic firms in the industry in question. See also *protected markets*. ABBRV. *VRAs*.

voluntary simplicity. N. A consumer lifestyle in which people have an ecological awareness, seek material simplicity and durability, strive for self-reliance, and purchase more inexpensive products.

voluntary wholesaler. N. A wholesaler who sponsors a voluntary chain and who are active in supplying numerous members. See also *voluntary chain*.

voucher. N. A written statement that bears witness or vouches for something (e.g., a voucher showing that services have been rendered or goods bought).

VPI. ABBRV. Very promotable item.

VPVH. ABBRV. Viewers per viewing household.

VRAs. ABBRV. Voluntary restraint agreements.

wagon distributor. N. See *truck jobber*.

wagon jobber. N. See *truck jobber*.

wagon retailer. N. A merchant middleperson engaged in selling anything for a profit. He or she conducts huckstering.

waiting line theory. N. An approach to maximizing the efficient servicing of arrivals at a service facility by balancing the costs associated with waiting time and idle time.

wait order. N. A request to a medium to hold an advertisement and not releasing it until a date in the future is named; used especially in newspapers.

waiver. N. The release signed by an inventor who wishes to get consideration of a nonpatented idea or product.

waiver of restoration premium. N. A provision in many contracts whereby the company agrees not to charge an additional premium for reinstating the amount of the contract after loss has occurred.

walk. N. *(slang)* A customer who fails to purchase something and walks out of the store.

walk-out. N. See *walk*.

want. N. Something that is lacking that is desirable or useful. It is formed by a person's experiences, culture, and personality. See also *wants*.

want ads (advertisements). N. Advertisements that describe an available position and benefits, identifies the employer or box number for response, and tells those who are interested how to apply.

wants. N. *(slang)* Needs learned by people during their lifetime. See also *want*.

want slip. N. Written statements submitted to buyers by salespersons indicating items not in stock that have been requested by customers.

warehouse. N. A structure where goods are stored prior to distribution. See also *bonded warehouse, public warehouse.*

warehouse, bulk. N. A warehouse for the tank storage of liquids and open, dry products (e.g., coal, sand, and stone).

warehouse, captive. N. See *warehouse, private.*

warehouse, commodity. N. A warehouse that stores commodity goods (cotton, wool, tobacco, and other grown items).

warehouse, company. N. See *warehouse, private.*

warehouse, private. N. A warehouse operated by an owner, which holds his or her goods. Synonymous with *warehouse, captive; warehouse, company.*

warehouse, state-bonded. N. A public warehouse, under government supervision, that has been licensed by a state prior to operation. Merchandise is stored there without payment of duties or taxes until it is withdrawn from the warehouse.

warehouse, U.S. Customs–bonded. N. A federal warehouse where goods remain until duty has been collected from the importer. Goods under bond are also kept there.

warehouse, U.S. Internal Revenue. N. A public warehouse in which the owner of goods has posted a bond guaranteeing payment of internal revenue tax on U.S.-produced items.

warehouse club. N. A no-frills, cash-and-carry discount store that operates in a poor location. To shop there, the customer must become a member and pay dues.

warehouse receipt. N. An instrument listing the goods or commodities deposited in a warehouse. It is a receipt for the commodities listed, for which the warehouse is the bailee. Warehouse receipts may be either nonnegotiable or negotiable.

warehouse replenishment time. N. The speed at which products sold from a warehouse are replaced by the factor.

warehouse retailing. N. High-volume, low-overhead mass merchandising with few customer services.

warehouse showroom. N. A discount store that follows a strategy based on low overhead and high turnover; customers pay cash and must transport the merchandise themselves.

warehouse stock. N. Goods held in quantity in a warehouse for reasons of economy.

warehouse store. N. (1) A no-frills supermarket that stocks a wide variety of food and nonfood items and sells them at lower prices than the typical supermarket price. (2) A simply furnished retail outlet that offers a limited assortment of items at discount prices as a result of special arrangements made with a producer. Synonymous with *box store*.

warehousing. N. Involves the physical facilities used primarily for the storage of goods held in anticipation of sales and transfers within a distribution channel.

wares. N. Items or commodities that are offered for sale.

warranty. N. (1) A statement, either written, expressed, or implied, that a certain statement identified in a contract is true or will be true. (2) In sales, a promise by a seller that the product or property that is being sold is as he or she has represented it. Usually a warranty is presented with the sold goods. See also *caveat* *emptor, express warranty, implied warranty, guaranty, product liability.*

warranty price. N. The price established for an item that is deemed fair and just by both seller and buyer.

wash sale. N. A spurious sale in which the seller becomes the purchaser of what he or she sells. The purpose is to create activity in the item or to establish a market price. A wash sale is prohibited by law.

was-is-pricing. N. See *psychological discounting*.

wastage. N. (1) Wear of property; loss because of usage, deterioration, and so on. (2) In marketing, people of no specific value to an advertiser because they are not part of the designed target market.

waste. N. Material or supplies considered unfit for their original use. Results from poor handling, errors in production, mishandling, etc. See also *scrap*.

waste circulation. N. (1) Advertising that is done in a location where there is no distribution for the advertised product. (2) The number of people in an audience who are not prospects, e.g., infants.

watermark. N. A distinctive mark or design produced in paper to identify the manufacturer.

wave scheduling. N. See *pulsation*.

waving. N. See *pulsation*.

weakest-link theory. N. The concept that the least durable component in a product will control its useful life. According to this theory, all components should be built so that their life span will be equal in all units of similar function and price. See also *functional obsolescence, planned obsolescence*.

weak market. N. A situation characterized by a greater demand for selling than for purchasing.

wealth. N. The value of a person's total possessions and rights in property.

wearout. N. (1) The tendency of consumer response to a sales promotion to diminish over time. (2) The point when an advertisement or advertising campaign is no longer effective; based on frequency of presentation, the target market, the quality of the advertisement, its novelty, etc. The length of deterioration varies from weeks to years.

Webb-Pomerene Act of 1918. N. Federal legislation exempting exporters' associations from antitrust regulations.

Weber's Law. N. A marketing concept used in the understanding of people's perception of brands; suggests that consumers determine a product's value not on its separate characteristics but instead on their perceived differences between it and alternative brands. See also *just noticeable difference*.

weekly. N. A periodical published weekly. See also *dailies*.

week's supply technique. N. One of the four primary methods of retailers for stock planning. When sales shift considerably, this approach is not very helpful because it provides for the stock level to vary directly with sales, a situation that may not occur.

weight. N. (1) The amount or quantity of heaviness or mass. (2) The thickness of paper stock. (3) In advertising, the number of exposures of an advertising message. (4) In advertising, the number of gross rating points an advertiser wishes to place in a market. See also *gross weight, media weight*.

weighted average. N. A periodic inventory cost flow assumption whereby the cost of goods sold and the ending inventory are determined to be a weighted-average cost of all merchandise available for sale during the period.

weighted-point method. N. Determining sources of supply be setting evaluation factors to which numbers can be assigned as relative weights.

weighting. N. In market research, the statistical method applied when units drawn with unequal probabilities to form a sample are assigned weights to make them comparable for analytical purposes. As there is a great difference in population size between locations, people have different probability levels of being chosen for a sample. Weights are assigned to the units from each area to make the entire combined sample representative of the geographic population from which it was drawn.

wet goods. N. Liquids.

Wheeler-Lea Amendment of 1938. N. Federal legislation, amending the Federal Trade Commission Act of 1914, to protect the consumer against unfair trade practices in interstate commerce and against false or misleading advertising of foods, drugs, and cosmetics. See also *phony list price*.

wheel of retailing. N. Theory that, when entering the market, new forms of retailing first emphasize lower prices but as time passes the prices rise, making the merchandise subject to competition from newer organizations, which commence operations with lower prices. See also *trading down, trading up*.

whiplash impact. N. Shifts in the demand for items causing excessive or inadequate inventories at differing points in the channel of distribution because of inadequate controls and data. See also *derived demand*.

whip shot. N. See *zip pan*.

white-coat ruling. N. A ruling from the Federal Trade Commission claiming that it is deceptive advertising to use actors attired in white laboratory smocks to appear as doctors when speaking in support of any product or service in an advertisement or commercial.

white goods. N. (1) Appliances of substantial size and cost (e.g., refrigerators, freezers, washing machines, and stoves). Its name comes from the white enamel finish used. (2) Sheets, pillowcases, and lines. Its name comes from the early tradition of manufacturing these items in only white. See also *brown goods, orange goods, red goods, yellow goods*.

white mail. N. Customer correspondence received in an envelope other than the one provided by the marketer; contains customer inquiries, complaints, or changes of address.

white space. N. Open space in a print advertisement; usually found in advertisements for luxury goods as advertisers believe empty space gives an appearance of elegance. Conversely, inexpensive items are often crowded together when advertised.

whiz. N. See *zip pan*.

whole market approach. N. Dealing with the full range of customers; does not recognize or make an effort to appeal to the differences between various segments. See also *market segmentation*.

wholesale. V. To sell goods in gross to retailers, who then sell the merchandise to customers.

wholesale cooperatives. N. Full-service merchant wholesalers owned by member firms to economize functions and offer broad support. There are producer-owned and retailer-owned wholesale cooperatives.

wholesale price. N. The price for goods that is paid by retailers to suppliers.

wholesale price index. N. A measure used by marketers, compiled by the U.S. Bureau of Labor Statistics, showing the average change in the price of approximately two thousand, two hundred commodities at the primary market level (usually the level at which the commodity is first sold commercially in substantial volume) compared to the average level in selected base years. See also *price index*. Synonymous with *producer price index*. ABBRV. *WPI*.

wholesaler. N. (1) An intermediary that distributes products primarily to commercial or professional users. (2) An individual who buys and sells goods to retailers and other users but does not sell in significant amounts to the consumer. There are: (a) full-service wholesalers—those who provide services such as carrying stock, maintaining sales forces, and offering management and credit assistance to purchasers, and (b) limited-service wholesalers—those who offer some, but not all, of the services provided by full-service wholesalers. See also *jobber, merchant wholesaler, cash and carry wholesaler, rack jobber, truck jobber*. Synonymous with *distributor*.

wholesale-sponsored voluntary chain. N. See *voluntary chain*.

wholesaling. N. (1) All the activities provided by wholesaling intermediaries involved in selling merchandise to retailers; to industrial, institutional, farm, and professional businesses; or, to other types of wholesaling intermediaries. (2) Selling merchandise to firms that purchase for reasons other than consumption, usually to resell the item for profit. See also *merchandise mart, wholesaling intermediary, retailing*.

wholesaling intermediary. N. Any firm that engages primarily in wholesaling activities. See also *wholesaling*.

wholly-owned subsidiary. N. A separate organization, owned and completely controlled by a parent firm.

width of a product mix. N. The number of different product lines a company offers.

windfall profit. N. An unexpected profit arising from causes that were not controlled by the recipient.

window dressing. N. (1) Statements that appear to be more positive than warranted. (2) A statement that makes something appear better than it is. See also *painting the bus*.

window streamer. N. An advertising banner hanging in a store window. Synonymous with *window strip*.

window strip. N. See *window streamer*.

win-win situation. N. Where both the purchaser and seller are pleased from their completed transaction.

withdrawals. N. Items sold or bought out of a consignment. Usually the consignee reports on and pays for these items on a periodic schedule.

without recourse. N. In sales, an agreement that the purchaser accepts all risks in the transaction and gives up all rights of recourse. See also *caveat emptor, with recourse*.

with-pack premium. N. Providing a free gift or other item placed inside or outside of another product. See also *in-pack, on-pack*.

with recourse. N. An agreement that if the seller is unable to meet his or her obligations, the purchaser has the right to endorse a claim against the seller for sustained damages. See also *without recourse*.

Wool Products Labeling Act. N. Federal legislation passed in 1939 and made effective in 1941; requires that items containing wool, with certain exceptions such as carpets and upholstery, must show labels on the merchandise indicating the percent of new wool, reused or reprocessed wool, and other fibers or fillers that are used.

word association. N. See *free association*.

word-of-mouth advertising. N. A promotion not paid for, where one satisfied customer of an item or service communicates his or her feelings to others who may in turn become buyers of the same item or service. In fact, not advertising, as it is not paid for by an advertiser. See also *nationally advertised brand*.

work flow. N. The sequence of jobs in an organization needed to produce the firm's goods or services.

working capital. N. The excess of current assets over current liabilities, representing the capital immediately available for the continued operation of a business.

working capital turnover. N. A measure of the amount of working capital used in sustaining the sales of a period, computed by dividing net sales by average working capital.

work-in-process inventory. N. All products that have begun the manufacturing process but have not been completed. Work-in-process inventory is the cost of partially completed production. See also *finished-goods inventory*.

work load analysis. N. (1) Estimating sales activities needed to fulfill the potential of a sales territory. (2) An approach to sales force design in which the size of the sales force is determined by dividing the total workload in hours by the number of selling hours available from each salesperson.

work unit. N. The smallest subdivision of a job or operation.

world price. N. The price at which a given item is selling internationally under market conditions in effect at the time of the sale.

worldwide firms. N. Organizations that are global, multinational, or transnational.

WPI. ABBRV. Wholesale price index.

wraparound. N. A decorative banner that is draped about or circles an in-store merchandise display. Wraparounds are an example of point-of-purchase advertising.

wrapper. N. (1) A label. (2) The sheet of flexible material (paper, foil, etc.) or lamination used to cover a product for storage, sale, or shipment.

wrap-up. N. *(slang)* A customer who buys readily.

write-off. N. An asset that has been determined to be uncollectable and therefore has been charged off as a loss. Sometimes it is the debt itself.

write-up. N. In sales, documentation of the making of a sale.

xenophobia. N. Impacts on global marketing and consumer activities; the fear of foreigners. It can express itself in unfair and illegal trade practices around the world, especially for people living and working within the border of competing nations.

yearly order. N. See *blanket order*.

yellow goods. N. Nonconsumable household items with a high profit margin, such as refrigerators, dishwashers, and ovens, that are costly and replaced after many years of service. At times they are also called white goods. See also *brown goods*, *orange goods*, *red goods*, *white goods*.

Yellow Page advertising. N. Advertisements placed in a telephone Yellow Pages directory. Yellow Pages advertisements are display advertisements that have copy providing the advertiser's address and telephone number, product/service offerings, brands carried, and hours of store opening. Sometimes there are illustrations. See also *directory advertising*.

yes, but technique. N. A sales approach to deal with objections, where the salesperson first sympathizes with the prospect, and then attempts to show how that point of view is inadequate. Synonymous with *agree and counterattack technique*, *agreeing and neutralizing technique*.

yes-no controls. N. Controls that allow for a screening process point at which specific approval is needed to permit the activity to continue.

yield. V. (1) To give up possession. (2) To pay.

yield management pricing. N. A form of demand-based pricing whereby a firm determines the mix of price-quantity combinations that generates the highest level of revenue for a given period.

YOU attitude. N. In advertising, the concept that all advertisements must appeal to individuals, not groups, for greatest impact and value.

youth market. N. People under 25 years of age, who are often interested in goods and services that are different, unusual, or suggest values other than those held by older people.

yuppie. N. Young urban professionals with money. A creation of the 1980s, the term refers to people who are in their mid-thirties and represent a target audience for some advertisers.

Z

zapping. N. Of great concern to marketers and advertisers, using a television remote control to change stations during a program's commercial breaks to avoid watching advertisements.

ZBB. ABBRV. Zero-based budgeting.

zero-based budgeting. N. (1) An approach to budgeting in which each part of the organization must justify each item in its budget before it will be granted the funds it needs. (2) A financial management technique to redirect funds from lower-priority current programs to higher ones to pinpoint opportunities for improved efficiency and effectiveness, to reduce budgets while raising operating performance, and to improve profitability. ABBRV. *ZBB*.

zero-based media planning. N. A media selection process that involves (a) listing and ranking media objectives in order of importance; (b) examining and ranking possible media components in terms of their compatibility with the stated media objectives; (c) forming decision packages (i.e., plans consisting of one or more of these components); (d) comparing the decision packages with other packages that are retained and compatible with objectives; and, (e) reviewing, making tradeoffs, and arriving at resolution of the plan.

zero defects. N. When no mistakes and waste of resources occur while discharging a production function—a rare occurrence. At times workers who perform well, are rewarded when there are zero defects found.

zero haven. N. A tax-haven nation that levies no taxes (or practically none) on income.

zip advertisement. N. See *outsert*.

zip code. N. The U.S. Postal Service's system of designating geographic areas for mail sorting and delivery. Short for *zoning improvement plan*. See also *zip code analysis*.

zip code analysis. N. Based on the assumption that people living in the same geographic area tend to exhibit similar buying patterns; assessing a direct-marketing effort in differing geographic locations based on zip codes where the firm reviews the number of orders received from different zip codes to determine the levels of sales from the areas. Impacts future direct-mail programs. See also *zip code*.

zip pan. N. In broadcasting, particularly television, the swift movement of the camera across a message or scene. Synonymous with *whip shot, whiz*.

zone delivered pricing. N. A pricing scheme where the supplier equalizes freight on shipments to all consumers, within a defined geographic area. See also *zoning price*.

zone pricing. N. See *zoning price*.

zoning improvement plan. N. See *zip*.

zoning price. N. (1) A geographic pricing policy in which the seller divides a geographic area into zones and charges each buyer in a given zone the base price plus the standard freight rate for that zone. (2) The result of a policy of separating a total marketing area in areas (zones) for which different prices are established. All buyers in a zone pay the same price. See also *market segmentation, zone delivered pricing*.

zooming. N. A device used in commercials on television where the picture is made to appear ever larger, until reaching the desired size.

Abbreviations

AAA. ABBRV. American Academy of Advertising.

AAAA. ABBRV. American Association of Advertising Agencies.

AA rating. ABBRV. Average audience rating.

ABA. ABBRV. Area-by-area allocation.

ABC. ABBRV. Audit Bureau of Circulations.

ACI. ABBRV. Advertising Council, Inc.

ACK. ABBRV. Acknowledgment.

ad. ABBRV. Advertisement.

AE. ABBRV. Account executive.

AFA. ABBRV. Advertising Federation of America.

AIO. ABBRV. Activities, interests, opinions.

AMA. ABBRV. American Marketing Association.

AMS. ABBRV. Analytical Marketing System.

ANA. ABBRV. Association of National Advertisers.

ARB. ABBRV. (1) Advertising Review Board. (2) American Research Bureau.

ASP. ABBRV. American selling price.

ATA. ABBRV. American Telemarketing Association.

avails. ABBRV. In advertising, availabilities.

BPI. ABBRV. Brand potential index.

BSR. ABBRV. Basal skin resistance.

BTA. ABBRV. Best times available.

CAD. ABBRV. Cash against documents.

CBD. ABBRV. Cash before delivery.

circ. ABBRV. Circular.

COD. ABBRV. (1) Cash on delivery. (2) Collection on delivery.

COG. ABBRV. Customer-owned goods.

COM. ABBRV. Customer's own merchandise.

co-op mailing. ABBRV. Cooperative mailing.

CPI. ABBRV. Consumer Price Index.

CPM. ABBRV. Critical path method.

CPSA. ABBRV. Consumer Product Safety Act.

cume. ABBRV. Cumulative audience.

CWO. ABBRV. Cash with order.

DAR. ABBRV. Day after recall.

demo. ABBRV. Demonstration.

DOF. ABBRV. Degree of freedom.

DPS. ABBRV. Double-page spread.

EBI. ABBRV. Effective buying income.

EC. ABBRV. European Community.

E.D. ABBRV. The abbreviation for a newspaper insertion order indicating that a particular advertisement be run every day.

E.D.D. ABBRV. The abbreviation for a newspaper insertion order indicating that a particular advertisement be run every other day.

E.D.D.T.F. ABBRV. The abbreviation for a newspaper insertion order indicating that a particular advertisement be run every other day until forbidden.

EDM. ABBRV. Electronic direct marketing.

EOQ. ABBRV. Economic order quantity model.

E.O.W.T.F. N. A newspaper insertion order directing that an advertisement be run every other week until forbidden.

EU. ABBRV. European Union.

Euro-Ad. ABBRV. Euro-Advertisement.

FAS. ABBRV. Free alongside ship.

Abbreviations

fax. ABBRV. Facsimile broadcasting.

FCC. ABBRV. Federal Communications Commission.

F.O.B. ABBRV. Free (freight) on board.

FSA. ABBRV. Foreign sales agent.

FTA. ABBRV. Free-trade agreement.

FTC. ABBRV. Federal Trade Commission.

FTZ. ABBRV. Foreign trade zone.

GAFF. ABBRV. Abbreviations for a store category including the general merchandise, apparel and accessory, and furniture and home furnishings and appliances stores.

GAFFO. ABBRV. See *GAFF*.

GRP. ABBRV. Gross rating point.

GTC. ABBRV. Good 'til canceled order.

HABA. ABBRV. Health and beauty aids.

HBA. ABBRV. Health and beauty aids.

HMS. ABBRV. Horizontal marketing system.

INP. ABBRV. Information-need-product.

I/PRO. ABBRV. For-profit corporation providing advertisers with verification and analysis of Internet website traffic.

IPRs. ABBRV. Intellectual property rights.

ISO. ABBRV. International Organization for Standardization.

JIT purchasing. ABBRV. Just-in-time purchasing.

JND. ABBRV. Just noticeable difference.

KBI. ABBRV. Key buying influence.

KD. ABBRV. Knocked down.

L/C. ABBRV. Letter of credit.

MADA. ABBRV. Money, authority, desire, access.

MBO. ABBRV. Management by objectives.

MOM. ABBRV. Middle of month dating.

MPC. ABBRV. Marginal propensity to consume.

MPI. ABBRV. Marginal propensity to invest.

MPS. ABBRV. Marginal propensity to save.

MRO. ABBRV. Maintenance, repair, and operating supply items.

MS. ABBRV. Multidimensional scaling.

N. ABBRV. The number of instances, of whatever sort, in the total population being studied.

n. ABBRV. The total number of cases or observations in a small group.

NAD. ABBRV. National Advertising Division.

NAFTA. ABBRV. North American Free Trade Agreement.

NAM. ABBRV. National Association of Manufacturers.

NARB. ABBRV. National Advertising Review Board.

net. ABBRV. (1) Broadcast network. (2) Net amount.

NGT. ABBRV. Nominal group technique.

NIFO. ABBRV. Next in, first out.

NPD. ABBRV. New product development.

NPV. ABBRV. Net present value.

NRP. ABBRV. Net rating point.

NSI. ABBRV. Nielsen station index.

NTB. ABBRV. Nontariff barrier.

NTI. ABBRV. Nielsen television index.

NTM. ABBRV. Nontariff measures.

Abbreviations

OEMs. ABBRV. Original Equipment Manufacturers.

OMAs. ABBRV. Orderly marketing agreements.

on-spec. ABBRV. On-speculation.

open ad. ABBRV. Open advertisement.

OPM. ABBRV. (1) Operations per minute. (2) Other people's money.

OS&D. ABBRV. Over, short, and damaged.

OTB. ABBRV. Open-to-buy.

P. ABBRV. Each of the Ps of the marketing mix: product, price, promotion, and place.

PERK. ABBRV. Perquisites.

PERT. ABBRV. Program evaluation and review technique.

PERT/COST. N. A modified PERT system that, in addition to time, deadlines, and schedules, includes all cost considerations.

PIMS. ABBRV. Profit impact of marketing strategy.

PLC. ABBRV. Product life cycle.

POP. ABBRV. Point-of-purchase.

POS. ABBRV. Point-of-sale.

POSDCORB. ABBRV. The seven functions of administration: planning, organizing, staffing, directing, coordinating, reporting, and budgeting.

POST. ABBRV. Point-of-sale terminal.

pub-set. ABBRV. Publication-set.

remit rate. ABBRV. Remittance rate.

rep. ABBRV. Representative.

ROG dating. ABBRV. Receipt-of-goods dating.

ROI. ABBRV. Return on investment.

ROP. ABBRV. Run-of-paper.

ROW. ABBRV. Run-of-week.

SBUs. ABBRV. Strategic business units.

SEA. ABBRV. Single European Act.

SIC. ABBRV. Standard Industrial Classification System.

SOH. ABBRV. Stock on hand.

specs. ABBRV. Specification.

SRDS. ABBRV. Standard Rate and Data Service, Inc.

TCPA. ABBRV. Telephone Consumer Protection Act.

TF. ABBRV. Till forbid.

three Bs. ABBRV. Better Business Bureau.

UBD. ABBRV. Undeliverable billing document.

UPC. ABBRV. Universal product code.

USP. ABBRV. Unique selling proposition.

VALS. ABBRV. Market information based on consumer's values and lifestyles.

VAR. ABBRV. Value-added reseller.

VAT. ABBRV. Value-added tax.

VERs. ABBRV. Voluntary export restraints.

VIEs. ABBRV. Voluntary import expansions.

VMS. ABBRV. Vertical marketing system.

VO. ABBRV. Voice over.

VPI. ABBRV. Very promotable item.

VPVH. ABBRV. Viewers per viewing household.

VRAs. ABBRV. Voluntary restraint agreements.

Abbreviations

WPI. ABBRV. Wholesale price index.
ZBB. ABBRV. Zero-based budgeting.